PERSUASION

PERSUASION

Psychological Insights and Perspectives

Edited by

Sharon Shavitt
*University of Illinois
at Urbana-Champaign*

Timothy C. Brock
The Ohio State University

Allyn and Bacon
Boston   London   Toronto   Sydney   Tokyo   Singapore

Vice-President, Publisher: Susan Badger
Editorial Assistant: Laura L. Ellingson
Editorial-Production Service: Communicáto, Ltd.
Manufacturing Buyer: Megan Cochran
Cover Administrator: Linda K. Dickinson
Cover Designer: Suzanne Harbison

Copyright © 1994 by Allyn and Bacon
A Division of Paramount Publishing
160 Gould Street
Needham Heights, Massachusetts 02194

Library of Congress Cataloging-in-Publication Data

Persuasion : psychological insights and perspectives / edited by
   Sharon Shavitt, Timothy C. Brock.
       p.   cm.
   Includes bibliographical references and index.
   ISBN 0–205–15143–4
   1. Persuasion (Psychology).   2. Influence (Psychology).
3. Interpersonal communication.   4. Communication—Psychological
aspects.   I. Shavitt, Sharon.   II. Brock, Timothy C.
BF637.P4P44   1994
153.8'52—dc20   94–186
                                                           CIP

Printed in the United States of America

10 9 8 7 6 5 4 3 2   99 98 97 96 95

CONTENTS

PREFACE

The explosion of interest and research in the psychology of persuasion in the 1980s and early 1990s led to the unique feature of this book—an invitation to many of the world's leading persuasion researchers to write engagingly and authoritatively about their work for readers who are not specialists in their fields. Thus, the authors were asked to write for the enlightened tradebook reader as well as for the undergraduate student in the social sciences. As the editors of this collection, we sought writing that would meet high standards for excitement, readability, and authoritativeness. We sought chapters that would highlight several important and influential perspectives on persuasion, rather than survey the field comprehensively.

The resulting book, *Persuasion: Psychological Insights and Perspectives*, is an odyssey among important contemporary centers of basic and applied persuasion research. Our expert contributors were asked to illustrate and promote their lines of inquiry, rather than to document them in detail. Thus, each chapter presents a selection of studies, incorporating classic findings with recent discoveries. Additional references are provided for readers who wish to learn more about these research programs.

Chapter 1 introduces the domains of persuasion; excerpts throughout the chapter introduce our expert contributors. The chapters that follow pursue a logical progression from issues of definition and measurement through basic theory and research. The book concludes with applications to the important domains of health, politics, and advertising.

Because each chapter has been written to stand alone, readers can cover the chapters in whatever order suits their own interests. However, many students may find our logical ordering of chapters to be helpful, as follows.

Begin with Chapter 1 (Brock, Shavitt, and Brannon), which provides an intuitive, anecdotal introduction to the various domains of persuasion. Focus next on the key objects of persuasion—attitudes and opinions—and learn how they are defined and measured in Chapters 2 (Ostrom, Bond, Krosnick, and Sedikides) and 3 (Cacioppo, Petty, Losch, and Crites). Consider the relations between attitudes and behavior, how each can influence the other, as addressed in Chapters 4 (Fazio and Roskos-Ewoldsen) and 5 (Cooper and Scher). Tie together what you have learned so far within the perspective of an influential general theory of how persuasion works, presented in Chapter 6 (Petty, Cacioppo, Strathman, and Priester). Use the next two chapters to discover how personal and situational conditions can affect persuasion: in Chapter 7, differences between individuals in how susceptible they are to persuasion (Wood and Stagner), and in Chapter 8, the effects of group settings on persuasion (Kitayama and Burnstein). As you will learn in Chapter 8, a group's influence on an individual is based on powerful principles of compliance and conformity. Chapter 9 (Cialdini) shows how compliance tactics are used effectively by sales professionals to get us to say "yes" to their requests. Finally, examine why persuasion succeeds and why it fails in important domains of life: health in Chapter 10 (Leventhal and Cameron), politics in Chapter 11 (Sears and Kosterman), and subliminal advertising in Chapter 12 (Brannon and Brock). Refer to the Glossary as needed; it provides a comprehensive compendium of all technical terms and phrases used in this book. Separate author and subject indexes provide direct access to detailed information about sources and topics.

We did not impose a stylistic uniformity on our authors. Indeed, we wanted these experts' personalities to shine through in their writing. Chapters were, however, carefully edited to eliminate redundancies in coverage across chapters, and authors were encouraged to include references to the content of other chapters wherever appropriate. We are deeply indebted to our contributors for their careful efforts and for their insight, input, and enthusiasm throughout the preparation of this book.

Note to College Instructors

Through repeated use of the prepublication manuscript, we found this volume to have a textbook suitability superior to that of most other contributed volumes. The suitability stems from the popular level at which the book is written and the stand-alone quality of each chapter (so that instructors can arrange chapters to suit their own purposes). Although contributors were encouraged to avoid technical terms, some such terms were necessary; these are fully defined in the comprehensive, chapter-length Glossary.

Our distinguished contributors were enjoined to write for undergraduate students in a variety of disciplines, including psychology, business, marketing, sociology, journalism, advertising, and political science. Thus, this book can be a useful supplement to traditional, comprehensive texts in these fields. It is also suitable as the main text in courses focusing on psychological research on persuasion. Because our contributors have described the ongoing directions of their research programs, this volume will also be a useful sourcebook for advanced students and researchers interested in persuasion.

Acknowledgments

We, the editors, are especially indebted to our distinguished roster of contributing authors. These persuasion experts have ensured that their respective chapters reflect current scholarship in the behavioral sciences; they have kept some of their best writing for this book, in spite of competing pressures and opportunities.

We are also indebted to the many students who helped us by reacting critically to earlier drafts of these pages.

Finally, we wish to thank those individuals who reviewed earlier versions of this book for Allyn and Bacon: Steve Chaffee, Stanford University; Dennis Regan, Cornell University; and Gary Wells, Iowa State University.

S. S.
T. C. B.

PERSUASION

1

GETTING A HANDLE ON THE AX OF PERSUASION

An Introduction

TIMOTHY C. BROCK
The Ohio State University

SHARON SHAVITT
*University of Illinois
at Urbana-Champaign*

LAURA A. BRANNON
The Ohio State University at Lima

> *"I think we ought to read only the kind of books that wound and stab us. . . . We need the books that affect us like a disaster, that grieve us deeply, like the death of someone we loved more than ourselves, like being banished into forests far from everyone, like a suicide. A book must be the axe for the frozen sea inside us."*
> —Franz Kafka, *Letter to Pollak* (1/27/1904)

No one escapes psychological "axwork," the constant reconfiguring of our beliefs, attitudes, intentions, and behavior by unrelenting and ubiquitous forces. These forces are our subject matter and are referred to in this book as *influence* and *persuasion* (see Figure 1-1).

Persuasion is constantly remaking us into persons who are measurably changed. Sometimes imperceptibly—ofttimes dramatically.

1

FIGURE 1-1   The human psyche is constantly being reconfigured in response to the variety of messages disseminated by various forces. These forces are the foundation for influence and persuasion.

Source: Reprint permission from The Columbus Advertising Federation of Columbus, Inc. Created by Debora Patton, Retter Patton and Associates, Inc., Bexley, Ohio.

Persuasion processes are at the heart of the social movements and social upheavals of our time. The ability of these processes to reconfigure millions of minds and hearts has enabled masters of persuasion and influence to become the leaders of the world—for ill or for good.

FIGURE 1-2   The recent revolution in the Soviet Union and continuing unrest in the Russian republics are vivid examples of the power of mass media persuasion and social influence.

Source: Maclean's Magazine, Maclean Hunter Ltd., Sept. 9/91, pages 16–17, © Ricki Rosen/Saba Photography. Used with permission.

The most important event of the twentieth century, in terms of lives lost and lives changed, is the rise of the Nazis and World War II. Mastery of rhetoric and its effective delivery enabled a fast-talking, failed housepainter, Adolf Hitler, and his propagandists to convert the relatively cultured, well-educated German people into agents and cooperators in an unprecedented genocide. *The Holocaust is sufficient justification for requiring understanding of the psychology of persuasion from everyone.* Such understanding may be the only sure defense against another Holocaust.

The two Soviet Union revolutions of 1917 and 1991 depended on persuasion from leaders and corresponding interpersonal influence at the grassroots level. Lenin sought to promote psychological involvement in Marxist ideology; Gorbachev and Yeltsin had to undo that same Marxist-Leninist commitment 70 years later. During these 70 years, the Stalin reign of terror derived part of its strength from manipulation of the Soviet media and the consequent stifling of dissenting views. Soviet citizens were forbidden to read Western newspapers and magazines and to see Western films; they were punished for informal, unsupervised contact with foreigners.

Decades later, opposition leader Boris Yeltsin's vivid and persuasive pleas to the Russian people, delivered uncensored through the Western media, helped doom the coup by Marxist hard-liners and hasten massive reforms, along with the disintegration of the Soviet Union (see Figure 1-2).

Mass media persuasion and social influence are powerful engines of historical change. Understanding how these forces operate can help us to understand the major events that shape our lives. We are not doomed to repeat the blunders of history if we can expose agents of terror and repression while they are still seeking recognition in an arena of public opinion or at the ballot box. The heat of counter-argument and the glare of public denunciation must be deployed in a timely fashion. If not, they may not be able to prevail later against cannons and mass incinerations. This book aims to lay bare the processes underlying belief formation and belief change so that an informed citizenry can better resist the demagogues of today and tomorrow.

The Domains of Persuasion and Influence, the Authorities, and Their Theories

Let us approach the psychology of persuasion by considering the immediate circumstances of our own lives. We will enter a variety of familiar domains, and, for each domain, we indicate, in an excerpt or two, a persuasion expert who has mastered that domain. Fortunately, these experts also serve as senior authors of the ensuing chapters.

Sharon Shavitt

Shavitt, senior editor of this book, has published articles about persuasion, consumer responses to advertising, and processes of social judgment in leading journals such as the Journal of Personality and Social Psychology, *the* Journal of Experimental Social Psychology, *the* Journal of Advertising, *and the* Journal of Consumer Psychology. *Her research has focused primarily on how personal motivations affect information processing and persuasion. Her experiments have helped to establish new methods for investigating the motivational bases of attitudes and have yielded implications for the persuasiveness of advertising messages. She is currently Associate Professor of Advertising and Psychology and Associate Director of the Cummings Center for Advertising Studies at the University of Illinois.*

The Wording of Questions to Tap People's Attitudes Matters More than You Realize: Measuring the Unmeasurable

The key targets of persuasion are our attitudes and opinions. These include attitudes toward political candidates, social policies, organizations, persons, consumer products—you name it, we have attitudes toward it. Those who seek to persuade us seek to create or to change our attitudes in a particular direction.

But how do we know when they have succeeded? How do we know what people's true attitudes or opinions are? Chapter 2 deals with the building blocks of the study of persuasion: the definition and measurement of attitudes. Thomas Ostrom, Charles Bond, Jon Krosnick, and Constantine Sedikides describe how we study the anatomy of the mind after persuasion has occurred and explain the complexities of opinion polling. You will learn that measuring opinions can often be tricky and that how you ask a question can have a dramatic impact on the responses you will receive.

For example, you might think people know how they feel about different political issues such as the economy and foreign affairs. Therefore, if you ask your roommate, "Which of the following do you consider to be the most important problem facing the United States today: unemployment, inflation, the threat of war, the government budget deficit, or crime?" you think you would get the same answer if you listed the response alternatives in the reverse order (i.e., crime, the government budget deficit, the threat of war, inflation, or unemployment). But you won't! Try it!

Thomas M. Ostrom

Ostrom's major contributions have been in the areas of social cognition, attitude theory, and attitude measurement. He has contributed to the differentiation between affective, behavioral, and cognitive components of attitudes; to the problem of how people overtly communicate private attitudes; to the mathematical analysis of impression formation; and to the cognitive basis of judgments, inferences, and decision making. His books include Psychological Foundations of Attitudes *(with A. G. Greenwald & T. C. Brock),* Person Memory: The Cognitive Basis of Social Perception *(with R. Hastie et al.),* Cognitive Responses in Persuasion *(with R. E. Petty & T. C. Brock), and* Social Cognition: Contributions to Classic Issues in Social Psychology *(in preparation, with P. Devine & D. Hamilton). Ostrom is currently Professor of Psychology and formerly Director of the Cognitive Science Center at The Ohio State University.*

Jon A. Krosnick

Krosnick's research has examined a variety of factors affecting the reliability of survey results, including the effects of question format and the impact of the order of response choices on answers to survey questions. His books include Introduction to Survey Research and Data Analysis *and* Thinking about Politics: Comparisons of Experts and Novices. *He is currently Associate Professor of Psychology and Political Science at The Ohio State University.*

Building Pipelines to Our Hearts and Minds:
The Lie Detector Professionals Are Close to Total Victory

Of course, people may not always be willing to answer honestly when an opinion pollster asks them, "How would you feel about a Black family moving into your neighborhood?" or "What is your attitude toward marijuana use?" How can we tell if someone is reporting their true attitudes when he or she may be motivated to lie?

The modern science of psychophysiology offers some answers. In Chapter 3, John Cacioppo, Richard Petty, Mary Losch, and Stephen Crites reveal new and reliable ways of detecting a person's true attitudes through examination of physiological events. It turns out that some well-placed electrodes can monitor thoughts, feelings, and attitudes that a respondent may be unwilling or unable to report. If you are a person with socially unacceptable beliefs, be sure you run fast, because if you are caught and measured, you can no longer hide your true feelings!

John T. Cacioppo

Cacioppo's articles and book chapters include seminal contributions to the study of attitude formation and change and to psychophysiological perspectives on social processes and individual differences. His books include Attitudes and Persuasion: Classic and Contemporary Approaches *(with R. E. Petty),* Social Psychophysiology: A Sourcebook *(with R. E. Petty),* Perspectives on Cardiovascular Psychophysiology *(with R. E. Petty),* Communication and Persuasion: Central and Peripheral Routes to Attitude Change *(with R. E. Petty), and* Principles of Psychophysiology: Physical, Social, and Inferential Elements *(with L. G. Tassinary). He is currently Professor of Psychology at The Ohio State University and President of the Society for Psychophysiology.*

Do We Do as We Say We Believe?
When and How Attitudes Guide Behavior

The Nazi movement that led to World War II succeeded in part because the masses who strew roses in the streets for Hitler in 1934 were willing to fling themselves into the trenches against the alleged "enemies of the Third Reich" six years later. Beliefs guided behavior.

So students who believe that cheating is wrong would not cheat on an exam, right? People who believe that energy conservation is important do not use as much energy as those who do not consider it to be a problem, right? People who do not like their jobs tend to show poor attendance at work, right? It makes so much sense, it is hardly worth mentioning that people behave consistently with their attitudes, right? You will be surprised to learn that, according to Russell Fazio and David Roskos-Ewoldsen in Chapter 4, none of these statements is necessarily correct. People often behave in ways that contradict their attitudes.

Upon reading their chapter, you will learn when and under what circumstances attitudes influence behavior. With this knowledge in hand, you will be able to distinguish whether people will behave consistently or inconsistently with their expressed attitudes. Sometimes changing a person's mind is *not* sufficient to change his or her behavior.

Russell H. Fazio

Fazio has published extensively on a number of central issues regarding attitudes. He has been concerned with the processes by which attitudes both follow from past behavior and guide subsequent behavior. He has developed a model of attitudes as object-evaluation associations in memory and shown that the strength of this association determines the likelihood that the attitude will be activated automatically from memory upon exposure to the attitude object, as well as the extent to which the attitude influences the processing of information regarding the object and behavior toward the object. He is currently Professor of Psychology at Indiana University.

A Funny Thing Happened After You Bought the Forum: How Our Actions Affect Our Attitudes

Have you ever had to make a difficult choice between two things that were equally desirable? For example, do you remember looking for a new home or apartment? You probably looked at several alternatives and, after "weeding out" the undesirables, had to decide between two equally nice places, apartment A and apartment B. After making a lengthy, detailed list of all of the pros and cons of each residence (location, cost, utilities, etc.), you finally made a painful choice and signed a contract to rent apartment A. Then a funny thing began to happen. Initially, you considered it a toss-up between the two apartments, but once you signed the contract, it all began to look crystal clear. Apartment A was much nicer than apartment B; after all, apartment B was not *that* much closer to where you work than apartment A, and the neighborhood probably was not as nice; and even though apartment B cost less in monthly rent, the utilities were probably exorbitant. Thank goodness you did not make a foolish mistake and actually choose apartment B! What could you have been thinking before you made your choice? Actually, the more appropriate question might be, what were you thinking *after* your decision?

As Joel Cooper and Steven Scher explain in Chapter 5, our actions and decisions have a way of changing our attitudes. You will discover how some reevaluation processes illustrated here can explain everything from fraternity "Hell Weeks" (why people sometimes come to love the most those who have treated them the worst) to dramatic religious conversions.

Joel Cooper

Cooper has published extensively in the area of cognitive dissonance. He has pursued the importance of decision freedom, personal responsibility, and aversive consequences in dissonance arousal. He has also conducted research on the psychological and physiological arousal properties of dissonance. His books include Understanding Social Psychology *(with S. Worchel & G. R. Goethals). He is currently Professor of Psychology and former Chair of the Psychology Department at Princeton University.*

Don't Get Lost in the Clutter: Using Persuasion Theory to Your Advantage

On a typical day, you may be exposed to hundreds of persuasive appeals. On television, in magazines and newspapers, on the radio, in your mailbox, on billboards, bench signs, bumper stickers, and bulletin boards—there is no escape from the efforts of people trying to influence you.

Chapter 6 focuses on the dizzying array of persuasive messages with which we are confronted each day and describes how we mentally navigate through the clutter. Clearly, you don't have the time and energy to pay attention and think carefully about each of those messages. You are constantly making choices about whether to read the newspaper editorial or turn the page, whether to watch the loud commercial or hit the "mute" button, whether to listen to the president's speech on the car radio or concentrate on your driving (. . . we hope you will choose the latter).

In Chapter 6, Richard Petty, John Cacioppo, Alan Strathman, and Joseph Priester present a general theory that predicts when individuals are likely to evaluate a message carefully, when they are not, and how persuasion works in each of these scenarios. It also provides you with specific criteria for gauging the efficacy of your own persuasive efforts.

Richard E. Petty

Petty has been a major contributor to and developer of the cognitive response approach to persuasion. His dissertation introduced the "two routes to persuasion" idea that, in collaboration with John Cacioppo, was expanded into the Elaboration Likelihood Model of persuasion. His books include Cognitive Responses in Persuasion *(with T. M. Ostrom & T. C. Brock),* Social Psychophysiology: A Sourcebook *(with J. T. Cacioppo),* Perspectives on Cardiovascular Psychophysiology *(with J. T. Cacioppo),* Communication and Persuasion: Central and Peripheral Routes to Attitude Change *(with J. T. Cacioppo), and* Attitude Strength: Antecedents and Consequences *(in preparation with J. Krosnick). He is currently Professor of Psychology and Chair of the Social Psychology Doctoral Program at The Ohio State University.*

Can We Identify the "Sucker Who Is Born Every Minute"?

If so, persuasion becomes easy work. But how can you pick the "pushover" out of a crowd? Are there particular characteristics you can look for? Do you think women are generally more easily persuaded than men? Do you believe that intelligent people are harder to persuade than less intelligent people? You will discover in Chapter 7, as Wendy Wood and Brian Stagner show, that identifying gullible, persuadable people based on their personality or social characteristics is not quite as easy as it may first appear. Sometimes men are more persuadable than women, and sometimes intelligent people are more persuadable than less intelligent people. You will learn that, in general, personality traits are surprisingly poor predictors of influenceability and that many stereotypes concerning "born pushovers" are unwarranted. (Such differences, when they do exist, tend to be quite small and variable.) However, you will also learn that you *can* predict whether a given individual will be persuaded by a message concerning a given topic if you know something about *how* that person thinks about the issue.

Wendy Wood

Wood's research has identified a variety of factors that can account for message recipients' predispositions to be influenced or to be resistant to change: recipients' overall self-esteem and intelligence, their knowledge concerning the influence topic, and the sex of the recipient. Her books include Process and Productivity in Groups *(with S. Worchel & J. Simpson). She is currently Associate Professor of Psychology at Texas A & M University.*

If You Can't Save the World, Then at Least Try to Change It

It is easy to believe that "one person can't make a difference; I'm just a little fish in a big pond; no one even notices me." We all feel that way, sometimes.

In fact, in group situations, we often assume that it is easy for people with a minority opinion to be swept away by the tide of the majority view. We are often overwhelmed by the apparent power of those in the majority and by the forces of group psychology—the desire to get along and to avoid "making waves."

In Chapter 8, you will learn from Shinobu Kitayama and Eugene Burnstein how one person *can* make a tremendous difference. You will learn when a minority of people can sway the majority. You will understand why majorities can be so influential and what a minority of individuals can do in order to be effective.

Once you understand the factors underlying group dynamics, you will be in a better position to act as a minority powerhouse, a gadfly who can use the majority's superior weight as leverage against itself. You *can* change the world.

Shinobu Kitayama

Along with a program focusing on the role of emotional factors in perceptual and cognitive processes, Kitayama has studied cognitive processes involved in social communication and social judgment. More recently, he has been investigating cultural variation in a variety of psychological processes, including self, social thinking, emotion, and social motivation. He is currently Professor of Psychology in the Faculty of Integrated Human Studies, Kyoto University, Japan.

Eugene Burnstein

Burnstein has done research on a variety of issues in group dynamics and interpersonal perception. In recent work, he has shown that whether others in a group influence us depends not so much on what they actually say but more on how we encode what they say. This kind of analysis has been used to make sense of a variety of psychological phenomena, ranging from opinions about other countries to group polarization. He is currently Chair of the Social Psychology Program and Professor of Psychology at the University of Michigan, as well as a research scientist in the Research Center for Group Dynamics at the Institute for Social Research.

One of Those Days on Which Everything Went Wrong: The Perils of Social Influence

Imagine that you have just returned home one morning from a draining business trip and are in an airport on your way to the baggage claim. A yellow-robed monk comes up to you, gives you a flower, and asks you for a donation. You are not sympathetic to the monk's cause; you are annoyed at being stopped and harassed in an airport; and you did not want a flower. Yet, you have an almost out-of-body experience as you look down upon yourself, reaching into your pocket and handing the annoying man a dollar. What just happened here? How is this possible? You pick up your luggage and decide to walk to a major intersection in order to wait for a cab. You are standing at a street corner, waiting for the crossing light to say "WALK," when a shabbily dressed man crosses the street without waiting for the signal. You sneer at the man with contempt at his disobedience of the law. A few moments later, a businessman carrying a briefcase and wearing a three-piece suit chooses to cross against the light, and you, almost mindlessly, follow him. It is not until you hear the screeching brakes of an oncoming car that you realize that you never would have followed the first man but were willing to follow the second man to your early grave. The ax of social influence fell twice before you even left the airport. You did things you really didn't want to do.

Safely at home and having regained your nerve, you decide to go to a department store with the intention of buying an advertised product at an exceptionally low price. When you get to the store, you learn that there was a misprint in the ad and that the product you wanted is no longer on sale. Yet, you buy it anyway, at the regular price. It is only when you get home that you realize that you could have bought the same product at a local discount store for less than you ended up paying for it, a store that was on your way home anyway.

Robert Cialdini, in Chapter 9, discusses the ways in which compliance-gaining professionals (people who make their livelihood separating the rest of us from our money) manage to influence us so effectively. You will learn how these people exploit our usual, almost mindless reliance on simple behavioral "rules of thumb": rules such as, you should "return gifts with gifts," "obey authority," "be consistent," and the like. During this process, you might even learn how to resist these common influence attempts and, hopefully, will be empowered with a new, strengthened ability to say, "*No*, thank you."

Robert B. Cialdini

Extensive scholarly training in the psychology of influence, together with 20 years of research into the subject, has earned Cialdini an international reputation as an expert in the fields of persuasion and compliance. He is currently Regents' Professor of Psychology at Arizona State University. His book Influence, *which was the result of a three-year program of study into the reasons that people comply with requests in natural settings, has appeared in numerous editions and in six languages.*

Proof That, at 23, You Were the World's Greatest Lover: The Dilemmas of Health Persuasion

Is the ax metaphor for a persuasive hit too strong? Here's a persuasive message you may want to sink into the head of every pubescent 14-year-old.

> Suppose you started having sex when you were 15 and had one new partner each year until you were 23. No big deal. Suppose that your partner at 15 and your new partners at 16, 17, 18, etc. had followed the same pattern. Now suppose, also, as the AIDS epidemic makes plain, that when you have sex with one person, you also come inevitably into contact with the biochemical residues of all that person's previous partners. At 15, your number of actual and phantom partners was merely 1 plus 0 for a total of 1. At sixteen, your number of actual partners was 2 and phantom partners, 1, for a cumulative total of 3. At 17, 3 actual and 4 phantoms for a cumulative total of 7: Your partner at 17 joined you with 3 phantoms of his or her own; and add the single phantom associated with last year's partner. Still no big deal? Please get out your pencil and calculator, because at 18, 19, 20, and onwards, up you went into the wild blue yonder. Result: At the still tender age of 23, with only 9 actual partners, your still-tender bloodstream was serving as fairgrounds for the entertainment and nourishment of hungry viruses and bacterial fellow travelers from no less than 502 phantoms!

Some of the greatest threats to public health in our society come from diseases that are linked to our lifestyles and behaviors. How does one convince people to adopt lifestyle behaviors that prevent or aid in the control of AIDS, lung cancer, or cardiovascular disease?

In Chapter 10, Howard Leventhal and Linda Cameron tackle the frustrating issues surrounding health persuasion and teach us how to help our friends, children, parents, and lovers to live healthier lives.

Howard Leventhal

Leventhal's early work focused on the attitudinal and behavioral effects of threat messages designed to promote health and avoid risky behaviors. His most recent work on the perception of and adaptive responses to ongoing and future illness threats (e.g., hypertension, breast cancer) has appeared in both medical and psychological journals. He is currently Professor of Psychology and Director of the Institute for Health, Health Care Policy, and Aging Research at Rutgers University.

Do We Really Have Ears to Hear and Eyes to See? Political Persuasion and the Mass Media

Media and their supporting persuasion industries help disseminate information in democracies. But the evidence indicates that the electorate is tuned out to political news, debates, and speeches. People are looking without seeing and hearing without listening. Why? Political psychology experts David Sears and Rick Kosterman delineate in Chapter 11 the "sink holes" of wasted media effort, particularly in the domain of political persuasion.

David O. Sears

Sears has published articles and book chapters on a wide variety of topics in social and political psychology, including attitude change, mass communications, ghetto riots, political socialization, voting behavior, and racism. His books include Public Opinion *(with R. E. Lane),* The Politics of Violence: The New Urban Blacks and the Watts Riot *(with J. B. McConahay),* Tax Revolt: Something for Nothing in California *(with J. Citrin), and* Political Cognition: The 19th Annual Carnegie Symposium on Cognition *(with R. R. Lau). Sears is currently Professor of Psychology and Political Science and former Dean of Social Sciences at the University of California, Los Angeles.*

You've Been Looking for the Breasts in the Icecubes Since 1957: The Continuing Saga of Subliminal Persuasion

Have you ever done or said something that you later regretted? Do you have any bad, or unhealthy, habits (such as smoking)? If it wasn't the devil that made you do it, then perhaps it was hidden messages that you were exposed to—perhaps it was subliminal advertising.

Imagine that you are watching a movie at a local theater and, all of a sudden, you have a strong craving for popcorn. You get up and purchase a large bucket of popcorn with extra butter and devour it all, despite the fact that you are on a diet! Was the movie altered so that certain frames, appearing too fast for you to consciously perceive them, suggested some word or phase (e.g., "Eat popcorn")? Alternatively, imagine that you have been trying to quit smoking for months. Yet despite all of your best efforts, you cannot seem to resist your cravings for cigarettes. Is your compulsion to smoke partly due to the magazine advertisements you read and the billboards you see on the way to work? Do these displays have suggestive words or body forms (with sexual connotations) embedded in their pictures? Even more frightening, are there evil messages hidden in rock music that encourage teenagers to rebel or even commit suicide? Are some forms of persuasion literally killing us?

Popular belief in the power of subliminal manipulation appears to be increasing. Ironically, the widespread belief in subliminal persuasion—despite the absence of scientific evidence—is based on the very factors that lead psychologists to doubt its effectiveness. In Chapter 12, Laura Brannon and Timothy Brock discuss the evidence for and against subliminal persuasion and explain why popular belief in it is likely to persist indefinitely.

Laura A. Brannon

Brannon's publications include a national field experiment published in Emotion in Advertising: Theoretical and Practical Explorations *(1990). She is senior author of a book in preparation,* Behavioral Compliance. *Her diverse interests in persuasion theory and applications (e.g., health, politics) are reflected in her authorship of articles appearing in* Psychological Science, Basic and Applied Social Psychology, New England Journal of Medicine, Journal of Social Issues, *and* American Political Science Review. *Currently Assistant Professor of Psychology at The Ohio State University (Lima), she was a National Science Foundation Graduate Fellow and an Ohio State University Presidential Fellow.*

Timothy C. Brock

Brock has published articles and book chapters on a wide variety of topics in the psychology of persuasion, including effects of salesperson-consumer similarity on purchasing behavior; the role of cognitive responses in determining acceptance of persuasive messages; processing of unintelligible persuasive messages; and the effect of cognitive tuning on attitude change persistence. His books include Order of Presentation in Persuasion *(with C. I. Hovland et al.),* Psychological Foundations of Attitudes *(with A. G. Greenwald & T. M. Ostrom),* Cognitive Responses in Persuasion *(with R. E. Petty & T. M. Ostrom),* Interdisciplinary Research and Doctoral Training *(with L. Comitas et al.), and* Attention, Attitude, and Affect in Response to Advertising *(with E. Clark & D. Stewart). Brock is currently Professor of Psychology at The Ohio State University and Past-President of the Society for Consumer Psychology, Inc.*

Epilogue and Invitation

Let us move out into the arenas of contemporary life and observe persuasion in action. In so doing, we will be guided by our authorities, the experts whose scientific contributions make and shape the moving front of knowledge of the psychology of persuasion.

We invited our experts to write about their lines of inquiry in the spirit of exciting promotion of ideas and interesting, timely illustrations of these ideas. Rather than furnish comprehensive documentation of pertinent studies or theoretical intricacies, we invited our authors to provide a view of the big picture that will be engaging and accessible to the nonpsychologist. Should you wish to "read more about it," each chapter also provides an extensive bibliography of the authors' primary sources for research and theory in the area.

Scientific terms are used sparingly in this volume, and readers will probably be familiar with most of them. However, you may occasionally find it instructive to refer to the Glossary in the back of this book. It furnishes clear and complete definitions of words and phrases that are part of the language of persuasion research.

Persuasion processes are fundamental to democratic and free-market societies. Persuasion processes are the mechanism through which individuals make critical decisions about their government, their marketplace, their community, and their lifestyle. By providing this glimpse into the psychology of persuasion, our goal is to sharpen your understanding of its workings and strengthen your appreciation of its role in our society.

2

ATTITUDE SCALES

How We Measure the Unmeasurable

THOMAS M. OSTROM
The Ohio State University

CHARLES F. BOND, JR.
Texas Christian University

JON A. KROSNICK
The Ohio State University

CONSTANTINE SEDIKIDES
University of North Carolina

Weldon and Babbs were in a pickle. The test results were clear cut. Babbs was pregnant. It was early in their relationship; they were still trying to find out just how well they liked each other. They had not yet discussed the possibility of marriage, much less the idea of having children. What to do?

One of the options they discussed was abortion. Babbs favored it, but Weldon had serious misgivings. Both of them came into the relationship with fairly well-developed attitudes about abortion. Babbs's good friend Cindy had previously had an abortion. The two of them had talked it over at some length before Cindy decided to go ahead with it. Fortunately, all had gone well. Cindy had become a vocal advocate of abortion rights. Babbs was sympathetic with her friend's views and once had even helped Cindy prepare materials for a pro-choice fund-raising drive.

Weldon's experiences had been quite different. His sister had an abortion two years ago, despite strong opposition from her parents. As a consequence of their angry reactions, she had moved to her own apartment and eventually stopped attending church with the family. Even though she still lived in the same city, she did not talk with Weldon or her parents more than once or twice a year. Weldon blamed the abortion for the breakup of his family.

Life experiences can lead people to acquire very different thoughts and feelings about the world around them. Babbs and Weldon have developed opposite attitudes about abortion, differences that lead them to take very different approaches to their present dilemma. And they are now in the midst of a new life experience that may well lead them to reshape the attitudes they brought into their relationship, either through becoming harder and more extreme or through revision and accommodation.

You, the reader, now have a sense of the differences in views toward abortion held by Babbs and Weldon. Their attitudes differ in fundamental ways and yet are not completely incompatible or irreconcilable. With those subtle hues and shadings in mind, consider the problem of the scientist whose objective is to study the nature of human attitudes. As scientists, we must move from the more impressionistic, evocative, and cinematic portrayal of Babbs's and Weldon's attitudes to a more rigorous and precise description. We must devise concrete ways to measure how attitudes differ from person to person. In short, we want to assign numbers to attitudes.

How Can We Know Another Person's Attitudes?

How did Babbs and Weldon manage to learn about each other's attitudes toward abortion? No doubt, most of their information came as a natural result of being together and talking about the things that matter to them. When the pregnancy occurred, the discussions became soul searching and intense.

There are at least four sources of information we draw upon to know another person's attitude. At first blush, the most straightforward is simply to ask the person. But as this chapter will show, direct questions do not always lead to direct (or correct) answers. A second source of information comes through observing how the person reacts to the attitude topic when it is raised in conversation or in other ways. For example, how does Weldon react to television news about a fire bombing of an abortion clinic? Is he indifferent, does he shake his head in disgust, or does he have a secret smile of satisfaction? Nonverbal reactions can convey volumes of information. Third, we can learn what kinds of actions the person will take when presented with the opportunity to help or harm the attitude object. For example, Babbs's helping Cindy with the pro-choice fund-raising drive clearly conveys a positive attitude. Fourth, people tend to associate with others who share their attitudes. So we can look at the attitudes held by the friends and family of a person to get an idea of his or her attitude.

Babbs and Weldon had spent a lot of time with one another, and so they could draw upon all four of these kinds of information to come to know how the other felt about abortion. To the extent that all four sources of information about a person's attitude tell the same story, then we can have some confidence that we have understood the attitude. But gathering all this information takes time.

Attitude researchers do not have the luxury of spending months, weeks, or even hours with a person. We have had to devise ways of measuring attitudes that can be administered in a very short time period. National surveys on political attitudes or consumer attitudes rarely devote more than a minute or two to measuring attitudes toward a particular political candidate or toward a new brand of toilet paper. Often such surveys will use just a single question to measure the attitude.

Why Measure Attitudes?

This book focuses on the persuasion process. It addresses the question of what leads people to change their attitudes. Persuasion occurs at the interpersonal level, such as when Babbs and Weldon struggle to come to some agreement about their abortion decision. It also occurs at the level of mass communications, as in the nationwide advertising campaigns of the pro-life and pro-choice groups. Mass media doubtlessly contributed to the development of Weldon and Babbs's current attitudes toward abortion.

Psychologists are striving toward a scientific understanding of attitudes and persuasion. We want to understand attitudes the way physicists understand molecules and neurophysiologists understand the brain. The starting point of any science is observation and measurement. We need to know what to look for and how to assign numbers to it.

There are two basic reasons why we need accurate and precise measures of attitudes. One is to test our theories of attitudes and persuasion. The primary way to evaluate the quality of a theory is through the accuracy of its predictions. Attitude measures provide the data we need to reveal the inadequacies of poor theories, confirm the quality of good theories, and (in the case of truly creative scientists) stimulate us to generate new theories.

The second reason we need measures of attitudes is for more practical, atheoretical purposes. You, the reader, have probably had some contact with applied attitude measurement. A phone call interrupting your dinner hour, a questionnaire in the mail, or a tap on the shoulder in the shopping mall often means that a list of questions will shortly follow. Consumer groups, political groups, government agencies, nonprofit organizations, the local zoo, the transit authority, and many other organizations inundate us with surveys designed to measure the public's attitudes. For example, research looks at political attitudes regarding policies and candidates, at consumer perceptions of different products, at employee morale in organizations, at levels of racial prejudice, and at college course evaluations. Political campaign strategies, product development decisions, supervisor salary raises, anti-discrimination legislation, and curriculum revision all depend on the accuracy of the techniques used to measure these opinions.

Three Fundamental Considerations

The measurement of attitude always involves three fundamental considerations (Davis & Ostrom, 1984). We will consider each in turn.

The Attitude Object

People hold attitudes toward all kinds of things. Abortion is just one example. We can have attitudes toward specific persons (e.g., our mother, a roommate, Marilyn Monroe, Bill Clinton, or even ourselves), toward social groups (e.g., African Americans, Baptists, Iraqis, or doctors), toward policy decisions (e.g., raising taxes, increasing military spending, or establishing diplomatic relations with Cuba), toward personal action decisions (e.g., having an abortion, going to a movie, or studying for an exam), toward abstract concepts (e.g., democracy, Christianity, or free private enterprise), and toward consumer products (e.g., Honda sedans, Ben and Jerry's ice cream, or Charmin toilet paper). Almost anything in our world can become the object of an attitude.

As is well documented in this book, attitude theories are assumed to apply equally well to all possible attitude objects, from persons to products. In the long run, this assumption may prove to be wrong, but for now, it vastly simplifies the measurement problem. The measurement techniques presented in this chapter are assumed to apply to all attitude objects.

Attitude Properties

Attitudes are complicated. People can have all sorts of thoughts and feelings toward the attitude object. And those reactions may well change over time. The first task of attitude measurement is to somehow simplify this complexity.

Asking a psychologist to measure an attitude is like asking a physician to measure a person. The physician is certain to say that this request makes no sense. It just is not specific enough. The physician needs to know what it is about the person you want measured. Is it the person's height or weight, the person's blood cholesterol level, the person's heart rate, or the body's chemical profile? A person has many such physical properties. Exactly the same problem exists if you ask an engineer to measure a car or ask a store manager to measure his or her supermarket. The measurement process cannot begin until the relevant properties are specified.

A psychologist faces a similar problem when asked to measure a person's attitude. Attitudes have a multitude of properties. However, there is one property that dominates attitude research and theory. Most of the time, when scholars use the term *attitude*, they are referring to the *evaluative* property. This is also what people in general think of when they use the term in their everyday lives. The evaluative property refers to how positively or negatively the person feels toward the attitude object. Measures of the evaluative property try to find out how pro versus con, favorable versus unfavorable, or supportive versus antagonistic people are toward the attitude object.

Weldon and Babbs, then, are each viewed as having an overall evaluative disposition toward abortion. Each person's overall attitude is the distilled essence of the many experiences, inferences, thoughts, and feelings he or she has had about the attitude object. Attitude is referred to as a *disposition* because it is thought to dispose people to react to the attitude object in an evaluatively positive or negative manner.

Each person's attitude can be located on the evaluative dimension. Attitudes can range anywhere on that dimension from extremely positive, through neutral, to extremely negative. That attitudinal point may vary from day to day (or even moment to moment), but at any given instant in time, the overall attitude is theoretically thought of as being fixed at one point on the evaluative dimension. The task of the researcher is to find a way to measure just where that point is located.

There is a diverse array of other properties of attitude that can be measured. Collectively, they are best thought of as being *nonevaluative.* Two people like Babbs and Cindy could actually hold the same overall evaluative disposition toward abortion (perhaps moderately in favor of it), but their attitudes might differ in a variety of other ways.

As one example, Babbs and Cindy could differ in the level of ego involvement (or importance) attached to their pro-choice attitudes. Babbs may be far less ego involved in her attitude than Cindy (at least during the period prior to her becoming pregnant). For Cindy, the attitude is linked to important social and moral values, whereas for Babbs, it is more an academic principle. Such differences in ego involvement could have important consequences. Babbs is probably more sympathetic to Weldon's persuasive arguments than Cindy would be. This is because, generally speaking, high ego involvement leads to high resistance to attitude change.

Another nonevaluative property is the dimensionality of the attitude. Attitudes usually have many beliefs associated with them. When we speak of *dimensionality,* we refer to the different dimensions (or belief clusters) that are present in a person's set of beliefs. Cindy's beliefs may contain a large number of dimensions, such as relevance to personal morality, freedom of choice, future responsibilities, women's liberation, and attitudes of intimate friends. Babbs's attitude, on the other hand, may be based on a far more impoverished set of beliefs. Her pro-choice stand may have been based solely on philosophical values regarding individual liberties. Dimensionality (or complexity of the underlying beliefs) can determine how people deal with persuasive communications, the kinds of arguments people raise when discussing the issue, and the kinds of life events that will make their attitude salient to them.

Many other nonevaluative properties have been explored by attitude researchers (e.g., ambivalence, intensity, and consistency). The reader should consult other sources if interested in more information about them (e.g., Scott, 1968; Smith, Bruner, & White, 1956).

Attitudes and persuasion researchers have been slow to investigate these nonevaluative properties in any systematic fashion. You will find very little treatment of them in this or other books in the field. Although we believe that nonevaluative properties will become an important area for future research activity, the present chapter nonetheless focuses on the more traditional evaluative measures.

Response Domain

The properties of an attitude, like evaluation, ego involvement, and dimensionality, are theoretical abstractions. That is, they cannot be directly observed. Instead, they must be inferred on the basis of observable (and therefore measurable) responses.

Researchers have identified three types of responses that people make when conveying their attitudes to others. They are referred to as the affective, cognitive, and conative components of attitude. This tripartite distinction has a long history in Western thought (Flemming, 1967; Ostrom, 1969). *Affective responses* refer to the emotional feelings and physiological consequences of encountering or thinking about an attitude object. These feelings vary from positive to negative on the evaluative dimension. *Cognitive responses* refer to the facts, knowledge structures, beliefs, inferences, and assumptions made about the attitude object. They vary from favorable to unfavorable on the evaluative dimension. *Conative responses* refer to behavioral intentions and overt actions taken in regard to the attitude object. They vary from supportive to hostile on the evaluative dimension. Different attitude measures give differential emphasis to the three components.

A Multitude of Attitude Measures

The remainder of this chapter is devoted to illustrating the variety of attitude measures that have been developed over the years. We will not give step-by-step instructions on how to construct or administer each measure. For this kind of information, the reader is directed to other sources (e.g., Edwards, 1957; Fishbein, 1967; Summers, 1970; Mueller, 1986). Nor will the chapter offer a comprehensive examination of all the research that has been directed toward developing and improving the field of attitude measurement. For this, the reader is directed to the chapters on attitude measurement in the two most recent editions of the *Handbook of Social Psychology* (Dawes & Smith, 1985; Scott, 1968). There are a number of attitude topics for which scales have already been developed (exclusively dealing with the evaluative property). Collections of these scales are found in Robinson, Athanasiou, and Head (1969); Robinson, Rusk, and Head (1968); Robinson and Shaver (1969); Robinson, Shaver, and Wrightsman (1991); and Shaw and Wright (1967).

Verbal Measures of Attitude

As noted previously, more than one property of attitude can be measured. However, most researchers are interested in the evaluative dimension. When people speak of attitude, they most frequently refer to this evaluative, favorable-unfavorable property.

Two general approaches have been developed for measuring this evaluative property. By far the most popular is through direct questions put to the respondent. We call these *verbal measures*. This is the approach used in questionnaires and surveys. The second approach is for the researcher to avoid directly talking to the respondent but rather to observe the overt actions, facial expressions, and physiological responses of the respondent. We call these *observational measures*. Using product purchases as an index of packaging attractiveness and channel switching as a measure of attitude toward soap operas are illustrations of this approach.

Direct Reports of Attitude

The simplest approach to discovering a person's attitude is to directly ask how he or she feels about the attitude object. This is what Weldon and Babbs are doing when they discuss their thoughts and feelings about abortion with one another.

Direct verbal measures can be divided into two categories: structured scales and unstructured scales. The main difference is that in *structured scales*, the respondent is given a limited number of answers to select from when responding to the question. For example, Babbs might ask Weldon to answer simply "yes" or "no," is abortion against his religious principles? *Unstructured scales* have an open-ended quality where respondents can elaborate their thoughts as fully as they wish when answering each question. For example, after Weldon said, "Yes, abortion is against my religious principles," Babbs might have asked him to explain more fully the kinds of inconsistencies that bothered him.

Structured Measures: Surveys and Single-Item Scales

People are generally most familiar with structured measures. This is the kind that is used most often in telephone surveys and "person-on-the-street" interviews. You are asked to think about your attitude and report it as accurately as you can. For example, the Gallup polls frequently measure Americans' attitudes toward the president's job performance. Gallup respondents have been asked: "Do you approve or disapprove of the way Clinton is handling his job as president?" Respondents who say "approve" presumably have positive attitudes toward President Clinton's performance, and those who say "disapprove" presumably have negative attitudes.

Structured scales have several advantages over unstructured scales. Since they can be printed in a booklet, they are easy to administer. Since they have a limited number of response options, they are easy to score. They have the additional advantage that they allow the investigator to focus on specific parts of an attitude that may be of special interest. For example, they can highlight specific beliefs related to the attitude object, or they can differentially highlight the affective, cognitive, or conative response domains.

The single-item, self-rating scale is the most widely used approach in attitude measurement. The scale acquired enduring fame when the movie *10* was released. Bo Derek came to define (or anchor) the top of Dudley Moore's 10-point scale of feminine pulchritude. This type of scale has been extensively adopted in both laboratory experimentation and nationwide surveys, for several reasons: It is quick and easy to construct, and it usually does the job as well as any of the multiple-item scales discussed later in this chapter.

A great deal of laboratory research uses seven-category rating scales. For many attitude topics, especially ones that people have thought about before, people seem to be able to identify about seven shades of attitude on the pro-to-con scale. More categories are meaningless, and fewer categories do not allow people to convey distinctions they know exist.

Some scales describe the pro-to-con dimension and ask people to check the category that best describes their overall attitude (see Figure 2-1, Panel A). Other scales provide a single statement of attitude or belief and ask how much the person agrees or disagrees with it (see Figure 2-1, Panel B). The scoring of these scales is simplicity itself. A number from 1 to 7 (or sometimes –3 to +3) is assigned to the person, depending on which category he or she checked.

Researchers feel that sometimes the respondent needs some help in visualizing attitudes as falling on a dimension. This is especially true for national surveys that may include a large number of respondents with poor reading skills. So the researchers try to create analogies between the attitude scales and other, more familiar concepts. Figure 2-2A shows a stair-step scale, and Figure 2-2B shows an opinion thermometer. Gradations in attitude parallel gradations in height or temperature. Some investigators feel that the use of such analogies allows a person to make more than seven distinctions on the attitude dimension. Typically, the thermometer scale provides 11 gradations of "temperature" (from 0 to 100).

Sometimes surveys are administered to groups that differ in their native language or to children too young to have good reading skills. In this case, rating scales may use pictorial ways of conveying gradations of positive to negative affect. Figure 2-3 illustrates one such scale.

Special Problems with Single-Item Measures of Attitudes.   The data provided by single items can sometimes be misleading. This is especially so in cases where the items are presented in oral form rather than in written form. During the last 20 years, researchers have identified many *biases in single-item measures*. These hidden biases have been identified by showing that seemingly trivial variations in the

FIGURE 2-1   Categorical single-item rating scales

Panel A: Favorability Scale

Question: How favorable or unfavorable do you feel toward legal abortion?
Instructions: Place a checkmark in one of the following categories.

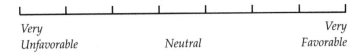

Very		*Very*
Unfavorable	*Neutral*	*Favorable*

Panel B: Agree-Disagree Scale

Question: How much do you agree or disagree that abortion should be legal?
Instructions: Please circle one of the following numbers.

–3	–2	–1	0	+1	+2	+3
Strongly			*Neither*			*Strongly*
Disagree			*Agree nor*			*Agree*
			Disagree			

FIGURE 2-2 Single-item scales with analogical formats

Panel A: Stair-Step Scale

Question: What is your attitude toward the pro-choice supporters of abortion rights?
Instructions: Place a check mark on the stairstep that best describes your attitude.

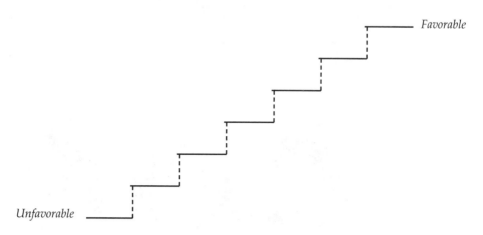

Panel B: Opinion Thermometer

Question: How do you feel toward the pro-choice supporters of abortion rights?
Instructions: Circle the number on the thermometer scale that best describes your feelings.

100	*Warm*
90	
80	
70	
60	
50	
40	
30	
20	
10	
0	*Cold*

1. _____   2. _____   3. _____   4. _____

5. _____   6. _____   7. _____

FIGURE 2-3   Pictures are sometimes better than words.

wording, format, and order of survey questions can have dramatic effects on the answers people give to them.

    Before we explain these biases, we would like you to answer a few short questions:

1. Do you agree or disagree with the following statement: "The civil justice system in the United States works very well and is in no need of repair."
2. Do you favor a law that would make abortion illegal, or do you believe that such a law would interfere too much with the rights of women to control their own bodies?
3. Which of the following do you consider to be the most important problem facing the United States today: unemployment, inflation, the threat of war, the government budget deficit, or crime?
4. Do you favor or oppose the Metallic Metals Act?
5. Do you think that the Japanese government should be allowed to set limits on how much U.S. industry can sell in Japan?

6. Do you think that the U.S. government should be allowed to set limits on how much Japanese industry can sell in the United States?

Do you think these questions would provide unbiased measurements of your opinions on the issues being addressed? Each one illustrates a particular type of bias, and we will discuss each below.

The problem with the first question is that some people seem to agree with everything, regardless of what a question asks. This tendency has come to be called *acquiescence bias* (see Schuman & Presser, 1981, ch. 8). This can be a problem when a statement is read to respondents and they are asked whether they agree or disagree with it.

Agree/disagree questions like this one about the civil justice system are often used in surveys. However, researchers have known for many years that the acquiescence bias can produce misleading results. In the case of the civil justice system question above, it would lead to overestimation of the number of people who have positive attitudes toward the civil justice system, since the statement is phrased positively. However, if the statement said instead, "The civil justice system has many serious problems and is greatly in need of repair," acquiescence response bias would lead to an overestimation of the number of people with negative attitudes.

Researchers are not yet certain about why some people show acquiescence response bias, though we have a number of theories. One possibility is that the tendency to acquiesce to any kind of social pressure is a part of these people's personalities (Couch & Keniston, 1960). According to this theory, these respondents listen to the interviewer read the statement about the civil justice system and infer that the interviewer believes it to be true; after all, she just said it, and she sounded like she believed it. This is not such an odd inference to make, in fact, because survey interviewers are trained to read statements in ways that make it sound as if they really do believe what they are saying. Respondents who think the interviewer believes the statement to be true and who have acquiescent personalities presumably say they agree with it because they feel social pressure from the interviewer (see Figure 2-4).

Because of this problem with agree/disagree questions, many survey researchers now believe that they should be avoided whenever possible. One is almost always able to rewrite an agree/disagree question in another format. For example, the civil justice system question above could be asked as follows:

Some people believe that the civil justice system works very well and needs no repairs. Other people believe the civil justice system has many problems and that many changes need to be made in it. Which point of view do you agree with more?

Unfortunately, you cannot be certain that you have eliminated the influence of acquiescence response bias just because a question does not ask respondents to agree or disagree with a statement. For example, consider the following question: "Do you favor a law that would make abortion illegal?" This question does not ask

Doonesbury

FIGURE 2-4   **The socially desirable wording of questions can produce acquiescence among respondents.**

Source: Doonesbury © 1989 G. B. Trudeau. Reprinted with permission of Universal Press Syndicate. All rights reserved.

respondents to agree or disagree with a statement, but people who are especially acquiescent might perceive the interviewer to favor the law and might therefore lean in the direction of saying "yes." Sure enough, some people say "yes" when asked whether they favor a law outlawing abortion and also say "yes" when asked whether they oppose a law outlawing abortion!

Researchers have therefore concluded that it is preferable to ask balanced questions. The abortion question above is unbalanced because it offers only one point of view. A simple way to make it balanced would be to say, "Do you favor or oppose a law that would make abortion illegal?" This presumably makes it more difficult for a respondent to infer the interviewer's attitude on an issue and therefore reduces the likelihood of acquiescence.

Asking a favor/oppose question like this one is probably the best way to balance an unbalanced question. Sometimes, though, researchers go a little too far in trying to do so. Consider question 2 earlier about abortion: "Do you favor a law that would make abortion illegal, or do you believe that such a law would interfere too much with the rights of women to control their own bodies?" The intention of this question is presumably to offer two contrasting points of view and to legitimize both of them.

However, there are two problems with this question. First, it offers a persuasive argument supporting the pro-choice point of view and offers no such argument supporting the pro-life point of view. This argument might persuade some respondents to express positive attitudes toward abortion (Bishop, Oldendick, & Tuchfarber, 1982). Because surveys are intended to measure attitudes and not to change them, this possibility could lead to misleading results. Second, the question actually makes it difficult for some pro-choice persons to express that point of view. Imagine that you believe abortion should not be made illegal because you feel there are too many laws and that no new laws should be passed. But you also do not believe that outlawing abortion would interfere too much with women's right to control their own bodies. How do you answer the question? Neither answer choice would express your views! Clearly, it is a badly written question. The lesson to be learned is that attitude questions work best (1) when they are balanced, (2) when they do not include persuasive arguments, and (3) when they offer points of view that cover all the opinions that people might have on an issue.

A second problem with single items can result from *omitting important response choices* from closed-ended questions. One of the most frequently asked questions in survey research is, "What do you consider to be the most important problem facing the United States today?" This is called an *open-ended question* because it allows respondents to give any answer they wish. When researchers analyze answers to such a question, their first step is to code the answers into categories and to tabulate the number of respondents who give each type of answer. This coding process can sometimes be quite difficult because rarely do two people give exactly the same answer. For example, one respondent might say "inflation" and another might say "high prices." Are these respondents saying the same thing? This is a judgment call that researchers must make.

Because these judgment calls are difficult to make with any confidence, many survey researchers advocate letting the respondent code his or her own answers into a category. This is done by asking closed-ended questions. Question 3 above is an example: "Which of the following do you consider to be the most important problem facing the United States today: unemployment, inflation, the threat of war, the government budget deficit, or crime?" This question asks respondents to choose among a set of offered alternatives and therefore does not require any coding by the investigator.

If a respondent's preferred answer to a question is not included among the alternatives, how will he or she answer? Some may rebel and state their preferred answer. But others will typically select one of the offered choices. So, for example, even if a man believes that drug abuse is the nation's most important problem, he may not insist on that answer. Rather, he may pick the one of the five mentioned problems he considers most important (Schuman, Ludwig, & Krosnick, 1986). It is therefore extremely important that the list of responses to a closed-ended, forced-choice question be as complete as possible.

Once a researcher has determined which answer choices should be offered in a closed-ended question, he or she must make another important decision: In what order should the response alternatives be read to the respondent? As it turns out, reading response alternatives in different orders can lead respondents to give different answers, even though the question seems to ask the same thing. This is called a *response order effect*.

Consider again the question about national problems: "Which of the following do you consider to be the most important problem facing the United States today: unemployment, inflation, the threat of war, the government budget deficit, or crime?" Which answer would you choose if an interviewer read it to you over the phone? Now, imagine that the interviewer instead read the list of choices to you in the reverse order: "crime, the government budget deficit, the threat of war, inflation, or unemployment?" Would you have given a different answer?

Survey researchers have shown in many studies that you may well have given a different answer. Two sorts of effects can occur—primacy effects and recency effects (Krosnick & Alwin, 1987). *Primacy effects* occur when respondents are biased toward choosing one of the first answer choices they hear. One reason why primacy effects occur is laziness: Respondents simply choose the first answer choice that seems acceptable. *Recency effects* occur when respondents are biased toward choosing one of the last answer choices they hear. One reason why recency effects occur is memory: After hearing a long list of answer choices, it is sometimes easier for respondents to remember the last ones read.

Response order effects can appear in questions like the "most important problem" question described above, and they also can occur in much simpler rating-scale questions. So, for example, asking respondents to indicate whether they feel "extremely favorable, very favorable, somewhat favorable, neither favorable nor unfavorable, somewhat unfavorable, very unfavorable, or extremely unfavorable" toward an economic policy can lead people to give a different answer than reading the response choices in the reverse order, from extremely unfavorable to extremely favorable. It is impossible to simply read a question and predict whether it has a response order bias built into it. The only way to be sure is to see whether respondents give different answers when the response alternatives are read in different orders.

How did you respond when answering question 4 above about the "Metallic Metals Act"? A particularly tricky problem with survey attitude measures is *non-attitudes* (Converse, 1964). Nonattitudes are opinions that people express that really do not reflect a pre-existing view they had on the issue. Rather, they concocted a response on the spot, based on little or no information about the issue. Some people who have no opinion on an issue tell interviewers that explicitly, but other people pretend to have an opinion instead. They do this, presumably, because they feel some pressure to portray themselves to the interviewer as thoughtful and knowledgeable. Unfortunately, some evidence suggests that the responses people whip up on the spot do not reflect meaningful opinions at all but rather are purely random choices from among the answer choices offered by a question. Consequently, these respondents would probably give a completely different answer if they were asked the same question a week or two later. (See Chapter 7 by Wood and Stagner for further discussion.)

When the results of polls are reported in the media, they usually ignore the possibility of nonattitudes completely. The usual practice is to report the proportion of citizens who favor or oppose a particular political candidate or government policy. These proportions are typically not based on the nation as a whole but rather on only those survey respondents who offered an opinion in response to the relevant survey question. The people who said "don't know" are not mentioned at all.

The proportion of people who say "don't know" can vary a great deal, depending upon exactly what attitude is being measured. Almost everyone offers opinions about abortion, gun control, and race relations policies, and very few people offer opinions about U.S. relations with Central American nations. Therefore, a poll report claiming that 60% of people oppose U.S. government aid to El Salvador and that 40% favor aid is likely to be misleading in its indication that a majority of Americans oppose aid. In fact, a majority of Americans might have said they had no opinion at all on the issue! For some attitude issues, therefore, it is a mistake to interpret the results of attitude surveys without knowing the proportion of respondents who offered opinions on each issue asked about.

It is hard to identify nonattitudes conclusively, but some studies have provided pretty convincing evidence that they exist. For example, in one study (Schuman & Presser, 1981), respondents in a national survey were asked whether they favored or opposed the "Agricultural Trade Bill." This was an obscure bill being considered by Congress that had received no national publicity at all and that the researchers believed no Americans would know about. Despite this likely ignorance, only 69% of respondents in the survey said they had no opinion toward the bill. Nineteen percent said they favored it, and 11% said they opposed it! When these people were asked why they favored or opposed it, their answers revealed that they did not know anything about the bill, that they had tried to guess what it was about, and that they had concocted an evaluation of it on that basis. Similar results have been produced when surveyors have asked Americans about other obscure pieces of legislation and, in some cases, about nonexistent pieces of legislation that the survey researchers made up, such as the "Metallic Metals Act" (Bishop, Tuchfarber, & Oldendick, 1986).

The *order in which questions are asked* can have a substantial effect on answers. One type of question order effect that is well-understood involves the norm of evenhandedness: the belief that all parties in a dispute should be treated equally (Schuman & Ludwig, 1983). Consider question 5 above: "Do you think that the Japanese government should be allowed to set limits on how much U.S. industry can sell in Japan?" Many Americans oppose such limits and say so when asked this question. However, the proportion of people who say so goes down substantially when this question is preceded by question 6 above: "Do you think that the U.S. government should be allowed to set limits on how much Japanese industry can sell in the United States?" Most Americans favor such limits and say so in response to this question. When it is followed by the question about allowing Japan to limit U.S. imports, many respondents realize that they ought to be evenhanded. Consequently, many who would have opposed allowing Japan to limit imports say they favor that right.

Question order effects have also been shown to occur in measures of public attitudes toward legalized abortion. Since the early 1970s, the University of Chicago's National Opinion Research Center has been asking Americans whether they favor or oppose legalized abortion under a variety of circumstances. A series of questions asks respondents whether it ought to be legal to get an abortion if there is a strong chance of a serious defect in the baby or if a woman is married and does not want any more children.

People's answers to the question about a married woman who does not want any more children are very different, depending on whether they are first asked about the case in which there is a strong chance of a birth defect (Schuman, Presser,

& Ludwig, 1981). Fewer people say they favor abortion for the married woman if they are first asked the birth defect question. One possible explanation for this question order effect is that the "married woman" reason seems less convincing when compared to the "defect" reason. Another explanation focuses on the possibility that many respondents may have ambivalent feelings about abortion. According to this explanation, most people favor legalized abortion in the case of a birth defect. However, because they feel some ambivalence about this, they say they oppose abortion in the case of the married woman in order to convey their mixed feelings to the interviewer. These examples make it clear that the answers people give to an attitude question in a survey can be partly influenced by the questions that came before it.

Structured Measures: Multiple-Item Scales

All of the biases discussed in the last section make it difficult to take a person's answer to a single question as a perfect indicator of his or her opinion on the issue. One way that researchers have learned to overcome these biases is to use *multiple-item tests*. The primary motivation for constructing multiple-item scales is to improve the reliability and accuracy of the testing instrument. It is common practice in other fields, such as the measurement of personality, intelligence, and scholastic achievement, to include a number of different items in the test. No teacher would ever give just one multiple-choice question as the entire final exam. The more items that are included, the more accurately test performance reflects students' knowledge.

The same principle holds true in attitude measurement. Where single-item scales ask for feelings in general, multiple-item scales include items that cover a variety of different feelings and beliefs the person may have toward the attitude object. Averaging across 5 or 10 separate items should provide a more valid index of the underlying attitude because the bias affecting any single item will have a relatively small effect on a person's total test score.

One of the earliest of the multiple-item scales was developed by Likert (1932). The Likert scale is probably the most used attitude measurement technique other than the single-item self-rating. To develop a Likert scale, the researcher begins by generating a large pool of belief statements for pretesting. The entire set of items is given to a sample of pretest subjects to indicate how much they agree or disagree with each item (see Figure 2-5). Each subject is presented with the statements and instructed to check only one of (usually) five possible responses for each statement (Strongly Agree, Agree, Undecided, Disagree, Strongly Disagree).

A provisional attitude score is computed for each of these subjects based on their answers to the entire item set. Only those individual items that correlate highest with the provisional score are selected for inclusion in the final scale. Usually, half the selected items are positive beliefs and half are negative beliefs. This minimizes distortions due to acquiescence bias (described in the previous section).

A great deal of the research reported in this book employs a variant on the Likert technique. These "message-based" Likert scales bypass the usual first step of pretesting a large group of items. This approach is taken when the researcher

FIGURE 2-5   Examples of Likert scale items

Instructions: Please read each statement and circle the level of agreement that best describes your reaction.

1. Women should have control over their own bodies.

   | Strongly Agree | Agree | Undecided | Disagree | Strongly Disagree |

2. Abortion should be legal throughout the United States.

   | Strongly Agree | Agree | Undecided | Disagree | Strongly Disagree |

3. Abortion is not a civilized act.

   | Strongly Agree | Agree | Undecided | Disagree | Strongly Disagree |

4. Abortion is no different than infanticide.

   | Strongly Agree | Agree | Undecided | Disagree | Strongly Disagree |

Note: The overall attitude score is calculated by adding the four items. A value of +2 is given to the strongest pro-choice response (*Strongly Agree* for items 1 and 2 and *Strongly Disagree* for items 3 and 4). A value of –2 is given to the opposite end of each scale, and the intermediate responses are given values of +1, 0, and –1.

wants to know the respondent's reactions to the specific arguments and conclusions presented in a persuasive communication (e.g., several arguments may have been given in support of the conclusion that tuition should be doubled next year).

In such cases, the investigator will prepare a small number of belief statements, each of which relates to a different argument in the message. In this manner, a scale of only two to six items may be prepared. There is some risk to this approach, however, because for the scale to be reliable, all the items must show positive correlations with one another. And since this can only be calculated after the study is complete, the entire study may have to be redone, should the measure prove invalid.

Why is the Likert scale so popular? It is easy to construct and, most importantly, it works. To construct a message-based Likert scale, researchers have to come up with just a few attitudinal statements. The scale works because researchers use common sense: They know what a "pro," an "anti," and a "neutral" item is, and they know how to avoid irrelevant items. As a result, Likert scales routinely show high correlations with other attitude scales.

There are a wide variety of alternative approaches to the construction of multiple-item attitude scales. Some are developed to be consistent with particular theories of attitude (e.g., Fishbein & Ajzen, 1975; Rosenberg, 1956; Thurstone, 1928). Others involve statistical refinements of the Likert approach, making use of modern item response theory in test construction (e.g., Lord, 1980). However, these treatments are too technical for our present purposes. (See Ostrom, 1989, for a more detailed discussion of these issues.)

Unstructured Measures

Likert scales, along with all the single-item measures, share an important feature: They impose a structure on the attitude they measure. A psychologist first selects the attitude items and then selects a fixed set of response alternatives. Respondents are not given the opportunity to qualify or expand on their answers.

Imagine what an impoverished picture we would have of Babbs's and Weldon's attitudes toward abortion if all we knew was how they rated themselves on the scales portrayed in Figures 2-1, 2-2, 2-3, and 2-5. These scales capture little of the flavor and subtle nuances of their attitudes. For example, Weldon may partly agree and partly disagree with Likert item 2 (Figure 2-5). His acceptance of legalized abortion may be conditional on the woman receiving parental consent if she is under the age of 21. Such concerns about family solidarity would be difficult to capture with a limited set of structured items.

Unstructured approaches to attitude measurement have been developed to overcome these problems. In open-ended questions, subjects have the opportunity to express themselves in their own terms. The respondent must provide an answer using his or her own vocabulary of thoughts and feelings. One use of the open-ended approach is with *focus groups*. In this case, the researcher meets with a small group of people and asks them to discuss the issue among themselves. The focused interaction among the group members often brings out subtleties and nuances in attitude that would otherwise be missed.

In questionnaires and one-on-one interviews, respondents are asked broad questions like "How do you feel about abortion?" or more specific belief questions such as those that appear on a Likert scale (see Figure 2-5). Respondents are allowed to say whatever they wish. Indeed, they are usually encouraged to expand beyond mere expressions of agreement or disagreement.

Responses are tape-recorded or transcribed verbatim by an interviewer who tries not to influence the subject in any way. The product of an open-ended interview is a typed transcription (referred to as a *protocol*) of everything the respondent said in answer to the questions. These protocols can yield important information—particularly if the attitude is one the person has thought about a lot and so has lots to say about it (Ericcson & Simon, 1980).

Subjects' responses to open-ended questions may be quirky and unique, depending on the special experiences each person may have had. The respondent may voice a number of thoughts that are related to one another in intricate ways. Consider, for example, one pro-life activist's response to a sociologist, when questioned about abortion:

> *One of the problems of abortion, I think, is the further degradation of women in society. . . . I think having abortion as an alternative—as a way out, I guess—makes it easier for men to exploit women than ever before. I think they are less inclined probably to take responsibility for their actions or to anticipate the consequences of their actions as long as abortion is available. And I think it makes it harder for women who do not choose to engage in premarital sex to say no, or to be accepted in society, because there's*

always this consideration that there's something wrong with them. (An activist, in Luker, 1984, p. 162)

As you can see, open-ended expressions of attitude are rich and diverse in the thoughts and feelings they express. There are two approaches to analyzing these protocols. One approach, called *content analysis*, tries to identify the variety of qualitative themes that are expressed. This involves thoughtful reading of all the protocols with the purpose of intuiting the underlying categories of religious, moral, practical, and psychodynamic concerns that are expressed there. It is like reading a novel and trying to analyze the motives of the main characters. One application (Shavitt & Brock, 1986) has examined people's reactions to advertisements and has identified categories of thoughts about the self, about the product, and about ad execution (i.e., how the ad was presented).

Once a set of categories is developed, it is taught to a small set of coders who then read through all the protocols and count the number of times each underlying category appears in each protocol. This way, we can analyze abortion attitudes to determine, for example, how the concerns of men differ from women, how the concerns of people who are affluent differ from those of people who are poor, or how the concerns of Blacks differ from those of Whites.

A second approach to analyzing protocols allows us to give each person an overall attitude score on the evaluative dimension. Cacioppo, Harkins, and Petty (1981) review a method for scoring open-ended responses to persuasive messages referred to as a *cognitive response analysis*. It is used in research reported elsewhere in this book (see Chapter 6 by Petty, Cacioppo, Strathman, and Priester).

The cognitive response procedure involves respondents' jotting down their attitude-relevant thoughts immediately after hearing or reading a persuasive message. They are asked to place their thoughts on separate lines in the thought-listing form. The kinds of beliefs and sentiments that people write turn out to be similar to the items that are used in Likert scales. However, people also write other things in their protocols, including comments about the communicator's credibility and about the accuracy of the arguments used in the persuasive message.

The key to scoring these protocols is to identify which of the listed thoughts are positive and which are negative toward the attitude object. Researchers have a choice of two ways to get this information. The simplest is to ask the respondent to go back and indicate whether each thought is positive or negative. The alternative is to have several independent raters read over the thoughts at a later point and code them as being positive or negative. The overall attitude score for each respondent is obtained by computing the proportion of the scored responses that are positive.

Indirect Reports of Attitude

Direct attitude measures are constructed and administered on the premise that participants are willing and able to give an accurate report of their attitudes. This assumption is probably valid in a large number of cases, especially where the experimenter has established good rapport, the respondent is motivated to be helpful, and anonymity is guaranteed.

Indirect techniques were developed to overcome problems that arise when respondents are either too embarrassed or too paranoid about their answers being used against them. People are likely to misrepresent their attitudes when it is in their self-interest to do so. This is unlikely to happen in the case of Babbs and Weldon, since they are earnestly seeking to share their sentiments with one another. However, Babbs may not be nearly as forthcoming when talking with Weldon's parents. If a person is given an attitude test in the context of an employment interview or if the person holds an attitude that is considered repulsive by society, that person may well deliberately distort the way he or she answers a questionnaire (see Figure 2-6).

*"Would you say Attila is doing an excellent job, a good job,
a fair job, or a poor job?"*

FIGURE 2-6   People know the truth can hurt.

Source: Drawing by Chas. Addams; © 1982 The New Yorker Magazine, Inc.

A number of indirect attitude measurement techniques have been developed to overcome these problems. They are all based on known ways in which attitudes affect normal human functioning. One approach uses the well-known Thematic Apperception Test pictures. This *projective* test works because powerful attitudes (e.g., racial prejudice) are known to influence the stories that respondents tell about the ambiguous pictures.

The *information error test* is based on people's known tendency to distort reality so that their perceptions agree with their attitudes (Hammond, 1948). The test capitalizes on that bias by looking at the direction of distortions. Do the distortions make the attitude object look good, or do they make the attitude object look bad?

The test presents respondents with a series of factual questions in a multiple-choice test format (see Figure 2-7). It is presented to the respondent as being a test of factual knowledge; no mention is made of the experimenter's interest in the respondent's attitudes. It appears to be an ordinary multiple-choice quiz of the type commonly used in educational settings.

FIGURE 2-7   Information error test

Instructions: This is a test of your factual knowledge about an important social issue. Please circle the correct answer for each of the following questions.

1. The number of pregnant women who die each year from legal abortions is:

   a. 376
   b. 704
   c. 1,875
   d. 5,397

2. The average annual donation to religious organizations by pro-choice advocates is:

   a. $520
   b. $318
   c. $280
   d. $78

3. The percent of pro-life supporters who approve of firebombing abortion clinics is:

   a. 1.6%
   b. 5.3%
   c. 9.6%
   d. 12.7%

4. The average month at which pregnancies are terminated by abortion is:

   a. 4.0 month
   b. 3.2 month
   c. 2.4 month
   d. 1.3 month

Note: The test is scored by assigning the numbers 1 through 4 to the selected answers. The most pro-choice response (alternative a for the first two questions and alternative d for the last two questions) is given a "4," and the most pro-life response is given a "1."

The trick here is that all the alternatives for each question are incorrect. In fact, the researcher may not even know what the correct answer actually is. The respondent is required to guess from among the several response options provided by the researcher. The set of alternatives vary in how flattering or unflattering they are toward the attitude object. Since exceedingly few respondents will know the correct answer, it is assumed that they will draw upon their attitude when selecting an alternative to each question. For example, the first item in Figure 2-7 refers to the number of pregnant women who die as a result of having an abortion. A low number of deaths is more likely to be selected by pro-choice persons, and a high number is more likely to be selected by pro-life advocates.

Persuasion researchers have not used indirect methods as much as direct methods. Techniques like the information error test are not as reliable as the direct measures. This is due in part to other factors (e.g., familiarity with the topic and amount of factual knowledge) contributing as much to the final score as does attitude. Another reason indirect methods are not used is because most persuasion research (like that in this book) is conducted in the context of nonsensitive attitude issues (e.g., consumer products, raising school tuition, and political candidates), where people are more willing to be forthright in reporting their attitudes.

We have now completed our review of verbal approaches to the measurement of the evaluative property of attitude. All these measures require the direct cooperation of the participants, and further, most require that the participants be able to read. This means that the participants have to be willing to give their time and also have to be cooperative. The literacy requirement means that these measures cannot be used with young children or people who are visually impaired or poorly educated.

Observational Measures of Attitude

Observational measures are designed to overcome the limitations inherent in verbal measures. The key difference between the two approaches is the question of who is doing the reporting. In all verbal measures, the participant whose attitude is being measured is providing all the evidence. The participant is the one who fills out the test or questionnaire. This is why verbal tests are sometimes referred to as *self-report measures*. In the case of observational measures, however, another person observes and records whatever data are needed to infer the participant's attitude. The person doing the observing is usually the experimenter, but it could be another person, like a parent, friend, peer, teacher, or supervisor. In contrast to the self-report nature of verbal measures, observational indices could be thought of as "other-report" measures.

Overt Behavior

One popular type of observational measure considers *overt behavior*. Here the investigator records whether or not certain activities are engaged in by the respondent. Social behaviors are selected that reflect either a favorable or unfavorable orientation toward the attitude object. As was noted by Ostrom (1969), these refer to the kinds of actions that are supportive of or antagonistic to the attitude object. As an example of social behavior in the case of abortion, we noted that Babbs had helped prepare promotional material for the pro-choice movement. Her friend Cindy may have contributed money or written her congressperson in support of pro-choice legislation.

Social psychologists have a long history of studying the relationship between attitudes and overt behavior (described in Chapter 4 by Fazio and Roskos-Ewold-sen). Some psychologists would take behavior as the "acid test" of all attitude measures and regard a person's actions as the only basis for inferring the person's attitudes. They would argue that "talk is cheap" and that one should "watch what people do, not what they say."

These psychologists seem to equate attitudes with behaviors. We do not. True, attitudes are defined as dispositions to respond (Campbell, 1950), but dispositions are just that—*dispositions*. Every behavior has multiple causes—of which an attitude is only one. The chapters by Fazio and Roskos-Ewoldsen (Chapter 4) and Cooper and Scher (Chapter 5) in this book detail the many complexities that arise in understanding the relation between attitudes and socially meaningful behaviors.

Although the relationship between attitudes and behavior is rarely one to one (Dawes & Smith, 1985), behavior can be used as an attitude measure: If Cindy demonstrates in favor of women's rights to abortion, we may infer that she supports those rights. Of course, our inference would be invalid if Cindy were only putting on a show for our benefit. More generally, behavioral measures may lack validity if the people who are exhibiting the behavior know that they are under observation by others who are important to them (Kelman, 1958; Roethlisberger, 1941).

The best behavioral measures are those that are unobtrusive. *Unobtrusive measures* are ones in which the respondents do not know they are being observed. People have no reason to distort their behaviors if they are unaware that others are watching and listening. For example, we may want to measure people's attitudes toward different art museum displays. Social desirability concerns may lead people to downplay their interest in erotic or obscene art when given verbal measures. Several behavioral options are available, including recording the average amount of time spent at each display or, more subtly, measuring the rate of wear on the carpet or floor tiles in front of the different displays. As another example, researchers might unobtrusively monitor the contents of a person's garbage can to estimate the household's attitude toward different food products or toward different reading materials (Webb, Campbell, Schwartz, Sechrest, & Grove, 1981). You might check the next time your own garbage is collected to see if one of the workers is carrying a clipboard!

It is often difficult to estimate a person's evaluative disposition on the basis of observing just one behavior (Fishbein & Ajzen, 1974; Ostrom, 1969). Babbs's helping her friend with pro-choice materials may have been nothing more than an act of friendship. This same problem of unreliability exists with single-item verbal measures. We would not want to construct a Likert scale with just one item. If all we knew was that Babbs agreed with the item "Abortions can lead to severe emotional distress," we would erroneously conclude that she held a pro-life attitude. Just as we are better off with multiple questionnaire items when estimating a person's attitude, so, too, are we better off obtaining multiple instances of a person's behavior.

Nonverbal Measures

Sometimes people conceal controversial attitudes and even go to the extent of saying things they do not believe. Babbs, for example, was speaking to her grandmother just the other day, when the topic of abortion came up. Granny voiced opposition to "murdering babies" and then asked for Babbs's view. Hoping to spare Granny and wanting to show respect, Babbs hid her support for abortion and actually expressed some mildly antiabortion beliefs. Could Granny tell that Babbs was lying? Would she discover Babbs's true attitude?

Attitudes can be inferred from nonverbal responses that are independent of the content of speech. Through paralinguistic cues, facial cues, and bodily cues, people convey attitudes that may contradict their verbalizations.

Paralinguistic cues include all audible characteristics of speech other than verbal content. Research has shown that deceptive verbalizations have a distinctive sound. Lies are high pitched, they are punctuated by hesitations, and they contain many speech errors like mispronunciations and the use of "ums" and "ahs" (Zuckerman, DePaulo, & Rosenthal, 1981). These cues to deception were probably used by Granny when listening to Babbs's faint-hearted agreement with Granny's pro-life views. Even Babbs's voice tone could have given her away. This was illustrated in a study by Weitz (1972). White students who had previously "bent over backwards" in verbally denying racial prejudice used a cold tone of voice when speaking to a Black person. Their *paralanguage* revealed a level of hostility concealed (perhaps even unconsciously) in their surface language.

Attitudinal affect (including feelings of pleasure and disgust) can also be expressed through *facial cues*. The eyes, the nose, the mouth, and the brows all have a universal language of their own. Research has found that facial expressions carry similar meanings across a variety of cultures (Ekman, 1985). Because we know that our face can be a road map to our feelings, we sometimes try to "stage manage" our expressions to conceal our true reactions. Babbs certainly tried to do this when talking to Granny. But research has shown that attitudes will leak out, despite our best efforts at concealment. One study videotaped students as they smelled pleasant and disgusting odors (Kraut, 1982). The students were instructed to assume facial poses that contradicted their personal reactions to the odors. They tried to pretend that the pleasant odors were disgusting and the disgusting odors were pleasant. But these ruses did not work. Despite students' attempts at self-control, their true attitudes could be detected by others who viewed the videotapes.

Affect is also conveyed through *bodily cues*. Shrugs, gestures, foot tapping, self-touching, and self-scratching can all reveal attitudes. In fact, people may reveal more with their bodies than with their faces because they rarely bother to control bodily cues. For example, in one study, student nurses saw a gruesome medical film and then were asked to describe the film as pleasant (Ekman & Friesen, 1974).

From videotapes of these deceptive descriptions, judges were asked to infer the nurses' affective reactions to the film. Judges who saw the nurses' bodies were able to detect their true negative reactions. In fact, these judges were more accurate than were judges who saw videotapes of the nurses' faces.

Physiological Measures

Measures of physiological functioning might be used as indices of attitudes. The tripartite view of attitude argues that the affective component (versus the cognitive and conative components) consists of emotional feelings and their physiological underpinnings. As Weldon and Babbs discuss their abortion decision, they may experience tenseness and generalized anxiety during some moments and surprise and relief at other times. The measurement of these responses is described in some detail in Chapter 3 by Cacioppo, Petty, Losch, and Crites.

Accessibility

In our earlier discussion of verbal measures, we noted that there is a special problem when it comes to nonattitudes. (Remember our asking you about your attitude toward the "Metallic Metals Act"?) People are not always willing to say that they have no opinion on a topic. The *accessibility* approach provides one way to address this issue that does not depend on self-awareness of one's own attitudes. This approach measures just how long (in milliseconds) it takes a person to answer a question about his or her attitudes. Will Babbs answer the question "Are you pro-choice?" faster than her friend Cindy, and what are we to make of this difference?

Fazio (1986; Chapter 4 in this volume) uses the accessibility approach for determining the presence or absence of an attitude. On a computer screen, the subject sees an attitude question, like "Do you favor a woman's right to have an abortion?" and the subject must hit a button to signal an answer of "yes" or "no." Fazio does not focus on which choice the participant selected; rather, he focuses on how long it took the person to make the choice. Across several studies, Fazio has demonstrated that subjects who are slow to answer an attitude question do not have a well-developed set of preexisting beliefs. Rather, they are generating an answer for the first time when asked the question. It is not that they are indifferent or ambivalent. Rather, they lack a set of predeveloped thoughts about the attitude object that would have enabled them to respond quickly. People with a long delay are thought of as not having an attitude prior to the question being asked. Thus, this approach could be used to distinguish attitudes from nonattitudes.

Attitudes can differ in accessibility even if they are equivalent on the evaluative dimension (Fazio & Williams, 1986). Although Babbs and her friend are both pro-choice, Cindy's attitude may be more accessible than Babbs's. If asked her stance on abortion, Babbs might deliberate for a while before expressing her pro-choice position. Cindy, on the other hand, would deliver her views swiftly, spontaneously, and in a wide variety of circumstances. Cindy's attitude, being more accessible, is more likely to be a guide to action than is Babbs's. Accessibility, then, is one of the factors that determine which attitudes are likely to affect behavior and which will not (see Chapter 4 for more details).

Summary

The attitudes held by Babbs, Cindy, and Weldon toward abortion differ from one another in many, many ways. That is the reality facing anyone who tries to measure attitudes on any topic. Our focus in this chapter has been to capture just one of those ways. Namely, we have focused on how people's attitudes differ in terms of their overall evaluative character. To *measure* attitudes is to assign a number to the attitude that reflects its evaluative character.

We hope that you, the reader, in having read our chapter are now convinced of two truths. One is that it is impossible to measure attitudes, and the other is that we manage to do the impossible pretty well. Attitudes have a quicksilver quality that allows them to change shape and makes them difficult to hold steady in the palm of your hand. They have a complexity due to the many thoughts, urges, and feelings they provoke. And they are intangible in the sense that they cannot be seen, heard, tasted, touched, or sniffed. Attitude researchers well understand that no single measure can ever capture attitudes in their full glory.

And yet the field has accepted the measurement challenge and has not done too badly. This chapter has provided you with a cafeteria of different methods. All have been shown to be valuable for studying some attitudes in some contexts. In fact, it may have been disappointing for you to learn that so many different approaches have been developed. Life would be a lot easier if there were just one technique that could be used for all purposes. However, one important lesson is that no single technique can be used for all purposes. Verbal techniques are better for some purposes, and observational techniques are better for other purposes.

In reading the other chapters in this book, you will note that different techniques are used by different researchers under different circumstances. Each has chosen a measurement approach that is best suited for the problems targeted by his or her research. Should you find yourself wanting to measure attitudes, we hope you will be equally thoughtful in your selection of measures.

References

Bishop, G. F., Oldendick, R. W., & Tuchfarber, A. J. (1982). Effects of presenting one versus two sides of an issue in survey questions. *Public Opinion Quarterly, 46*, 69–85.

Bishop, G. F., Oldendick, R. W., & Tuchfarber, A. J. (1983). Effects of filter questions in public opinion surveys. *Public Opinion Quarterly, 47*, 528–546.

Bishop, G. F., Tuchfarber, A. J., & Oldendick, R. W. (1986). Opinions on fictitious issues: The pressure to answer survey questions. *Public Opinion Quarterly, 50*, 240–250.

Cacioppo, J. T., Harkins, S. G., & Petty, R. E. (1981). The nature of attitudes and cognitive responses and their relationships to behavior. In R. E. Petty, T. M. Ostrom, & T. C. Brock

(Eds.), *Cognitive responses in persuasion* (pp. 31–54). Hillsdale, NJ: Lawrence Erlbaum Associates.

Campbell, D. T. (1950). The indirect assessment of social attitudes. *Psychological Bulletin, 47,* 15–38.

Converse, P. E. (1964). The nature of belief systems in mass publics. In D. E. Apter (Ed.), *Ideology and discontent.* New York: Free Press.

Couch, A., & Keniston, K. (1960). Yeasayers and naysayers: Agreeing response sets as a personality variable. *Journal of Abnormal and Social Psychology, 60,* 151–174.

Davis, D., & Ostrom, T. M. (1984). Attitude measurement. In R. J. Corsini (Ed.), *Wiley encyclopedia of psychology.* New York: Wiley.

Dawes, R. M., & Smith, T. L. (1985). Attitude and opinion measurement. In G. Lindsay & E. Aronson, (Eds.), *The handbook of social psychology* (3rd ed., Vol. 1, pp. 509–566). New York: Random House.

Edwards, A. L. (1957). *The social desirability variable in personality assessment and research.* New York: Dryden.

Ekman, P. (1985). *Telling lies: Clues to deceit in the marketplace, politics, and marriage.* New York: Norton.

Ekman, P., & Friesen, W. V. (1974). Detecting deception from the body or face. *Journal of Personality and Social Psychology, 29,* 288–298.

Ericcson, K. A., & Simon, H. A. (1980). Verbal reports as data. *Psychological Review, 83,* 37–64.

Fazio, R. H. (1986). How do attitudes guide behavior? In R. M. Sorrentino & E. T. Higgins (Eds.), *The handbook of motivation and cognition: Foundations of social behavior.* New York: Guilford Press.

Fazio, R. J., & Williams, C. J. (1986). Attitude accessibility as a moderator of the attitude-perception and attitude-behavior relations: An investigation of the 1984 presidential election. *Journal of Personality and Social Psychology, 51,* 505–514.

Fishbein, M. (Ed.). (1967). *Readings in attitude theory and measurement.* New York: Wiley.

Fishbein, M., & Ajzen, I. (1974). Attitude toward objects as predictors of single and multiple behavioral criteria. *Psychological Review, 81,* 59–74.

Fishbein, M., & Ajzen, I. (1975). *Belief, attitude, intention and behavior: An introduction to theory and research.* Reading, MA: Addison-Wesley.

Flemming, D. (1967). Attitude: The history of a concept. *Perspectives in American History, 1,* 287–365.

Hammond, K. R. (1948). Measuring attitudes by error-choice: An indirect method. *Journal of Abnormal and Social Psychology, 43,* 38–48.

Kelman, H. (1958). Compliance, identification, and internalization: Three processes of attitude change. *Journal of Conflict Resolution, 2,* 51–60.

Kraut, R. E. (1982). Social presence, facial feedback, and emotion. *Journal of Personality and Social Psychology, 42,* 853–863.

Krosnick, J. A., & Alwin, D. F. (1987). An evaluation of a cognitive theory of response order effects in survey measurement. *Public Opinion Quarterly, 51,* 201–219.

Likert, R. (1932). A technique for the measurement of attitudes. *Archives of Psychology, 140,* 1–55 (whole).

Lord, F. M. (1980). *Applications of item response theory to practical testing problems.* Hillsdale, NJ: Erlbaum.

Luker, K. (1984). *Abortion and the politics of motherhood.* Berkeley, CA: University of California Press.

Mueller, D. J. (1986). *Measuring social attitudes: A handbook for researchers and practitioners.* New York: Teacher's College Press.

Ostrom, T. M. (1969). The relationship between the affective, behavioral, and cognitive components of attitude. *Journal of Experimental Social Psychology, 5,* 12–30.

Ostrom, T. M. (1989). Interdependence of attitude theory and measurement. In A. Pratkanis, S. Breckler, & A. Greenwald (Eds.), *Attitude structure and function* (pp. 11–36). Hillsdale, NJ: Erlbaum.

Robinson, J. P., Athanasiou, R., & Head, K. B. (1969). *Measures of occupational attitudes and occupational characteristics.* Institute for Social Research, University of Michigan.

Robinson, J. P., Rusk, J. G., & Head, K. B. (1968). *Measures of political attitudes.* Institute for Social Research, University of Michigan.

Robinson, J. P., & Shaver, P. B. (1969). *Measures of*

social psychological attitudes. Institute for Social Research, University of Michigan.

Robinson, J. P., Shaver, P. R., & Wrightsman, L. S. (1991). *Measures of personality and social psychological attitudes.* New York: Academic Press.

Roethlisberger, F. (1941). *Management and morale.* Cambridge, MA: Harvard University Press.

Rosenberg, M. J. (1956). Cognitive structure and attitudinal affect. *Journal of Abnormal and Social Psychology, 53,* 367–372.

Schuman, H., & Ludwig, J. (1983). The norm of even-handedness in surveys as in life. *American Sociological Review, 48,* 112–120.

Schuman, H., Ludwig, J., & Krosnick, J. A. (1986). The perceived threat of nuclear war, salience, and open questions. *Public Opinion Quarterly, 50,* 519–536.

Schuman, H., & Presser, S. (1981). *Questions and answers in attitude surveys.* New York: Academic Press.

Schuman, H., Presser, S., & Ludwig, J. (1981). Context effects on survey responses to questions about abortion. *Public Opinion Quarterly, 45,* 216–223.

Scott, W. A. (1968). Attitude measurement. In G. Lindzey & R. E. Aronson (Eds.), *The handbook of social psychology* (2nd ed., Vol. 2, pp. 204–273). Reading, MA: Addison-Wesley.

Shavitt, S., & Brock, T. C. (1986). Self-relevant responses in commercial persuasion: Field and experimental tests. In J. Olson & K. Sentis (Eds.), *Advertising and consumer psychology* (Vol. 3, pp. 149–171). New York: Praeger.

Shaw, M. E., & Wright, J. M. (1967). *Scales for the measurement of attitude.* New York: McGraw-Hill.

Smith, M. B., Bruner, J., & White, R. (1956). *Opinions and personality.* New York: Wiley.

Summers, G. F. (1970). *Attitude measurement.* Chicago: Rand McNally.

Thurstone, L. L. (1928). Attitudes can be measured. *American Journal of Sociology, 33,* 529–544.

Webb, E. J., Campbell, D. T., Schwartz, R. D., Sechrest, L., & Grove, J. B. (1981). *Nonreactive measures in the social sciences* (2nd ed.). Boston: Houghton Mifflin.

Weitz, S. (1972). Attitude, voice and behavior: A repressed affect model of interracial interaction. *Journal of Personality and Social Psychology, 24,* 14–21.

Zuckerman, M., DePaulo, B. M., & Rosenthal, R. (1981). Verbal and nonverbal communication of deception. In L. Berkowitz (Ed.), *Advances in experimental social psychology* (Vol. 14, pp. 1–59). New York: Academic Press.

3

PSYCHOPHYSIOLOGICAL APPROACHES TO ATTITUDES

Detecting Affective Dispositions When People Won't Say, Can't Say, or Don't Even Know

JOHN T. CACIOPPO
The Ohio State University

RICHARD E. PETTY
The Ohio State University

MARY E. LOSCH
University of Iowa

STEPHEN L. CRITES
The Ohio State University

You have been recommended for a promotion to a position you have long coveted. Before making a final ruling on your promotion, however, you have been asked to submit to a lie detection test to ensure you are a person of good morals and are loyal to company and country. You suspected that refusing would be tantamount to admitting fault, but the wires, electrodes, and interrogative style of the examiner are more stressful than you anticipated. "Have you ever lied when filing your tax returns?" "Have you ever used any illicit drug?" "Have you ever considered having an extramarital affair?" "Have you ever considered violating a professional confidence?" "When filing your tax returns last year, did you overstate your deductions by approximately: $10? $100? $500? $1,000? $5,000? Over $5,000?" "Do you want this promotion because of: the vacation time? the money? the power? the creative opportunities? the status?" You can feel the coveted promotion slipping through your clammy hands.

While taking your seat on an airplane, you notice the person next to you is a very attractive member of the opposite sex. You notice, too, that this person expresses indifference as you are seated, but you also detect that the person clearly blushed. Does the person wish to be ignored, or would your effort to start a conversation be welcomed?

Both of these stories involve psychophysiological responses. Psychophysiology is the scientific study of human thought, emotion, and behavior as revealed or implemented in physiological events. Attitude researchers have traditionally been interested in psychophysiology for its presumed ability to measure how people truly feel about a person, object, or issue. Although the power to know what others are thinking might seem very desirable, there are few invasions of privacy more serious than the invasion of a person's innermost thoughts and feelings. Stable social relationships and exchanges may be served well by the fact that people's thoughts and feelings are not always apparent to those with whom we interact. Still, we have all encountered instances in which it would have been helpful if we could have gotten beyond what someone was saying to know what their true attitudes were. Attitude researchers face this problem in every study they conduct, for the self-report measures discussed by Ostrom et al. in Chapter 2 are of use only to the extent that they are valid reflections of people's true attitudes.

This chapter concerns the theory behind and several strategies for studying people's thoughts, feelings, and attitudes through the examination of physiological processes and events. This approach is somewhat unique. Consider, for instance, that most of the research discussed in this book involves manipulating situations and asking people to report their attitudes. Such an approach assumes that people are willing and able to tell you their true attitudes. Indeed, even discrepancies between self-reported attitudes and behaviors are not interpreted as questioning the validity of the self-reports but rather as indicating that alternative forces such as habits and social norms also influence individuals' behaviors. In contrast, a major theme of the present chapter is that attitudes and their consequences extend beyond what individuals are willing and, in some cases, are able to tell in words. Among the topics discussed in this chapter are the utility of psychophysiology in measuring and investigating attitudes people are unwilling to report and its possible utility in the study of attitudes people are unable to report.[1]

Attitude Assessment: Lessons from Lie Detection

Lie detection is perhaps the best known psychophysiological approach (actually, a class of approaches) to the problem of trying to determine what someone really thinks or knows. The term *lie detection* evokes images of polygraphs (devices for measuring physiological responses) and criminal investigations, with good reason.

The Department of Defense alone administers tens of thousands of such tests each year, most in specific incidents of suspected crimes. Television and films depict lie detection tests as capable of revealing deep secrets (e.g., criminal guilt, paternity), and famous lawyers such as F. Lee Bailey exalt the virtues of lie detection tests. Contrary to this public image, however, the major use of physiological measurement for the purpose of lie detection is in screening employees for government and businesses (see Figure 3-1). Several million such tests are given each year, in fact, and the number is growing (Lykken, 1981). Is anything to be learned from this work for the study of attitudes?

Bogus Pipeline

Lessons from the Detection of Deception

According to Hassett (1978), the use of lie detection to investigate crimes may have begun with a clever prince centuries ago. The suspects in a crime were brought to his palace, were lined up with their hands behind them, and were informed that, in an adjacent room, there was a sacred donkey that would bray when the guilty person pulled its tail. The suspects were told to go in turn into the darkened room alone with the donkey, to pull its tail, and to return then to their position in line, with hands clasped behind. In fact, the donkey was neither sacred

GERBERG
USA

"No. It's my polygraph."

FIGURE 3-1   Business ups and downs?

Source: Gerberg USA; Cartoonists & Writers Syndicate.

nor did it bray when a guilty person pulled its tail. These details, however, were of no consequence for the determination of the suspects' guilt or innocence. This is because the prince had dusted the donkey's tail with black powder; the theory was that only the suspect with something to hide would enter the darkened room and, out of fear of being detected, would only pretend to pull the donkey's tail. Hence, once all the suspects had returned to their place in line, the prince had them extend their hands in front of them, palms up. The suspect with clean hands was presumed guilty.[2]

Attitude Assessment

An analogous modern-day procedure for measuring attitudes is known as the *bogus pipeline*—so called because people are led to believe that a machine (rather than a sacred donkey) has a pipeline to their thoughts and attitudes. Gerard (1960; cited Gerard, 1964) may have been the first contemporary social psychologist to convince subjects he could measure their true feelings with a polygraph. In Gerard's study, subjects were told their task was to make a choice between two alternatives by pressing a button with either the left or right index finger. The alternatives were multipointed stars projected side by side on a screen for one-fifth of a second, and subjects were to choose the star with the greater number of points. Subjects were told that the study concerned not their considered judgments but their first impulses. All subjects had electrodes attached to their right and left forearms and were led to believe that the highly sensitive physiological recording equipment would register their first impulse by indicating their initial tendencies to press a button. Hence, there was little use in subjects not pressing the button that reflected their true choice between the alternatives.

This procedure has been used to obtain more truthful reports of feelings and attitudes that subjects might otherwise have been unwilling to give:

> The paradigm is based on the simple premise that no one wants to be second guessed by a machine. If a person could be convinced that we do have a machine that precisely measures attitudinal direction and intensity, we assume that he would be motivated to predict accurately what the machine is saying about him. (Jones & Sigall, 1971, p. 349)

In a demonstration of this procedure, Sigall and Page (1971) had some subjects report their attitudes on standard paper-and-pencil rating scales (see Chapter 2 by Ostrom et al. in this volume) and others report their attitudes under bogus pipeline conditions. Subjects in the bogus pipeline conditions were told to hold a steering wheel connected to a pointer. Turning the wheel allowed the pointer to move from 0 to any point on the attached −3 to +3 attitude rating scale. Electrodes were attached to subjects' forearms, and they were told that the physiological recordings could predict how far in either direction they would turn the wheel. A few practice trials were conducted in which bogus physiological data, "predicting" the subjects' true attitudes toward the stimuli, were presented. (This accurate prediction of the subjects' attitudes was possible because, unknown to the subjects, the investigator had access to their opinions from a previous questionnaire.) Subjects were even asked to try to fool the "physiological measure" on one of these early trials. Of course, since the attitude predictions were based on subjects' responses to a questionnaire administered previously, they were uniformly unsuccessful in trying to "beat the machine."

Once the subjects were convinced that the machine could read their attitudes, the attitudes that were really of interest were measured. Half of the subjects, all of whom were white females, were asked to judge whether or not certain traits (e.g., honesty) were characteristic of Americans, and half were asked if the traits were characteristic of Blacks. Results revealed that Americans were rated more favorably by the bogus pipeline than the nonpipeline (paper-and-pencil scale only) group, whereas Blacks were rated less favorably by the bogus pipeline than nonpipeline group.

But how can one tell which set of judgments is really more valid (paper-and-pencil ratings or bogus pipeline)? The investigators did not actually have unique access to the truth. This, of course, was a problem in the prince's use of the donkey, as well. It would be better to create particular beliefs in subjects and then use rating scales and the bogus pipeline to determine which best reflected these known beliefs. This is exactly what was done in a study by Quigley-Fernandez and Tedeschi (1978). Subjects were first informed about how to perform well on an experimental test. They were later given a chance to cheat on the test and were subsequently asked if they possessed any prior information about the test. Subjects questioned under the bogus pipeline conditions confessed more often than those who were not. Hence, these data appear to confirm the theory underlying the bogus pipeline.

Summary

The accumulated evidence suggests that the bogus pipeline procedure may be effective in getting people to reveal information that they might normally be unwilling to report. There are three important limitations to this procedure, however. First and foremost, the subject's belief in the procedure is crucial to its success. As the procedure becomes more widely known or as people become more skeptical about lie detection, the incentive for their telling how they actually feel will be lost and the procedure will no longer be effective. Second, just as the innocent suspects who were asked to pull the donkey's tail must certainly have suffered anxious moments, evidence points, too, to the bogus pipeline as inducing negative arousal in subjects (Gaes, Kalle, & Tedeschi, 1978). This unfortunate feature might make the bogus pipeline inappropriate in certain settings (e.g., in studies of cognitive dissonance, where it might serve as a misattribution cue; see Chapter 5 by Cooper and Scher in this volume). Finally, the procedure is not particularly useful when a person's attitude toward a person or issue is not readily accessible—that is, when the person is unable to report his or her true attitude. Indeed, just as the anxiety created by a class examination can make it difficult to remember the answers to difficult test questions, the anxiety aroused by the bogus pipeline procedure may hinder one's ability to recall actual attitudes.

Physiological Arousal in Lie Detection and Attitude Assessment

There are important parallels between the detection of deception and the detection of attitudes. First, we saw in the preceding section that a person's belief in the validity of procedures is important for the effectiveness of the bogus pipeline procedure. As we shall see, this is also the case for the polygraph in contemporary lie detection. It would be nice if, instead, some simple physiological measure could be identified that would occur if and only if the person told a lie (see Figure 3-2). Unfortunately, there is no known bodily response or set of bodily responses that occurs when and only when one lies, just as there is none that provides a readout of and only of one's attitudes. To get around this limitation, physiological responses are observed under specially contrived circumstances in order to *infer* a person's honesty or attitudes based on unusual increases in bodily arousal in response to a question or stimulus.

STEINER
USA

FIGURE 3-2   Psychologists wish they could identify a simple physiological response that would occur if and only if a person told a lie.

Source: Steiner USA; Cartoonists & Writers Syndicate.

One theory that has guided inferences in both studies of deception and studies of attitudes is that strong emotions are associated with physiological arousal (specifically, activation of the sympathetic nervous system). To the extent that lying or the threat of being detected while lying is emotionally arousing, then one would expect lying to be associated with greater physiological arousal than truth-telling. Before proceeding to examine how this theory has been applied to studies of attitudes, we illustrate its application in attempts to detect deception.

Lessons from the Detection of Deception

Most lie detection tests involve recording measures such as a person's heart rate, blood pressure, respiration, and electrodermal activity (sweating) in an attempt to detect evidence of unusual tension or stress that can be associated with lying. Prior to connecting a suspect (or potential employee) to the polygraph, a pretest interview is conducted (Iacono & Patrick, 1988). Many people find themselves so apprehensive about the threat of exposure that they admit to misdeeds during this period. For those who do not, sensors are attached, and a demonstration is staged to convince the subject that it is futile to try to fool the machine. For instance, the person selects a card from several and is told to deny having selected the card when it is presented again. Although there are several variations in procedures, the individual might be shown each of the cards, during which time physiological measures are monitored with chart and pens. When the card selected by the individual is presented, the polygrapher points to the changes in bodily response, charted by the polygraph, which purportedly foiled the individual's attempt to conceal this information. The examiner invariably can find a segment of the record to which to point to show *physiological activation* when the individual tried to lie because there are fluctuations in normal physiological activity even when people are sitting quietly.

As in the bogus pipeline, the creation of the *belief* in the ability of the machine to read the individual's innermost thoughts and feelings enhances the likelihood the individual will tell the truth; and for those who are still not compelled to tell the truth by the fear of exposure, the creation of the belief that they might well be exposed makes the individual even more nervous about anything he or she hopes to conceal. This nervousness, coupled with the special significance associated with the information one is trying to conceal, increases the likelihood that the individual will show a strong bodily response—for example, increased sweating, irregular breathing, and elevated blood pressure—when subsequently asked a question about something he or she wishes to conceal.

Attitude Assessment

The theory that strong emotions are associated with activation of the sympathetic nervous system also suggests that to the extent the presentation of a person or object evokes strong feelings, its presentation should be associated with greater physiological arousal than should presentations of people or objects toward which the person does not feel strongly. This theory has been of interest to attitude researchers because it suggests that extremely positive and extremely negative attitudes might be associated with increased sympathetic activity, regardless of what people say about these attitudes. It is also conceivable that even more specific inferences about a person's thoughts or feelings can be suggested by a person's bodily responses if the situation in which these responses are measured is constructed appropriately.

One procedure for measuring sympathetic activation involves the measurement of sweat gland activity. A very small electrical current is applied across two electrodes that are attached to the hand. (The current is so small that subjects are unaware of it, and the current presents no threat of shock or trauma to the subject.) Changes in the resistance of the skin to the flow of electric current reflect changes in the activation of a particular class of sweat glands (eccrine glands). The more these glands are activated, the more filled they are with sweat (a good conductor), and the lower the resistance to current flow. This *electrodermal* measure became a favorite among attitude researchers because it was easy and inexpensive to record; with appropriate equipment, changes were easy to detect with the eye and to quantify by hand; the measure was assumed to reflect general physiological arousal; and the measure had a direct link to what common sense indicated should be related to such subjective experiences as stress and emotion, namely, sweating (but see Cacioppo & Sandman, 1981). However, the measure did not reflect the direction (favorable versus unfavorable) of the emotion.

The earliest applications of this theory supported the expectation that emotionally laden words and statements evoked larger electrodermal responses (EDRs) (e.g., larger increases in sweating). Syz (1926–1927), for instance, found that a group of medical students showed larger EDRs[3] to emotionally laden words such as *prostitute*. Similarly, Dysinger (1931; see McCurdy, 1950) presented both pleasant and unpleasant words and found that the sizes of the EDRs were correlated with the extremity of the words but could not predict whether the words were rated as being pleasant or unpleasant.

This result has been found to hold for a variety of attitude objects and, more interestingly, has been extended to show that more information about a person's attitude could be inferred if one knew in general terms whether the person felt positively or negatively about the attitude object. For instance, Rankin and Campbell (1955) measured EDRs while subjects were voicing whatever thoughts came to mind. The manipulation involved having an experimental assistant appear to adjust a set of bogus electrodes on the subject's hand. Following each adjustment, average EDRs were calculated. Rankin and Campbell found that the EDRs were larger following the adjustments made by a Black assistant than those made by a White assistant. Later investigations demonstrated that people with negative attitudes toward Blacks showed larger EDRs to pictures of Blacks than did people with relatively favorable attitudes, presumably because the negative attitudes were more extreme (e.g., Vidulich & Krevanick, 1966; Westie & DeFleur, 1959).

It is important to recognize, however, that in all these studies the EDRs are not a direct consequence (or measure) of attitudes—just as was the case in the use of physiological measures to detect lying. Most individuals, whether guilty or innocent, will show a bodily response (e.g., increased EDRs) when asked if they murdered a close friend or relative, and large differences between people in their general anxiousness and physiological responsivity can make it difficult to separate the guilty party from the innocent party based on such a question. Similarly, the novelty, unexpectedness, or significance of stimuli can affect bodily responses such as people's EDRs, regardless of their attitude toward these stimuli. It would be no more appropriate, therefore, to conclude that a large electrodermal response following the introduction of the issue of nuclear power necessarily reflected an underlying emotional feeling about the issue than it would be to conclude that a particular individual was lying simply because a large increase in physiological activity was observed following a question.

Summary

Whether or not an individual responds physiologically to an attitude object or how much the individual responds to the object can be influenced by a number of factors besides the individual's attitude toward the object. These other factors include such things as an individual's concern about making a good impression, the novelty or unexpected nature of the stimulus, the significance of the stimulus to the individual, anger or embarrassment evoked by the stimulus, and the physiological (e.g., electrodermal) responsiveness of the individual. As we have seen, many of these problems can be overcome by the careful investigator.

For example, what if you wanted to know how strongly a friend felt about civil rights? Monitoring the changes in your friend's physiological response when you mention civil rights would not be very informative, because changes in bodily response could be due to the novelty of the question and testing situation, the individual's general physiological responsiveness, and so on. However, what if you were to monitor the changes in physiological response when you sequentially presented a larger number of attitude objects, some for which your friend's attitudes were known beforehand? You might be able to determine whether the changes in physiological response were reflecting something about your friend's already known attitudes (e.g., the extremity of the attitudes). If physiological changes were greater when objects or issues about which the individual felt strongly were presented, then you would have greater confidence (though not complete certainty) that similar physiological responses evoked by other attitude objects reflected similarly intense attitudes toward the objects (see Cacioppo & Tassinary, 1990). It is the discrepancies between verbal reports and physiological responses that are often of the greatest interest. If your friend were to report the complete absence of prejudicial feeling toward an ethnic group but were to show strong physiological responses to members of the group, then greater caution and perhaps additional inquiries would be in order before accepting the validity of your friend's verbal reports or paper-and-pencil ratings.

The Significant Information Test

A related theory that has guided inferences in studies of deception in crime suspects is that a stimulus that is (or is made) highly significant to a person (e.g., the instrument used to murder someone) evokes stronger physiological responses (e.g., larger EDRs) than does a stimulus that is not significant. Furthermore, the presentation of this stimulus would be expected to be associated with greater physiological responsivity only in the guilty individual to the extent that (a) the stimulus is familiar and has special significance only to the guilty individual and (b) the presentation of this information uniquely threatens to expose this individual as being the guilty party. Before proceeding to examine how this theory can be applied to studies of attitudes, we examine its application in attempts to detect deception in criminal investigations.

Lessons from the Detection of Deception

The theory outlined above has led to a technique for detecting deception called the *Guilty Knowledge Test (GKT*; see Lykken, 1981). In the GKT, subjects are not asked whether or not they committed a particular misdeed, but rather they are asked a series of questions about the crime. Each question concerns one feature of the crime, with multiple-choice alternatives including the correct answer as well as other plausible but incorrect choices. For instance, a suspect in a homicide might be asked whether the victim had been killed with a machete, hunting knife, butcher's knife, paring knife, or ice pick. All questions and response options are reviewed with the suspect prior to beginning the GKT. Only an individual who knows the details of the crime (that is, has guilty knowledge) is expected to respond most physiologically to the correct answer because this information has special significance only to the guilty individual, and its presentation threatens to expose the individual's guilt.

As noted in the preceding section, even an innocent individual may respond to a particular piece of guilty knowledge for some irrelevant reason (e.g., chance, prior history in an unrelated case), so GKTs consist of 10 such questions. This greatly reduces the likelihood that an innocent person would react most strongly to the relevant item in each of the 10 questions (Iacono & Patrick, 1988). One corresponding limitation of the GKT, however, is that the investigator (e.g., the police) must know several bits of information that are known by the guilty party but are not known by innocent individuals.

Attitude Assessment

The limitation of the GKT in criminal investigations is not as serious an obstacle for the attitude researcher. If one assumes that individuals know their true attitudes or at least that their attitudes have special significance to them (much as their own name or the sound of their voice does), then one can think of this knowledge as analogous to knowing a particular detail about a crime. Knowledge of one's attitude is not likely to have as much significance for individuals as knowledge about a crime they committed. An individual's attitude might be made even more significant, however, by instructing the individual to memorize his or her attitude, think about the feelings that characterize it, and imagine a personal behavior that exemplifies it (e.g., see Ben-Shakhar & Gati, 1987). In the assessment phase, the individual is presented with a sequence of attitude positions, only one of which represents the individual's own personal position. This attitude position would be expected to evoke more physiological responsivity than other positions because the person's own attitude has the greatest familiarity and personal significance.

As we noted above, the presentation of this information might also increase responsivity if individuals believed its presentation threatened to expose their personally or socially unacceptable feelings. That is, as in the case of the GKT, physiological responsivity to the presentation of their attitude position may be enhanced when individuals are motivated to avoid having their attitudes "exposed" by the polygraph during questioning. However, this threat does not appear necessary (Ben-Shakhar & Gati, 1987). Because the key to this procedure is the familiarity and special significance of a person's attitude position, rather than the threat of exposure of a particular piece of guilty knowledge, the test, when applied to the study of attitudes, might be termed the *Significant Information Test (SIT)*.

Gur and Sackeim (1979) reported an interesting study that illustrated the potency of stimulus significance in evoking physiological responses, even when individuals could not identify which of the stimuli to which they were exposed was their significant stimulus. People listened to tape recordings of their own voice and to tape recordings of others whose voices sounded generally similar. The individuals were asked to try to identify the tape recording of their own voice, and EDRs were recorded during the presentation of all of the tape recordings. Many of the individuals who participated in this study were able to identify correctly which was their own voice, but not all were able to do so. Interestingly, the presentation of the individual's voice was associated with larger EDRs than was the presentation of other people's voices, even for individuals who were unable to identify the recording of their own voice. This result raises the possibility that using the SIT for attitude assessment could provide information about attitudes that individuals themselves might have difficulty specifying.

Summary

Research has demonstrated that an effective test for detecting deception is the guilty knowledge test (Lykken, 1981). The SIT for attitude assessment is based on the same theory as the GKT: Physiological responding peaks when a person's true attitude is presented because this information has special significance to the individual. The SIT, therefore, is a potentially powerful procedure for probing attitudes that individuals are unwilling to report. Moreover, given recent research suggesting that familiar, significant information can evoke physiological reactions, even though the person may be unable to recognize the information, the SIT may also provide a means for probing attitudes that individuals are unable to report. Of course, like the GKT, attitude assessments based on the SIT require that several questions be used to ensure the reliability of the assessment.

Event-Related Brain Potential Responses

As people process information, their brain generates electrical signals, which can be recorded from the scalp. Investigators have tried to use these signals, which can be recorded using electroencephalography (EEG), to explore the activities of the brain and mind. The reasoning was that if the brain wave activity associated with two stimuli is different, the brain must have processed these stimuli differently. Although in theory, comparing the brain wave activity evoked by the stimuli may appear simple, in practice, it is complicated because the specific brain wave activity associated with a given stimulus (e.g., positive or negative attitude object) is very small, and the brain is doing many things in addition to evaluating the stimulus. These other activities can mask the activity evoked by the stimulus. For instance, the electrical signals from the brain change slightly about 300 milliseconds after the presentation of an item when the item differs from the category of items previously presented (e.g., a high-pitched tone presented after a series of low-pitched tones; a disliked item presented after a set of liked items). The change in brain wave activity is small and reflects only one of many operations being performed by the brain. Thus, one cannot see this change in brain wave activity when a single item is presented.

One method of "mining" this small electrical signal out of the other electrical activity being generated by the brain involves exposing people to an item (e.g., positive or negative attitude objects) many times while brain wave activity is recorded. The theory underlying this technique is that the brain will respond similarly to each presentation of the item and that the brain wave activity that is unrelated to the item will vary in a more haphazard way (i.e., randomly about zero). By averaging the brain wave activity associated with the presentation of many such items, the small changes in electrical signals evoked by these items become measurable. (This is because the measures of brain wave activity not associated with or time-locked to the item total zero using this technique.) The small changes in the brain wave activity that are left after averaging are called *event-related brain potentials* because they reflect changes in brain activity that are linked to some event (e.g., the presentation of a tone or an attitude object). These small event-related changes in brain wave activity have potentially important implications for the measurement of attitudes.

Lessons from the Detection of Deception

A recent paper by Farwell and Donchin (1991) examined the applicability of using brain wave activity for assessing deception. In their experiment, half of the subjects were induced to participate in a mock crime, and the remaining subjects were not induced to participate in that mock crime. Subsequently, the subjects were shown a series of stimuli, with a few crime-related stimuli included, while EEG activity was recorded. To subjects who *had not* participated in the mock crime (and who, therefore, were unaware of what the mock crime involved), the crime-related and crime-unrelated items on the list were indistinguishable. However, to subjects who *had* participated in the mock crime, the crime-related stimuli were distinctive and important (i.e., because the subjects were trying to conceal the fact that they had knowledge of the mock crime). Averaging the EEG activity revealed that the brain wave activity evoked by the crime-related items was different than the brain wave activity evoked by the crime-unrelated items but only for the subjects who had participated in the mock crime. For subjects who had not participated in the mock crime and who had no knowledge of the mock crime, similar patterns of brain wave activity were observed for the crime-related and crime-unrelated items.

Rosenfeld, Angell, Johnson, and Qian (1991) also used brain wave activity for the purposes of lie detection, but they used slightly different procedures than did Farwell and Donchin. In Rosenfeld et al. (1991), for example, subjects were told that they were suspected of committing four antisocial behaviors. Half of the subjects were known to have committed one of these antisocial behaviors, and the other subjects were known to have committed none of the antisocial behaviors. The antisocial behavior a subject was known to have committed was considered a "guilty-item" (e.g., smoked pot monthly), whereas any antisocial behavior that a subject was known not to have committed was considered an "innocent-item" (e.g., stole some clothes, took friend's money). Subjects were then shown a series of descriptions of antisocial behaviors while EEGs were recorded. Rosenfeld et al. compared the brain wave activity evoked by the guilty-items with the electrical activity evoked by the innocent-items and found the brain wave activity differed for those subjects who were, in fact, guilty of the antisocial behavior described in the guilty-items. Allen, Iacono, and Danielson (1992) recently conducted three experiments that produced similar results.

Attitude Assessment

As the preceding studies illustrate, unexpected and important stimuli evoke brain wave activity that differs slightly from the brain wave activity evoked by expected and unimportant stimuli. We have recently examined whether these findings could be used to investigate (and possibly assess) human attitudes. In an illustrative experiment (Cacioppo, Crites, Berntson, & Coles, 1993), subjects rated their attitudes toward a large number of objects and issues (e.g., pizza, raising tuition). These ratings were used to identify 75 items toward which the subject held positive attitudes and 75 items toward which the subject held negative attitudes. Next, EEG activity was recorded from each subject while items from this list of 150 attitude objects were presented on a computer screen located in front of the subject. These items were presented one at a time in blocks of 6 while the subject counted either the number of positive or negative items in the block. Sometimes all 6 items were liked by the subject, sometimes all 6 items were disliked, sometimes 5 of the 6 items were liked, and so on. In this way, many of the blocks of items contained mostly positive or mostly negative items.

The key question in this study was, What happens to brain wave activity when a positive item is presented in the middle of a list of negative items or when a negative item is presented in the middle of a list of positive items? The studies described in the previous section indicated that brain wave activity differed when an item from a different informational category (crime related or crime unrelated) was presented, but would the brain wave activity differ when an item from a different attitudinal category was presented? The results suggested yes; the brain wave activity differed when an item was presented that evoked the opposite feelings as had the preceding items. Indeed, this was the case, even though the brain wave activity evoked by the positive items did not differ from the brain wave activity evoked by the negative items. It was not the items per se but the context in which these items were presented that led to different forms of brain wave activity. We have now repeated these results using personality trait descriptions (Cacioppo et al., 1993), and we have even found differences in the amplitude of the evoked brain potentials that reflect the intensity of subjects' feelings about an attitude object (Cacioppo, Crites, Gardner, & Berntson, under review).

Summary

The contemporary use of brain wave activity to investigate concealed information and attitudes is based on the theory that certain features of how an item is categorized are reflected in small but measurable changes in brain wave activity. When an item in a list of items does not fit or is *inconsistent* with an activated category, then the brain wave activity is different (i.e., it contains a larger, slow, positive potential that trails the stimulus presentation by about 300 milliseconds) than when the item fits or is *consistent* with the activated category. Of course, this only works if people are paying attention to the items in the list, so subjects in these studies are usually given a task that requires they respond to the stimuli based on the feature or categorical dimension that is of interest (e.g., counting the number of positive or negative words in a list). Recent studies have applied this theory to the detection of lying with some early success, and the application of this theory to attitude assessment also appears promising thus far. Additional research is required, however, before the value and limitations of this new approach to attitude assessment are known.

Physiological Indicators of Affective Direction

Overt Bodily Responses as a Function of Affective Direction

Physiological measures have thus far been viewed as useful only in assessing general physiological arousal or responsivity. This view, which has a long tradition in the field of attitudes, assumes that physiological measures can reflect the intensity but not the positive or negative nature of people's emotional reactions (see review by Cacioppo, Petty, & Geen, 1989). Yet anyone who has ever watched the facial expression of someone who just tasted something they truly disliked or the expression of a person who has just seen someone they truly love and have missed might suspect that a person's physical actions and expressions can reveal whether one feels positively or negatively about an object or person (see Chapter 2 by Ostrom et al.).

In the earliest studies along these lines, investigators did indeed watch people's visually observable expressions of emotion (e.g., smiles, posture, interpersonal spacing) to gauge people's attitudes toward others (e.g., Darwin, 1872; Galton, 1884). Galton, for instance, wrote:

When two persons have an "inclination" to one another, they visibly incline or slope together when sitting side by side, as at a dinner table, and they then throw the stress of their weights on the near legs of their chairs. It does not require much ingenuity to arrange a pressure gauge with an index and dial to indicate changes in stress. . . . I have made some crude experiments, but being busy with other matters, have not carried them on. (1884, p. 184)

More recently, Ekman, Friesen, and Ancoli (1980) were able to gauge how much individuals liked particular segments of a videotape by monitoring when and to what extent subjects smiled while watching the videotape.

Electromyographic Responses as a Function of Affective Direction

Not all emotional processes are accompanied by visually or socially perceptible expressions or actions, however, and this fact has limited the utility of research on the outward expressions of emotions. For instance, Graham (1980) attempted to assess viewers' emotional responses to television advertisements using a comprehensive scoring procedure for measuring people's observable facial actions. Graham found that, for most of his subjects, there were too few observable facial expressions to the ads to make further analyses worthwhile.

There is now evidence, however, indicating that emotional reactions that are too fleeting or subtle to evoke an outward expression can nevertheless be measured physiologically (Cacioppo et al., 1989). Neural activation of the striated (e.g., facial) muscles results in electrical impulses that can be detected using electromyography (EMG), even when there are no perceptible muscle contractions. For instance, Love (1972) videotaped people's facial expressions while they were exposed to a proattitudinal or counterattitudinal appeal; he reported finding no differences in outward facial expressions, despite the fact that individuals reported more positive attitudes toward the proattitudinal than counterattitudinal communications. Cacioppo and Petty (1979) later replicated Love's finding while also demonstrating that the level of EMG activity recorded over selected muscle regions of facial expression (e.g., brow, cheek; see Figure 3-3) differentiated subjects who anticipated and were exposed to a message consistent with their attitudes from those who anticipated and were exposed to a counterattitudinal message.[4]

But what if individuals were reading an editorial in the newspaper or watching a political debate on television? Are these individuals not emitting miniature smiles or frowns? Recent research suggests there are small but measurable responses that can reflect the positive or negative nature of individuals' emotional reactions, even though these responses are more primitive in form than the more familiar, easily recognizable outward expressions of emotion (e.g., Cacioppo, Petty, & Marshall-Goodell, 1984; McHugo, Lanzetta, & Bush, 1991). Cacioppo et al. (1984), for instance, instructed subjects to imagine reading an editorial with which they agreed or disagreed or to read a page of (neutral) text as if they agreed or disagreed with it. Results indicated that there was more EMG activity over the brow

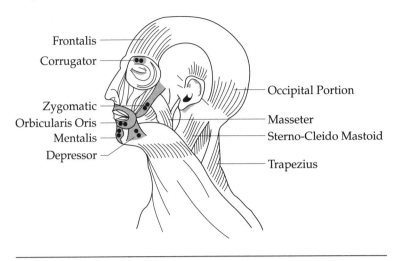

Frontalis

Corrugator

Zygomatic

Orbicularis Oris

Mentalis

Depressor

Occipital Portion

Masseter

Sterno-Cleido Mastoid

Trapezius

FIGURE 3-3   Sample facial EMG placements

Source: From "Electromyograms as Measures of Extent and Affectivity of Information Processing" by J. T. Cacioppo and R. E. Petty, 1981, *American Psychologist, 36,* pp. 441–456. Copyright 1981 by the American Psychological Association. Reprinted by permission.

region and less EMG activity over the cheek region when subjects imagined or actually read text with a negative rather than positive attitudinal instruction. Moreover, the EMG activity over muscles that have less of a role in the nonverbal communication of positive or negative feelings (e.g., the forearm flexors, lip muscle) was not altered by the attitudinal instruction followed by the subjects during the task. This suggests that there is a precise and eloquent orchestration of neural impulses to specific muscles, not simply a tension or general arousal response to emotional events.

EMG activity appears to vary as a function of the intensity as well as the direction of the emotional reaction. Evidence for this notion was provided in studies by Cacioppo, Petty, Losch, and Kim (1986; see also Cacioppo & Petty, 1979). Subjects were exposed to slides of moderately unpleasant, mildly unpleasant, mildly pleasant, and moderately pleasant scenes. Among the unpleasant scenes were pictures of litter along highways, trash dumps, and environmental wastelands, whereas among the pleasant scenes were white-sand beaches, colorful butterflies, and arching rainbows. Subjects viewed each slide for five seconds and rated how much they liked the scene that was depicted, how familiar the scene appeared, and how aroused it made them feel. Independent judges, who did not know which scenes subjects had seen, rated videorecordings of subjects' facial actions during the five-second presentations of scenes. The judges could not tell from looking at the videotapes of subjects whether the subjects were viewing positive or negative photographs. This result suggests that the scenes were so mild that outwardly perceptible facial expressions were not evoked. Nevertheless, analyses of facial EMG revealed that the activity over the muscles of facial expression varied according to the direction *and* intensity of the individuals' emotional reactions to the slides: The more subjects liked the scene, the lower the level of EMG activity over the brow region; EMG activity over the cheek region tended to be greater for liked than disliked scenes; and EMG activity was higher around the eye when moderately liked than mildly liked or disliked scenes were presented (see Figure 3-4).

Summary

Attitude researchers have long sought to identify naturally occurring physiological responses that reflect both the direction and intensity of a person's feelings about an attitude object, but previous efforts to identify such measures have been unsuccessful (e.g., Hess, 1965; see reviews by Cacioppo & Sandman, 1981; Janisse, 1977; Petty & Cacioppo, 1983). This history makes particularly interesting the more recent studies suggesting that positive and negative emotional states have effects on facial muscle patterns that are so subtle they may not be detectable to the naked eye. There is even some evidence to suggest that these subtle effects on the facial muscles, especially the muscles around the eyes and brow, are not easy for people to suppress (Cacioppo, Bush, & Tassinary, 1992; see also Ekman & Friesen, 1982). It is possible that facial EMG can be informative about a person's emotional responses to something whether or not the individual is willing or able to report his or her underlying feelings. Further research is needed to test this possibility.

In addition, one should recognize that the context in which these measures are made remains important in studies of emotions and attitudes (Cacioppo, Martzke, Petty, & Tassinary, 1988; Cacioppo et al., 1986). Facial expressions are clearly controllable, and facial expressions can serve to communicate nonemotional information and to deceive as well as to communicate emotional states. It would be an error, based on these studies, therefore, to infer that the observation of increased EMG activity over the brow region *necessarily* meant the individual disliked something. It may, for instance, simply mean the person is concentrating on or is perplexed by the attitude stimulus rather than disliking it. Moreover, if the response did reflect disliking, the emotional response might be transient, specific, and completely irrelevant to the attitude object. Thus, although this research has been informative, it should be remembered that the context in which the recordings are made is important to consider when interpreting such physiological responses (Cacioppo & Tassinary, 1990).

Classically Conditioned Physiological Responses

In the preceding sections, we saw how researchers have attempted to measure and study attitudes by observing physiological responses that are the natural result of experience with attitude objects. We also noted that a major limitation of these approaches is the absence of some simple physiological response that would vary only according to a person's evaluation (or attitude) toward a person, object, or issue. Russian psychologists, however, have adopted a different strategy to the problem of detecting a particular thought, feeling, or attitude (see Cacioppo & Petty, 1983). The theory underlying their approach is that a physio-

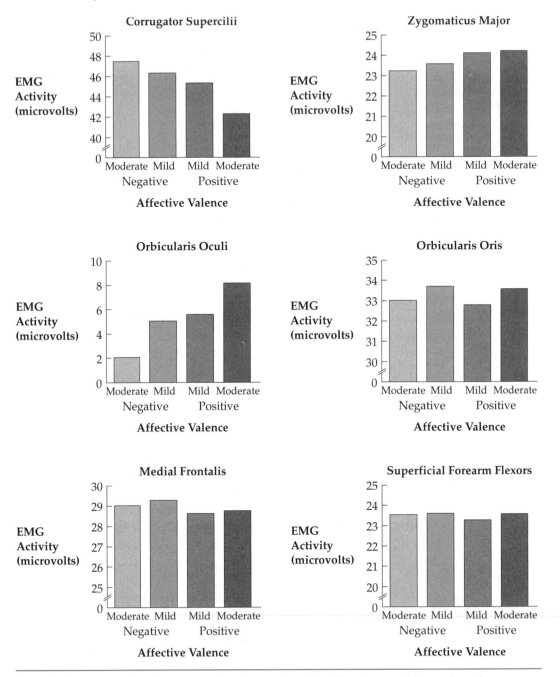

FIGURE 3-4   Facial EMG activity as a function of the direction and intensity of affective reactions

Source: From "Electromyographic Activity over Facial Muscle Regions Can Differentiate the Valence Intensity of Affective Reaction" by J. T. Cacioppo, R. E. Petty, M. E. Losch, and H. S. Kim, 1986, *Journal of Personality and Social Psychology, 50*, pp. 260–268. Copyright 1986 by the American Psychological Association. Adapted by permission.

logical response (e.g., salivation) could be linked uniquely to a particular meaning, such as *good*. By artificially creating a unique link between a physiological response and a concept such as *good*, one could then measure a person's attitude toward an object, person, or issue by recording the size of the physiological response that followed the presentation of the attitude object. The artificial linking of a physiological response (e.g., salivation) to a concept (e.g., *good*) was done with a variation of classical conditioning termed *semantic conditioning*, and the measurement of a person's attitude relied on a process called *semantic generalization*. Before describing some of the actual studies that have been conducted using this approach, we review the topics of semantic conditioning and generalization.

Semantic Conditioning and Generalization

Classical conditioning involves learning to associate an initially neutral stimulus (called a *conditioned stimulus*, or *CS*) with some evocative stimulus (called an *unconditioned stimulus*, or *UCS*). The evocative, or unconditioned, stimulus is so named because its presentation alone evokes a response of some kind (called an *unconditioned response*, or *UCR*) in the person or animal. These relationships are illustrated in Figure 3-5.

Repeated pairings of the conditioned stimulus with the unconditioned stimulus results in the CS evoking the same response (called the *conditioned response* or *CR*) as does the unconditioned stimulus (see the top panel in Figure 3-5). Meat powder, for example, evokes salivation (UCR) in the dog. If the dog is presented with both a 1,000 Hz tone (CS) and meat powder (UCS) on repeated occasions, eventually the presentation of the 1,000 Hz tone alone will cause the dog to salivate (CR). Once this has been accomplished, presentation of similar test stimuli (e.g., a 900 Hz tone) can also evoke the conditioned response (salivation), although the less similar the test stimulus is to the original conditioned stimulus (1,000 Hz tone), the smaller the conditioned response that is evoked. This phenomenon is known as *stimulus generalization*.

In this example, tones of varying frequencies have served as the conditioned stimulus. Importantly, words such as *good* or *bad* can also be used as conditioned stimuli. Prior to the conditioning, a word such as *good* has no power to evoke a physiological response, such as salivation. Following conditioning (in which *good* serves as the CS, cranberry sauce injected into the mouth serves as the UCS, and salivation serves as the UCR), the presentation of the word *good* evokes salivation (i.e., the CR). This is called *semantic conditioning* because the meaning of the word, rather than simply the physical letters constituting the word, has become empowered to evoke the conditioned response (see the bottom panel in Figure 3-5). Words and objects similar in meaning to the conditioned stimulus can also evoke a response similar in form to the conditioned response. As was the case with the tones in the example above, the more similar in meaning the test word is to the conditioned stimulus, the more similar the observed response is to the conditioned response evoked by the test word. This effect, which is a special case of stimulus generalization, is called *semantic generalization*.

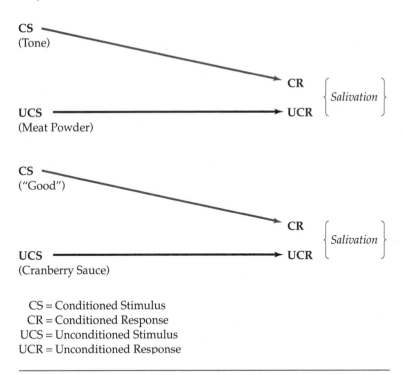

CS = Conditioned Stimulus
CR = Conditioned Response
UCS = Unconditioned Stimulus
UCR = Unconditioned Response

FIGURE 3-5   Top panel: Illustration of the classical conditioning of salivation to a bell. Bottom panel: Illustration of the classical conditioning of salivation to the word *good*. After repeated pairings of the conditioned stimulus (CS) and unconditioned stimulus (UCS), the CS alone elicits salivation.

Attitude Assessment

The classical conditioning approach to the assessment of thoughts, feelings, and attitudes grew out of the work of the Soviet laboratories of Kragnogorsky and Ivanov-Smolensky in the late 1920s and early 1930s, when, according to Razran (1961), it was observed that a conditioned response elicited by the sound of a metronome was also evoked by the announcement of the word *metronome* and vice versa. Razran (1961) also summarizes an early Soviet study in which semantic conditioning was adapted for measuring a person's attitudes toward political slogans. According to Razran, a 13-year-old boy was classically conditioned using cranberry sauce as the UCS to salivate to the work *khorosho* ("well, good") and to differentiate this word and response from the word *plokho* ("poorly, badly, bad"). That is, *khorosho* served as the reinforced stimulus, and *plokho* served as the unreinforced stimulus.

    To validate the conditioning procedure, the boy's secretion of saliva was monitored for 30 seconds beginning with the spoken sentence *Khorosho uchenik otvechayet* ("Well the student answers") and similarly for the spoken sentence

Plokho vorobey poyot ("Poorly the sparrow sings"). The boy was reported to secrete 14 drops of saliva following the statement containing the word *khorosho* and only 3 drops of saliva following the statement containing the word *plokho*. This outcome provided evidence that the investigators had successfully linked the act of salivation to an evaluative meaning.

Over the course of the next several days, the boy's attitudes toward various local and national issues were examined without asking the boy to tell them anything but simply by measuring the boy's salivary responses to slogans and sentences (see Table 3-1). Theoretically, large salivary responses would indicate the boy felt positively about the statements, whereas small salivary responses would indicate the boy felt negatively. For instance, if little or no salivation was found following statements such as *The Soviet Constitution is the most democratic* and *The Soviet people love their Motherland*, then the boy's attitudes and loyalty to the Soviet Union might be questioned. That is, through semantic generalization, the *concepts* of good and bad were now associated with a physiological response. Hence, liked and disliked political slogans were now linked to this physiological response.

The data reported by Razran are summarized in Table 3-1. Inspection of these results reveal considerable support for the theory that physiological responses

TABLE 3-1   Salivation to Statements Following Conditioning

*Test Statement**	*Drops of Saliva*
Negative Statements	
The pupil was fresh to the teacher	0
Brother is insulting sister	1
The pupil failed to take the examination	2
The Fascists destroyed many cities	2
The pupil broke the glass	2
My friend is seriously ill	2
Intermediate Statement	
The pupil passed the examination with a mediocre grade	10
Positive Statements	
The pupil studies excellently	14
Leningrad is a wonderful city	15
The Soviet Constitution is the most democratic	17
The Soviet people love their Motherland	17
The fisherman caught many fish	18
The children are playing well	19
The Soviet army was victorious	23
The pioneer helps his comrades	23
The enemy army was defeated and annihilated	24

Source: Adapted from Razran, 1961.

*In addition to these statements, the word *khorosho* was announced seven times and elicited an average of 14.7 drops of saliva, whereas the word *plokho* was announced two times and elicited an average of 1.5 drops during the 30-second recording interval.

(salivating) can be artificially induced to reflect a thought or attitude. The secretion of saliva during the 30-second period beginning with the announcement of the statements with which the boy was likely to agree averaged 18.8 drops of saliva, compared to 1.5 drops for statements with which the boy was likely to disagree. These results indicated that the boy had a positive attitude toward the Soviet Union.

Notice, too, that the statement *The pupil passed the examination with a mediocre grade* resulted in 10 drops of saliva. This suggests the possibility that the boy was not one of the better students. Although one would want to measure the response to several such statements before drawing any conclusions about the boy's thoughts and feelings about school, his intermediate level of salivation following the statement that the pupil performed middling on a test suggests that the boy would not be displeased with mediocre performances in school. You can see, then, how measures of the artificially induced physiological response can be used to make inferences about a person's thoughts, feelings, and attitudes.

The report of this Soviet research involved only a single individual. Is the same result observed when several individuals are tested under more controlled procedures? Subsequent research in Western laboratories has been promising. Acker and Edwards (1964), for instance, conducted a study in which a *vasomotor response* (constriction of the blood vessels in the left index finger) was classically conditioned to the word *good* or *bad*. Following conditioning, subjects were exposed to words that had been rated previously on an attitude scale. Thus, the investigators knew from this scale which words subjects thought were good and which words they thought were bad. In the subsequent test phase, the words were presented to subjects while vasomotor activity was monitored. Results indicated the appropriate generalization of vasoconstriction to words: Subjects for whom *good* had served as the CS showed vasoconstriction when words with positive connotations were presented, whereas subjects for whom *bad* had served as the CS showed vasoconstriction when words with negative connotations were presented.

Summary
An alternative to monitoring a naturally occurring physiological response to an attitude stimulus is to (a) link a unique physiological response (e.g., salivation) to the mental event of interest (e.g., a particular attitude) using semantic conditioning and (b) assess the extent to which this conditioned response is observed when various stimuli are presented. Although the classical conditioning approach is cumbersome in regard to the equipment involved and the initial conditioning that must be done, these costs may well be worth it to obtain a more accurate and complete mapping of a person's attitudes. Interestingly, this approach has seen some application in the study of attitudes but none, to our knowledge, in the area of lie detection. This may be one instance, therefore, in which there are lessons from the study of attitudes for investigators interested in the detection of deception.

Conclusions

Most of what is known about attitudes is the result of investigators asking people to report their attitudes. These reports might be made by responding aloud, as in telephone interviews, or by marking a position on a scale with a pencil. But do the responses people give truly represent their attitudes? For instance, research on attitudes and behaviors indicates that attitudes—as assessed by self-report measures—are sometimes predictive of intentional behaviors. Furthermore, research has shown that attitudes that come to mind quickly can have more impact on self-reports and short-term behaviors than those that come to mind more slowly (see Chapter 4 by Fazio and Roskos-Ewoldsen). However, just as long-term memories can influence a person's behavior subtly even when the person cannot tell you what those memories are, an attitude may also exert subtle influences on behavior even when the person is unable to identify or report the attitude. Although we have found it useful to ask subjects in our studies of persuasion to report their attitudes (see Chapter 6 by Petty, Cacioppo, Strathman, and Priester, this volume), we have not considered self-reports of attitudes to be the standard against which the validity of all other approaches should be measured (see Cacioppo, 1991; Cacioppo & Petty, 1986; see also Banaji & Greenwald, 1991).

How then can one study attitudes if one cannot always believe what people say? In attempting to answer this question, we have noted parallels between the study of attitudes and the study of concealed information (i.e., lie detection), and we have outlined several theoretically based approaches to detecting people's attitudes when they will not say, cannot say, or do not even know. Did former President Richard Nixon know about the Watergate burglary from the outset, or did he simply become an unwitting participant in a cover-up that ultimately cost him his presidency? Was Gordon Liddy, the convicted Watergate burglar, being loyal to the United States, as he claimed, or more specifically to his boss, Richard Nixon?

Different tactics discussed in this chapter might be the most appropriate to obtain answers to these questions. President Nixon claimed from 1971 through 1975 that he was unaware of the planning of the Watergate break-in and that he had not participated in any cover-up to protect himself or the participants. If Nixon had denied having advanced knowledge about the break-in using the bogus pipeline procedure, one would have greater confidence that he was telling the truth. We would still not know the answer to the key question, however: Had Nixon been informed of the break-in and did he help orchestrate the Watergate cover-up?

The SIT might have proved a more expedient probe of this question than the years of interviewing witnesses, plea bargaining for testimony, and investigative reporting that were required to implicate Nixon. This is because specific questions about the Watergate cover-up and the principals involved should have had greater significance to Nixon if he had been involved in the Watergate cover-up than if he had not been involved. Gordon Liddy was so cool and controlled under questioning, on the other hand, that linking physiological responses to a concept such as loyalty or favorability through semantic conditioning may have proven more informative.

As we have noted in the present chapter, to date, these procedures have sufficient limitations that the outcomes of such tests should be considered suggestive rather than definitive. But it is not difficult to imagine that, in the not too distant future, a sample of persons from the population might be tested physiologically to gauge the honesty of responding to key questions in national surveys or that facial EMG responses or event-related brain responses might be used to measure feelings that people are unwilling or unable to report accurately. With such advances will come new and challenging ways of thinking about attitudes and persuasion, exciting new developments in theory and applications, and, most importantly, social and ethical responsibilities to ensure individual rights and privacy.

Notes

1. Due to space limitations, the present chapter deals with the role of bodily responses as a means of studying attitudes and does not deal with the role of bodily responses in the development, maintenance, and changing of attitudes. Interested readers may wish to consult Buck (1984), Cacioppo, Petty, Losch, and Kim (1986), Petty and Cacioppo (1983), and Zajonc and Markus (1982) for discussions of how bodily responses might influence attitude change and resistance to change.

2. Of course, this procedure has some problems. For example, an innocent person who did not believe in the reliability of the donkey might refuse to pull the tail, thereby appearing guilty. Alternatively, a guilty person who did not believe in the donkey might comply with pulling the tail, thereby appearing innocent.

3. The skin resistance response (SRR) is the reciprocal of the skin conductance response (SCR). Measurement of electrodermal activity in units of skin conductance is preferable because it is less affected by the background level of electrodermal activity, is more linearly related to sweat secretion (Darrow, 1964), and tends to be more normally distributed (Edelberg, 1972). For the sake of simplicity here, we use the term *electrodermal responses (EDRs)* to refer to phasic increases in the sympathetic activation of the eccrine (sweat gland) system whether SRRs or SCRs were employed.

4. Although we shall refer to general facial areas (e.g., cheek, brow) rather than to specific muscle regions, we do so here for didactic purposes only. Fcr instance, the *cheek* is of interest because the zygomaticus major muscle, which when contracted pulls the corners of the mouth upward and back (i.e., into a smile), is associated with positive emotional states, whereas the *brow* is of interest because the corrugator supercilii muscle, which when contracted pulls the brows together and down (i.e., into a frown), is associated with negative emotional states. Discussion of the actual placements and recording procedures are beyond the scope of this chapter, although interested readers might consult Cacioppo, Tassinary, and Fridlund (1990).

Acknowledgment

Preparation of this chapter was supported by National Science Foundation Grant No. BNS-8940915 and DBS-9211483.

References

Acker, I. E., & Edwards, A. I. (1964). Transfer of vasoconstriction over a bipolar meaning dimension. *Journal of Experimental Psychology, 67*, 1–6.

Allen, J. J., Iacono, W. G., & Danielson, K. D. (1992). The identification of concealed memories using the event-related potential and implicit behavioral measures: A methodology for prediction in the face of individual differences. *Psychophysiology, 29*, 504–522.

Banaji, M. R., & Greenwald, A. G. (1991). *Measuring implicit attitudes.* Paper presented at the American Psychological Society, Washington, DC.

Ben-Shakhar, G., & Gati, I. (1987). Common and distinctive features of verbal and pictorial stimuli as determinants of psychophysiological responsivity. *Journal of Experimental Psychology: General, 116*, 91–105.

Buck, R. (1984). *The communication of emotion.* New York: Guilford Press.

Cacioppo, J. T. (1991). *Attitudes.* Invited address, Midwestern Psychological Association, Chicago, IL.

Cacioppo, J. T., Bush, L. K., & Tassinary, L. G. (1992). Microexpressive facial actions as a function of affective stimuli: Replication and extension. *Personality and Social Psychology Bulletin, 18*, 515–526.

Cacioppo, J. T., Crites, S. L., Berntson, G. G., & Coles, M.G. H. (1993). If attitudes affect how stimuli are processed, should not they affect the event-related brain potential? *Psychological Science, 4*, 108–112.

Cacioppo, J. T., Crites, S. L., Jr., Gardner, W. L., & Berntson, G. G. (under review). Bioelectrical echoes from evaluative categorization: I. A paradigm in which a late positive brain potential varies as a function of attitude valence and extremity.

Cacioppo, J. T., Martzke, J. S., Petty, R. E., & Tassinary, L. G. (1988). Specific forms of facial EMG response index emotions during an interview. From Darwin to the continuous flow hypothesis of affect-laden information processing. *Journal of Personality and Social Psychology, 54*, 592–604.

Cacioppo, J. T., & Petty, R. E. (1979). Attitudes and cognitive response: An electrophysiological approach. *Journal of Personality and Social Psychology, 37*, 2181–2199.

Cacioppo, J. T., & Petty, R. E. (1981). Electromyographic specificity during covert information processing. *Psychophysiology, 18*, 518–523.

Cacioppo, J. T., & Petty, R. E. (1983). Soviet contributions to social psychophysiology. In J. T. Cacioppo & R. E. Petty (Eds.), *Social psychophysiology: A sourcebook.* New York: Guilford Press.

Cacioppo, J. T., & Petty, R. E. (1986). Social processes. In M.G.H. Coles, E. Dochin, & S. W. Porges (Eds.), *Psychophysiology.* New York: Guilford Press.

Cacioppo, J. T., Petty, R. E., & Geen, T. (1989). Attitude structure and function: From the tripartite to the homeostasis model of attitudes. In A. R. Pratkanis, S. J. Breckler, & A. G. Greenwald (Eds.), *Attitude structure and function* (pp. 275–309). Hillsdale NJ: Erlbaum.

Cacioppo, J. T., Petty, R. E., Losch, M. E., & Kim, H. S. (1986). Electromyographic activity over facial muscle regions can differentiate the valence and intensity of affective reactions. *Journal of Personality and Social Psychology, 50*, 260–268.

Cacioppo, J. T., Petty, R. E., & Marshall-Goodell, B. (1984). Electromyographic specificity during simple physical and attitudinal tasks: Location and topographical features of integrated EMG responses. *Biological Psychology, 18*, 85–121.

Cacioppo, J. T., Petty, R. E., & Tassinary, L. G. (1989). Social psychophysiology: A new look. *Advances in Experimental Social Psychology, 22*, 39–91.

Cacioppo, J. T., & Sandman, C. A. (1981). Psychophysiological functioning, cognitive responding, and attitudes. In R. E. Petty, T. M. Ostrom, & T. C. Brock (Eds.), *Cognitive response in persuasion.* Hillsdale, NJ: Erlbaum.

Cacioppo, J. T., & Tassinary, L. G. (1990). Inferring psychological significance from physiological signals. *American Psychologist, 45*, 16–28.

Cacioppo, J. T., Tassinary, L. G., & Fridlund, A. J.

(1990). The skeletomotor system. In J. T. Caccioppo & L. G. Tassinary (Eds.), *Principles of psychophysiology: Physical, social, and inferential elements* (pp. 325–384). New York: Cambridge University Press.

Darrow, C. W. (1964). The rationale for treating the change in galvanic skin response as a change in conductance. *Psychophysiology, 1,* 31–38.

Darwin, C. (1872). *The expression of emotions in man and animals.* London: Murray.

Dickson, H. W., & McGinnies, E. (1966). Affectivity in the arousal of attitudes as measured by galvanic skin response. *American Journal of Psychology, 79,* 584–587.

Dysinger, D. W. (1931). A comparative study of affective responses by means of the impressive and expressive methods. *Psychological Monographs, 41,* 14–31.

Edelberg, R. (1972). Electrical activity of the skin. In N. S. Greenfield & R. A. Sternbach (Eds.), *Handbook of psychophysiology.* New York: Holt, Rinehart, & Winston.

Ekman, P., & Friesen, W. V. (1982). Felt, false, and miserable smiles. *Journal of Nonverbal Behavior, 6,* 238–258.

Ekman, P., Friesen, W. V., & Ancoli, S. (1980). Facial signs of emotional experience. *Journal of Personality and Social Psychology, 39,* 1125–1134.

Farwell, L. A., & Donchin, E. (1991). The truth will out: Interrogative polygraphy ("lie detection") with event-related brain potentials. *Psychophysiology, 28,* 531–547.

Gaes, G. G., Kalle, R. J., & Tedeschi, J. T. (1978). Impression management in the forced compliance situation. *Journal of Experimental Social Psychology, 14,* 493–510.

Galton, F. (1884). Measurement of character. *Fortnightly Review, 42,* 179–185.

Gerard, H. B. (1960). *Acts, attitudes, and conformity.* Symposia Study Series No. 4, The National Institute of Social and Behavioral Science, September.

Gerard, H. B. (1964). Psychological measurement in social psychological research. In P. H. Leiderman & D. Shapiro (Eds.), *Psychobiological approaches to social behavior.* Stanford, CA: Stanford University Press.

Graham, J. L. (1980). A new system for measuring nonverbal responses to marketing appeals. *1980 AMA Educator's Proceedings, 46,* 340–343.

Gur, R. C., & Sackeim, H. A. (1979). Self-deception: A concept in search of a phenomenon. *Journal of Personality and Social Psychology, 37,* 147–169.

Hassett, J. (1978). *A primer of psychophysiology.* San Francisco: W. H. Freeman.

Hess, E. H. (1965). Attitude and pupil size. *Scientific American, 202,* 46–54.

Iacono, W. G., & Patrick, C. J. (1988). What psychologists should know about lie detection. In A. K. Hess & I. B. Weiner (Eds.), *Handbook of forensic psychology* (pp. 205–233). New York: Wiley.

Janisse, M. P. (1977). *Pupillometry: The psychology of the pupillary response.* Washington, DC: Hemisphere Press.

Jones, E. E., & Sigall, H. (1971). The bogus pipeline: A new paradigm for measuring affect and attitude. *Psychological Bulletin, 76,* 349–364.

Love, R. E. (1972). *Unobtrusive measurement of cognitive reactions to persuasive communication.* Unpublished doctoral dissertation, The Ohio State University.

Lykken, D. T. (1981). *A tremor in the blood: Uses and abuses of the lie detector.* New York: McGraw-Hill.

McCurdy, H. G. (1950). Consciousness and the galvanometer. *Psychological Review, 57,* 322–327.

McHugo, G. J., Lanzetta, J. T., & Bush, L. K. (1991). The effect of attitude on emotional reactions to expressive displays of political leaders. *Journal of Nonverbal Behavior, 15,* 19–41.

Petty, R. E., & Cacioppo, J. T. (1983). The role of bodily responses in attitude measurement and change. In J. T. Cacioppo & R. E. Petty (Eds.), *Social psychophysiology: A sourcebook.* New York: Guilford Press.

Quigley-Fernandez, B., & Tedeschi, J. T. (1978). The bogus pipeline as a lie detector: Two validity studies. *Journal of Personality and Social Psychology, 36,* 247–256.

Rankin, R. E., & Campbell, D. T. (1955). Galvanic skin response to Negro and white experimenters. *Journal of Abnormal and Social Psychology, 51,* 30–33.

Razran, G. (1961). The observable unconscious and the inferable conscious in current Soviet psychophysiology. *Psychological Review, 68,* 81–147.

Rosenfeld, J. P., Angell, A., Johnson, M., & Qian, J. (1991). An ERP-based, control-question lie detector analog: Algorithms for discriminating effects within individuals' average waveforms. *Psychophysiology, 28,* 319–335.

Sigall, H., & Page, R. (1971). Current stereotypes: A little fading, a little faking. *Journal of Personality and Social Psychology, 18,* 247–255.

Smith, C. A. (1936). A study of the autonomic excitation resulting from the interaction of individual opinion and group opinion. *Journal of Abnormal and Social Psychology, 31,* 138–164.

Syz, H. (1926–1927). Observations on unreliability of subjective reports of emotional reactions. *Journal of Psychology, 17,* 119–126.

Thurstone, L. L., & Chave, E. J. (1929). *The measurement of attitude.* Chicago: University of Chicago Press.

Vidulich, R. N., & Krevanick, R. W. (1966). Racial attitudes and emotional response to visual representations of the Negro. *Journal of Social Psychology, 68,* 85–93.

Westie, F. R., & DeFleur, M. L. (1959). Autonomic responses and their relationship to race attitudes. *Journal of Abnormal and Social Psychology, 58,* 340–347.

Zajonc, R. B., & Markus, H. (1982). Affective and cognitive factors in preferences. *Journal of*

4

ACTING AS WE FEEL

When and How Attitudes
Guide Behavior

RUSSELL H. FAZIO
Indiana University

DAVID R. ROSKOS-EWOLDSEN
University of Alabama

Consider each of the following statements. Do you believe the statement to be true or false?

1. College students who disapprove of cheating do not cheat on tests; it is only the students who view cheating as acceptable who do cheat.
2. When segregation was still legal, hotel and restaurant owners with racial stereotypes toward Chinese people would not serve them food or allow them to stay at their establishments.
3. How well people like their jobs is predictive of their job attendance. People who like their jobs are less likely to miss a day of work.
4. During the 1970s, people who felt that the energy crisis was a significant problem used less energy than those people who did not really believe that there was a crisis.
5. Regardless of whether an employer makes a snap judgment or deliberates extensively about a hiring decision, if the employer has a negative attitude toward working women, a female candidate will not be hired.

All of these common-sense statements assume that people's attitudes influence their actions and decisions. In fact, as we shall see in this chapter, *none* of these five statements is correct. The basic finding of decades of research is that sometimes people act in accordance with their attitudes, and other times, they act in ways that are quite inconsistent with their attitudes.

In this chapter, we shall address three fundamental questions regarding the attitude-behavior relation (see Zanna & Fazio, 1982). (1) *Is* there a relation? That is, do attitudes influence behavior? (2) *When* is such a relation to be expected? In other words, what variables determine the degree to which attitudes might influence behavior? To the extent that attitudes do predict behavior, this question concerns the identification of other factors that play a role in this relationship. Finally, (3) *How* do attitudes guide behavior? By what psychological processes do attitudes exert these influences? If we are to understand the relation between attitudes and behavior, we need to develop models and theories of the psychological processes that link attitudes to behavior.

Is There a Relation Between Attitudes and Behavior?

For a number of decades now, the field of social psychology has had reason to question the intuitively reasonable assumption that people behave consistently with their attitudes. During the early 1930s, LaPiere (1934) conducted what has become probably the most widely cited study of the attitude-behavior relation. While traveling across the western United States in the company of a Chinese couple, LaPiere stopped at over 200 hotels and restaurants. The Chinese couple was refused service at only one establishment. Some six months later, LaPiere wrote to each of the establishments, asking if they served Chinese guests. Surprisingly, 92% of those who responded indicated that they did not accommodate Chinese guests. Thus, there was a startling inconsistency between the attitude responses to LaPiere's letter and the actual behavior toward the Chinese couple with whom LaPiere had traveled. In a very similar study concerning an African American person, instead of Chinese guests, Kutner, Wilkins, and Yarrow (1952) also observed much discrepancy between people's reports of their attitudes and their actual behavior.

Although these findings seem to indicate a lack of correspondence between attitudes and behavior, the relevance of these classic studies to the issue of attitude-behavior consistency has been questioned. For example, the point has been raised that the person who waited on the Chinese guests in the LaPiere study or the African American guest in the Kutner et al. study may not have been the same person who responded to the attitude question (Ajzen, Darroch, Fishbein, & Hornik, 1970; Dillehay, 1973). In addition, it can be argued that the specific individuals who were admitted to the establishments in these studies were not representative of what came to the proprietor's mind when asked in an abstract mailing about admitting a Chinese or African American person (Lord, Lepper, & Mackie, 1984). That is, the proprietor may have imagined a slovenly, unappealing person when responding to the attitude question, in contrast to the pleasant appearance of the specific individuals who were admitted.

However, these studies are by no means the only ones to challenge the assumption that individuals typically behave consistently with their attitudes. For example, Corey (1937) examined the relationship between students' attitudes toward cheating and their actual cheating behavior. The students took a series of true-false examinations, which they self-scored at a later class meeting. Unbeknown to the students, however, the instructor had scored the exams during the interim period. Thus, the difference between the scores that students assigned to themselves and the scores assigned by the instructor served as the measure of students' cheating behavior. The correlation between the students' attitudes toward cheating and actual cheating was essentially zero. Attitudes toward cheating did not in the least bit predict the actual behavior. Instead, cheating was related to test performance; the more poorly the student had done on the exam, the more likely the student was to cheat in scoring the exam.

Corey's findings are not unusual. Indeed, in a highly influential paper, Wicker (1969) reviewed 31 investigations of the attitude-behavior relation and concluded that,

> *Taken as a whole, these studies suggest that it is considerably more likely that attitudes will be unrelated or only slightly related to overt behaviors than that attitudes will be closely related to actions. . . . Correlation coefficients relating the two kinds of responses are rarely above .30, and often are near zero. (p. 65)*

Wicker's review, along with others (e.g., Deutscher, 1973), led to considerable skepticism—sufficiently so that some suggested that "it may be desirable to abandon the attitude concept" (Wicker, 1971, p. 29).

Nonetheless, this skepticism does not appear to have been fully warranted. Although it cannot be denied that a large number of studies suggest that attitudes do not influence behavior, sometimes attitudes *do* predict behavior. For example, studies of voting behavior consistently have indicated a substantial relation between preelection attitudes and voting. Basically, people vote for the candidate they like. Kelley and Mirer (1974) analyzed data concerning the four presidential elections from 1952 to 1964 and found that voting behavior could be predicted accurately from preelection attitudes for 85% of the respondents.

A study by Goodmonson and Glaudin (1971) measured attitudes toward organ transplantation and later made a series of successively more difficult and more committing requests of the respondents, ranging from a request that they schedule an appointment to be interviewed about organ transplants, to their participating in the interview, and culminating in the actual signing of a legal document providing posthumous organ donation. The number of behavioral steps that the respondent took toward this final goal served as the index of behavior. The correlation between attitudes and behavior was 0.58. In a study of homeowners' actual energy consumption, a negligible correlation was found between the perceived severity of the energy crisis and energy usage, but a correlation of 0.65 was observed between energy usage and homeowners' attitudes regarding the necessity of air conditioning in maintaining their health and comfort (Seligman et al., 1979).

Even this brief sampling of positive findings indicates that attitude-behavior correlations can and sometimes do exceed the 0.30 ceiling claimed by Wicker (1969). Consideration of positive findings of this sort has led to a far more optimistic outlook about the usefulness of attitudes in predicting behavior (Calder & Ross, 1973; Fazio & Zanna, 1981; Schuman & Johnson, 1976; Zanna, Higgins, & Herman, 1982). The blanket statement that attitudes have little to do with behavior is often contradicted by studies in the literature. Research has revealed everything from findings of no relation whatsoever (e.g., Corey's 1937 study of cheating behavior) to the nearly perfect relation observed in the context of voting behavior.

Thus, the answer to the question "Is there a relation between attitudes and behavior?" is a resounding "sometimes." Given the range of findings, it becomes apparent that the question of attitude-behavior consistency has to be approached differently.

> *Rather than asking whether attitudes relate to behavior, we have to ask "Under what conditions do what kinds of attitudes of what kinds of individuals predict what kinds of behavior?" . . . We need to treat the strength of the attitude-behavior relation as we would treat any other dependent variable and determine what factors affect it. (Fazio & Zanna, 1981, p. 165)*

When Do Attitudes Guide Behavior?

This question calls for identifying factors that determine whether the relation between attitudes and behavior will be relatively strong or weak. Such factors are typically referred to as *moderating variables*—they moderate the relation between attitudes and behavior. As was hinted earlier, moderators of the attitude-behavior relation include qualities of the behavior, qualities of the person, qualities of the situation in which the behavior is exhibited, and qualities of the attitude itself. We shall review briefly the evidence regarding each of these classes of potential moderating variables.

Qualities of the Behavior

The behaviors that a social psychologist might be interested in predicting from knowledge of a person's attitudes can range from the very specific (e.g., will the person attend church services this week?) to the very general (e.g., how many religious behaviors will the person perform over the next month?). In a highly influential analysis, Ajzen and Fishbein (1977) have noted the importance of measuring attitudes and behavior at equivalent levels of specificity. A specific behavior is best predicted by an attitudinal question that is equivalently specific to the action in question, the target of the action, the context in which the action is performed, and the time of the action (e.g., "How do you feel about attending church this Sunday?"). In a study conducted prior to the mandated use of lead-free gasoline, Heberlein and Black (1976) found that the actual purchase of lead-free gas was better predicted by questions asking specifically about buying lead-free gas than by questions assessing more general attitudes toward ecology.

In contrast, a general pattern of behavior is best predicted by a general attitude measure. For example, Fishbein and Ajzen (1974) examined the relation between subjects' attitudes toward "being religious" and their reports of having performed each of 100 specific behaviors relevant to religion, such as praying before or after meals and donating money to a religious institution. The correlation between the general attitude toward religion and any specific *single* action was a mere 0.15, on the average. In contrast, the correlation between attitude and the *general* behavior pattern (i.e., the number of religious actions performed) was 0.71. In their review of the literature, Ajzen and Fishbein (1977) noted that studies that employed attitude and behavior measures that were equally specific typically found higher attitude-behavior correlations than did studies in which one of the two measures was more specific than the other. Thus, the degree of match between the attitude and the behavior we wish to predict affects the strength of the attitude-behavior relation that will be observed. The same may be true for the relation between personality and persuasion, as described by Wood and Stagner in Chapter 7.

Qualities of the Person

It is also the case that some kinds of people typically display greater attitude-behavior consistency than do other kinds of people. In general, two classes of individuals have been considered—those who were aware of and guided by their internal feelings versus those who tend to rely heavily upon cues in the situation to decide how to behave. Generally speaking, the people who are aware of their feelings display greater attitude-behavior consistency than do people who rely upon situational cues.

Obviously, this is a very rough distinction. Any given behavior of an individual can be guided both by the individual's internal feelings and by external cues. Yet a number of personality scales have been developed and used successfully to assess whether a given person *tends* to rely more heavily upon one type of cue or the other. Although some important differences exist among the personality traits that have been explored as possible moderators of the attitude-behavior relation, each relates to this general distinction. For example, there is some evidence suggesting that the personality dimension of *locus of control* relates to attitude-behavior consistency. Locus of control refers to the amount of control that people perceive themselves having over their lives and environment. Individuals with an external locus of control perceive the environment and events external to themselves as controlling their lives. "Internals," on the other hand, feel that they govern their lives and environment. Individuals characterized by an internal locus of control display greater consistency between their attitudes and their actions than externals (Saltzer, 1981).

Level of moral reasoning has also been found to affect the relation between attitudes and behavior (Rholes & Bailey, 1983). More advanced moral reasoning is characterized by principled, morally responsible thought based on one's own general principles of moral action. Lower levels of reasoning focus on the general positive or negative consequences of a particular action or on a feeling of being bound by social or legal rules. Individuals who depend on their own feelings and principles to make moral judgments act much more consistently with their attitudes toward moral issues than do people who rely upon external standards to determine what is moral.

The personality dimension that has received the greatest attention in the context of the attitude-behavior issue is Snyder's (1987) *self-monitoring* dimension. Individuals with low scores on the self-monitoring scale claim to be guided by dispositions (their inner feelings); they agree with such statements as "My behavior is usually an expression of my true inner feelings, attitudes, and beliefs." In contrast, individuals who score high on the self-monitoring scale view their behavior as stemming typically from a pragmatic concern with what is appropriate in each situation. They agree with such statements as "In different situations and with different people, I often act like very different persons." Thus, these individuals are said to *monitor* the impression that they make on other people and adjust that impression to fit with others' expectations. (See also Chapter 7 for evidence that high self-monitors are more influenceable than low self-monitors.) A number of studies have indicated that low self-monitors behave more consistently with their attitudes than do high self-monitors (Ajzen, Timko, & White, 1982; Snyder & Kendzierski, 1982; Snyder & Swann, 1976; Zanna, Olson, & Fazio, 1980). For example, Snyder and Swann (1976) observed a correlation among low self-monitors of 0.42 between attitudes toward affirmative action and judgments of liability in a simulated sex discrimination case. Among high self-monitors, the correlation was a negligible 0.03.

To reiterate, all three of these personality types vary on the extent to which the individual pays attention to or is influenced by his or her internal feelings. As one would expect, people who focus upon themselves tend to act more consistently with their attitudes (e.g., people characterized by an internal locus of control, high moral reasoning, and/or low self-monitoring). On the other hand, people who are guided more by the environment or other external factors often do not act in a manner that is consistent with their attitudes (e.g., individuals with an external locus of control, low levels of moral reasoning, and/or high self-monitors).

Qualities of the Situation

A number of situational variables also affect the strength of the attitude-behavior relation. These include normative factors, the extent to which individuals have a vested interest in the attitude issue, time pressure to reach a decision, and situational cues that remind the individual of the relevance of his or her attitudes.

The Effect of Norms

Norms—that is, beliefs about how one should or is expected to behave in a given situation—can exert a powerful influence upon behavior. Fishbein and Ajzen (1975) have proposed a model, which we shall review more fully in a later section, that views norms as having a major influence upon behavior (see Figure 4-1).

"Not eating your Cheezies, Miller?"

FIGURE 4-1 Norms can have a strong influence on our behavior, regardless of our attitudes.

Source: Drawing by Gahan Wilson; © 1986 The New Yorker Magazine, Inc.

Much evidence has been found in support of this view (see Ajzen & Fishbein, 1980, for a review). We often behave as we believe others expect us to behave.

Norms can constrain an individual's behavior to the point that it is unlikely that the person will display behavior consistent with his or her attitudes. Indeed, the norms may be so strong and so universally held that virtually everyone in the situation behaves the same, regardless of their attitudes. For example, we may wish that someone were dead, but we would very rarely act on this attitude. Hence, attitude-behavior consistency is low. Consider also the relation between job satisfaction and work attendance. At first glance, one might expect people who like their jobs to be less likely to miss a day of work. Yet the normative pressure (in addition to the potential financial pressure) to attend work every day is strong. Thus, with the exception of illnesses, people generally go to work every day, even people who do not like their jobs. Indeed, studies of job satisfaction have found little relation between attitudes toward one's job and absenteeism (e.g., Vroom, 1962).

However, consider what might happen on a day on which an unforeseen event does free individuals from their sense of obligation to attend work. A severe snow-storm strikes, making travel very difficult and also making it clear that not every-one will get to work that day. Smith (1977) studied precisely such a situation in a company on the day following a major snowfall in the city of Chicago. The atten-dance rate that day was approximately 70%, and work attitudes did predict atten-dance. Averaging across six different attitude measures, the correlation between work attitudes and attendance was 0.46. In contrast, a comparison sample from the same company's office in the city of New York, in which no snowstorm had occurred on this particular day, had an attendance rate of approximately 96% and revealed an average correlation between attitudes and behavior of only 0.08.

Vested Interest

The degree to which someone has a vested interest in an issue also has a profound impact upon attitude-behavior consistency. A person has a vested interest in an issue because actions relevant to that issue could have a strong impact on the indi-vidual. For example, in a situation investigated by Sivacek and Crano (1982), the issue concerned pending legislation in the state of Michigan that would raise the minimum drinking age from 18 to 20. A student who is already 20 years old would not be affected by the new law. However, a younger student who likes to drink would, indeed, have a vested interest in seeing the bill defeated. Sivacek and Crano studied a sample of students, ranging in age, who had earlier reported being against the proposed law. When these students were telephoned by a presumed organization that was campaigning against the proposal and were asked to help the campaign efforts, those with a vested interest (the younger students) were more likely to follow through on their attitudes. More of the younger students were willing to help, and they pledged to make more phone calls attempting to persuade others to vote against the proposal than did students with no vested interest in the issue.

Time Pressure

In a series of experiments, Zanna and his colleagues observed that individuals are more likely to base their decisions on their attitudes when they are under time pressure (see Jamieson & Zanna, 1989, for a review). It appears that time pressure pushes people away from a careful examination of the available information and toward a reliance upon their preexisting attitudes. For example, in one study, sub-jects were asked to consider job applications from both male and female job candi-dates. Bechtold, Naccarato, and Zanna (1986) manipulated the amount of time that the subjects had to reach a decision about whom they would recommend hiring. When there was no time pressure and, hence, subjects could consider all the details carefully, their personnel decisions were unrelated to their attitudes toward work-ing women. That is, subjects whose earlier reported attitudes indicated some prej-udice against women were just as likely to recommend hiring a female candidate as were subjects who did not hold prejudiced attitudes. In striking contrast, when subjects were under time pressure to make a hiring recommendation, an attitude-behavior relation was apparent. Subjects prejudiced against women were less likely to recommend hiring a female candidate.

This is an interesting study because it points out that, from a societal perspective, there are some instances when we do not want attitude-behavior consistency. In this instance, acting in accordance with an attitude leads to discrimination against certain groups within our society. Jamieson and Zanna (1985) also found that, in a simulated sex discrimination suit and a simulated trial involving a mandatory death penalty, if the defendants were judged guilty, attitudes toward affirmative action were predictive of judgments in the sex discrimination suit and attitudes toward capital punishment were predictive of judgments of guilt in the trial—provided that subjects were under time pressure to read the case material and reach a decision. Thus, in three situations in which one would hope that individuals would consider the details of a case objectively and be free of the bias of their attitudes, subjects were able to do so—when they were allowed to examine the case material at their own pace. However, when under time pressure, the subjects were strongly biased by their existing attitudes.

Cues in the Situation

Situations sometimes contain what can be termed *attitude relevance cues* (i.e., prompts that lead an individual to consider the relevance of his or her attitude in the immediate situation). It is not uncommon to be told in elections to "vote your conscience." Such an appeal may be an attempt to make people's attitudes relevant at the time of an election. For example, in 1980, supporters of John Anderson's presidential campaign often urged people to ignore practical considerations (the fact that Anderson did not have a chance to win the election) and vote for the candidate they liked.

Snyder and Kendzierski (1982) examined the impact of such an attitude relevance cue. They arranged for each subject to overhear a conversation between two accomplices of the experimenter while the subject and the accomplices were in a waiting room. The conversation concerned a notice posted on the wall that requested volunteers to participate in a psychological experiment. When one accomplice indicated that he did not know whether to volunteer or not, the other replied in one of two ways. In one condition, to make the attitude relevant, the accomplice answered: "[It's] really a question of how worthwhile you think experiments are." In the control condition, the reply was simply: "Beats me—it's up to you." Although all the subjects in the experiment felt positively about psychological research, those in the cue condition were more likely to act on those attitudes. That is, they were more likely to volunteer to participate in the research referred to on the notice than were subjects in the control condition.

Qualities of the Attitude

Some kinds of attitudes appear to be stronger than other kinds of attitudes (Raden, 1985). In this context, *stronger* is not used in the sense of the attitude being more extreme. Instead, *stronger* refers to the apparent influence that the attitude has upon the individual's behavior. In fact, in all of the research that we will summarize, groups of subjects with different degrees of attitude strength were compared, but the distributions of attitude scores (i.e., the extremity of attitudes) in the two or more groups were equivalent to one another.

The Role of Direct Experience

One attitudinal quality that has been investigated extensively is the *manner of attitude formation* (see Fazio & Zanna, 1981, for a review). On the one hand is attitude formation through direct behavioral experience with the attitude object, and on the other hand is attitude formation through indirect, nonbehavioral experience with the attitude object. For example, a child may form an attitude toward a toy by playing with the toy (direct experience) or on the basis of a friend's or an advertisement's description of the toy (indirect experience).

Attitudes based upon direct experience have been found to be more predictive of later behavior than attitudes based upon indirect experience. This was first shown in a study that took advantage of an actual event at Cornell University (Regan & Fazio, 1977). Due to a campus housing shortage, many freshmen had spent the first few weeks of the academic year in temporary housing. Typically, these accommodations consisted of a cot in the lounge of a dormitory. Relative to the freshmen who were immediately assigned to permanent housing, those in temporary quarters had much more direct experience with the housing crisis. Those assigned permanent quarters, on the other hand, had learned about (and formed their attitudes toward) the housing shortage only through discussions with others and through reading the frequent articles that appeared in the campus paper. Thus, a naturally occurring event had created two groups that differed in their manner of attitude formation. The two groups were compared for the extent to which they displayed behavior that was consistent with their attitudes toward the housing crisis (e.g., agreeing to sign a petition calling upon the university to alleviate the shortage, obtaining the signatures of other students, or writing a letter to the university housing office). Attitude-behavior consistency was much greater among those who had been assigned to temporary housing (the direct experience group) than among those who had been assigned to permanent housing (the indirect experience group). This was true even though the two groups, on the average, had equally negative attitudes toward the housing shortage.

A second experiment by Regan and Fazio (1977) manipulated the manner of attitude formation in the laboratory. Subjects were introduced to a set of five intellectual puzzles in one of two ways. Some subjects were presented previously solved examples of each puzzle and listened to the experimenter describe the type of puzzle and the specific example and solution (indirect experience condition). The remaining subjects were given an opportunity to actually work the same example puzzles, thus forming their attitudes through direct behavioral experience. After attitudes toward each of the five types of puzzles were assessed, all subjects participated in a *free-play* situation. They were given numerous samples of each puzzle type and instructed to play with any that they wished. On the average, the relation between a given subject's attitude toward a puzzle and the amount of free-play behavior with the puzzle was greater in the direct than in the indirect experience condition (see also Fazio & Zanna, 1978).

One thing that differentiates attitudes based on direct versus indirect experience is how *accessible* the attitudes are from memory. By *accessibility*, we mean how easily the attitude comes to mind. Some attitudes come to mind without any conscious effort on our part. When someone sees a cockroach, the "yuck" response probably comes to mind immediately. This attitude would be highly accessible from memory. But sometimes we have to deliberate quite extensively about what our attitude is toward some object. If you are asked which of several restaurants is the best Tibetan restaurant, you may have to think extensively about which one you like the best. This attitude would not be at all accessible from memory.

As these examples illustrate, one way to measure how accessible an attitude is from memory is by how long it takes people to answer if they like or dislike something. Using a measure of response latency (response time), Fazio, Chen, McDonel, and Sherman (1982) found that attitudes based on direct experience tend to be more accessible from memory. Subjects who had direct experience with puzzles were able to respond more quickly to inquiries about their attitudes toward the puzzles than were subjects who had indirect experience. As will be discussed later, attitude accessibility plays a major role in the attitude-behavior relation.

Amount of Information

The more information that people have about the attitude object, the greater the attitude-behavior consistency that they display. This has been shown in a series of studies by Davidson, Yantis, Norwood, and Montano (1985). In one study, investigators examined the relation between attitude toward obtaining a flu shot and actually being vaccinated. The more informed subjects reported being about flu shots, the more consistency they exhibited. Again, this is despite the fact that the attitudes across the two groups of subjects were essentially equivalent. Interestingly, those who had received flu shots in the past and thus had direct experience with the attitude object also displayed more consistency. Furthermore, the effects of these two factors were found to be independent of one another. That is, amount of information was related to attitude-behavior consistency apart from the effect of direct experience, and direct experience was related to attitude-behavior consistency apart from the effect of information.[1]

The essential point made by these various findings about the qualities of attitudes is that identical attitude scores, as measured by some questionnaire, do not necessarily reflect the same underlying attitudes. The attitudes may have been formed in different manners or may be based upon different amounts of information. As a result, these individuals' attitudes may vary in terms of how well they predict subsequent behavior.

Summary

The findings we have reviewed make it abundantly clear that attitudes do sometimes relate to behavior. Extreme pessimism regarding the value of attitudes as predictors of behavior is unwarranted. Furthermore, we now have a lengthy catalog of situational, personality, attitudinal, and behavioral qualities that appear to determine the strength of the attitude-behavior relation.

What is missing, however, is any sense of *why* these various factors exert their influence. Why do only certain kinds of attitudes or certain kinds of situations promote attitude-behavior consistency? These concerns raise a very basic question regarding the attitude-behavior relation: How do attitudes guide behavior? By what processes do attitudes influence our behaviors?

If we had an understanding of such processes, then it would be far easier to understand why only certain kinds of attitudes of certain kinds of individuals in certain kinds of situations seem to guide behavior. It is to this point that we now turn.

How Do Attitudes Guide Behavior?

Two different mechanisms by which attitudes can influence behavior will be discussed. The major distinction between the two centers upon the extent to which the behavior is thoughtfully planned in advance of its actual performance as opposed to being a spontaneous reaction to one's perception of the immediate situation. That is, an individual may reflect and deliberate about a behavioral plan and may decide how he or she intends to behave. In so doing, the person may consciously consider the implications of his or her attitude. For example, when buying a car or deciding which college to attend, people extensively deliberate about the decision and consider all the advantages and disadvantages before making a behavioral decision. Alternatively, the individual may not actively reflect upon his or her attitude, but that attitude may influence how the person interprets the event that is occurring and, in that way, affect the behavior. When choosing between a pistachio and chocolate ice cream cone, people rarely analyze the positive and negative features of each flavor. Instead, their attitudes toward the different flavors determine which flavor looks better at that moment in time. The former type of process is the essence of Ajzen and Fishbein's (1980) *theory of reasoned action*. The latter is depicted in Fazio's (1986) *model of the attitude-to-behavior process*.

Ajzen and Fishbein's Theory of Reasoned Action

As implied by its name, the theory of reasoned action assumes that people deliberate about the wisdom of a given course of action.

> *We argue that people consider the implications of their actions before they decide to engage or not engage in a given behavior. For this reason we refer to our approach as a "theory of reasoned action." . . . We make the assumption that most actions of social relevance are under volitional control and, consistent with this assumption, our theory views a person's* intention *to perform (or to not perform) a behavior as the immediate determinant of action. (Ajzen & Fishbein, 1980, p. 5)*

According to this theory, then, an individual's behavioral intention is the single best predictor of the person's eventual behavior. The theory goes on to specify the dimensions that an individual considers in forming a behavioral intention. The person considers, weighs, and combines (a) his or her attitude toward the behavior in question and (b) subjective norms regarding the behavior (see Figure 4-2). The second component, subjective norms, involves *both* the person's beliefs about what important others think that he or she should do *and* the person's motivation to comply with the wishes of these others. In deciding whether to attend college, an individual may consider what his or her friends and parents think about attending college *as well as* how important it is to comply with the parents' and friends' wishes.

The first component, the attitude component, refers specifically to the behavioral choice under consideration (e.g., buying a Sony television), not the general attitude toward the object (e.g., a Sony television). The reason the model differentiates between attitudes toward behavior and attitudes toward the object is that we may have a positive attitude towards Sony televisions but not toward *purchasing* a Sony television because of the costs involved in such a behavior (e.g., increased credit payments). According to the theory, the individual constructs this attitude toward the behavior by a careful analysis of available information. The attitude is a function of the person's beliefs concerning the likely outcomes to result from performing the behavior and the person's positive or negative feelings about those outcomes.

As an example, consider a young couple that is deciding whether to have a baby. According to the theory, the couple would consider the outcomes that are likely to occur if they were to have a baby (e.g., having to nurture the baby, less time to engage in leisure activities, playing with the baby, strain on the family bud-

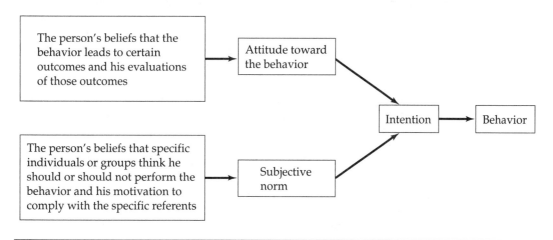

FIGURE 4-2   A schematic diagram of Ajzen and Fishbein's theory of reasoned action

Source: Icek Ajzen/Martin Fishbein, *Understanding Attitudes and Predicting Social Behavior,* © 1980, p. 8. Reprinted by permission of Prentice-Hall, Englewood Cliffs, New Jersey.

get) and their evaluations of these outcomes. From this information, they would construct an attitude toward having a baby. The couple would also consider how people who are important to them (family and friends) would feel about their having a child. Are they pressuring the couple to have a child? Would such significant others be supportive? The more positively the couple views the prospect of having a baby and the more support they perceive from others for their doing so, the more likely the couple is to arrive at the intention to have a child.

Davidson and Jaccard (1979) applied the theory of reasoned action to just such a situation in the context of a two-year study of family planning behavior. The investigators found that the correlation was high between the behavioral intentions to have a child among a sample of women and their actual childbearing over the two-year period. Furthermore, these behavioral intentions were highly related to measures of the attitudinal and normative components specified by the theory. This investigation, along with a number of other studies reviewed by Ajzen and Fishbein (1980), provides impressive support for the theory of reasoned action.

Fazio's Attitude-to-Behavior Process Model

The theory of reasoned action assumes that attitudes guide behavior through conscious consideration of and deliberation about one's attitude and its implications for a given course of action. In contrast, the process model proposed by Fazio and his colleagues (Fazio, 1986; Fazio, Powell, & Herr, 1983) suggests that attitudes can guide a person's behavior even when the person does not actively reflect and deliberate about the attitude. When someone sees a cockroach, he or she probably does not consider the beliefs about how unsanitary cockroaches are, nor is he or she likely to reason out what other people think of smashing the cockroach. If people did engage in such extensive thinking, the cockroach would disappear before anyone had a chance to decide how to react. Instead, in very basic terms, the Fazio model argues that the individual's attitude toward cockroaches would define this situation as an unpleasant one and the person would act upon this feeling or impulse.

According to the model, the precursor of behavior is the individual's definition of the event that is occurring. That is, the individual's interpretation of what is happening is assumed to determine how the individual responds. The classic research of Latané and Darley (1970) concerning bystander intervention provides a useful illustration of this principle. In one experiment, subjects were led into a room and asked to fill out a questionnaire, while the experimenter waited outside the room. A short time later, smokelike vapors started to enter the room through a vent in the wall. Some subjects perceived the vapors as harmless, while other subjects interpreted them as actual smoke from a fire. Definition of the event as a fire was found to be a critical step if an individual was to react to the emergency situation by notifying the experimenter. In this "smoke-filled room" experiment, subjects who failed to define the smokelike vapors as an indicant of a fire were unlikely to report the incident, even though the vapors eventually became so dense that individuals had difficulty reading their questionnaires! Thus, how we perceive a situation has a profound impact on our behavior. You can take the same set of people, in the same physical setting, and have them respond very differently.

Within the process model, this *definition of the event* consists of two components—the individual's perceptions of the attitude object in the immediate situation and the individual's definition of the situation. *Definition of the situation* refers to the storehouse of knowledge that the individual possesses concerning behaviors that are to be expected and that are appropriate in the particular situation. For example, when smoke enters a room due to a fire, the norm is that people should report the fire. It is in this way that norms can influence behavior.

Perceptions of the attitude object in the immediate situation also influence our definition of an event and provide the means for a potential impact of attitudes. A vast literature indicates that attitudes can guide how and what we perceive (see Fazio, 1986, for a review). In the words of Smith, Bruner, and White (1956), an attitude provides "a ready aid in 'sizing up' objects and events in the environment" (p. 41).

Earlier, we discussed the notion that attitudes can vary in how accessible they are from memory. The idea that attitudes vary in their accessibility from memory is an integral aspect of the process by which attitudes can influence what we perceive. The Fazio process model views an attitude as an association in memory between the attitude object and one's evaluation of the object. The strength of this association can vary and determines the accessibility of the attitude from memory. To illustrate, consider an example outside the context of attitudes—the association between *bacon* and *eggs*. If someone mentions bacon to you, you probably cannot help but think of eggs because the two are so strongly associated. On the other hand, if I say "sidewalk," you are much less likely to think of "eggs," despite the old saying that sometimes it is so hot you can fry an egg on the sidewalk. The *bacon/eggs* association is much stronger in memory than is the association between *sidewalk* and *eggs*. Likewise, the strength of the association between an attitude object and one's evaluation of the object can vary. As discussed earlier, the association (e.g., *cockroach* and *yuck*) can be so strong that the evaluation immediately and spontaneously comes to mind when you encounter the attitude object.

The process model maintains that the attitude must be activated from memory (i.e., it must come to mind) when the individual sees the attitude object, if the attitude is to exert any influence. If the attitude is activated from memory, then it serves as a filter through which the object is viewed at that moment in time. As a result, immediate perceptions of the attitude object will be consistent with the attitude. In contrast, if the attitude is not activated, then the immediate perceptions will be based on momentarily noticeable features of the attitude object that may not be consistent with the attitude. For example, when noticing a grocery item toward which you do not have an accessible attitude, features such as the type of wrapping, the position of the item on the shelf, or whether the item is on sale are likely to influence your immediate perception of the item (see Figure 4-3).

According to the model, then, the initiation of the attitude-to-behavior process depends upon whether the attitude is activated from memory. There are a number of ways that attitudes can be activated from memory. Such activation can

"That's just our opinion, but I believe the public feels the same way."

FIGURE 4-3   Attitudes guide our perceptions and judgments.

Source: Drawing by Saxon; © 1986 The New Yorker Magazine, Inc.

occur as a result of situational cues (Snyder & Kendzierski, 1982). When we are told to vote our feelings, our attitudes are likely to be activated from memory. However, attitude activation also can occur without the benefit of prompting from a situational cue—if the attitude is sufficiently accessible from memory. As we discussed earlier, we smash cockroaches because our dislike of cockroaches comes to mind immediately—the attitude is highly accessible. Attitudes involving strong object-evaluation associations (*cockroach/yuck*), then, are highly accessible from memory and can be activated from memory automatically or effortlessly merely upon seeing the attitude object. It is such attitudes that are capable of initiating the attitude-behavior process, even without prompting from any situational cue. Once activated from memory, the attitude can influence one's perceptions of the object in the immediate situation, one's definition of the event, and ultimately, one's behavior (see Figure 4-4).[2]

The model predicts that attitude accessibility will determine the relation between attitudes and perceptions or judgments of an object. The relation is

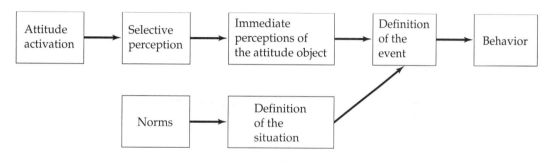

FIGURE 4-4   A schematic diagram of Fazio's attitude-to-behavior process model

Source: From "How Do Attitudes Guide Behavior?" by R. Fazio, 1986, in R. M. Sorrentino and E. T. Higgins (Eds.), *The Handbook of Motivation and Cognition: Foundations of Social Behavior* (pp. 204–243). Reprinted by permission of the Guilford Press.

expected to be stronger if the attitude is accessible from memory than if not. The model makes a similar prediction regarding the attitude-behavior relation. Both of these hypotheses have been supported in research (see Fazio, 1989, for a full review of this research). For example, Fazio and Williams (1986) examined the relation between attitudes toward former President Reagan and judgments of the performance of the candidates in the televised debates during the 1984 election campaign. The attitudes of a sample of townspeople were assessed, along with the accessibility of those attitudes as indicated by how long people took to respond to an attitude question. Following the debates, the respondents were mailed postcards that asked them to indicate which candidate had performed better in the debates. As one would expect, these judgments were biased by people's attitudes. The more positive the attitude toward Reagan, the more likely the person was to judge Reagan and the Republican vice-presidential candidate George Bush to have performed better than their opponents. (See Chapter 11 by Sears and Kosterman for more examples.) More importantly, as predicted by the model, this bias conferred by one's attitude was stronger among respondents whose attitudes toward Reagan were relatively accessible from memory than among those with less accessible attitudes (see Figure 4-5).

This same study also found evidence for the predicted impact of attitude accessibility on the attitude-behavior relation. After the election, the respondents were telephoned and asked how they had voted. The relation between attitudes toward Reagan, as measured in midsummer, and voting was much higher among individuals with accessible attitudes than among those with less accessible attitudes.

A recent study by Fazio, Powell, and Williams (1989) provided more evidence for this point. Subjects' attitudes toward a variety of products and the accessibility of those attitudes were measured. This measure involved assessment of the latency (length of time) with which individuals indicated their attitudes. The faster the latency, the more accessible the attitude. As a token of appreciation for having participated in the study, subjects were shown 10 products at the end of the study and allowed to select 5 of them to take home. The available products included such items as Snickers and Mounds candy bars, Sun-Maid Raisins, Planters Peanuts, and V-8

DUNAGIN'S PEOPLE

"NO, I DIDN'T WANT WATCHING THE DEBATES TO INFLUENCE MY OPINION ABOUT WHO WON THEM."

FIGURE 4-5   Judgments of the outcome of the presidential debates

Source: Reprinted with special permission of North America Syndicate.

Juice. Which products the subjects selected served as the behavior measure. The relation between attitude toward a given product and whether the subject chose the given product as a gift was examined. As predicted by the model, this relation was found to increase as the accessibility of the attitude increased. The more accessible the subject's attitude, the more likely it was that the subject's decision about whether to select the product was consistent with the attitude. For example, a subject who reported liking Planters Peanuts but who took a relatively long time to report that attitude was less likely to choose Planters as his or her free gift than someone who reported liking Planters Peanuts equally well but reported that attitude faster.

New Directions

Although much research has yet to be conducted, the two models that have been discussed do provide the potential for addressing *why* some of the factors we discussed earlier affect the attitude-behavior relationship. For example, the theory of reasoned action can explain the impact of various personality factors on the attitude-behavior relation by reference to how much importance an individual places on the attitude versus the normative component in forming a behavioral intention. Some kinds of people (e.g., low self-monitors) might typically give more weight to their attitudes and less weight to their normative beliefs than do other kinds of people (e.g., high self-monitors). Likewise, situational factors such as vested interest and the presence of attitude relevance cues might lead individuals to weigh more heavily the attitude component.

The attitude-behavior process model proposed by Fazio (1986) also provides a way to integrate these various factors into a theory. Viewed in the context of this model, the personality factors exert their influence either because they identify people for whom norms will greatly influence their definition of the event and/or because they identify people who are generally likely to hold attitudes that are highly accessible from memory. In fact, there is some evidence to indicate that low self-monitors generally hold attitudes that are more accessible than the attitudes of high self-monitors (Kardes, Sanbonmatsu, Voss, & Fazio, 1986).

Two different processes by which attitudes can guide behavior have been discussed. One clearly focuses upon deliberate, planned, reasoned action in which an attitude exerts an impact on behavior because the individual reflects upon the attitude. The other concerns an influence of attitude that need not stem from reflection but instead from the attitude's influence upon one's perception of objects and situations, which in turn affects one's behavior. Clearly, not all social behavior is deliberate and reasoned. Just as clearly, not all behavior is an impulsive reaction to one's definition of the event.

Given that both processes occur, under what conditions is each process likely to operate? In brief, we would argue that which process occurs depends upon both motivation and opportunity (see Fazio, 1986). The deliberate process proposed by the theory of reasoned action obviously requires extensive cognitive work. As a result, it seems reasonable to propose that some motivation is necessary to induce individuals to engage in this effortful reasoning process. Such motivation is likely to exist when one's behavioral decision will have important consequences. When the cost of making a bad decision is perceived to be high, individuals appear motivated to engage in careful reasoning (Kruglanski & Freund, 1983). Without such inducement, individuals may see little cost to permitting behavior to flow spontaneously from their interpretation of the event. Of course, the motivation to engage in effortful reasoning is not sufficient in and of itself. The opportunity to do so also must exist. Situations that require one to make a behavioral response quickly can deny one the chance to engage in much reasoning. (See Chapter 6 in this volume by Petty et al. for a discussion of similar factors affecting responses to persuasive messages.)

In sum, when the situation both motivates the individual to consider his or her action carefully and allows the individual the opportunity to do so, the process described in the theory of reasoned action may occur. Attitudes would affect behavior by being one of the elements that the individual actively considers in arriving at a behavioral plan. Without such motivation or opportunity, the model of the attitude-behavior process proposed by Fazio (1986) appears applicable.

Whether the attitude directs behavior would depend upon whether the attitude is activated from memory and the extent to which the attitude colors the individual's definition of the event. Through such a process, attitudes can serve as remarkably functional tools for individuals. Attitudes that are accessible from memory can guide an individual's behavior in a satisfying direction without the individual having to engage in conscious, deliberative reasoning. In this way, attitudes can simplify ongoing, everyday life.

Notes

1. A number of additional qualities of the attitude also have been shown to relate to attitude-behavior consistency. These include (a) how confidently the attitude is held (e.g., Fazio & Zanna, 1978; Sample & Warland, 1973), (b) how clearly defined the attitude is (e.g., Fazio & Zanna, 1978; Sherif, Kelly, Rodgers, Sarup, & Tittler, 1973), (c) how consistent the individual's affect and beliefs concerning the attitude object are (e.g., Norman, 1975), and (d) how stable the attitude is over time (e.g., Schwartz, 1978).

2. Research findings concerning attitudes as object-evaluation associations and attitude accessibility have led to two conclusions. First, the accessibility of an attitude and the likelihood that the attitude will be activated from memory upon mere observation of the attitude object depends upon the strength of the object-evaluation association (Fazio, Chen, McDonel, & Sherman, 1982; Fazio et al., 1983; Fazio, Sanbonmatsu, Powell, & Kardes, 1986). Second, the strength of the object-evaluation association can be reasonably estimated by measuring how quickly an individual can respond to an inquiry about his or her attitude toward the object (Fazio et al., 1982; Powell & Fazio, 1984; Fazio et al., 1986). Relatively fast responses indicate strong associations and relatively high accessibility from memory.

Acknowledgments

Preparation of this chapter was supported by Grant MH 38832 and by Research Scientist Development Award MH 00452 from the National Institute of Mental Health. The authors thank Carol Williams for her helpful comments on an earlier version of the chapter.

References

Ajzen, I., Darroch, R., Fishbein, M., & Hornik, J. (1970). Looking backward revisited: A reply to Deutscher. *American Sociologist, 5,* 267–273.

Ajzen, I., & Fishbein, M. (1977). Attitude-behavior relations: A theoretical analysis and review of empirical research. *Psychological Bulletin, 84,* 888–918.

Ajzen, I., & Fishbein, M. (1980). *Understanding attitudes and predicting social behavior.* Englewood Cliffs, NJ: Prentice-Hall.

Ajzen, I., Timko, C., & White, J. B. (1982). Self-monitoring and the attitude-behavior relation. *Journal of Personality and Social Psychology, 42,* 426–435.

Bechtold, A., Naccarato, M. E., & Zanna, M. P. (1986). *Need for structure and the prejudice-discrimination link.* Paper presented at the annual meeting of the Canadian Psychological Association, Toronto.

Calder, B. J., & Ross, M. (1973). *Attitudes and behavior*. Morristown, NJ: General Learning Press.

Corey, S. M. (1937). Professed attitudes and actual behavior. *Journal of Educational Psychology, 28*, 271–280.

Davidson, A. R., & Jaccard, J. J. (1979). Variables that moderate the attitude-behavior relation: Results of a longitudinal survey. *Journal of Personality and Social Psychology, 37*, 1364–1376.

Davidson, A. R., Yantis, S., Norwood, M. & Montano, D. E. (1985). Amount of information about the attitude object and attitude-behavior consistency. *Journal of Personality and Social Psychology, 49*, 1184–1198.

Deutscher, I. (1973). *Why do they say one thing, do another?* Morristown, NJ: General Learning Press.

Dillehay, R. C. (1973). On the irrelevance of the classical negative evidence concerning the effect of attitudes on behavior. *American Psychologist, 28*, 887–891.

Fazio, R. H. (1986). How do attitudes guide behavior? In R. M. Sorrentino & E. T. Higgins (Eds.), *The handbook of motivation and cognition: Foundations of social behavior* (pp. 204–243). New York: Guilford Press.

Fazio, R. H. (1989). On the power and functionality of attitudes: The role of attitude accessibility. In A. R. Pratkanis, S. J. Breckler, & A. G. Greenwald (Eds.), *Attitude structure and function* (pp. 153–179). Hillsdale, NJ: Erlbaum.

Fazio, R. H., Chen, J., McDonel, E. C., & Sherman, S. J. (1982). Attitude accessibility, attitude-behavior consistency, and the strength of the object-evaluation association. *Journal of Experimental Social Psychology, 18*, 339–357.

Fazio, R. H., Powell, M. C., & Herr, P. M. (1983). Toward a process model of the attitude-behavior relation: Accessing one's attitude upon mere observation of the attitude object. *Journal of Personality and Social Psychology, 44*, 723–735.

Fazio, R. H., Powell, M. C., & Williams, C. J. (1989). The role of attitude accessibility in the attitude-to-behavior process. *Journal of Consumer Research, 16*, 280–288.

Fazio, R. H., Sanbonmatsu, D. M., Powell, M. C., &

Kardes, F. R. (1986). On the automatic activation of attitudes. *Journal of Personality and Social Psychology, 50*, 229–238.

Fazio, R. H., & Williams, C. J. (1986). Attitude accessibility as a moderator of the attitude-perception and attitude-behavior relations: An investigation of the 1984 presidential election. *Journal of Personality and Social Psychology, 51*, 505–514.

Fazio, R. H., & Zanna, M. P. (1978). Attitudinal qualities relating to the strength of the attitude-behavior relationship. *Journal of Experimental Social Psychology, 14*, 398–408.

Fazio, R. H., & Zanna, M. P. (1981). Direct experience and attitude-behavior consistency. In L. Berkowitz (Ed.), *Advances in experimental social psychology* (Vol. 14, pp. 162–202). New York: Academic Press.

Fishbein, M., & Ajzen, I. (1974). Attitudes toward objects as predictors of single and multiple behavioral criteria. *Psychological Review, 81*, 59–74.

Fishbein, M., & Ajzen, I. (1975). *Belief, attitude, intention and behavior: An introduction to theory and research*. Reading, MA: Addison-Wesley.

Goodmonson, C., & Glaudin, V. (1971). The relationship of commitment-free behavior and commitment behavior: A study of attitude toward organ transplantation. *Journal of Social Issues, 27*, 171–183.

Heberlein, T. A., & Black, J. S. (1976). Attitudinal specificity and the prediction of behavior in a field setting. *Journal of Personality and Social Psychology, 33*, 474–479.

Jamieson, D. W., & Zanna, M. P. (1985). *Moderating the attitude-behavior relation: The joint effects of arousal and self-monitoring*. Paper presented at the annual meeting of the Canadian Psychological Association, Halifax.

Jamieson, D. W., & Zanna, M. P. (1989). Need for structure in attitude formation and expression. In A. R. Pratkanis, S. J. Breckler, & A. G. Greenwald (Eds.), *Attitude structure and function* (pp. 383–406). Hillsdale, NJ: Erlbaum.

Kardes, F. R., Sanbonmatsu, D. M., Voss, R., & Fazio, R. H. (1986). Self-monitoring and attitude accessibility. *Personality and Social Psychology Bulletin, 12*, 468–474.

Kelley, S., & Mirer, T. W. (1974). The simple act of voting. *American Political Science Review, 68,* 572–591.

Kruglanski, A. W., & Freund, T. (1983). The freezing and unfreezing of lay-inferences: Effects on impressional primacy, ethnic stereotypic and numerical anchoring. *Journal of Experimental Social Psychology, 19,* 448–468.

Kutner, B., Wilkins, C., & Yarrow, P. R. (1952). Verbal attitudes and overt behavior involving racial prejudice. *Journal of Abnormal and Social Psychology, 47,* 649–652.

LaPiere, R. T. (1934). Attitudes vs. actions. *Social Forces, 13,* 230–237.

Latané, B., & Darley, J. M. (1970). *The unresponsive bystander: Why doesn't he help?* New York: Appleton-Century-Crofts.

Lord, C. G., Lepper, M. R., & Mackie, D. (1984). Attitude prototypes as determinants of attitude-behavior consistency. *Journal of Personality and Social Psychology, 46,* 1245–1266.

Norman, R. (1975). Affective-cognitive consistency, attitudes, conformity, and behavior. *Journal of Personality and Social Psychology, 32,* 83–91.

Powell, M. C., & Fazio, R. H. (1984). Attitude accessibility as a function of repeated attitudinal expression. *Personality and Social Psychology Bulletin, 10,* 139–148.

Raden, D. (1985). Strength-related attitude dimensions. *Social Psychology Quarterly, 48,* 312–330.

Regan, D. T., & Fazio, R. H. (1977). On the consistency between attitudes and behavior: Look to the method of attitude formation. *Journal of Experimental Social Psychology, 13,* 38–45.

Rholes, W. S., & Bailey, S. (1983). The effects of level of moral reasoning on consistency between moral attitudes and related behaviors. *Social Cognition, 2,* 32–48.

Saltzer, E. B. (1981). Cognitive moderators of the relationship between behavioral intentions and behavior. *Journal of Personality and Social Psychology, 41,* 260–271.

Sample, J., & Warland, R. (1973). Attitude and prediction of behavior. *Social Forces, 51,* 292–304.

Schuman, H., & Johnson, M. P. (1976). Attitudes and behavior. *Annual Review of Sociology, 2,* 161–207.

Schwartz, S. H. (1978). Temporal instability as a moderator of the attitude-behavior relationship. *Journal of Personality and Social Psychology, 36,* 715–724.

Seligman, C., Kriss, M., Darley, J. M., Fazio, R. H., Becker, L. J., & Pryor, J. B. (1979). Predicting summer energy consumption from homeowners' attitudes. *Journal of Applied Social Psychology, 9,* 70–90.

Sherif, C. W., Kelly, M., Rodgers, H. L., Sarup, G., & Tittler, B. I. (1973). Personal involvement, social judgment, and action. *Journal of Personality and Social Psychology, 27,* 311–328.

Sivacek, J., & Crano, W. D. (1982). Vested interest as a moderator of attitude-behavior consistency. *Journal of Personality and Social Psychology, 43,* 210–221.

Smith, F. J. (1977). Work attitudes as predictors of attendance on a specific day. *Journal of Applied Psychology, 62,* 16–19.

Smith, M. B., Bruner, J. S., & White, R. W. (1956). *Opinions and personality.* New York: John Wiley & Sons.

Snyder, M. (1987). *Public appearances/private realities: The psychology of self-monitoring.* New York: Freeman.

Snyder, M., & Kendzierski, D. (1982). Acting on one's attitude: Procedures for linking attitude and behavior. *Journal of Experimental Social Psychology, 18,* 165–183.

Snyder, M., & Swann, W. B., Jr. (1976). When actions reflect attitudes: The politics of impression management. *Journal of Personality and Social Psychology, 34,* 1034–1042.

Songer-Nocks, E. (1976). Situational factors affecting the weighting of predictor components in the Fishbein model. *Journal of Experimental Social Psychology, 12,* 56–69.

Vroom, V. H. (1962). Ego-involvement, job satisfaction, and job performance. *Personnel Psychology, 15,* 159–177.

Wicker, A. W. (1969). Attitudes versus actions: The relationship of verbal and overt behavioral responses to attitude objects. *Journal of Social Issues, 25,* 41–78.

Wicker, A. W. (1971). An examination of the "other variable" explanation of attitude-behavior inconsistency. *Journal of Personality and Social Psychology, 19,* 18–30.

Zanna, M. P., & Fazio, R. H. (1982). The attitude-behavior relation: Moving toward a third generation of research. In M. P. Zanna, E. T. Higgins, & C. P. Herman (Eds.), *Consistency in social behavior: The Ontario Symposium* (Vol. 2, pp. 283–301). Hillsdale, NJ: Erlbaum.

Zanna, M. P., Higgins, E. T., & Herman, C. P. (Eds.). (1982). *Consistency in social behavior: The Ontario Symposium* (Vol. 2). Hillsdale, NJ: Erlbaum.

Zanna, M. P., Olson, J. M., & Fazio, R. H. (1980). Attitude-behavior consistency: An individual difference perspective. *Journal of Personality and Social Psychology, 38,* 432–440.

5

WHEN DO OUR ACTIONS
AFFECT OUR ATTITUDES?

JOEL COOPER
Princeton University

STEVEN J. SCHER
University of the Cariboo

Clyde Barrow had a relatively normal childhood for a boy growing up in a large, poor family in Dallas in the 1920s and 1930s. He was a bit mischievous and he skipped school occasionally, but there was little in his behavior to suggest that he would eventually become a bank robber and violent murderer. Nothing that would lead anyone to expect he would die on a quiet Louisiana road in a shootout with six policemen. And nothing to indicate that he would be half of America's most famous criminal duo—Bonnie and Clyde (see Figure 5-1).

But Clyde's life changed in the spring of 1926. By then, Clyde had met his first love, a schoolgirl named Anne. And after their first lovers' quarrel, Anne fled to her aunt's farm in the small town of San Augustine. Clyde rented a car to make the 170 mile trip to reconcile with Anne. Anne quickly forgot her differences with her boyfriend, and the couple stayed on in the country for an extra two days.

From Clyde Barrow's vantage point, all was right with the world. But the car rental company began to worry when Clyde did not show up to return their automobile. They called the police, who eventually tracked Clyde down in San Augustine. When they arrived, Clyde realized that he had been responsible for stealing the car. He ran out of the farmhouse and across the fields. The police drew their pistols and fired several shots. Clyde made it to the woods and hid until the police left. When he returned to the farm, he saw the hopeless situation he was in. Everyone saw him as a criminal—including Anne, who would now leave him for good.[1]

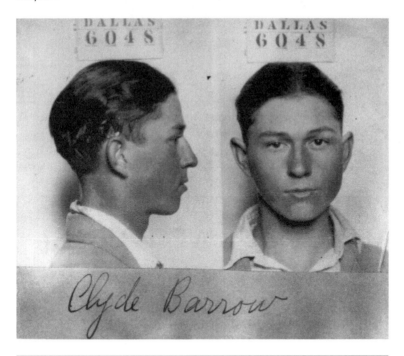

FIGURE 5-1   Mug shots of Clyde Barrow in his youth

Source: From the collections of the Texas/Dallas History and Archives Division, Dallas Public Library.

And so began the adult life of a criminal who, by the time of his death, would be responsible for countless robberies and murders. Clyde quickly persuaded himself that crime was not so bad. He began stealing cars whenever necessary. Soon he graduated to robbing drugstores and finally to bank robbery and murder. Each step of the way, Clyde justified his actions by changing his attitudes.

Throughout most of this book, the authors discuss methods used to change attitudes because it is normally assumed that to change behavior, it is sufficient to change people's attitudes. Fazio and Roskos-Ewoldsen (Chapter 4) have summarized research showing that the relationship between changes in attitudes and changes in behavior is not always as straightforward as has been assumed. That is, attitude changes do not lead directly to behavior changes. In this chapter, we will show that sometimes the relationship between attitudes and behaviors flows in the opposite direction: That is, changes in behavior can actually lead to changes in attitudes.

What is important about Clyde Barrow's first run-in with the police? Clyde's behavior—stealing the car and running from the approaching police—was in conflict with his belief in the law. More importantly, perhaps, his thoughts about his actions and his thoughts about his attitudes were in conflict.

Leon Festinger (1957) proposed a theory to explain what would happen in a situation like this. His theory, called the theory of *cognitive dissonance*, states that whenever a person holds cognitions or thoughts that are inconsistent or in conflict with one another, the person will feel tension. The tension will be experienced as a drive (similar to what we feel when we are hungry) and will result in efforts to reduce the inconsistency between these two cognitions. Festinger claimed that the amount of dissonance experienced (and therefore the intensity of the drive to reduce the dissonance) will be based on the number of discrepant cognitions one has (weighted by the importance of those cognitions) divided by the number of consistent, consonant cognitions one has (weighted by *their* importance). This could be thought of as a mathematical formula:

$$D = \frac{w_1(\text{\# dissonant cognitions})}{w_2(\text{\# consonant cognitions})}$$

In this formula, D stands for the total amount of dissonance, and w_1 and w_2 represent weights for how important these cognitions are to the person.

Think of Clyde again. He held two cognitions that were discrepant. These were "I believe the law should be obeyed" and "I stole a car and I am running from the police." According to Festinger, this should have led Clyde to be motivated to reduce the discrepancy. There were several ways that Clyde's overall dissonance (D, from the formula) could have been reduced. One way would have been for him to add consonant cognitions. This would have raised the denominator of the dissonance equation and thus lowered the overall value. For example, Clyde could have remembered all the times that he obeyed the law. Or he could have made a donation to the policeman's benevolent society. Any of these activities could have reduced dissonance.

However, there was another possibility. Clyde could have changed one of the discrepant cognitions so that it would be more in line with the other. This would have lowered the numerator of the dissonance equation. Which cognition would he change? Festinger argued that people will change the cognition that is "least resistant to change." Although sometimes people are able to change their memory for some behavior they have done, this is usually not very easy. It would have been hard for Clyde to deny that he ran from the police. On the other hand, it would have been easier to change his attitude about obeying the law. Clyde could have reduced his dissonance by coming to believe that it is all right to be a criminal. This is probably the most common way that dissonance is reduced—by changing attitudes. It is this aspect of dissonance theory that makes it relevant to the psychology of persuasion.

Although Festinger claimed that when any two cognitions were discrepant, dissonance would be aroused, almost all of the research done on this topic has included at least one cognition about one's own behavior. For example, in a classic experiment by Festinger and Carlsmith (1959), subjects were asked to come into the lab and perform an extremely boring task. Specifically, subjects spent 20 minutes turning empty thread spools on pegs on a board, then turning square pegs one-quarter turn to the left and right. Then, they were asked to tell a new subject (who was actually working for the experimenters) that the task was really interesting and exciting. They were paid the nominal sum of one dollar to tell the lie to the waiting subject. These activities created two discrepant cognitions for the subject—"This task was dull" and "I told someone that the task was interesting." Compared to subjects who had done the spool-turning task but had not told anyone that it was interesting, the subjects who lied (and therefore were expected to be feeling dissonance) later reported that the spool task was interesting. That is, they reduced their dissonance by changing their attitudes about the task.

However, the Festinger and Carlsmith experiment included another important condition. Recall that the subjects described above were paid one dollar for telling the accomplice that the task was interesting. Another group of subjects were also asked to tell another person that the task was interesting. However, these subjects were offered 20 dollars to tell the lie. What relevant cognitions did these subjects have? They still had the same dissonant cognitions that the one dollar subjects had—"The task was dull" and "I told someone that the task was interesting." However, these subjects also had an additional consonant cognition—"I received 20 dollars to tell this lie." Since the addition of this consonant cognition should have reduced the amount of dissonance felt by these subjects (recall the formula), they should have been less likely to change their attitudes about the task. As predicted by Festinger and Carlsmith, these subjects rated the task to be just as boring as the subjects who never told anyone that the task was interesting.

In Festinger and Carlsmith's study and many similar studies, a person is induced to comply with a request that is contrary to his or her attitude. These studies are now known as *induced compliance* studies, and they have many parallels in everyday life. For example, lawyers may have to argue for a client or for some legal position that is contrary to their beliefs. People may claim to support some issue because they want to impress someone who believes in that position (like a boss or a potential romantic partner). Politicians may have to make specific arguments that they do not believe in order to win votes. In all these situations, according to cognitive dissonance theory, people will experience dissonance and may reduce it by changing some attitude to be more in line with the content of their statements. This type of situation has been the most frequently used experimental method to study cognitive dissonance in the lab.

Cognitive dissonance theory also makes clear predictions about the consequences of choices that we make. Every time we choose between two or more alternative courses of action, we experience some dissonance. The dissonance is caused by the negative elements of the course of action chosen and the positive elements of the course that was not chosen (Brehm, 1956). Suppose you were trying to decide what car to buy. Perhaps you have narrowed your choices to a turbo-charged Mazda RX-7 and a Ford Fiesta. A list of the pros and cons of each purchase might look like Table 5-1. Notice that there are a few less negative and a few more positive elements to the Mazda. Looking at this list, you go to the car dealer and make your purchase. However, there are some negative things about the Mazda that you will have to live with, and there are some positive things about the Ford that you must do without. These rejected positive elements and accepted negative elements should lead to cognitive dissonance.

Brehm (1956) found in his research that when subjects had to choose between two gifts, both of which they had originally rated as fairly desirable, subjects' rat-

TABLE 5-1   Some possible pros and cons involved in choosing between two cars

Mazda Rx-7		Ford Fiesta	
Pros	*Cons*	*Pros*	*Cons*
Speed	Expensive	Good gas mileage	Ugly
Looks good		Roomy	Needs repairs often
Many colors			

ings after their decision showed a "spreading of the alternatives." That is, the chosen gift was seen as more desirable than it had initially been rated and the foregone gift was rated less positively than it had been rated prior to the choice. Brehm claimed that these people were reducing cognitive dissonance by adding more thoughts that were consistent with their choice. They tried to think of more positive things about the gift they chose and more negative things about the unchosen gift. Making a choice between the two gifts led to changes in attitudes about those gifts.

We make choices all the time in everyday life. And the more there is to like about the options we do not choose and the more there is that we do not like about the option we do choose, the more unwanted consequences we will be responsible for causing. Thus, after we make a choice, we tend to think it is better and the things we rejected are worse than we thought before. This may explain why people sometimes seem very closed minded about the things they have bought or chosen. After you buy the RX-7, your attitudes about it and the other cars you considered will be changed, and you may think that the Mazda is the best car in the world.

Now, let us consider a different type of dilemma to which cognitive dissonance has been applied. What are the consequences of people working hard—perhaps suffering—to achieve a goal? Dissonance theory predicts that people will come to like things better the more they have suffered to attain them (see Figure 5-2). Imagine that you are trying to be admitted to a club, sorority, or fraternity. You are confronted with an elaborate pledge period, replete with a number of difficult or embarrassing activities. The behavior, which is effortful, is inconsistent with people's general attitude to do things that are pleasant. And suppose that it turned out that the fraternity or sorority had some genuinely unattractive features: The other members were dull, the food was bad, and the parties were mediocre. How can you deal with the dissonance between the suffering involved in pledging, the attitude that one does not like to suffer, and the unattractive features of the group? One way to deal with the dissonance is to alter your perception of the group so that, in your eyes, it becomes the world's best fraternity or sorority. Suffering would make sense if it were done to gain access to the world's best social group.

Aronson and Mills (1959) tested this proposition by designing an experiment in which female subjects had to read aloud either sexually explicit or sexually non-explicit words in order to gain admission to a discussion group that was discussing sexual topics. After their "initiation," the subjects listened to a boring discussion among group members about the secondary sexual characteristics of lower verte-

FIGURE 5-2   Cognitive dissonance at work

Source: GARFIELD reprinted by permission of UFS, Inc.

brates. Subjects who had had to read aloud the more embarrassing, sexually explicit material experienced dissonance. In order to reduce the tension, they rated the boring discussion as more enjoyable and rated the participants as more attractive than subjects who had read nonexplicit (nonembarrassing) material.

There are other situations where expending effort may lead to cognitive dissonance and persuasion (see Figure 5-3). For example, when people have to go through a strenuous interview process to get a job, they may reduce their dissonance by liking the job more. Retailers may also make use of the dissonance produced by effort justification, and this may occur on more occasions than we usually think. If retailers make their products difficult to get or make the prices of their products very high, people who do get the products may develop more positive attitudes toward the products than if they had not put so much effort (or money!) into getting them. Several examples of this have taken place in the past—whether intentionally or inadvertently.

One of the most striking may have occurred during the Christmas season of 1983. You may recall that the hottest toy fad was the Cabbage Patch Doll. The dolls were in short supply, relative to the demand, and parents had to travel to toystores all over their area, searching for the dolls for their children. They paid premium prices, and on some occasions, there were almost riots over the purchase of the dolls. The news media reported several cases of families (some of lower income) who traveled overnight to London and other European cities to purchase dolls because they were not available locally. These efforts to get the dolls only raised the perceived attractiveness of the doll and the importance of getting one that Christmas—*attitudes were changed to justify the effort expended.*

FIGURE 5-3 Could effort justification processes explain the dedication of these Peace Corps members?

Source: Courtesy of the Peace Corps and The Advertising Council, Inc.

For 25 years, our people have endured long hours and tough working conditions for virtually no pay.

And 9 out of 10 would do it again.

A lot of corporations would like to claim that kind of loyalty.

But only the Peace Corps gives you the chance to immerse yourself in a totally different culture while helping to make an important difference in other people's lives.

So join us in celebrating the 25th Anniversary of the Peace Corps, and all the remarkable people who made it possible.

Or better yet, join us yourself. Call **1-800-424-8580** to find out more.

Peace Corps.
Still the toughest job you'll ever love.

In the Head or In the World: The Role of Consequences

Festinger originally argued that the only requirements for cognitive dissonance are inconsistent cognitions. According to this point of view, cognitive dissonance could be aroused merely by two thoughts, two elements that start and end in one person's mind. For example, the two beliefs "I believe in the U.S. Constitution" and "I do not believe in free speech" would be seen as dissonant. However, you may have noticed that in all of the research described in this chapter so far, the dissonance arises between an element inside the head (a belief or attitude) and an element outside the head (a behavior—a choice, talking to another subject, etc.). In fact, it is now known that not only must some behavior take place for dissonance to be aroused but that that behavior must produce some undesired consequence (Cooper & Fazio, 1984).

Research has confirmed that dissonant or discrepant thoughts are not sufficient conditions for dissonance to occur. As suggested above, a person must behave in a way that produces an aversive consequence—that is, some outcome that the person wishes had not occurred (Goethals & Cooper, 1972)—in order for dissonance to be aroused (see Collins & Hoyt, 1972; Cooper & Fazio, 1984; Scher & Cooper, 1989). Cooper and Worchel (1970), for example, repeated the Festinger and Carlsmith induced compliance study, where a subject is asked to tell another subject (actually an accomplice of the researchers) that a boring task is interesting. In this situation, the aversive consequence is deceiving a fellow student into expecting an exciting time, when a boring one is actually going to follow. Cooper and Worchel reasoned that this outcome would only be the result of the lie to the accomplice if the accomplice appeared to believe the subject. So, they had the accomplice tell some subjects that he was convinced that the task would be interesting, but he told other subjects that he was not convinced. Dissonance was only aroused in those conditions where he appeared convinced. That is, only when subjects thought they had produced the bad outcome of convincing the accomplice was there any change in subjects' attitudes toward the task.

As this and other studies suggest (e.g., Cooper, Zanna, & Goethals, 1974), just arguing for a position that is inconsistent with your attitudes will not produce dissonance by itself. Some aversive outcome must result for there to be dissonance. We have recently taken this notion one step further (Scher & Cooper, 1989): We asked college students either to write essays that were consistent or essays that were inconsistent with their attitudes toward a disliked policy. Some students were then led to believe that their essays (whether consistent or inconsistent with their attitudes) would have an unwanted effect, leading to adoption of the policy. When students were told that their essays would have this unwanted effect, dissonance was aroused, regardless of the positions that they took in their essays. In other words, the unwanted outcome was more important than the inconsistency of the essay-writing behavior in producing cognitive dissonance and changing attitudes to justify that outcome.

The Role of Responsibility

However, the arousal of cognitive dissonance is not caused just by producing aversive consequences. A person must also feel *personally responsible* for producing the consequences. If a person produces some aversive consequence but only because another person held a gun to his or her head, he or she should not experience cognitive dissonance. It is only when people feel responsible for the consequences that they will be motivated to change their view of the world in order to accommodate this violation of the normal course of events (Cooper & Fazio, 1984). And this change in world view is typically accomplished by changing one's attitudes.

In order for people to feel dissonance, then, they must interpret their behavior so that they see themselves as responsible for the bad consequences. However, it seems that people would not want to see themselves as being responsible for producing an aversive consequence (cf. Ross & DiTecco, 1975; Schlenker, 1982), and if the assignment of responsibility is not completely straightforward or obvious, people may try to reinterpret the events so that they do *not* feel responsible. If anything about the dissonance-arousing situation will let them deny (to themselves) that they are responsible, they will grab on to this fact and not change their attitudes (Insko et al., 1975). By denying their responsibility for the bad consequences, people can avoid dissonance-produced attitude change.

Research in dissonance has looked at some of the factors that will keep people from changing their attitudes even when they produce some aversive consequences. For example, Linder, Cooper, and Jones (1967) showed that if people in the induced compliance situation described earlier felt they were *coerced* into giving a speech or writing an essay, they would not feel dissonance.[2] Furthermore, several studies (Cooper, 1971; Cooper & Brehm, 1971; Cooper & Goethals, 1974; Goethals, Cooper, & Naficy, 1979) have shown that *foreseeability* of the aversive consequences is necessary for dissonance-related attitude change to occur.[3] Having free choice over one's behavior and being able to foresee the consequences of that behavior are major elements of being responsible for some outcome (Heider, 1958; Shaver, 1985). As we discussed, when something allows people to deny their responsibility for the unwanted outcome in the induced-compliance situation, they do not change their attitudes.

Aside from free choice and foreseeability, however, there are other aspects of the perception of responsibility that have been addressed. Shaver (1985), for example, has identified three other *dimensions of responsibility*. A person will be seen as responsible for an action to the extent that a person is seen as the *cause* of some outcome, that the action was *intended*, and that the person had an *"appreciation of the moral wrongfulness* of his or her conduct" (p. 102, emphasis in original). There has not been research in the dissonance literature to determine if these elements are also necessary for dissonance to be aroused. However, the reinterpretation of the theory that we have summarized here (Cooper & Fazio, 1984) suggests that these would be fruitful avenues for further research.

Returning to the story with which we started this chapter, what are the crucial elements that led to Clyde Barrow's changing attitudes about crime? He was *responsible* for the *unwanted consequences* of being chased by the police, losing his girlfriend Anne, and gaining a reputation as a car thief. These are the crucial elements in arousing cognitive dissonance, and these may have contributed to his subsequent antisocial attitudes and behaviors.

The Role of the Self in the Arousal of Dissonance

For what sorts of outcomes are people willing to accept responsibility? A good deal of research suggests that people will protect their self-esteem and image in the eyes of others by claiming that their successes were caused by something about themselves and that their failures were caused by something about the environment or situation (cf. Bradley, 1978; Zuckerman, 1979 for reviews). Similarly, people may deny responsibility for bad things. A few studies have confirmed this notion (Harvey, Harris, & Barnes, 1975; MacDonald & Davies, 1983).

In fact, some have claimed that this desire to protect self-esteem or self-image is the real reason that people change their attitudes in dissonance-arousing situations. Two recent perspectives on dissonance theory claim that dissonance-related persuasion is really caused by threats to a person's self-concept or *identity image*: "a theory . . . that is constructed about how one is and should be perceived, regarded, and treated in social life" (Schlenker, 1982, p. 194). Steele's (1988) *self-affirmation theory* and Schlenker's (e.g., 1980; 1982; 1985) theory of *self-identification* both attempt to account for dissonance research in a similar way. Schlenker (1982) argues that the induced compliance paradigms "usually induce subjects to lie, cheat, harm others, refrain from doing what they obviously prefer to do, do something they obviously would prefer to avoid doing. . . . In short, the paradigms place subjects in situations where they might appear to have *violated personal or public standards for conduct and threatened their identities*" (p. 209, emphasis in original). Likewise, Steele (1988) says that dissonance motivation is aroused because a dissonant act implies that a person is not "morally adequate" and it makes the person "feel foolish, raises doubts about one's competence, adaptive coherence, self-control, and other self-concepts" (p. 278). According to these views, feeling personally responsible for an aversive outcome connects that outcome with a person's image of himself or herself, making him or her feel inadequate in some way. As a result, that person wishes to reaffirm his or her self-adequacy in some way.[4] According to these views, attitude change in response to cognitive dissonance affirms the self or protects one's image.

Steele and Liu (1981; 1983) provided some evidence for the notion that dissonance is really aroused because of concerns about the self. They demonstrated that if subjects in a typical dissonance situation are given a chance to show that they are good people, or to affirm their positive values, they do not change their attitudes, even when the self-affirmation they make has nothing to do with the attitudes involved in arousing the dissonance. Although these studies are very interesting, they are not conclusive proof that dissonance motivation comes from a feeling that the self is inadequate. What they do show is that dissonance-induced attitude change can be forestalled. Further research is needed to identify the role that self-image plays in dissonance processes.

Cognitive Dissonance and Ideology

So far in this chapter, we have discussed the fact that when people feel personally responsible for some unwanted or aversive consequence, cognitive dissonance is aroused, which can lead to attitude change. In all of the research we have discussed, however, only one attitude was really changed. That is, the typical situation is that subjects take one action (e.g., convincing another person that a boring task was exciting), and then the researchers measure how much one attitude was changed (e.g., how much the subject like the task).

However, in many (if not most) situations, several attitudes and behaviors are related to each other. If Clyde Barrow was really an innocent boy before the incident with the rental car, the minor change in his attitude about crime could not have led to the extensive crime spree that eventually resulted. Clyde would have had to adopt a set of attitudes about crime and the behaviors he eventually committed, in other words, a *criminal ideology*. An *ideology* is "a systematic scheme or coordinated body of ideas or concepts especially about human life or culture" (*Webster's Third*, 1966). Clyde may have developed a set of systematically interrelated attitudes about crime and criminal activity.

Cognitive dissonance theory seems particularly suited to explaining how people develop and bolster particular ideologies and related behavioral patterns because of an ever-escalating cycle of action to attitude change to action. Each change in attitude leads to further changes in behavior, leading directly to further dissonance, and soon the person's entire ideology is changed.

Let us suppose that after his run-in with the police over the rental car, Clyde's attitude toward law and order changed just a little. This attitude change (based on action) would, under the right conditions, lead to behavior change (see Chapter 4 by Fazio & Roskos-Ewoldsen). Clyde's new attitude about the police might have led him, at first, to commit some minor crimes—shoplifting or jaywalking, for instance. However, these minor crimes may have led to further unwanted consequences, and this would have led to further attitude change. Perhaps at some point, in fleeing a burglary scene, Clyde killed someone. Feeling responsible for *this* aversive event may have led to changes in other attitudes—about human life and murder. This cycle could have continued until Clyde Barrow developed into the full-fledged criminal that he became (see Figure 5-4).

When Prophecy Fails: Cognitive Dissonance and the End of the World

In 1956, Festinger, Riecken, and Schachter reported a fascinating real-life study on the role of cognitive dissonance in shaping ideology. These authors and several students working with them had infiltrated a strange cult of people who had predicted the end of the world. What happened to this cult and its members illustrates the power of cognitive dissonance processes to influence ideology and behavior.

FIGURE 5-4   Clyde Barrow as he looked in 1933

Source: UPI/BETTMANN.

Mrs. Marian Keech was a middle-aged woman living with her husband in the suburban town of Lake City.[5] She had long expressed an interest in a variety of occult and psychic phenomena, and so it was not completely surprising when she began receiving messages from her deceased father. As Mrs. Keech explained it, "Without knowing why, I picked up a pencil and a pad that were lying on the table near my bed. My hand began to write in another handwriting. . . . I realized that somebody else was using my hand" (p. 33). Despite lack of encouragement from her husband and her mother, Mrs. Keech continued to wait for messages from other worlds. Soon, she began hearing from other spiritual beings, whom she came to call "the Guardians," who resided at "lower densities" on the planets of Clarion and Cerus.

Mrs. Keech discussed her messages with several people, and eventually word of her powers spread to a small group of followers. They believed that Mrs. Keech's messages came from creatures of superior intelligence living on planets beyond our solar system. The followers, whom she called "the Seekers" but whom the Guardians called "sibets," learned from the Guardians that by December 21, the great lost continents of Atlantis (in the Atlantic) and Mu (in the Pacific) would rise and that the world would be flooded. But the true believers had no need to worry about the coming disaster. Those who were "the chosen" would be saved. Wherever they were, the spaceships would come and rescue them.

The sibets made many sacrifices as the day of Armageddon approached. At first, there were small, undesirable consequences of being a sibet: Many of the student-believers gave up vacations or had to deal with scorn and anger from their parents. Others made financial and time commitments—traveling to and from Lake City, attending meetings with Mrs. Keech, and typing, mimeographing, and studying the many lessons that Mrs. Keech would receive. The believers were also told to give up smoking and eating meat. Although the specific behaviors in preparation for the cataclysm were dictated by the Guardians, each member made his or her own decision to be a member of the Seekers. Each *chose* to follow the Guardians' instructions with the concomitant unpleasant consequences.

Cognitive dissonance, therefore, must have been aroused. The Seekers' dissonance could be reduced by strengthening their attitudes about the messages of the Guardians. This attitude change occurred and led to further behaviors consistent with the attitudes.

As the date of the flood got even closer, members made greater sacrifices. Many gave away large sums of money or paid off all of their debts. Soon, they would not need money. Several of the believers quit their jobs to dedicate themselves full time to waiting for the prophecy and preparing themselves for the arrival of the spacemen. Early in December, Mrs. Keech had received the word that those who were going on the spaceship could not wear any metal on their person. The members of the group began to remove any metal from their clothing. They cut off their zippers, removed their shoes (because of nails and metal soles), and some of the women removed their bra straps.

Mrs. Keech made several of the group move into her home and take care of her. One poor soul was told by the Guardians that he could not go outside at all and that he could eat nothing but nuts. He strictly obeyed these prohibitions until they were revoked, several days later. In mid-December, a prominent member of the group was fired from his job at a nearby college because of his involvement with the group. This news and therefore news about the beliefs of Mrs. Keech's followers was heavily reported in the area press.

Up to this point, the group interpreted the undesired effects in such a way as to keep dissonance to a minimum. Everything was seen as part of the highly positive outcome—rescue from disaster. However, this interpretation became seriously threatened by the events leading up to December 21, the day of the predicted cataclysm and rescue. Several times, Mrs. Keech predicted the arrival of the rescuing spacemen; the sibets waited in the cold night, and each disappointment was later interpreted as a test of their readiness to be rescued.

Finally, the last day of the world arrived. The sun rose and the sun set. December 21 came and went. No floods occurred; nothing rocked the core of the globe. Neither Atlantis nor Mu rose up, as had been predicted. The scene at the Keech house at midnight, the hour of the appointed rescue by the spaceships from Clarion, was desperate. First, the group disbelieved their watches, assuming that the passing of midnight did not occur. When they were struck by the obvious disconfirmation of their strongly held belief, there was tremendous tension. It remained for Mrs. Keech to receive a series of messages from the Guardians that tried to resolve this disconcerting disconfirmation. The "Christmas Message to the People of the Earth" stated, in part, "And mighty is the word of God—and by his word have ye been saved—for from the mouth of death have ye been delivered and at no time has there been such a force loosed upon the Earth" (p. 169). In other words, the firm belief of the sibets had led the Creator to call off the destruction of the world!

We can now examine the effects of dissonance among the sibets and how the events of the last four days of the world changed those effects. The initial dissonance caused by the sacrifices of Mrs. Keech and her followers had been resolved by developing an ever more complex system of attitudes about the coming cataclysm. If they were going to spend the rest of their lives on planets at different densities, they did not need their money, their jobs, or the metal in their clothes. If the spacemen did not come when originally expected, then the followers were being tested. However, when the apocalypse was finally called off, all of these consequences once again mattered, and new consequences arose. The lives of the Armstrongs, the family of the man who had been fired from the college, had been irrevocably damaged. Besides the loss of money and Dr. Armstrong's job, his reputation had been ruined. Furthermore, his sister had begun legal proceedings to have him and Mrs. Armstrong committed and to gain custody of their two younger children. Mrs. Keech also had suffered, and all of the committed members of the group suffered consequences to some degree. The dissonance was extremely high for all of the seekers.

The group members used various strategies to deal with the cognitive dissonance that arose because of the disconfirmations. The official doctrine of the group was reinterpreted. An attempt was made to gain increased social support for this reinterpreted ideology, and to *diffuse the responsibility* for the consequences.

The "Christmas Message" from the Guardians was in essence a reinterpretation of the group's beliefs. The actions taken by the group did not lead to *undesired* consequences but to a highly desirable outcome. The group's faith and the actions taken to maintain that faith led directly to the salvation of the earth. How could the events be undesirable if this was the result? Furthermore, in order to bolster this reinterpretation, for the first time, effort was made to recruit new members. As Festinger, Riecken, and Schachter (1956) put it, "If more people can be persuaded that the system of belief is correct, then clearly it must [at least in the minds of the believers] be correct" (p. 28).

The reinterpretation was not the only way the sibets tried to reduce dissonance. Aside from reducing the aversive nature of the events, they also attempted to reduce their personal responsibility for the consequences. They did this by *diffusing responsibility*. In other words, they tried to spread the responsibility for the events among as many people as possible. After one of the early disconfirmations,

Mrs. Keech deemed that all of the followers should gather at her home. It became increasingly important that all of the members remain together. In this way, the responsibility for the disconfirmation could be spread among as many people as possible. The attempts at recruiting new members, if they had been successful, would have set up a further diffusion of responsibility for future bad events.

Here we have seen how cognitive dissonance can explain a naturally occurring change in a complex set of beliefs and behaviors. In this situation, the persuasion that took place was almost *accidental*. No one tried to get Mrs. Keech's followers to change their beliefs. Nonetheless, the events that took place aroused dissonance, leading to major ideological changes and reinterpretations.

Conclusion

It is clear that actions have effects upon attitudes. The research in cognitive dissonance theory has been the most notable approach in demonstrating the link between the two. Chapter 4 in this volume described the effect that attitudes can have on actions. In the current chapter, we have shown that, when conditions are right, people's actions cause changes in their attitudes. Factors such as responsibility and the type of consequences that are brought about by the actions are necessary preconditions for attitudes to be affected by actions. Was the crime spree of Bonnie and Clyde caused by the series of chance events that led Clyde Barrow to take actions that later led to his adopting the attitudes of a criminal? Perhaps we cannot seriously offer such a reconstruction of history. But we can be certain that the actions that people take can cause fundamental restructuring of their attitudes.

Notes

1. This story is the one told by Clyde's sister. Other evidence suggests that Clyde Barrow had already had trouble with the law and was something of a delinquent. However, for purposes of illustration, we will stick to this version of Clyde's younger days (Treherne, 1984).

2. This is the reason that we prefer the term *induced compliance* to the term Festinger and Carlsmith (1959) originally used—*forced compliance*. If the behavior is really forced, dissonance will not be aroused.

3. However, the consequences do not actually need to have been *foreseen* (Goethals et al., 1979).

4. The two theories have a slightly different focus. Schlenker (e.g., 1985) believes that people's behavior in these situations is motivated by threats to their image—either their image as presented to others or as presented to themselves. Steele (1988) places more emphasis on people's sense of their own identity. Otherwise, the perspectives are quite similar, especially as they relate to cognitive dissonance theory and persuasion.

5. In order to protect the participants, Festinger, Riecken, and Schachter (1956) changed the names of the participants and most of the locations that play a part in their story. We use the aliases in this account.

References

Aronson, E., & Mills, J. (1959). The effect of severity of initiation on liking for a group. *Journal of Abnormal and Social Psychology, 59,* 177–181.

Bradley, G. W. (1978). Self-serving biases in the attribution process: A re-examination of the fact or fiction question. *Journal of Personality and Social Psychology, 35,* 56–71.

Brehm, J. W. (1956). Post-decision changes in desirability of alternatives. *Journal of Abnormal and Social Psychology, 52,* 384–389.

Collins, B. E., & Hoyt, M. G. (1972). Personal responsibility for consequences: An integration and extension of the "forced compliance" literature. *Journal of Experimental Social Psychology, 8,* 558–593.

Cooper, J. (1971). Personal responsibility and dissonance: The role of foreseen consequences. *Journal of Personality and Social Psychology, 18,* 354–363.

Cooper, J., & Brehm, J. W. (1971). Prechoice awareness of relative deprivation as a determinant of cognitive dissonance. *Journal of Experimental Social Psychology, 7,* 571–581.

Cooper, J., & Fazio, R. H. (1984). A new look at dissonance theory. In L. Berkowitz (Ed.), *Advances in experimental social psychology* (Vol. 17, pp. 229–266). New York: Academic Press.

Cooper, J., & Goethals, G. R. (1974). Unforeseen events and the elimination of cognitive dissonance. *Journal of Personality and Social Psychology, 29,* 441–445.

Cooper, J., & Worchel, S. (1970). Role of undesired consequences in arousing cognitive dissonance. *Journal of Personality and Social Psychology, 16,* 199–206.

Cooper, J., Zanna, M. P., & Goethals, G. R. (1974). Mistreatment of an esteemed other as a consequence affecting dissonance reduction. *Journal of Experimental Social Psychology, 10,* 224–233.

Festinger, L. (1957). *A theory of cognitive dissonance.* Stanford, CA: Stanford University Press.

Festinger, L., & Carlsmith, J. M. (1959). Cognitive consequences of forced compliance. *Journal of Abnormal and Social Psychology, 58,* 203–210.

Festinger, L., Riecken, H., & Schachter S. (1956). *When prophecy fails.* Minneapolis, MN: University of Minnesota Press.

Goethals, G. R., & Cooper, J. (1972). The role of intention and postbehavioral consequences in the arousal of cognitive dissonance. *Journal of Personality and Social Psychology, 23,* 293–301.

Goethals, G. R., Cooper, J., & Naficy, A. (1979). Role of foreseen, foreseeable, and unforeseeable behavioral consequences in the arousal of cognitive dissonance. *Journal of Personality and Social Psychology, 37,* 1179–1185.

Harvey, J. H., Harris, B., & Barnes, R. D. (1975). Actor-Observer differences in the perceptions of responsibility and freedom. *Journal of Personality and Social Psychology, 32,* 22–28.

Heider, F. (1958). *The psychology of interpersonal relations.* New York: Wiley.

Insko, C. A., Worchel, S., Folger, R., and Kutkus, A. (1975). A balance theory interpretation of dissonance. *Psychological Review, 82,* 169–183.

Linder, D., Cooper, J., & Jones, E. E. (1967). Decision freedom as a determinant of the role of incentive magnitude in attitude change. *Journal of Personality and Social Psychology, 6,* 245–254.

MacDonald, L. M., & Davies, M. F. (1983). Effects of being observed by a friend or stranger on felt embarrassment and attributions of embarrassment. *Journal of Psychology, 113,* 171–174.

Ross, M., & DiTecco, D. (1975). An attributional analysis of moral judgments. *Journal of Social Issues, 31,* 91–109.

Scher, S. J., & Cooper, J. (1989). Motivational basis of dissonance: The singular role of behavioral consequences. *Journal of Personality and Social Psychology, 56,* 899–906.

Schlenker, B. R. (1980). *Impression management: The self-concept, social identity, and interpersonal relations.* Monterey, CA: Brooks/Cole.

Schlenker, B. R. (1982). Translating action into attitudes: An identity-analytic approach to the explanation of social conduct. In L. Berkowitz (Ed.), *Advances in experimental social psychology* (Vol. 15, pp. 193–247). New York: Academic Press.

Schlenker, B. R. (1985). Identity and self-identification. In B. R. Schlenker (Ed.), *The self and social life* (pp. 65–99). New York: McGraw-Hill.

Shaver, K. G. (1985). *The attribution of blame: Causality, responsibility, and blameworthiness*. New York: Springer-Verlag.

Steele, C. M. (1988). The psychology of self-affirmation: Sustaining the integrity of the self. In L. Berkowitz (Ed.), *Advances in experimental social psychology* (Vol. 21, pp. 261–302). New York: Academic Press.

Steele, C. M., & Liu, T. J. (1981). Making the dissonant act unreflective of the self: Dissonance avoidance and the expectancy of a value-reaffirming response. *Personality and Social Psychology Bulletin, 7,* 393–397.

Steele, C. M., & Liu, T. J. (1983). Dissonance processes as self-affirmation. *Journal of Personality and Social Psychology, 45,* 5–19.

Treherne, J. (1984). *The strange case of Bonnie and Clyde*. London: Jonathan Cape.

Webster's Third New International Dictionary of the English Language. (1966). Springfield, MA: G. C. Merriam Company, Publishers.

Zuckerman, M. (1979). Attribution of success and failure revisited: or The motivational bias is alive and well in attribution theory. *Journal of Personality, 47,* 245–287.

6

TO THINK OR
NOT TO THINK

Exploring Two Routes to Persuasion

RICHARD E. PETTY
The Ohio State University

JOHN T. CACIOPPO
The Ohio State University

ALAN J. STRATHMAN
University of Missouri

JOSEPH R. PRIESTER
The Ohio State University

Hamlet is reading a magazine. His eye is caught by an ad for the Great Dane sword. The ad pictures Fortinbras raising the sword in battle. The ad proclaims:

10 REASONS WHY THE GREAT DANE OUTPERFORMS ITS COMPETITORS

The ad continues:

REASON #1—BECAUSE OF ITS SHARPER BLADE, THE GREAT DANE KILLS FASTER AND MORE DECISIVELY.

Hamlet, who had never heard of the Great Dane before, thinks to himself:

I need a sword that kills quickly and decisively. With such a mighty sword, I could rectify wrongs that have been committed. By rectifying the wrongs, there would be one less villainous, adulterous, murderer of kings. After I have rectified the wrongs, I would be free of these thoughts that are driving me mad. Yes, a sword that kills faster and more decisively is precisely what I need.

Hamlet continues to read the other nine reasons, thinking about each in a manner similar to the way in which he thought about the first.

Laertes is reading the same magazine, and his eye is also caught by the Great Dane ad. Laertes, who was also unfamiliar with the Great Dane, thinks to himself:

Fortinbras looks very fierce in this picture, and many advantages of the Great Dane are listed. It must be a fine sword.

Laertes continues past the ad, without stopping to read any of the arguments.

In the scenario above, if we had assessed Hamlet's and Laertes's attitudes toward the Great Dane sword before and after they were exposed to the ad, it is probable that we would have observed attitude change in both of them. That is, both may have changed from a neutral or slightly negative attitude toward the Great Dane before reading the ad (sometimes we are skeptical of things with which we are unfamiliar) to a very positive evaluation after the message. For example, both Hamlet and Laertes might have rated the Great Dane a "4" on a 9-point scale (1 = very unfavorable; 9 = very favorable) before looking at the ad, but an "8" afterwards. But what do these "8's" mean? Clearly, Hamlet spent more time thinking about the sword than did Laertes. And the nature of Hamlet's thoughts was quite different than the type of thinking that Laertes did about the sword. But does the quantity and quality of thinking matter? After all, both Hamlet and Laertes rated the sword an identical "8."

Current research on persuasion suggests that, indeed, the amount and nature of the thinking matters greatly. The purpose of this chapter is to describe a theory of persuasion that says that not all attitude changes that look the same really are. This theory, called the *Elaboration Likelihood Model* (or ELM, for short), says that the amount and nature of the thinking that a person does about a persuasive message (such as an advertisement) has an important influence on the kind of persuasion that occurs (Petty & Cacioppo, 1981, 1986). By the end of this chapter, you should have a better understanding of why all "8's" are not alike and also have a framework for appreciating why certain factors have the impact on attitude change that they do.

In order to understand the ELM, it is first important to understand an assumption that the ELM makes about the nature of humans in general. That assumption is that people have neither the ability nor the motivation to evaluate everything carefully. Think about it. You are a busy person with many things to do. Add to this busyness the fact that you live in a complex world. You will probably agree that you cannot take the time nor do you have the mental energy to analyze carefully each and every decision you make or piece of information you encounter.

But this causes a potential problem, because you, like other people, have hundreds of little decisions to make each day. For example, a trip to the typical supermarket confronts the shopper with over 25,000 possible items from which to select. Can the shopper read the labels on all of the products in a given category to find the one that has the best price, combination of ingredients, and the like? Of course not. Instead, people reserve their effortful thought processes and energy for those tasks that they feel are most deserving and those situations that permit time for reflection. In other instances, they rely on relatively simple *cues* in the situation, such as whether their favorite sports hero is pictured on the cereal box or how *many* reasons are listed to buy a product on an in-store display. This is the strategy that Laertes followed in forming his attitude about the Great Dane sword.

In the typical situation in which persuasion might take place, a person or a group of people (i.e., the *recipient*, or audience) receives a communication (i.e., the *message*) from another individual or group (i.e., the *source*) in a particular setting (i.e., the *context*). The communication usually presents reasons or arguments in favor of or against a particular object (e.g., the Great Dane sword), person (e.g., a presidential candidate), or issue (e.g., abortion). The message may be delivered in person or via some print (e.g., newspaper), audio (e.g., radio), or video (e.g., television) medium (i.e., the *channel*). For example, a team of attorneys may present the closing arguments for the conviction of an accused murderer to a 12-member jury in a packed and noisy courtroom, or a solitary child may sit in a tranquil bedroom and watch a commercial for a new sugar-coated cereal with a prize in the box. Each of the various aspects of the persuasion situation (i.e., source, message, recipient, channel, context) has been studied in depth and has been shown to be of some importance in influencing attitudes (McGuire, 1969, 1985). In this chapter, we will explain how these factors or variables work to produce persuasion by using the ELM.

Overview of the Elaboration Likelihood Model (ELM) of Persuasion

The ELM is based on the notion that people want to have correct attitudes and beliefs, since these will normally prove to be most helpful in dealing with everyday problems. For example, if we liked evil people or thought highly of shoddy products, we surely would have difficulties. The ELM describes two rather different ways by which a person might come to hold a reasonable attitude (i.e., one that seems right to the person). One procedure, referred to as following the *central route* to persuasion, involves carefully thinking about and examining information pertinent (or central) to the merits of a topic. The second strategy, called the *peripheral route* to persuasion, involves less cognitive effort and occurs when a person relies on a relatively simple cue in the situation, such as whether the source appears to be an expert or whether a product comes in an attractive package (i.e., relying on information that permits a reasonable decision without requiring the person to undertake a careful and effortful analysis of the true merits of the issue or product). (Recall that, in describing the ways that attitudes can guide behavior, Fazio and Roskos-Ewoldsen in Chapter 4 also distinguish between two processes that differ in the cognitive effort required.)

The Central Route to Persuasion

Consider Hamlet's thoughts in response to the Great Dane advertisement. Hamlet relates the information in the ad (e.g., "Kills faster and more decisively") to knowledge and information that he already possesses (e.g., "Wrongs that have been committed") to arrive at new ideas that were present neither in the ad nor in his previous knowledge (e.g., "I would be free of these thoughts that are driving me mad"). This type of thinking is called *elaboration* and is the hallmark of the central route to persuasion.

The effortful elaboration that is necessary to take the central route involves paying careful attention to the relevant information in the message and relating that information to previous knowledge stored in memory (e.g., Is the message consistent or inconsistent with other facts that I know?) and generating new implications of the information (e.g., What does this mean for my life?). The ultimate goal of this effort is to determine if the position taken by the source has any merit. For example, consider the advertisement encountered by Hamlet and Laertes. One of the arguments presented was that it was a good sword because of its sharper blade. In addition, the argument continued that, because of the sharp blade, the sword had the potential to kill faster and more decisively. The thoughts that a person has in response to an argument are often referred to as *cognitive responses* (Greenwald, 1968; Perloff & Brock, 1980; Petty, Ostrom, & Brock, 1981). These cognitive responses might be favorable toward the message (e.g., "With such a mighty sword, I could rectify wrongs that have been committed"), or they might be unfavorable (e.g., "I need a sword strictly for fencing. Having a sharp blade is the last thing that I need"). The process of elaboration, or generating cognitive responses, may be thought of as a private dialogue in which the person reacts to the information presented (Festinger & Maccoby, 1964) (see Figure 6-1).

As we will describe shortly, considerable research supports the view that persuasion may depend on the nature of the thoughts generated in response to a message. In general, we will refer to the act of generating issue-relevant cognitive responses to a message in an attempt to assess the true merits of the position taken as following the central route to persuasion.

In order to evaluate the merits of the arguments presented in a message, a person has to be both *motivated* and *able* to do so. Not every message is sufficiently interesting for us to think about, and not every situation provides us with sufficient time for careful reflection. When people are motivated and able to follow the central route, they carefully appraise the extent to which a message provides information that is fundamental or central to the true merits of the person, object, or issue under consideration. Of course, the particular type of information that is perceived central to the merits of any particular issue may vary from person to person and from situation to situation (cf., Katz, 1960). For example, research has shown that when some people think about the topic of capital punishment, religious considerations and arguments are particularly persuasive, but for others, legalistic arguments carry the most weight (Cacioppo, Petty, & Sidera, 1982). Likewise, research has shown that when evaluating consumer products, some people are particularly

"Who the hell do you think you're kidding?"

FIGURE 6-1   **People are sometimes very active processors of the messages that they receive. The thoughts that a message elicits can be favorable, unfavorable, neutral, or some combination of these.**

Source: Drawing by Modell; © 1975 The New Yorker Magazine, Inc.

concerned about how usage of the product will affect the image that they project; for other people, this dimension is unimportant (Snyder & DeBono, 1985, 1989). Just as people may differ in the dimensions central to their attitudes, different situations may cause different attributes to be central. For example, in judging a person's prospects for admission to graduate school, intelligence is central, whereas attractiveness is not. On the other hand, when judging the same person's prospects for a modeling career, the opposite may hold.

The important point here is that sometimes attitudes are formed or changed by a rather thoughtful process in which people carefully attend to the arguments presented, examine them in light of their relevant experiences and knowledge, and evaluate them along the dimensions they perceive to be central to the merits of the objects.[1] Attitudes formed via this central route are expected to have a number of distinguishing characteristics. In particular, these attitudes are expected to be (a) relatively easy to be called to mind (accessible); (b) relatively persistent and stable over time; (c) relatively resistant to challenge from competing messages; and (d) relatively predictive of the person's attitude-relevant behavior.

The Peripheral Route to Persuasion

Consider Laertes's thoughts in response to the advertisement. Laertes's thoughts focus primarily on the endorser of the sword and the mere number of features the sword is said to have. Thus, Laertes's attitude is not the result of effortfully considering the actual merits of the information about the sword! Instead he is relying on the simple cues of *source attractiveness* and *message length*. The type of attitude formation and change that occurs in the absence of effortful message elaboration is referred to as taking the *peripheral route* to persuasion.[2] But why would anyone form or change an attitude based solely on information such as who is pictured with a product and how many reasons appear to favor it?

The peripheral route to persuasion recognizes that it is neither adaptive nor possible for people to exert considerable mental effort in thinking about all of the persuasive communications to which they are exposed (cf., Miller, Maruyama, Beaber, & Valone, 1976). Just imagine if you thought carefully about *every* television or radio commercial you heard or ad you came across in newspapers or magazines. If you ever made it out of the house in the morning, you probably would be too mentally exhausted to do anything else! In a perfect world, we might hold opinions only on those topics that we had considered carefully. As we noted above, however, this ideal is impossible because, in the course of daily life, we are called upon to express opinions and to act on issues that have little direct interest to us and about which we have had little time to think.

In order to function in contemporary society we must often act as "lazy organisms" (McGuire, 1969) or as "cognitive misers" (Taylor, 1981). This means that we must at times have some relatively simple means for deciding what is good and what is bad. For example, consider a patriotic American who is watching television when an ad comes on for one of the many candidates in the Democratic primary election for the House of Representatives. In a sincere voice and with the American flag in the background, the candidate gives his views on domestic spending priorities. Since it is several months before the election and our television viewer is an "independent" voter who does not plan to vote in the primary anyway, there is little reason for him to think about the message carefully. Imagine that following the commercial, the phone rings and the viewer is asked to respond to a political poll. The viewer reports a favorable attitude toward the candidate, not because of an evaluation of the views expressed toward domestic spending but because the sincere voice and the American flag triggered positive associations or allowed a simple inference that the candidate was probably worthy. Thus, both our television viewer and Laertes formed their attitudes via the peripheral route. That is, their opinions are the result of their use of simple cues rather than thinking about the substantive arguments presented.

According to the ELM, attitudes formed or changed via this peripheral route are less accessible, persistent, resistant, and predictive of behavior than are attitudes formed or changed by the central route. Figure 6-2 diagrams the two routes

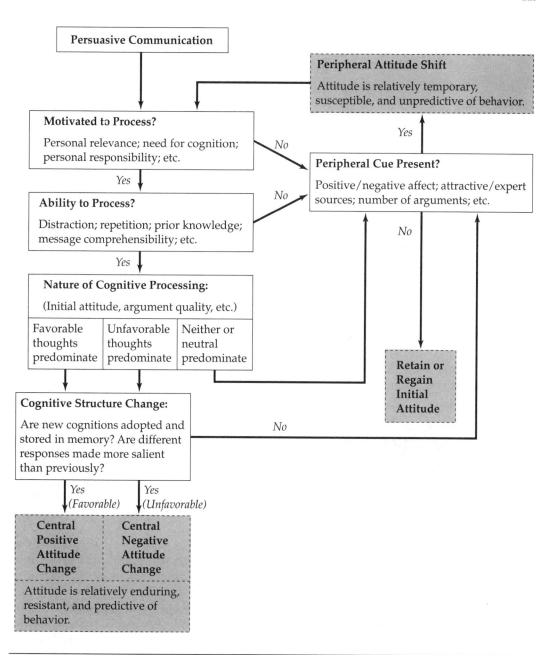

FIGURE 6-2 **The two routes to persuasion. This diagram depicts the possible endpoints after exposure to a persuasive communication according to the Elaboration Likelihood Model (ELM) (i.e., central attitude change, peripheral change, no change).**

Source: From *Communication and Persuasion: Central and Peripheral Routes to Attitude Change* by R. E. Petty and J. T. Cacioppo, 1986, New York: Springer Verlag. Copyright 1986 by Springer Verlag. Reprinted by permission.

to persuasion. It shows that the central route occurs when people possess both the motivation and ability to elaborate carefully the arguments presented but that the peripheral route is more likely to occur when either motivation is low or ability is impaired.

Evidence for the Two Routes to Persuasion

According to the ELM, then, the likelihood of elaborating on a persuasive communication (or *elaboration likelihood*), as determined by a person's motivation and ability to think about the arguments in the communication, determines the route to persuasion. When the elaboration likelihood is high (i.e., a person is both motivated *and* able to process a communication), the central route to persuasion occurs, but as the elaboration likelihood decreases, the peripheral route becomes more powerful.

Research on the ELM has proceeded in several stages. First, attempts were made to demonstrate that numerous variables could have an impact on persuasion by affecting the extent to which people were motivated or able to think about the arguments in a message. Next, studies demonstrated that the impact of peripheral cues on persuasion would be greater when the elaboration likelihood was low rather than high. Finally, evidence was obtained for the different consequences of the two routes to persuasion. For example, did central-route attitudes really last longer than peripheral-route attitudes? Each of these streams of research is described in the following sections.

Modifying Attitudes by Affecting Message Elaboration

One of the most important and integrative principles of the ELM is that variables can affect persuasion by affecting how much thinking a person is doing about a message (a lot or a little) and what kinds of thoughts (favorable or unfavorable) are generated in response to the message. Table 6-1 presents a way of categorizing variables that affect message elaboration.

As shown in Table 6-1 (and also Figure 6-2), we can distinguish variables that affect *motivation* to process a message from those variables that affect *ability* to process. Simply stated, variables influencing motivation are those that affect a person's rather conscious intentions and goals in processing a message. In other words, do people choose to exert the necessary effort to process the message arguments? In contrast, the question of ability is one of whether the person has the necessary skills, knowledge, and opportunity to evaluate the message. Motivational and ability variables can be further divided into (1) those variables that are part of the persuasion situation versus those that are part of the individual recipient of persuasion and (2) those variables that affect the amount of thinking (i.e., increasing or decreasing thinking in a relatively objective manner) versus those variables that motivate or enable a bias to the thinking that is underway (i.e., making it more or less favorable than it otherwise would be). We will deal with each of these distinctions.

TABLE 6-1   Categorization and examples of factors affecting elaboration likelihood

	Motivational Factors		Ability Factors	
	Situational	*Dispositional*	*Situational*	*Dispositional*
Relatively Objective Processing	Personal relevance	Need for cognition	External distraction	General intelligence
Relatively Biased Processing	Forewarning of intent	Open/closed mindedness	Head movements	Issue relevant knowledge or schema

Source: Adapted from Petty, Unnava, & Strathman, 1991.

Situational Impact on Motivation to Think

What are some of the possible situational variables that might have motivated Hamlet to scrutinize the Great Dane ad more than Laertes? One possibility is that Hamlet had been thinking about purchasing a sword before he ever saw the ad. That is, he already intended to buy a sword and was trying to decide which sword to buy. This intention rendered the ad more personally relevant to Hamlet. Laertes, on the other hand, had no intention of purchasing a sword, so the ad had little personal relevance to him. Could self-relevance be a difference that led Hamlet to process the ad more than Laertes?[3]

Some of the persuasive messages that we confront have direct personal implications for our lives, whereas others do not. For example, a new proposal to raise the state sales tax affects just about everyone; a proposal to close a state park affects mostly nature lovers; and a proposal to prohibit having alligators as pets affects hardly anybody. People should be especially motivated to think about proposals with direct personal implications. After all, if we can process only a limited number of the many communications we receive, it would be most adaptive to devote the most time and energy to those with the most personal consequences (Petty, Cacioppo, & Haugtvedt, 1992). (See, for example, the research on vested interest reviewed by Fazio and Roskos-Ewoldsen in Chapter 4.)

If people were divided into groups for which a message was either high or low in personal relevance, which group would be easier to persuade if we wanted to produce persuasion by the *central route*? Since the central route requires extensive thinking about the information presented, and high relevance should enhance thinking, it would seem that this group would show more persuasion. However, this reasoning assumes that the thoughts (elaborations) generated in response to the message are favorable, such as would be the case if the message presented arguments that were compelling when scrutinized. What if the message contained arguments that were not very persuasive and did not hold up under a careful examination? If people in the high-relevance group are engaged in considerable thought about weak or specious arguments, they should show *less* agreement than a group that is not thinking about the arguments because they will better realize the flaws in the message.

Testing this reasoning requires developing two sets of arguments on some topic. For example, in one study, both strong and weak arguments were developed on the topic of instituting a comprehensive exam for college seniors (Petty & Cacioppo, 1979b). The comprehensive exam was described as a test of what students had learned in their major area, and passing it was proposed as a requirement for graduation. Not surprisingly, most undergraduates were initially opposed to the institution of these exams. However, a message with strong arguments was developed to elicit mostly favorable cognitive responses when the students were *instructed* to think about them. For example, the strong arguments pointed out, among other things, that job placements and starting salaries improved at colleges with the exams. In stark contrast, a set of *weak* arguments was designed to elicit mostly unfavorable cognitive responses. The weak messages argued, for example, that the exams should be instituted because parents wanted them and that the exams were a tradition dating back to the ancient Greeks. As you might expect, when students were asked to think about these reasons for instituting the exams, their thoughts were quite negative.

Although preliminary testing assured that students were able to distinguish the strong from the weak arguments when they were instructed to do so, it said nothing about whether increasing the personal relevance of the message would make them more likely to think *spontaneously* about the implications of the arguments and form attitudes based on these thoughts. The ELM hypothesis, of course, was that when the message was high in personal relevance, the students would naturally scrutinize the arguments even when they were not instructed to do so, but when the message was low in personal relevance, devoting effort to thinking about the arguments would be less likely.

Given that strong and weak messages on the topic of senior comprehensive exams were developed successfully, the experiment next required a procedure to vary whether the message was perceived as being high or low in personal relevance. To accomplish these differences in personal relevance, some of the students (high-relevance group) were led to believe that the exam proposal was for their own university whereas other students (low-relevance group) were led to believe that the exam proposal was for a comparable but distant university (cf., Apsler & Sears, 1968). All of the participants in the study were told that their job was to rate the "sound quality" of radio editorials about the proposed exam that were sent to the journalism school from universities throughout the nation. These instructions were given so that complying with the study would not require thinking about the content of the message. Each participant sat in a private cubicle and was randomly assigned to listen through headphones to one of the four editorials required by the experimental design (high relevance with strong arguments; high relevance with weak arguments; low relevance with strong arguments; low relevance with weak arguments). Following exposure to one of the messages, the students were asked to list the thoughts they had while listening to the tape (see Cacioppo & Petty, 1981, for a description of the thought-listing procedure).

The attitude results from this study are graphed in Figure 6-3. Just as expected, when the speaker advocated that the exams should be instituted at a distant uni-

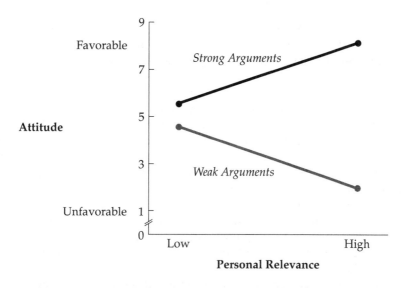

FIGURE 6-3 Postmessage attitudes as a function of personal relevance and argument quality. The figure shows that argument quality is a more important determinant of persuasion when personal relevance is high rather than low.

Source: Data from Petty & Cacioppo, 1979b, experiment 2.
Note: Data presented on transformed metric.

versity (i.e., low personal relevance), the students' attitudes were not affected very much by whether the speaker provided strong or weak arguments. However, when the message was of high personal relevance, argument quality was an important determinant of attitudes. Also, the thoughts that the students listed after message exposure suggested that the more extreme attitudes were accompanied by more extreme thoughts. That is, when the arguments were strong, students exposed to the high-relevance message produced more than twice as many favorable thoughts as low-relevance subjects, even though both groups were exposed to the *identical* arguments. When the arguments were weak, high-relevance subjects generated almost twice as many unfavorable thoughts as subjects exposed to the low-relevance version of the message.

Because the pilot testing for this study showed that the students were capable of distinguishing the strong from the weak arguments when they were instructed to do so, the study indicates that people become more likely to engage *spontaneously* in this effortful evaluation process as the perceived personal relevance of the message increases (Petty & Cacioppo, 1990). That is, as the personal relevance of a message increases, individuals are more likely to decide to think about the message on their own. In fact, research suggests that simply changing the pronouns in a message from the third person (e.g., *one* or *he and she*) to the second person (e.g., *you*) is sufficient to increase thinking about the message

(Burnkrant & Unnava, 1989). This fact has not been lost on advertisers, of course, who have made extensive use of advances in computer-assisted mailings to individualize and personalize the messages they send to potential customers (see Figure 6-4).

Although the personal relevance of a message is a major determinant of people's motivation to think about the arguments presented, it is not the only one. Studies have uncovered several other factors that can be employed to increase the elaboration likelihood. For example, when people believe they are the only ones responsible for judging a message, they exert more effort in thinking about it than when they are part of a group that is responsible. As a result, the quality of the arguments in a message has a greater impact on the attitudes of individual rather than group evaluators (Petty, Harkins, & Williams, 1980).

Apparently, when people are jointly responsible for making an evaluation (such as when they are serving on a committee), they may feel that their input is less important or needed, and thus they work less hard (Harkins & Petty, 1982; Latané, Williams, & Harkins, 1979). In a similar vein, people put more effort into thinking about messages that come from multiple sources rather than just one source (Harkins & Petty, 1981). People appear to reason that information that comes from multiple sources is more likely to be valid and therefore worthy of processing than information that comes from only one person (Harkins & Petty, 1987).

As a final example, research indicates that when people are not normally motivated to think about the message arguments, more thinking can be provoked by summarizing the major arguments as *questions* rather than *assertions* (Petty, Cacioppo, & Heesacker, 1981). For example, rather than concluding your argument by saying, "And therefore, instituting comprehensive exams for seniors would increase the prestige of the university," you could ask, "Wouldn't instituting comprehensive exams for seniors increase the prestige of the university?" (See also Burnkrant & Howard, 1984; Howard, 1990.) Summarizing an argument as a question causes people to engage in greater thought about the merits of the argument.

The use of rhetorical questions, of course, could lead to more or less agreement with the advocated position, depending upon whether thinking about the argument leads to favorable or unfavorable cognitive responses. In the 1980 presidential election, Republican candidate Ronald Reagan asked voters whether they were better off now or four years ago. (The previous four-year term of Democrat Jimmy Carter was characterized by high inflation and interest rates.) By posing a question, Reagan likely achieved greater issue-relevant thinking (and negative attitudes toward the Carter administration) than if he had simply told voters that they were *not* better off (Myers, 1983).

Individual Differences in Motivation to Think

Could personality factors have accounted for the fact that Hamlet thought about the Great Dane ad to a greater extent than Laertes? Consider that, aside from the ad in the magazine, Hamlet ruminates about a wide variety of things, even when there is little situational motivation for him to do so. Consider also that Laertes, aside from the ad in the magazine, rarely thinks about things unless the situational motivation is intense. Is it possible that Hamlet thought about the ad more than

FIGURE 6-4   Personalized messages are particularly effective in engaging information processing.

NOTICE FOR RECEIPT

From: R. K. Barnum, Gift Distribution Committee

Mr. & Mrs. Richard E. Petty
3104 Oaklawn Street   Date Sent: September 17, 1993
Columbia, MO 65203   Gift Processing #: "One Thousand"

Dear Mr. & Mrs. Petty,

Several weeks ago, we attempted to notify you of your selection in a sweepstakes program we were conducting. You and your family had been selected to represent the Midwest region of the United States. What this meant was that you had either won the Chrysler Convertible or one of the other three gifts listed below:

(1) Chrysler Convertible   **(3) $1,000 Cash**
(2) 45″ Giant Screen TV Projection System   **(4) Electrasport Boat (claimed)**

Note: Unless our records are incorrect, you did not claim your gift. Due to the nature in which you were selected, you will have one last opportunity to claim your gift.

Please note that the 10 foot Electrasport Boat has recently been claimed. Therefore, your gift is one of the three remaining gifts . . . which are:

(1) Chrysler Convertible   **(2) 45″ Giant Screen Projection System**

Don't buy that new car until you visit us.   Enlarge your favorite programs as
Equipped with automatic transmission,   big as life. The dual lens system
air, AM-FM radio/cassette player, and   provides the ultimate in quality
more. Available in the color of   and clarity for your viewing
your choice.   pleasure.

(3) $1,000 Cash
A gift that's always welcome. Treat
yourself to that something special
you've been waiting for!

IMPORTANT: To determine whether you'll receive the Chrysler Convertible or one of the other two final gifts, you must visit **Lake View Resort**, located near Branson, Missouri. When you meet the Details of Participation, visit any day except Wednesday. For your convenience, plan your visit at 10AM, 12 noon, 2PM, or 4PM.

If not claimed by October 13, 1993, this offer will be forfeited and reissued. Any special offer made is valid only on the day of your visit.

When you receive the **Chrysler Convertible** or the **45″ Giant Screen TV Projection System**, we ask that you allow us to use your name in our future promotions.

P.S. The special Bonus Gift pictured is yours and will be presented at the time of your visit for your consideration in visiting and touring **Lake View Resort**.

URGENT: Bring this notice to Lake View Resort for your gift presentation.
See reverse for Details of Participation, retails, odds and map.

Laertes simply because Hamlet is the type of person who likes to think, whereas Laertes is the type of person who generally dislikes thinking?

Recent research shows that some people generally enjoy thinking in a wide variety of situations, but others do not. The *Need for Cognition Scale* (Cacioppo & Petty, 1982) measures this difference between individuals. Some of the items from this scale are presented in Table 6-2.

If people were divided into groups that typically enjoyed or did not enjoy thinking, which group would be more persuadable if persuasion occurred by the *central route*? The predictions for this individual variable should be similar to the predictions for the situational variables (e.g., personal relevance) that we have already discussed. Specifically, if people high in need for cognition do more thinking about the arguments than people low in need for cognition, they should be more persuaded when the arguments are strong, but when the arguments are weak, they should be less persuaded than people low in need for cognition.

In order to test this reasoning, an experiment was needed similar to the one on personal relevance that we described earlier. This time, strong and weak arguments were developed on the topic of raising university tuition (Cacioppo, Petty, & Morris, 1983). As in the study on personal relevance, the strong arguments elicited mostly favorable elaborations when people were instructed to think about them, whereas the weak arguments elicited mostly unfavorable thoughts. For example, the strong arguments emphasized that inflation and high interest rates were eroding the ability of the university to keep its top faculty and that the reputation of the faculty was directly related to the prestige of the university and, ultimately, to the starting salaries of its graduates. The weak message argued, among other things, that tuition should be increased to take the unfair burden off state taxpayers and the additional revenue should be used to improve the roads leading to the new university sports arena!

Again, although preliminary testing assured that students were able to distinguish the strong from the weak arguments when they were instructed to do so, it

TABLE 6-2   Sample items from the Need for Cognition Scale

1. I would prefer a task that is intellectual, difficult, and important to one that is somewhat important but does not require much thought.
2. Learning new ways to think doesn't excite me much.*
3. The idea of relying on thought to make my way to the top doesn't appeal to me.*
4. I only think as hard as I have to.*
5. I really enjoy a task that involves coming up with new solutions to problems.
6. I like tasks that require little thought once I've learned them.*

Source: From "The Need for Cognition" by J. T. Cacioppo and R. E. Petty, 1982, *Journal of Personality and Social Psychology, 42*, 116–131. Copyright 1982 by the American Psychological Association. Reprinted by permission.
Note: Items are followed by a scale on which people rate the extent to which each statement is characteristic of them (e.g., –3 = very uncharacteristic, +3 = very characteristic). Items followed by an asterisk (*) are reverse scored.

still was not clear if there were individual differences in people's *natural tendencies* to think about the message arguments. Testing this hypothesis required presenting subjects with high and low needs for cognition with the strong and weak arguments, without giving them any specific instructions to think about the message. In the study, students who were classified as high or low in need for cognition (those scoring in the top and bottom thirds of the distribution of students who completed the personality scale) were told that their task was to read one of various policy statements prepared by the Office of Student and Academic Affairs and rate it for readability. Each participant sat in privacy and read the message presenting either strong or weak arguments for raising tuition. Following exposure to one of the messages, the students were asked to express their own attitudes about raising tuition.

The attitude data from this study are shown in Figure 6-5. As you can see, people who differed in need for cognition acted just as predicted. Specifically, the attitudes of people high in need for cognition were more affected by the quality of the message arguments than the attitudes of people who were low in need for cognition. Of course, it would be impossible even for people high in need for cognition to process *every* message they received, but these data indicate that, on average, people high in need for cognition are more likely to base their attitudes on a thoughtful assessment of message arguments than are people low in need for cognition.[4]

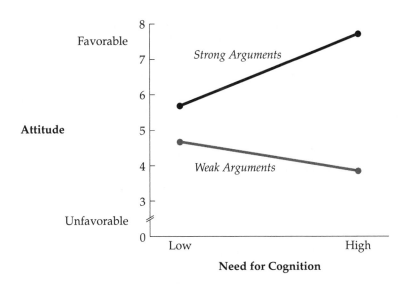

FIGURE 6-5   Postmessage attitudes as a function of need for cognition and argument quality. The figure shows that argument quality is a more important determinant of persuasion for people high rather than low in need for cognition.

Source: Data from Cacioppo, Petty, & Morris, 1983, experiment 2.

Ability Factors That Affect Elaboration

What if Hamlet had come across the Great Dane ad while listening to the radio as he drove down a busy highway, rather than coming across the ad in a magazine? We already suspect that Hamlet is high in need for cognition and that the message is of high personal relevance to him. According to the analysis we have provided thus far, Hamlet clearly is motivated to think about the arguments in the commercial. However, what if, just as the message comes on, a thunderstorm arises? Ordinarily, this highly motivated prince would be able to think about the message and drive at the same time, since driving would engage few of his cognitive resources. However, the thunder, lightning, wet pavement, dark skies, and reduced visibility all make driving a more difficult and cognitively demanding task. The increased distractions of driving should render Hamlet less able to scrutinize the message, even though there is high motivation to do so. What should the effects of this distraction be on persuasion? As we shall see, distraction can sometimes actually improve the persuasiveness of a message. At other times, it can make a message less persuasive.

In order to understand the effects of distraction, it is important to realize that having the necessary motivation to process a message is not sufficient for the central route to persuasion to occur. People must also have the *ability* to think about the message—distraction may adversely affect this ability. As was the case with motivational factors, ability factors may be divided into those that are part of the persuasion situation and those that are best viewed as part of the individual (see Table 6-1). Since the amount of distraction can vary from situation to situation, distraction falls under the domain of situational ability factors.

Although the initial research on distraction showed that distraction sometimes increased and sometimes decreased persuasion, it was not particularly clear *why* these effects occurred (see Petty & Brock, 1981).[5] The ELM approach is to ask: What is the expected effect of distraction on the thoughts people generate? Although some previous research had suggested that distraction might disrupt the process of counterarguing a message (see Figure 6-1; Festinger & Maccoby, 1964; Osterhouse & Brock, 1970), the ELM suggests a more general formulation. That is, distraction should disrupt whatever the dominant thoughts are to a communication, be they favorable or unfavorable. If the communication would normally elicit mostly unfavorable elaborations (counterarguments), distraction should disrupt these negative thoughts and result in *greater* agreement than if no distraction were present. However, if the communication would normally elicit mostly favorable elaborations, distraction should disrupt these positive thoughts and result in less agreement than if no distraction were present.

To test this analysis of distraction, college students were exposed to a message arguing that tuition should be cut in half at their university. In this study, the students listened over headphones to a message that contained either strong or weak arguments that were presented under conditions of either minimal or moderate levels of distraction (Petty, Wells, & Brock, 1976). In the moderate-level-of-distraction conditions, subjects were instructed to track the positions of X's that were flashed rapidly on a screen before them. In the minimal-level-of-distraction conditions, the subjects were given the same instructions. However, the X's were flashed at a much slower rate.

The attitude results from this study are graphed in Figure 6-6. As you can see, the effects of this distraction on persuasion were quite different depending upon the arguments in the message. When the message was weak, people who were distracted showed *more* agreement with the message than people who were not distracted! However, when the message was strong, increased distraction was associated with decreased influence. In addition, analyses of subjects' thoughts provided evidence for the view that distraction disrupted the predominant type of thought. When the message was strong, increasing distraction produced a significant decline in the number of favorable thoughts that subjects listed. When the message was weak, increasing distraction produced a significant decline in the number of unfavorable thoughts listed.

It is important to note that distraction had no effect on the number of message arguments that subjects could recall. This finding is interesting because it shows that, even though all subjects were equally aware of the arguments, as distraction increased, subjects were less able to think about the arguments and thus their attitudes were less affected by the strength of the information presented. Distraction, then, is an especially useful technique when one's arguments are poor because people may be aware that some arguments were presented (which is good for persuasion), but they may be unaware that the arguments were not very compelling.

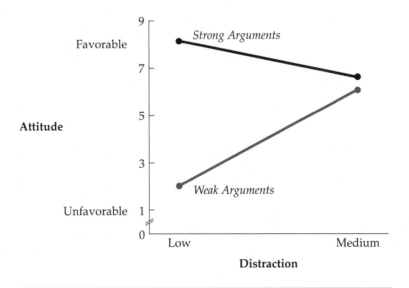

FIGURE 6-6   Postmessage attitudes as a function of distraction and argument quality. The figure reveals that distraction disrupts elaboration of the message.

Source: Data from Petty, Wells, & Brock, 1976, experiment 2.

Distraction, of course, is just one variable that has an impact on a person's ability to think about a persuasive communication. A number of other factors can influence persuasion by modifying a person's ability to process the message. For example, if a person were unable to realize the full implications of a message with one exposure, a few additional exposures might be beneficial for message elaboration. Repetition would only be helpful to persuasion, however, if the additional thinking resulted in the generation of more favorable thoughts. When weak arguments are repeated, additional exposures should lead to further thoughts that are unfavorable and, therefore, result in less persuasion (Cacioppo & Petty, 1989).[6]

As noted in Table 6-1, individual as well as situational factors can contribute to a person's ability to think about a message. For example, the higher a person's level of intelligence, all else equal, the more a person should be able to appreciate the merits of a truly brilliant argument and the more proficient the person should be in detecting the flaws in feeble reasoning. Also, the more objective knowledge that people have about some topic, the more they should be able to distinguish strong from weak arguments. (See Chapter 7 by Wood and Stagner for more information about the effects of these factors on persuasion.)

Relatively Objective versus Relatively Biased Elaboration

Consider the possibility that Horatio, Hamlet's good friend, has advised him to engage in some unusual behavior in public so that others will think he is mad. Specifically, Horatio tells Hamlet to move his head up and down throughout the entire day. As a result, when Hamlet reads the ad in the magazine, he is nodding his head up and down. Could something as simple as head nodding affect persuasion? If so, how? What if Hamlet had been shaking his head from side to side? We will address these questions shortly.

We have now seen that there are both situational and individual variables that can affect a person's motivation and ability to process the arguments in a persuasive communication. Importantly, all of the variables that we have discussed so far have affected motivation or ability to process a message in a relatively *objective* manner. In the strictest sense, if a person is thinking in an objective manner, this means that the person is trying to seek the "truth," wherever it might lead. Of course, there is no guarantee that attempting to be objective will actually lead to the truth. When a person has the ability to think about a message in a relatively objective or balanced manner, the person has the requisite skills and opportunity to consider the arguments impartially. This *objective* processing is what we strive for, though perhaps do not achieve, in jury deliberations, for example.

In contrast to this relatively objective processing, some variables impart a systematic *bias* to the information processing. That is, the variable encourages or inhibits the generation of either favorable or unfavorable thoughts in particular. When a variable affects processing in a biased fashion, this means that individual or situational factors make it more likely that one side of an issue will be supported over another.

Forewarning of Persuasive Intent. As shown in Table 6-1, variables that bias thinking can be divided into those that work by affecting motivation versus ability and those that are tied to situations versus individuals. A few examples should help to demonstrate how certain variables can bias a person's thoughts about a message.

Consider first the effect of a variable labeled *forewarning* by persuasion researchers. Forewarning occurs when a message recipient is informed in advance about some aspect of the persuasion situation. One type of forewarning occurs when people are informed in advance that the speaker is deliberately going to try to persuade them (Papageorgis, 1968). For example, a defense attorney might think that it is effective to begin his opening remarks with confidence by exclaiming that, "Before the end of this trial, I am going to convince you that my client is innocent!" One possibility is that when people learn that someone is going to try to persuade them, they decide that they should exert some effort in scrutinizing the message in order to decide if it is worth accepting. However, research suggests that the thinking induced by a forewarning of persuasive intent does not proceed in this impartial manner. Instead, when confronted by a person who expresses a strong desire to change our attitudes, we become motivated to *defend* our positions, at least if the attitude threatened is important to us (Brehm, 1966).

In one experiment testing this hypothesis, students were either forewarned or not warned of the persuasive intent of a speaker featured in a taped radio editorial (Petty & Cacioppo, 1979a). Some subjects were told that the editorial "was designed specifically to try to persuade you and other college students of the desirability of changing certain college regulations" (forewarned group). Others were simply told that the tape was prepared as part of a journalism class project (unwarned group). The personal relevance of the message was also varied. Subjects were led to believe either that the change in regulations would be implemented at their university next year (high relevance) or 10 years in the future (low relevance). All subjects heard a message containing five arguments in favor of requiring seniors to take a comprehensive exam in their major area as a prerequisite for graduation. All of the arguments were selected on the basis of pretesting so that they would be strong. Following exposure to the message, subjects expressed their own opinions and listed their thoughts.

Figure 6-7 presents the attitude results from this study. When the issue was low in relevance, the warning had no impact on attitudes. However, when the issue was of high relevance, the forewarning reduced persuasion. Under high relevance, the warned group generated over twice as many negative thoughts and half as many positive thoughts as the unwarned group. It is important to note that the warning reduced the persuasive impact of the message under high-relevance conditions, even though the message arguments were strong. Figure 6-7 shows quite clearly the very different effects of personal relevance and forewarning on attitude change. When the subjects were not warned, increasing personal relevance increased persuasion. This finding replicates the study graphed in Figure 6-3 and is to be expected if increasing personal relevance enhances the relatively objective processing of the strong message arguments. However, when the forewarning of

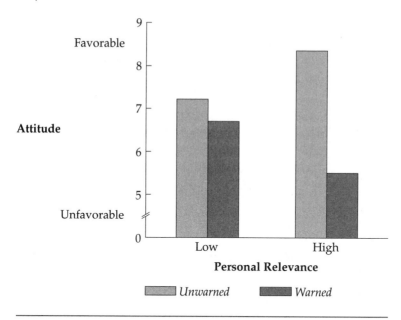

FIGURE 6-7   Postmessage attitudes as a function of personal relevance and forewarning. The figure shows that there is no difference in persuasion as a function of forewarning under low personal relevance. However, forewarning leads to reduced persuasion under conditions of high personal relevance (biased elaboration).

Source: Data from Petty & Cacioppo, 1979a.

persuasive intent was combined with personal relevance, the increased processing took on a negatively biased tone.[7]

Other Variables That Bias Thinking.   Just as some variables (such as forewarning of persuasive intent) affect a person's motivation to generate one kind of thought over another, other variables affect a person's ability to generate particular kinds of thoughts. For example, in one study, it was found that positive attitudes toward a message were facilitated when students were instructed to move their heads in a vertical (up-and-down) fashion but that negative attitudes were encouraged when students were instructed to move their heads in a horizontal (side-to-side) fashion during the presentation of a message (Wells & Petty, 1980). This rather unusual manipulation was introduced without suspicion by leading the subjects to believe that they were participating in a consumer test of the performance of some new headphones designed for people engaged in movement (e.g., exercise, dancing). The student subjects put on their headphones and began to move their heads as instructed (up and down or side to side) when an editorial was presented during the radio program they were listening to. How were attitudes affected by the head movements?

The results of the study were consistent with the hypothesis that vertical head movements facilitate the production of favorable thoughts (since people are used to thinking positive thoughts when they move their heads up and down) but are incompatible with and disrupt the production of unfavorable thoughts. The opposite holds for horizontal head movements (since people are used to thinking disagreeing thoughts when moving their heads from side to side). Thus, returning to Hamlet, it is probable that Hamlet's head nodding resulted in the generation of more favorable cognitive responses than if he had made no movements while reading the message. If he had been told by Horatio to shake his head from side to side, his cognitive responses would have been more negative than without any movements and the amount of persuasion would have been reduced.

Finally, it is important to note that just as situational variables such as a forewarning and head movements can bias thinking, so, too, can individual variables. For example, consider two people, Jack and Jill, who have the same attitude toward a political candidate, but Jill has much more information in support of her opinion than does Jack. Both encounter a strong attack on their favored candidate from an opposition leader. It would probably not surprise you much to learn that Jill is affected less by this attack than is Jack. Since Jill has more information behind her attitude, she is better able to counterargue messages that are opposed to her view and defend those that are consistent with it (e.g., Lord, Lepper, & Ross, 1979; Wood, 1982). However, if people have much information on an issue but the information does not consistently support their attitudes, such as if their feelings and their beliefs are inconsistent with each other (Chaiken & Yates, 1985; Rosenberg, 1960), then they should have a more difficult time defending their positions from attack than if the informational basis of their attitudes is consistent. (Chapter 7 in this book describes the important role of an attitude's information base in conferring resistance to persuasion.)

So far in our discussion of the variables that affect thinking about a persuasive message, we have considered the effect of each variable in isolation. In many real-life contexts, however, many variables are operating jointly to determine the extent of thinking. Also, many variables that can be separated in the laboratory often occur together in the natural environment. For example, people who like to think about issues (high need for cognition) will tend to have more information on a topic than people who do not like to think (Cacioppo, Petty, Kao, & Rodriguez, 1986). Also, people will tend to have more information about issues that are personally relevant than issues that are irrelevant (Wood, 1982). Thus, in order to assess how much thinking a person will do in any particular persuasion situation and whether that thinking will be relatively objective or biased, it is necessary to consider all of the categories of factors outlined in Table 6-1.[8]

Modifying Attitudes by the Use of Peripheral Cues

Now that it is clear that numerous variables can have an impact on persuasion by affecting the amount of thinking and whether that thinking is relatively objective or biased, we can turn to persuasion effects that occur in the *absence* of much thinking about the issue. We have seen that when individual and situational factors produce a high likelihood of thinking, persuasion effects depend on the nature of the issue-relevant thoughts elicited. Whether the thoughts are largely favorable or unfavorable will depend on the quality of the arguments provided and the operation of any biasing factors. On the other hand, when the elaboration likelihood is low, persuasion should be a function of the peripheral cues in the persuasion context.

For example, Laertes formed a favorable attitude toward the Great Dane sword without thinking about the arguments presented. Instead, his attitude was based on the fact that a fierce warrior was pictured holding the sword and that many arguments were listed in the ad. *Peripheral cues* are aspects of a persuasion situation that allow attitude change in the absence of argument elaboration. Testing the idea that simple cues can affect attitudes when people are either unmotivated or unable to process message arguments involves comparing people's reactions to simple cues when the elaboration likelihood is high versus when it is low.

In one investigation of peripheral cues, college students were asked to listen to a message over headphones that advocated that seniors be required to pass a comprehensive exam in their major as a requirement for graduation (Petty, Cacioppo, & Goldman, 1981). Three variables were manipulated in the study: the personal relevance of the message, the quality of the arguments presented, and the expertise of the source. Relevance was manipulated as described before by having the speaker advocate either that the new exam policy should be instituted at the students' own university next year (high relevance) or 10 years in the future (low relevance). The students were exposed either to eight strong or eight weak arguments that were attributed either to a report prepared by a local high school class (low expertise) or to a paper prepared by the Carnegie Commission on Higher Education, which was chaired by a Princeton University professor (high expertise). The expertise of the source provides a simple cue that students might use to judge the validity of the message without evaluating the arguments themselves.

After the students heard the tape-recorded message, they rated their attitudes toward the exams. The attitude results from this study are presented in Figure 6-8. The graph in the left panel shows that when the message was of low personal relevance, increasing source expertise increased agreement, regardless of argument quality. Of most interest is the finding that even when the arguments were weak, having an expert present them led to more persuasion. In the right panel of the figure, it can be seen that when the message was of high relevance, source expertise had no significant impact on attitudes; only argument quality was important. The results suggest that when people are *not* motivated to think about a message (e.g., low personal relevance), they rely more on peripheral clues (e.g., source expertise) and are less affected by argument quality. On the other hand, when people are motivated to think about the message (e.g., high personal relevance), they are less affected by peripheral cues but instead are more influenced by the strength of the arguments.

Several similar findings have been reported. For example, in one study, students were presented with print advertisements for a new disposable razor. Some students were led to believe that the razor would soon be available in their town and that they would get to select one brand of razor as a gift at the end of the exper-

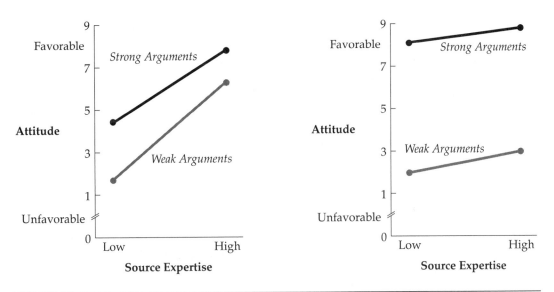

LOW PERSONAL RELEVANCE

HIGH PERSONAL RELEVANCE

FIGURE 6-8 Postmessage attitudes as a function of personal relevance, argument quality, and source expertise. The left panel shows that attitudes are affected by source expertise under conditions of low personal relevance. The right panel shows that attitudes are affected by argument quality under conditions of high personal relevance.

Source: Data from Petty, Cacioppo, & Goldman, 1981.

iment (high relevance of razor ad), whereas other students were led to believe that the razor would not be available in their area soon and that they would select a different product at the end of the study (low relevance of razor ad; Petty, Cacioppo, & Schumann, 1983). The razor ad depicted either a pair of liked (celebrity athletes) or neutral (average citizens) endorsers and presented either strong or weak arguments for the product. As in the previous study, argument quality was a more important determinant of persuasion when the relevance of the ad was high rather than low, but the celebrity status of the endorsers was a more important determinant of influence when the relevance of the ad was low rather than high (see also Chaiken, 1980; Rhine & Severance, 1970).

Recall that Laertes responded not only to the attractiveness of the endorser of the Great Dane sword but also to the apparent number of arguments contained in the message. A similar approach was used in a recent automobile ad that proclaimed that there are "21 Logical Reasons to Buy a SAAB." The ad went on to list the 21 reasons, ranging from technological advances to safety features to aesthetic concerns to price. It is unlikely that most people will think about *all* of these reasons, but the ad is impressive nonetheless. Will people be impressed by the fact that there are a large number of reasons to buy the car, or will the quality of the reasons make a difference?

Based on the research we have presented so far, it should be clear that the mere number of arguments should serve as a simple cue when the elaboration likelihood is low, but the number of arguments should be relatively unimportant when the likelihood of argument elaboration is high. In fact, this prediction has been supported. In a study that varied number of arguments, quality of arguments, and personal relevance (Petty & Cacioppo, 1984), it was found that increasing the number of either strong or weak arguments led to more persuasion when the personal relevance of the message was low. When relevance was high, however, increasing the number of strong arguments led to more persuasion, but increasing the number of weak arguments led to less persuasion. That is, the arguments were scrutinized when relevance was high and quality of arguments mattered. Under low relevance, all that mattered was the number of reasons given![9]

Multiple Roles for Variables in the ELM

We have now seen that there are two fundamentally different routes to persuasion. Before discussing the consequences of attitude changes by one route or the other, we will discuss an important contribution of the ELM—the idea that any one variable can assume more than one role.

First, variables can have an impact on persuasion by serving as *arguments*. An argument is a piece of information that says something about the true merits of the position taken. If the spokesperson for a beauty cream says, "If you use this cream you will look like me," the person's beauty serves as relevant information for evaluating the effectiveness of the product. If a travel ad shows pictures of a beautiful beach and sunset and says, "Visit Maui," the stunning pictures provide a good reason to visit that location. That is, the attractiveness of the person and scene serve as issue-relevant arguments.

Second, these same variables can sometimes have an impact on persuasion, not by providing information relevant to the true merits of the object but by serving as *peripheral cues*. Consider an advertisement featuring an attractive person who says, "Get your next car loan at my bank," or an ad featuring a new car on a beautiful beach with a gorgeous sunset. Here the attractiveness of the source and beach scenery indicate nothing about the true merits of the bank or car but nevertheless may allow favorable attitude formation in the absence of a diligent consideration of the merits of the products. A person's attraction to the source or scene may become attached to the bank and car by a simple association process (e.g., Staats & Staats, 1957). For example, you may have noticed how the pleasant feelings induced by a fine meal in a majestic setting may become attached to the person with whom you are dining, even though these feelings are really irrelevant to the merits of your companion.

A third way in which a variable can have an impact on persuasion according to the ELM is by determining the *amount of thinking* that you do about the message. For example, some people may be more curious about what an attractive person says than what an unattractive person says and do more thinking about the message when the arguments are presented by an attractive source (DeBono & Harnish, 1988; Puckett, Petty, Cacioppo, & Fisher, 1983). Conversely, some people may be put in such a good mood by pleasant scenery or may be so distracted by it that they fail to think about the arguments presented for the product (Mackie & Worth, 1989).

Finally, a variable can have an impact on persuasion by determining the kinds of thoughts that come to mind, or the *bias in thinking* (Petty & Cacioppo, 1990). For example, some people may be very biased against attractive people and try to counterargue and derogate everything they say. Other people may be fascinated with attractive people and attempt to find only good things in what they say. Similar biases in thinking can be induced by exposure to pleasant or unpleasant pictures that produce positive or negative mood states (see Petty & Wegener, 1991).

Implicit in the above discussion is that some variables can take on more than one role in persuasion situations. That is, certain variables have a chameleonic quality—they induce different processes in different situations. Thus, any given variable should not be thought of as exclusively fulfilling any one role. As seen in the example, the attractiveness of the source can function not only as an argument in some circumstances but as a peripheral cue in others, as a determinant of the amount of thinking in other situations, and as a determinant of bias in thinking in still other circumstances.

It is crucial to specify the general conditions under which variables such as source attractiveness act in each of the distinct roles. For source attractiveness, the available evidence can be summarized as follows: Under conditions of *low elaboration likelihood*, source attractiveness, if it has any impact at all, will serve as a peripheral cue (Haugtvedt et al., 1988). Under conditions of *high elaboration likelihood*, source attractiveness will not serve as a simple cue but may instead serve as a persuasive argument, if it provides information central to the merits of the attitude object (Petty & Cacioppo, 1980), or may bias the ongoing information-processing activity. Finally, under conditions of *moderate elaboration likelihood*, source attractiveness will influence the amount of argument elaboration (DeBono & Harnish, 1988; Puckett et al., 1983).

As a second example, consider how a person's mood might affect persuasion in each of the ways postulated by the ELM. What if you heard a commercial in the context of a very pleasant television program? Would you like the product advertised any more than if you heard the same commercial in the context of a more neutral program? And if so, would your more positive attitude be the result of the central or the peripheral route to persuasion? In a study examining this question (Petty, Schumann, Richman, & Strathman, 1993), subjects watched a commercial for a new pen that was embedded in either a pleasant program (an episode of the Bill Cosby show) or a neutral-mood documentary (about computers and robotics). Some subjects were led to believe that they would get to select one brand of pen as a free gift for participating in the study, so these subjects would presumably be motivated to think about the pen ad when it was presented (high elaboration likelihood group). Other subjects were led to believe that they would select their gift from a different product category, so they would not be particularly motivated to think about the pen ad (low elaboration likelihood group).

Interestingly, both the high- and the low-elaboration groups were more positive toward the pen when the commercial was seen during the pleasant than during the neutral program. Importantly, mood produced the effect for different reasons in the high- and low-elaboration groups. When people were motivated to think about the pen ad, positive mood increased the number of favorable thoughts that they generated—that is, mood biased thinking. The more positive subjects felt, the more positive thoughts they generated, and the more favorable their attitudes were. When people were not motivated to think about the pen ad, however, mood had no effect on positive thoughts, even though it did have an impact on attitudes. That is, attitudes became more positive in the absence of favorable thinking about the merits of the pen.

What is going on here? When the elaboration likelihood is low, people appear to use their mood as a cue to how they feel about the message. Thus, they may come to agree with the message to the extent that they are feeling good or to disagree if they are feeling bad. When the elaboration likelihood is very high, on the other hand, and people are thinking about the message, mood appears to bias the kinds of thoughts that come to mind. That is, favorable thoughts come to mind more easily when you are feeling good, but more unfavorable thoughts come to mind when you are feeling bad (cf. Bower, 1981).[10] This is similar to the idea that favorable thoughts are more likely to come to mind when you are moving your head up and down rather than from side to side.

What would happen if the elaboration likelihood were moderate rather than very high or low and the subjects were unsure as to whether the message was worth thinking about? Under these circumstances, some research suggests that a person's mood determines how much thinking will occur (Bless et al., 1990; Mackie & Worth, 1989). For example, people in a good mood might deliberately decide not to think about the message, especially if they anticipate that such thinking would destroy their good mood (see Petty, Gleicher, & Baker, 1991, for further discussion).

To summarize more generally, when the elaboration likelihood is low, people typically know that they do not want and/or are not able to evaluate the merits of the arguments presented. Thus, if any evaluation is formed, it is likely to be the result of the relatively simple associations or inferences permitted by variables serving as peripheral cues (e.g., source attractiveness, mood). On the other hand, when the elaboration likelihood is high, people typically know that they want and are able to evaluate the merits of the arguments presented. Thus, evaluations are formed as the result of careful argument scrutiny, and variables such as attractiveness and mood have relatively little impact as peripheral cues. Rather, these variables, if relevant to the central merits of the topic under consideration, can serve as persuasive arguments or, alternatively, bias the ongoing information-processing activity. Finally, when the elaboration likelihood is moderate, people may be uncertain as to whether the message warrants or needs scrutiny and whether they are capable of providing this analysis. In these situations, they may examine the persuasion context for indications of whether they should attempt to think about the message (e.g., Is this source worth listening to? How will the message make me feel?). In short, in order to anticipate what role some variable will play in persuasion, it is important to know the overall elaboration likelihood.

Consequences of the Route to Persuasion

As we noted above, the existing research is quite consistent with the view presented in this chapter that there are two rather different routes to persuasion. One occurs when a person engages in a careful analysis of the arguments that are central to the true merits of the position advocated, whereas the other occurs when peripheral cues in the persuasion context produce attitude change without much argument scrutiny.[11] Importantly, changes induced by these different routes may appear quite similar immediately after message exposure, but according to the ELM, attitudes formed by the two different routes should have quite different properties. The attitudes of Hamlet and Laertes are not really the same even though they are both "8's."

Recall that Hamlet processed the information in the Great Dane ad carefully because he planned to buy a sword in the near future and he is high in the need for cognition. Laertes had no current interest in purchasing a sword but reasoned that the Great Dane must be good because of the peripheral cues in the ad. According to the ELM, these two people have followed two very different routes to persuasion. Hamlet's attitude is a result of diligently thinking about the features of the sword, but Laertes's attitude is a result of making a simple inference about quality based on the cues featured in the ad.

The ELM predicts that the process responsible for attitude change has very important consequences. First, attitudes changed by the central route should last longer, all other things being equal, than attitudes changed by the peripheral route. In the relevant conditions of one study testing this hypothesis, college students were exposed to a message arguing for senior comprehensive exams under conditions of either high or low personal relevance (see Petty & Cacioppo, 1986). The message in this study contained strong arguments and was attributed to a prestigious and expert source. Attitudes were measured immediately after message exposure and again 10 to 14 days later under the guise of a phone opinion survey. A separate group of control subjects was not exposed to any message, but their attitudes were measured at the same points in time as the experimental subjects.

As shown in Figure 6-9, on the initial measure of attitudes taken right after the message, both the high- and low-relevance groups became more favorable toward the exams than the control group. In fact, both the high- and low-relevance groups changed to the same extent (just as Hamlet and Laertes change the same amount). Based on what you know about the ELM so far, however, you would expect these changes to have occurred for different reasons. That is, the high-relevance subjects presumably became more favorable because of carefully thinking about the strong arguments presented, but the low-relevance group presumably became more favorable because of the expert source who endorsed the exams.

More interesting is what happened when attitudes were assessed again two weeks later. An analysis of the attitudes of subjects in the high-relevance group

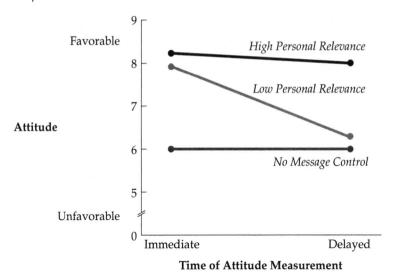

FIGURE 6-9   Immediate and delayed postmessage attitudes as a function of personal relevance. The figure shows that attitude change persists longer when the message is initially processed under high rather than low personal relevance (elaboration likelihood) conditions.

Note: See Petty & Cacioppo, 1986.

showed that their newly favorable attitudes remained relatively stable over time. However, an analysis of the attitudes of subjects in the low-relevance group revealed a lack of persistence. They were no longer any more favorable than the subjects who received no message at all! In short, the high-relevance subjects who formed their initial attitudes based on a careful consideration of issue-relevant arguments (central route) showed greater persistence of attitude change than the low-relevance subjects whose attitudes were based primarily on the source expertise cue (peripheral route).[12]

Recent research has also supported other consequences of attitudes changed by the central versus the peripheral route. Specifically, attitudes changed by the central route, in addition to lasting longer, have been shown to come to mind more readily and are more resistant when they are attacked than are attitudes changed by the peripheral route (e.g., Wu & Shaffer, 1987). In addition, people whose attitudes have been changed by the central route are more likely to act on their new attitudes than are people whose attitudes have been changed by the peripheral route (Cacioppo et al., 1986; Petty et al., 1983). These effects have been observed whether situational or personality factors influencing the route to persuasion have been investigated. So, people high in need for cognition, for example, show attitude changes that are more persistent over time and resistant to counterpersuasion than people low in need for cognition (Haugtvedt & Petty, 1992).[13]

Conclusions

In this chapter, we have outlined two different routes to persuasion and have shown that variables can serve in several distinct roles in affecting attitudes. Importantly, the ELM suggests that different strategies will be more or less effective in producing change, depending upon the elaboration likelihood. Furthermore, just knowing a person's attitude will not always be sufficient, since the basis of the attitude change (either centrally or peripherally formed) can lead to drastically different consequences. That is, research supports the following different implications of attitudes changed by the central versus the peripheral routes. Central-route attitudes will (1) predict behavior better, (2) come to mind more easily, (3) last longer, and (4) be more resistant to counterpersuasion attempts. Thus, it is useful to know not only how positive or negative someone's attitude is but also the extent of message elaboration that formed that attitude. In other words, a critical issue for understanding persuasion is whether attitude change is a result of the central or the peripheral route to persuasion.

To think, or not to think? That was the question facing Hamlet and Laertes when they came across the Great Dane ad. Can you guess what the consequences were of the different strategies Hamlet and Laertes used to form their ratings of "8" on the scale of attitudes toward the sword?

As Hamlet's attitude was changed via the central route, he not only had a positive attitude toward the sword, but he purchased one that afternoon and practiced intensively, hoping to free himself of the thoughts driving him mad. In contrast, Laertes's attitude was changed via the peripheral route, and he did not purchase the sword.

The next day, Hamlet and Laertes engaged in a duel and were asked to choose among two swords—the Great Dane and Brand X. Because his attitude came to mind more readily, Hamlet reached quickly and confidently for the Great Dane, whereas Laertes hesitated, winding up with the Brand X.

When the duel began, Hamlet scored easily, wielding his sword with competence and practice.

Unfortunately, Laertes cheated, striking Hamlet with a poisoned sword between bouts. Hamlet, angered by this ungentlemanly act, grabbed Laertes's sword and struck Laertes in a similar manner. Consequently, both died within minutes. Thus, no data can be given on the relative persistence or resistance of their attitudes.

Notes

1. Of course, this extensive scrutiny provides no guarantee that an *objectively* accurate opinion will be formed (see Petty & Cacioppo, 1986, for further discussion).

2. One type of peripheral process occurs when a person retrieves from memory a particular decision rule that can be used to evaluate the message (e.g., "Experts are usually cor-

rect, so I'll go along"). This is referred to as *heuristic processing*, which is distinguished from the *systematic processing* that occurs under the central route (see Chaiken, 1987).

3. We consider this kind of personal relevance to be situational because it is a momentary relevance. When the situation changes, so does the relevance. That is, once Hamlet purchases a sword, new sword ads will no longer have the same relevance as when he was in a decision-making mode. On the other hand, the relevance that stems from a chronic interest in some issue (e.g., a parent who is always concerned about her child) is better thought of as contained within the person rather than the situation. Most of the older research on self-relevance examined chronic self-relevance (e.g., Sherif & Cantril, 1947; Sherif & Sherif, 1967; but see Krosnick, 1988), whereas much of the newer research examines situational self-relevance (see Petty, Cacioppo, & Haugtvedt, 1992). The effects of these variables are quite similar, however, in that, as self-relevance of either type increases, people pay more attention to the arguments in a message (see Johnson & Eagly, 1989; Petty & Cacioppo, 1990).

4. You may be wondering if people who differ in need for cognition also differ in intelligence. Although there is a modest correlation between need for cognition and verbal intelligence (as might be expected), need for cognition contributes *independently* to message processing and persuasion. Readers interested in learning more about need for cognition should consult Petty and Cacioppo (1984; 1986, Chapter 2).

5. For example, learning theorists emphasized that distraction should inhibit persuasion by decreasing learning and comprehension (e.g., Regan & Cheng, 1973), whereas dissonance theorists emphasized that distraction should increase persuasion, since people would feel a need to justify to themselves exerting extra effort to hear the message, especially if it was disagreeable (Baron, Baron, & Miller, 1973; see also Chapter 5 in this volume).

6. The first few exposures should be maximally beneficial to processing strong arguments. After all of the implications of the arguments have been realized with moderate repetition, increasing exposures become tedious and tend to elicit negative responses, regardless of argument quality. Tedium can be forestalled by varying the nature of the information provided in each repeated version of the ad, however. When the elaboration likelihood is low, peripheral cues should be varied, but when the elaboration likelihood is high, strong arguments should be varied for maximal effectiveness (Schumann, Petty, & Clemons, 1990).

7. A statement of the persuasive intent of a speaker is effective in reducing influence when it is presented before the message but not when it is presented after (Kiesler & Kiesler, 1964). This finding, of course, is consistent with the view that an indication of persuasive intent biases the processing of the message. When the statement of the speaker's intent comes after the message, it is too late to bias thinking about the information presented.

8. It is important to note that often you just cannot *add* the effects of two variables to predict the result on elaboration. For example, research shows that for messages that are not self-paced (e.g., a message on radio), adding rhetorical questions to a message can increase elaboration mostly when people normally would not be thinking about the message (e.g., low-relevance message). On the other hand, adding rhetorical questions can disrupt elaboration if thinking ordinarily would have been high (e.g., high-relevance message; Petty, Cacioppo, & Heesacker, 1981).

9. Of course, variables other than personal relevance should be capable of influencing the power of simple cues to affect attitudes. In fact, any variable that decreases the elaboration likelihood should make the use of peripheral cues more likely. Thus, people who are low in need for cognition show more reliance on simple cues than people high in need for cognition (Axsom, Yates, & Chaiken, 1987; Haugtvedt, Petty, Cacioppo, & Steidley, 1988). People are also more likely to rely on simple cues when they lack the *ability* to think about a message, such as when the message is difficult to comprehend (e.g., Kiesler & Mathog, 1968;

Moore, Hausknecht, & Thamodaran, 1986; Ratneshwar & Chaiken, 1991) or when people have little or no prior information about the attitude object (e.g., Cacioppo, Marshall-Goodell, Tassinary, & Petty, 1992; Wood, Kallgren, & Priesler, 1985).

10. When the elaboration likelihood is high, people may also deliberately examine their mood to see if it is relevant to the attitude object. For example, reflection about the amount of fear that a message on AIDS has produced may help convince a person of how dangerous the consequences are (see Chapter 10 in this book).

11. For purposes of exposition, we have emphasized the central and peripheral routes as operating separately. This is true mostly at the high and low ends of the elaboration continuum. Of course, in many situations, the elaboration likelihood is moderate, and persuasion is determined in part by the central route and its processes and in part by the peripheral route and its processes.

12. In general, attitudes based on issue-relevant thinking should persist longer than attitudes based on simple cues. Two factors may produce exceptions to this principle, however. First, relative persistence may result from the *repeated* pairing of a peripheral cue with a particular position. These attitudes, though persistent in a vacuum, would likely be highly susceptible to counterpropaganda because people would have great difficulty defending their positions if attacked with strong arguments. Second, enduring attitudes may be classically conditioned with one exposure if the cue is sufficiently intense (e.g., fear of water may be conditioned by one near-drowning experience). Persuasive communications are rarely associated with such powerful cues, however.

13. The consequences of the route to persuasion may make it appear that the central route is invariably the attitude change strategy of choice, despite the potential difficulty in motivating and enabling people to think about the message. However, sometimes the peripheral route may be the only strategy possible. For example, there are some issues or objects for which there are few strong arguments (e.g., imagine trying to sell cigarettes with a high tar content). It is not surprising that, in these cases, ads typically contain hardly any information about the merits of the product (since there are none) but rather contain attractive endorsers or majestic scenery.

Acknowledgment

Preparation of this chapter was supported by National Science Foundation Grants BNS-8718038 and -9021647.

References

Apsler, R., & Sears, D. O. (1968). Attitudes. In C. Murchison (Ed.), *A handbook of social psychology* (pp. 798–844). Worcester, MA: Clark University Press.

Axsom, D., Yates, S., & Chaiken, S. (1987). Audience response as a heuristic cue in persuasion. *Journal of Personality and Social Psychology, 9*, 162–166.

Baron, R. S., Baron, P., & Miller, N. (1973). The relation between distraction and persuasion. *Psychological Bulletin, 80*, 310–323.

Bless, H., Bohner, G., Schwarz, N., & Strack, F. (1990). Mood and persuasion: A cognitive response analysis. *Personality and Social Psychology Bulletin, 16*, 332–346.

Bower, G. H. (1981). Mood and memory. *American Psychologist, 36*, 129--148.

Brehm, J. W. (1966). *A theory of psychological reactance.* New York: Academic Press.

Burnkrant, R. E., & Howard, D. J. (1984). Effects of the use of introductory rhetorical questions versus statements on information processing. *Journal of Personality and Social Psychology, 47,* 1218–1230.

Burnkrant, R. E., & Unnava, H. R. (1989). Self-referencing: A strategy for increasing processing of message content. *Personality and Social Psychology Bulletin, 15,* 628–638.

Cacioppo, J. T., Marshall-Goodell, B., Tassinary, L., & Petty, R. E. (1992). Rudimentary determinants of attitudes: Classical conditioning is more effective when prior knowledge about the attitude stimulus is low than high. *Journal of Experimental Social Psychology, 28,* 207–233.

Cacioppo, J. T., & Petty, R. E. (1979). Effects of message repetition and position on cognitive response, recall and persuasion. *Journal of Personality and Social Psychology, 37,* 97–109.

Cacioppo, J. T., & Petty, R. E. (1981). Social psychological procedures for cognitive response assessment: The thought listing technique. In T. Merluzzi, C. Glass, & M. Genest (Eds.), *Cognitive assessment* (pp. 309–342). New York: Guilford.

Cacioppo, J. T., & Petty, R. E. (1982). The need for cognition. *Journal of Personality and Social Psychology, 42,* 116–131.

Cacioppo, J. T., & Petty, R. E. (1989). Effects of message repetition on argument processing, recall, and persuasion. *Basic and Applied Social Psychology, 10,* 3–12.

Cacioppo, J. T., Petty, R. E., Kao, C. F., & Rodriguez, R. (1986). Central and peripheral routes to persuasion: An individual difference perspective. *Journal of Personality and Social Psychology, 51,* 1032–1043.

Cacioppo, J. T., Petty, R. E., & Morris, K. J. (1983). Effects of need for cognition on message evaluation, recall, and persuasion. *Journal of Personality and Social Psychology, 45,* 805–818.

Cacioppo, J. T., Petty, R. E., & Sidera, J. (1982). The effects of a salient self-schema on the evaluation of proattitudinal editorials: Top-down versus bottom-up processing. *Journal of Experimental Social Psychology, 18,* 324–338.

Chaiken, S. (1980). Heuristic versus systematic information processing and the use of source versus message cues in persuasion. *Journal of Personality and Social Psychology, 39,* 752–766.

Chaiken, S. (1987). The heuristic model of persuasion. In M. Zanna, J. Olson, & C. Herman (Eds.), *Social influence: The Ontario symposium* (Vol. 5, pp. 3–39). Hillsdale, NJ: Erlbaum.

Chaiken, S., & Yates, S. (1985). Affective-cognitive consistency and thought induced attitude polarization. *Journal of Personality and Social Psychology, 49,* 1470–1481.

DeBono, K. G., & Harnish, R. J. (1988). Source expertise, source attractiveness and the processing of persuasive information: A functional approach. *Journal of Personality and Social Psychology, 55,* 541–546.

Festinger, L., & Maccoby, N. (1964). On resistance to persuasive communications. *Journal of Abnormal and Social Psychology, 68,* 359–366.

Greenwald, A. G. (1968). Cognitive learning, cognitive responses to persuasion, and attitude change. In A. G. Greenwald, T. C. Brock, & T. M. Ostrom (Eds.), *Psychological foundations of attitudes* (pp. 147–170). New York: Academic Press.

Harkins, S. G., & Petty, R. E. (1981). The effects of source magnification on cognitive effort and attitudes: An information processing view. *Journal of Personality and Social Psychology, 40,* 401–413.

Harkins, S. G., & Petty, R. E. (1982). Effects of task difficulty and task uniqueness on social loafing. *Journal of Personality and Social Psychology, 43,* 1214–1229.

Harkins, S. G., & Petty, R. E. (1987). Information utility and the multiple source effect in persuasion. *Journal of Personality and Social Psychology, 52,* 260–268.

Haugtvedt, C., Petty, R. E., Cacioppo, J. T., and Steidley, T. (1988). Personality and ad effectiveness. *Advances in Consumer Research, 15,* 209–212.

Haugtvedt, C. P., & Petty, R. E. (1992). Personality and persuasion: Need for cognition moderates the persistence and resistance of attitude changes. *Journal of Personality and Social Psychology, 63,* 308–319.

Howard, D. J. (1990). Rhetorical question effects on message processing and persuasion: The role of information availability and the elicitation of judgment. *Journal of Experimental Social Psychology, 26,* 217–239.

Johnson, B., & Eagly, A. H. (1989). Effects of involvement on persuasion: A meta-analysis. *Psychological Bulletin, 106,* 290–314.

Katz, D. (1960). The functional approach to the study of attitudes. *Public Opinion Quarterly, 24,* 163–204.

Kiesler, C. A., & Kiesler, S. (1964). Role of forewarning in persuasive communications. *Journal of Abnormal and Social Psychology, 68,* 547–549.

Kiesler, C. A., & Mathog, R. (1968). The distraction hypothesis in attitude change. *Psychological Reports, 23,* 1123–1133.

Krosnick, J. A. (1988). Attitude importance and attitude change. *Journal of Experimental Social Psychology, 24,* 240–255.

Latané, B., Williams, K., & Harkins, S. G. (1979). Many hands make light the work: The cases and consequences of social loafing. *Journal of Personality and Social Psychology, 37,* 322–332.

Lord, C. G., Lepper, M. R., & Ross, L. (1979). Biased assimilation and attitude polarization: The effects of prior theories on subsequently considered evidence. *Journal of Personality and Social Psychology, 37,* 2098–2109.

Mackie, D. M., & Worth, L. T. (1989). Processing deficits and the mediation of positive affect in persuasion. *Journal of Personality and Social Psychology, 57,* 27–40.

McGuire, W. J. (1969). The nature of attitudes and attitude change. In G. Lindzey, & E. Aronson (Eds.), *The handbook of social psychology* (2nd ed., Vol. 3, pp. 136–314). Reading, MA: Addison-Wesley.

McGuire, W. J. (1985). Attitudes and attitude change. In G. Lindzey & E. Aronson (Eds.), *Handbook of social psychology* (3rd ed., Vol. 2, pp. 233–346). New York: Random House.

Miller, N., Maruyama, G., Beaber, R. J., & Valone, K. (1976). Speed of speech and persuasion. *Journal of Personality and Social Psychology, 34,* 615–624.

Moore, D. L., Hausknecht, D., & Thamodaran, K. (1986). Time compression, response opportunity, and persuasion. *Journal of Consumer Research, 13,* 85–99.

Myers, D. G. (1983). *Social Psychology* (2nd ed.). New York: McGraw-Hill.

Osterhouse, R. A., & Brock, T. C. (1970). Distraction increases yielding to propaganda by inhibiting counterarguing. *Journal of Personality and Social Psychology, 15,* 344–358.

Papageorgis, D. (1968). Warning and persuasion. *Psychological Bulletin, 70,* 271–282.

Perloff, R. M., & Brock, T. C. (1980). And thinking makes it so: Cognitive responses to persuasion. In M. E. Roloff & G. R. Miller (Eds.), *Persuasion: New directions in theory and research.* Beverly Hills, CA: Sage.

Petty, R. E., & Brock, T. C. (1981). Thought disruption and persuasion. In R. E. Petty, T. M. Ostrom, & T. C. Brock (Eds.), *Cognitive responses in persuasion* (pp. 55–79). Hillsdale, NJ: Erlbaum.

Petty, R. E., & Cacioppo, J. T. (1979a). Effects of forewarning of persuasive intent and involvement on cognitive responses and persuasion. *Personality and Social Psychology Bulletin, 5,* 173–176.

Petty, R. E., & Cacioppo, J. T. (1979b). Issue involvement can increase or decrease persuasion by enhancing message-relevant cognitive responses. *Journal of Personality and Social Psychology, 37,* 1915–1926.

Petty, R. E., & Cacioppo, J. T. (1980). Effects of issue involvement on attitudes in an advertising context. In G. Gorn & M. Goldberg (Eds.), *Proceedings of the division 23 program* (pp. 75–79). Montreal: American Psychological Association.

Petty, R. E., & Cacioppo, J. T. (1981). *Attitudes and persuasion: Classic and contemporary approaches.* Dubuque, IA: Wm. C. Brown.

Petty, R. E., & Cacioppo, J. T. (1984). The effects of involvement on response to argument quality and quantity: Central and peripheral routes to persuasion. *Journal of Personality and Social Psychology, 46,* 69–81.

Petty, R. E., & Cacioppo, J. T. (1986). *Communication and persuasion: Central and peripheral routes to attitude change.* New York: Springer/Verlag.

Petty, R. E., & Cacioppo, J. T. (1990). Involvement and persuasion: Tradition versus integration. *Psychological Bulletin, 107,* 367–374.

Petty, R. E., Cacioppo, J. T., & Goldman, R. (1981). Personal involvement as a determinant of argument-based persuasion. *Journal of Personality and Social Psychology, 41,* 847–855.

Petty, R. E., Cacioppo, J. T., & Haugtvedt, C. (1992). Involvement and persuasion: An appreciative look at the Sherifs' contribution to the study of self-relevance and attitude change. In D. Granberg & G. Sarup (Eds.), *Social judgment and intergroup relations: Essays in honor of Muzafer Sherif* (pp. 147–174). New York: Springer/Verlag.

Petty, R. E., Cacioppo, J. T., & Heesacker, M. (1981). The use of rhetorical questions in persuasion: A cognitive response analysis. *Journal of Personality and Social Psychology, 40,* 432–440.

Petty, R. E., Cacioppo, J. T., & Schumann, D. W. (1983). Central and peripheral routes to advertising effectiveness: The moderating role of involvement. *Journal of Consumer Research, 10,* 134–148.

Petty, R. E., Gleicher, F., & Baker, S. M. (1991). Multiple roles for affect in persuasion. In J. Forgas (Ed.), *Emotion and social judgment* (pp. 181–200). London: Pergamon.

Petty, R. E., Harkins, S. G., & Williams, K. D. (1980). The effects of group diffusion of cognitive effort on attitudes: An information-processing view. *Journal of Personality and Social Psychology, 38,* 81–92.

Petty, R. E., Ostrom, T. M., & Brock, T. C. (1981). Historical foundations of the cognitive response approach to attitudes and persuasion. In R. E. Petty, T. M. Ostrom, & T. C. Brock (Eds.), *Cognitive responses in persuasion* (pp. 1–29). Hillsdale, NJ: Erlbaum.

Petty, R. E., Schumann, D. W., Richman, S. A., & Strathman, A. J. (1993). Positive mood and persuasion: Different roles for affect under high and low elaboration conditions. *Journal of Personality and Social Psychology, 64,* 5–30.

Petty, R. E., Unnava, R., & Strathman, A. J. (1991). Theories of attitude change. In T. S. Robertson & H. H. Kassarjian (Eds.), *Handbook of Consumer Behavior* (pp. 241–280). Englewood Cliffs, NJ: Prentice Hall.

Petty, R. E., & Wegener, D. T. (1991). Thought systems, argument quality, and persuasion. In R. S. Wyer & T. K. Srull (Eds.), *Advances in social cognition* (Vol. 4, pp. 147–161). Hillsdale, NJ: Erlbaum.

Petty, R. E., Wells, G. L., & Brock, T. C. (1976). Distraction can enhance or reduce yielding to propaganda: Thought disruption versus effort justification. *Journal of Personality and Social Psychology, 34,* 874–884.

Puckett, J., Petty, R. E., Cacioppo, J. T., & Fisher, D. (1983). The relative impact of age and attractiveness stereotypes on persuasion. *Journal of Gerontology, 38,* 340–343.

Ratneshwar, S., & Chaiken, S. (1991). Comprehension's role in persuasion: The case of its moderating effect on the persuasive impact of source cues. *Journal of Consumer Research, 18,* 52–62.

Regan, D. T., & Cheng, J. B. (1973). Distraction and attitude change: A resolution. *Journal of Experimental Social Psychology, 9,* 138–147.

Rhine, R., & Severance, L. (1970). Ego-involvement, discrepancy, source credibility, and attitude change. *Journal of Personality and Social Psychology, 16,* 175–190.

Rosenberg, M. J. (1960). A structural theory of attitude dynamics. *Public Opinion Quarterly, 24,* 319–341.

Schumann, D., Petty, R. E., & Clemons, S. (1990). Predicting the effectiveness of different strategies of advertising variation: A test of the repetition-variation hypothesis. *Journal of Consumer Research, 17,* 192–202.

Sherif, M., & Cantril, H. (1947). *The psychology of ego-involvements: Social attitudes and identification.* New York: Wiley.

Sherif, M., & Sherif, C. W. (1967). Attitude as the individual's own categories: The social judgement-involvement approach to attitude and attitude change. In C. W. Sherif & M. Sherif (Eds.), *Attitude, ego-involvement, and change.* New York: Wiley.

Snyder, M., & DeBono, K. G. (1985). Appeals to image and claims about quality: Understanding the psychology of advertising. *Journal of Personality and Social Psychology, 49,* 586–597.

Snyder, M., & DeBono, K. (1989). Understanding the functions of attitudes: Lessons from personality and social behavior. In A. R. Pratkanis, S. J. Breckler, & A. G. Greenwald (Eds.), *Attitude structure and function* (pp. 339–360). Hillsdale, NJ: Erlbaum.

Staats, C. K., & Staats, A. W. (1957). Meaning

established by classical conditioning. *Journal of Experimental Psychology, 54,* 74–80.

Taylor, S. E. (1981). The interface of cognitive and social psychology. In J. H. Harvey (Ed.), *Cognition, social behavior, and the environment.* Hillsdale, NJ: Erlbaum.

Wells, G. L., & Petty, R. E. (1980). The effects of overt head-movements on persuasion: Compatibility and incompatibility of responses. *Basic and Applied Social Psychology, 1,* 219–230.

Wood, W. (1982). Retrieval of attitude-relevant information from memory: Effects on susceptibility to persuasion and on intrinsic motivation. *Journal of Personality and Social Psychology, 42,* 798–810.

Wood, W., Kallgren, C. A., & Priesler, R. M. (1985). Access to attitude-relevant information in memory as a determinant of persuasion: The role of message attributes. *Journal o f Experimental Social Psychology, 21,* 73–85.

Wu, C., & Shaffer, D. (1987). Susceptibility to persuasive appeals as a function of source credibility and prior experience with the attitude object. *Journal of Personality and Social Psychology, 52,* 677–688.

7

WHY ARE SOME PEOPLE EASIER TO INFLUENCE THAN OTHERS?

WENDY WOOD and BRIAN STAGNER
Texas A&M University

Are you easily influenced? Do salespeople, airport groupies, shady contractors, hawkers of fraudulent tax shelters, and door-to-door solicitors identify you as a "soft touch" and an easy mark? Or do would-be persuaders spot you as resistant and unyielding and pass you by in favor of other, more responsive targets?

The idea that people differ in how easily they can be influenced has great practical significance. Lawyers selecting jurors, advertisers targeting audiences, and demagogues seeking followers are all interested in identifying those who will be most susceptible to their appeals. Indeed, even before there were drive-ins, adolescent males were asking "Who is most readily influenced?"—though perhaps not in exactly these words.

As the cartoon in Figure 7-1 illustrates, it is sometimes easy to discern whether a person is susceptible to an influence attempt. In this chapter, we will consider a variety of characteristics of people that can be used to predict acceptance of or resistance to appeals. We will also consider the processes by which individual differences affect ease of influence.

The chapter presents two general routes by which personal attributes can affect persuasion and conformity. The first approach identifies how attributes of recipients affect processing of persuasive appeals. We will begin our discussion with a consideration of general personality traits, such as self-esteem and anxiety, and general abilities, such as intelligence and social sensitivity. For example, when

"No, I would not welcome a contrasting point of view."

FIGURE 7-1   Sometimes individual differences in influence are easy to spot.

Source: Drawing by Bernard Schoenbaum; © 1985 The New Yorker Magazine, Inc.

defending an unpopular client accused of lurid crimes ("Showgirl Arrested After Elderly Senator Dies in Fantasy Sex Games"), an attorney using this approach might consider how jurors would react to the case and select those who have a strong capacity to empathize with a "victimized, innocent girl." On the other hand, the prosecutor, also considering jurors' attributes that might affect message processing, would look for stable individuals who are cool, businesslike, "just-the-facts" sort of persons.

    We will then consider how message processing is affected by what we know about an issue and the way this information is organized in memory. To see how this *topic-bound* approach (Janis & Hovland, 1959) might work, imagine a car dealer talking with a young couple. The husband has been conscientiously reading all the new car performance data from *Road and Track* and *Hot Rod* for the past few months. He repeats these statistics to the dealer and explains why he will buy only a certain model. In response, the dealer shifts her attention to the wife, inquiring if the wife has any questions she could answer. The dealer later explains to one of her salespeople:

> "That guy knows a lot about cars—he already had all the information he needed and obviously had made his own decision. No way I was going to change his mind. If he had been automotively mystified like his wife, I might have swayed him with gentle anecdotes and nontechnical reassurances and maybe sold him a more expensive model. Even though I can't change that guy's mind about cars, I bet I could sell him products in areas in which he is not so well versed—toupees or elective surgery."

Our second general approach to understanding individual differences in influence considers the impact of social expectations. Just as social norms and expectations regulate other kinds of social interaction, they affect how people respond to influence. We will consider the expectations that arise from recipient attributes like sex and age. For example, we know a 70-year-old woman who was recently approached by a supposed investment advisor, attempting to help her with her investments. He clearly assumed that she was a widow who was not accustomed to making her own decisions and therefore vulnerable and easy to influence. His tactics included a mix of bullying and supportive friendship, a style nicely suited to sway the typical lonely older woman. Although a strategy of relying on sex and age to select targets might often be effective, we are happy to report that, in this particular case, the "con" was not successful.

Message Processing: Effects of General Personality and Abilities

It is pretty easy to make predictions about the effects of general personality attributes and abilities. For example, do you think a highly anxious person is more easy or less easy to influence than a less anxious one? You might come up with a good hypothesis about this. But consider, does it matter whether the message is personally threatening (e.g., reporting serious health risks) or whether it is trivial (e.g., concerning laundry detergents)? And does it matter whether the message is so simple that everyone can understand it or so complex and difficult that only the most able people can comprehend it? Suddenly simple, intuitive hunches may seem less plausible. To understand the effects of recipients' personality and abilities, we must account for their responses to each of these variables. A group of researchers at Yale (Hovland, Janis, & Kelley, 1953) and later McGuire (1969a, 1969b, 1985) proposed a model of information processing to handle just such complexities (see also Converse, 1962).

According to this model, persuasion is a result of a series of steps one goes through when one is exposed to a message, and recipient attributes may have a different effect on each of these steps. To change opinions, the recipient must first pay attention to the message, then comprehend its content, and finally yield to the persuasive suggestion. Of course, other steps may be relevant to adopting the recommended position (e.g., liking or expressing interest in the message). Yet research on recipient attributes has focused most on attention, comprehension, and yielding.

Attention to and comprehension of the message are difficult to study independently and consequently have usually been combined into a single variable labeled *reception*. Reception can be measured through recipients' recall of the content of the message. Yielding can be measured through the recipients' favorable or unfavorable evaluation of the communication position. In practice, then, the Yale-McGuire model typically considers two processes, reception and yielding, that mediate the effect of recipient attributes on opinion change. To illustrate the model, we will consider how people's intelligence and self-esteem relate to their influenceability.

Intelligence

A simple prediction about intelligence is that highly intelligent people should be easier to persuade than less intelligent ones. This is because intelligence should enhance reception; it should provide the ability to comprehend and interpret messages. People who lack intelligence presumably lack the ability to understand any but the simplest messages, and consequently, they should not be influenced by most communications.

Apparently, advertisers subscribe to the notion that readers' intelligence affects reception and persuasion. Both of the advertisements in Figure 7-2 present research on the effectiveness of skin cream, but the ad in Part A is very simple in its presentation and the one in Part B is much more detailed. The first ad appeared in *Seventeen* magazine and the second in *Senior Scholastic Magazine*.

Research testing the intelligence-influence link typically measures recipients' intelligence with an intelligence (IQ) test or a related instrument and then measures opinion change. For example, an early study examined the effects of anti-German propaganda films during World War II on army recruits. Those with higher educational levels (and presumably higher intelligence) were more persuaded by the films than recruits with less education (Hovland, Lumsdaine, & Sheffield, 1949). Those with better education also comprehended more of the message than the less educated, suggesting that it is because the more intelligent men were able to learn more from the message that they were more persuaded by it.

But what about yielding? The key to the Yale-McGuire model is that intelligence is negatively related to yielding but positively related to reception. Persons with high intelligence are more likely to attend to and comprehend the message position but are also less likely to yield to it. The low level of yielding occurs because intelligent individuals possess knowledge contradicting the message and can use this information to refute message arguments. The importance of yielding in the propaganda study (Hovland et al., 1949) mentioned above is apparent in the men's reactions to individual arguments in the message. Better educated men were more likely than those less educated to be persuaded by convincing, high-quality arguments such as "Appeasement of Germany by Britain and France would only make things worse in the long run." Better educated men were less persuaded by silly arguments such as "The Germans, if victorious, would try to control our country completely and force Americans to work as slaves" (Hovland et al., 1949).

In general, then, given a complex, well-reasoned message, the people who understand the message position should be more likely to adopt it. The enhanced reception associated with high intelligence should result in such individuals being more influenced by a complex message than those with low intelligence. Alternately, if the message is easy to understand and not well reasoned, yielding becomes the crucial factor, and less intelligent recipients should be more readily persuaded.

Overall, the opposing effects of intelligence on reception and on yielding lead to the prediction that moderate levels of intelligence should result in the greatest persuasibility. Low intelligence hinders reception, and high intelligence hinders yielding. People with moderate intelligence should show the optimum combined levels of reception and yielding.

If intellectual sophistication affects reception and yielding, one would expect a connection between age and influence. Indeed, as parents of toddlers are relieved to learn, influence in early years appears to increase with children's age (McGuire, 1985). As children's capacity to attend to and comprehend messages increases, so does their influenceability. However, according to McGuire (1985), maximum influence tends to be obtained at around 9 to 12 years of age and declines thereafter. He argues that, as intellectual prowess increases, young children are better able to process material. After a point, however, yielding declines because children become sufficiently sophisticated to analyze and reject weak, specious arguments.

Television advertisers thus should find it relatively simple to influence 6-year-olds; they just show their product in the proximity of other happy children who exclaim, "Wow!" and "Really fun." By about age 12, such ploys should no longer be effective.

Self-Esteem

Self-esteem is considered to be a personal estimate of worthiness, or an evaluation of oneself in a positive or negative way. High self-esteem reflects an overall positive evaluation, and low self-esteem reflects a negative evaluation. Self-esteem is often assessed by questionnaires that tap agreement with statements such as "I feel I have a number of good qualities," "I am able to do things as well as most other people," and "I take a positive attitude toward myself" (Rosenberg, 1965).

Early research on self-esteem assumed that people with high self-esteem are more difficult to influence than those with low self-esteem, but there have been many different explanations for why this should occur. For example, low-self-esteem persons may be more concerned about potential disapproval for deviating from the opinions of others. Those with high self-esteem believe others think well of them, and so they are less concerned about social rejection (Hovland, Janis, & Kelley, 1953). Another explanation is that high-self-esteem persons have more confidence in their own judgments than those with low self-esteem and consequently

FIGURE 7-2, Part A   This ad, which appeared in *Seventeen* magazine, presents little about the study evaluating skin cream effectiveness except its conclusion.

Source: © The Procter & Gamble Company. Used by permission.

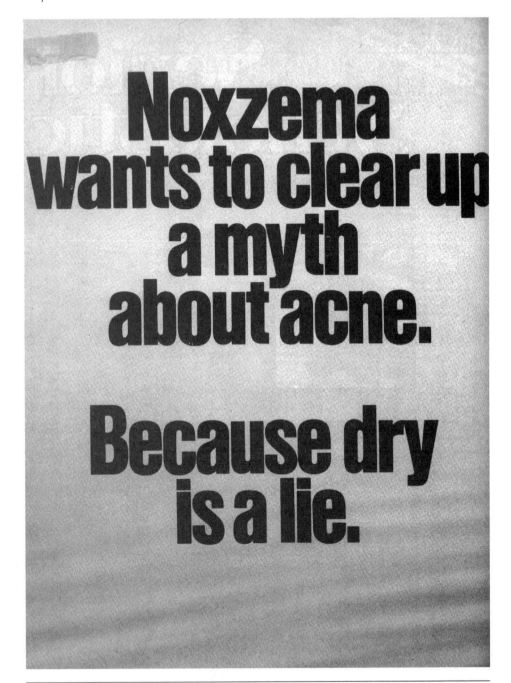

FIGURE 7-2, Part B   This ad, which appeared in *Senior Scholastic Magazine*, presents considerably more detailed, complex information about the study to evaluate skin cream effectiveness.

Source: © The Procter & Gamble Company. Used by permission.

Independent test proves the Noxzema moisturizing system clears up acne better. *Finally, there's proof. A scientifically-controlled study found that moist skin responded better to acne treatment than dry skin. And that the Noxzema moisturizing acne system is clearly superior to Oxy or the leading soap.*

How Noxzema beat Oxy and the leading soap. *The test took teenagers with active acne conditions and divided them into groups. Each group followed a washing and treatment program. Some washed with Oxy Wash and treated with Oxy 10, some washed with the leading soap and treated with a 10% benzoyl peroxide product, and the lucky ones, the clear winners, washed with Noxzema® Skin Cream and treated with Noxzema® 12 Hour Acne Medicine. And ended up with better skin and fewer blemishes. Better skin and fewer blemishes!*

Why Noxzema won. *You see, dry skin is damaged skin. That may interfere with the treatment process. But Noxzema Skin Cream washes moisture into your skin every time you wash. And it's*

Percent of times rated best by dermatologist.*		
4% Soap Program.	36% Oxy Program.	52% Noxzema Program.

4% Leading soap and a 10% benzoyl peroxide product.
36% Oxy Wash and Oxy 10.
52% Noxzema Skin Cream and Noxzema 12 Hour Acne Medicine.

moisture that makes your skin soft and supple. Then when you apply Noxzema 12 Hour Acne Medicine, a 10% benzoyl peroxide lotion with an added skin softener, it gets right to the blemishes and starts to work instantly. It's that simple.

You don't have to dry out your skin to clear up your acne. Not if you use moisturizing Noxzema. Because scientific testing has finally proved it: Dry is a lie!

*Based on biostatistical analysis of 23 competitive events during the study.

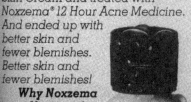

The Noxzema Moisturizing Acne Care System.

are less influenced by others' opinions (Cox & Bauer, 1964). You should recognize these predictions as involving yielding; essentially, they suggest that high-self-esteem people yield less than those with low self-esteem.

According to the Yale-McGuire model, the link between self-esteem and influence should not be so simple because we need to consider both reception and yielding. People with high self-esteem should attend to and comprehend messages better than low-self-esteem individuals. This is because low-self-esteem people should be withdrawn, preoccupied with their own troubles, and distracted by personal feelings of worthlessness, so that they have difficulty attending to and comprehending the message arguments (McGuire, 1969a).

We would anticipate, then, that high-self-esteem people would be more likely than those of low self-esteem to comprehend a complex, well-reasoned message. In this situation, in which reception (attention and understanding) of the points made in the message is crucial, high-self-esteem people should be easier to persuade. Alternately, if the message is simple, yielding becomes a more important factor than reception. Given that low-self-esteem people typically yield more than high-self-esteem ones, low-self-esteem people should then be easier to influence. Overall, the opposing effects of self-esteem on reception and on yielding lead us to expect, as in our discussion of intelligence, that people with moderate levels of this attribute will be easiest to persuade.

Does the Information-Processing Model Work?

The Yale-McGuire model is important theoretically because it identifies the information-processing steps by which recipient attributes affect opinion change. It provides a theoretical bridge between attitude change and recipients' personality and abilities. Furthermore, it explains complex relations between influence and these recipient attributes; simple-minded attempts to link such attributes with influence (e.g., "Highly intelligent people are more influenceable") are unlikely to be successful because influence is dependent on both reception and yielding.

However, a good theory does not ensure good prediction. A recent review examined the support for the Yale-McGuire model across 56 studies that linked self-esteem or intelligence to influence (Rhodes & Wood, 1992). Only a handful of these studies attempted to tap reception, and thus it was difficult to test directly the processes specified in the model. Yet the few studies that did assess recipients' self-esteem and recall of message arguments revealed, as expected, that people with high self-esteem received more of the message content than did those with low self-esteem.

The review also examined whether, across all studies, amount of opinion change conformed to the model's predictions. Self-esteem did seem to relate to influence in the anticipated manner. People low in self-esteem showed relatively little opinion change (presumably because of low levels of reception), and people high in self-esteem showed little change (presumably because of low yielding). As expected, the greatest persuasion was found with those of moderate levels of self-esteem.

Unfortunately, Rhodes and Wood (1992) were not able to locate enough studies of the effects of intelligence to test the model's predictions. The few studies they did find revealed that smarter people were more resistant to influence than less intelligent ones. This pattern fits the model, if we assume that people of higher intelligence yielded less than those of lower intelligence, but high- and low-intelligence persons did not differ in reception of messages (i.e., attention to or comprehension of appeals).

The unexpected pattern in which high- and low-intelligence people did not seem to vary in reception could be due to the procedures used in laboratory research. Reception of messages may be quite high for all participants in influence studies (Eagly & Chaiken, 1993). In real-world settings, where many stimuli compete for our attention and analysis, greater variability may occur in reception. Compare the probable reception of a typical, highly able college student subject, sitting in a barren laboratory cubicle with only the persuasive message to read, with that of an average moviegoer, sitting next to friends, eating popcorn, and trying to hear the soundtrack of the film over the catcalls of the adolescents in the front row. In real-world settings, then, we might find that less intelligent people, like those who have little self-esteem, would be difficult to influence because of their minimal attention to and comprehension of most appeals (see Converse, 1962).

In summary, global personality and ability attributes of recipients affect influence in part because of their effects on processing of persuasive appeals. Yet message processing is also the result of more specific attributes of recipients, such as the extent and the structure of attitude-relevant information in memory. In the next section, we consider these topic-bound predictors of influence. Although most of the research we will present was not designed with the Yale-McGuire model in mind, it would not be too much of a distortion to describe this research as investigating the effects of recipient attributes on yielding-type processes. Perhaps so little of this research has examined the attention and comprehension stages of the Yale-McGuire model because of the difficulties we noted in measuring these processes in the laboratory.

Message Processing: Extent and Structure of Attitude-Relevant Information

On ABC's "Nightline," Ted Koppel frequently uses a debate-type format to present issues, with proponents of one side presenting their views and then proponents of the other side getting their turn. Imagine that the issue is one about which you have little information and no clear opinion, say, an international dispute over territorial waters involving the smelt fishing industry. When the secretary of state from one of the countries first presents her views, you may find them convincing because the position seems well thought out and eminently reasonable—that is, until the opposing arguments are presented. The secretary of the interior from the other country in the dispute also presents highly plausible arguments, and you may think, Why didn't that occur to me? Contrast your response to that of the two experts whose livelihood is based on their ongoing debate on the topic (and who may have faced off against each other for McNeil/Lehrer, Dan Rather, or Tom Brokaw earlier in the evening). While the first speaker is outlining her views, the second is most probably busy countering each of the arguments. The speakers rarely convince each other to change positions; they do not experience the uncomfortable flip-flop in opinions of many of the viewers.

The different reactions of the viewers and speakers may derive in part from the way they organize in memory the information relevant to their attitudes. When you are familiar with an issue and you have thought about it repeatedly and organized your beliefs, feelings, and experiences into a coherent position, you are likely to have a well-articulated stance and to recall easily the basis for your views. When you know little about an issue, your reactions are not likely to be organized in memory in a coherent way, and you may be unable easily to recall relevant information.

Consistency Between Attitudes and Supporting Beliefs

An early perspective on attitude organization and structure focused on whether one's evaluation of an issue is consistent with one's beliefs about it (Rosenberg, 1960, 1968). Rosenberg argued that people who are interested in an issue tend to have well-articulated, well-thought-out opinions. That is, if they are in favor of an issue, they believe it promotes goals or outcomes they support and blocks goals they reject. For example, you may be in favor of public support for mass transit because you believe public transportation is energy efficient (promotes desired outcome) and relatively nonpolluting (blocks undesired outcome).

According to Rosenberg, people who are not particularly interested in an issue tend not to have well-considered opinions. If asked for their evaluations, however, they are unlikely to admit apathy and to say they do not have any strong views. Instead, they may try to cover up their indifference and confusion by stating some position (see Chapter 2 by Ostrom et al.). Attitude statements for these people are *empty* in the sense that they do not reflect an enduring, stable disposition. Such empty responders can be identified by a high level of inconsistency between their evaluation and their beliefs. For example, just prior to the 1992 presidential election, one of us got into a political discussion with our hairstylist. He asserted his intention to vote for Ross Perot. When asked if he was in favor of decreased military spending, he replied, "No." In favor of a 50 cent per gallon gasoline tax? "No." "Then why are you in favor of Perot?" "Because I feel that the 1990s are Perot's time," he replied.

Evaluative-cognitive consistency (consistency between one's attitudes and one's beliefs) differs from the global personality and ability variables we considered in the prior section because it is topic bound; if people are high in consistency on one issue, this indicates little about their consistency on another topic (Chaiken & Yates, 1985; Norman, 1975).

What effect does evaluative-cognitive consistency have on opinions? In general, attitudes high in consistency appear to be more stable over time than those low in consistency (Norman, 1975; Rosenberg, 1968). This is because low-consistency attitudes are likely to be based on temporary factors, such as the position that appears most popular or one's current mood state. Most importantly, people low in evaluative-cognitive consistency are also more susceptible to persuasion attempts (Chaiken, 1982; Rosenberg, 1968) as well as more conforming to others' opinions (Norman, 1975).

Attitudes characterized by high evaluative-cognitive consistency are resistant to influence attempts in part because of the wealth of available information supporting the evaluation (see Chaiken, Pomerantz, & Giner-Sorolla, in press; Chaiken & Yates, 1985). These accessible attitude-supportive beliefs and ideas can be used to defend one's views. When presented with a challenging message, people high in consistency do not yield, because they are better able to generate arguments supporting their own beliefs and countering those in the message than people low in consistency.

High-consistency people also differ from low-consistency ones because they seem actively aware of all positions on the issue, even those that oppose their own. When high-consistency people indicate their beliefs, they are more likely to attempt spontaneously to discount opposing information by, for example, noting that it has little validity (Chaiken & Yates, 1985). For example, a high-consistency person might anticipate opposition to her support of mass transit by indicating that, "Yes, it is expensive but not as expensive as maintaining highways for individually owned automobiles." People low in consistency tend just to mention the information inconsistent with their beliefs and make little attempt to integrate it with their overall position. Thus, our hairstylist friend did acknowledge that Mr. Perot's views on specific issues opposed his own but did not try to reconcile this inconsistency.

Working Knowledge

The amount of information that people possess about an issue also determines how easy they are to influence. The extent of attitude-relevant beliefs and experiences that people spontaneously bring to mind when confronted with an attitude object has been termed *working knowledge* (Wood, 1982; Wood, Rhodes, & Biek, in press). For example, when asked about their opinions toward mass transit, people high in working knowledge might note that automobile exhaust is partially responsible for the smog over many major cities, and they might remember traveling on the clean, efficient subway system in Washington, D.C. In contrast, people with little working knowledge, when considering their attitude toward mass transit, find it relatively difficult to recall details of relevant beliefs and experiences.

Working knowledge differs from standard knowledge, as measured by tests that evaluate the objective accuracy of one's information. Indeed, as may be painfully apparent when you discuss your beliefs with people who disagree with you, there is often little correspondence between the extent of someone's knowledge and its accuracy. People with a minimal grasp of objective facts may possess considerable working knowledge that represents their subjectively valid understanding of and experiences with an attitude topic. Indeed, for many attitude issues, the correctness of critical components of knowledge is unclear. On the topic of abortion, for example, it is difficult to determine the relative accuracy of the pro-life position that life begins at conception with the pro-choice view that life begins when the fetus is independently viable.

To measure the information base that underlies attitudes, people are given a short period of time to list the relevant beliefs and experiences they can recall. The number of beliefs and experiences people mention represents their working knowledge.

It is relatively difficult to change the opinions of knowledgeable people, whereas people with little knowledge change more readily (Biek, Wood, Nations, & Chaiken, 1993; Wood, 1982; Wood & Kallgren, 1988; Wood, Kallgren, & Preisler, 1985). Although low-knowledge people may state the same attitude position as someone high in knowledge, their opinion is not derived from an extensive information base and is more responsive to appeals to change.

Working knowledge is not just linked to amount of opinion change; it also predicts the strategy recipients use to analyze a persuasive message (Wood & Kallgren, 1988; Wood et al., 1985). Knowledgeable recipients do not yield; they have the ability and motivation to generate arguments countering an opposing position and bolstering their own views. Because knowledgeable people can marshal the internal support necessary to critically evaluate new information, they can see the fallacies in weak, specious arguments and are little persuaded by them (Wood et al., 1985). But people with extensive knowledge are not resistant to all messages. A well-reasoned message supported by facts may present arguments that are difficult to refute. Knowledgeable recipients would likely find such a message persuasive and change their opinions. In general, then, opinion change for these recipients is a function of their evaluation of message arguments (Petty & Cacioppo, 1986; Chaiken, Liberman, & Eagly, 1989). (Chapter 6 by Petty et al. describes the importance of message argument strength in persuasion when a message is processed in a systematic, effortful way.)

In contrast, people with minimal knowledge find it difficult to evaluate the validity of message arguments. They show similar levels of persuasion to strong and to weak messages. Rather than evaluating message quality, low-knowledge people appear to rely on simple rules of thumb or cognitive heuristics when processing a message (Chaiken et al., 1989; see also Chapter 6). They might focus on the communicators' attributes, reason that "I agree with those I like," and be more persuaded by friendly than unfriendly communicators (Wood & Kallgren, 1988). Alternately, they might rely on the length of the message, invoking the rule "Message length implies strength," and be more persuaded by long than short appeals (Wood et al., 1985).

Like evaluative-cognitive consistency, working knowledge is topic bound and does not appear to reflect a general cognitive style, such as verbosity or intelligence (Biek et al., 1993; Wood, 1982; Wood et al., in press). Working knowledge on one topic, such as abortion, does not predict opinion change on another topic, like preservation of the environment.

Cognitive Structures and Schemas

Consider the following paragraph:

> *The structure is actually quite simple. First you arrange items into different groups. Of course one pile may be sufficient depending on how much there is to do. If you have to go somewhere else due to lack of facilities that is the next step; otherwise, you are pretty well set. It is important not to overdo things. That is, it is better to do too few things at once than too many (Bransford & Johnson, 1972, p. 722).*

This description becomes much more interpretable once you know what activity is being described: washing clothes. Now that you know the topic of the paragraph, read it again. It should make a great deal more sense.

Why is it that the label for this paragraph has such a major impact on our understanding? According to one perspective, the label invokes a knowledge structure, or *schema*, for the activities associated with cleaning clothes. We can then use our prior knowledge to interpret the new information. A *schema* is a cognitive structure that represents organized knowledge about a concept. Schemata contain both the attributes of a concept and relations among the attributes. Schemata are thought to guide the perception of new information, memory for old information, and social inferences (Fiske & Taylor, 1991). Such knowledge structures guide message processing and enhance recall of one's own position on the issue and recall of the reasons for this evaluation.

Rather than assessing schemata directly, it is possible to demonstrate the effects of such a structure (as we did with the washing example) and reason that, if the effects occur, a schema must be present. One consequence of a schema is that it should direct one's memory for relevant information. This is because new information is often remembered better when you can relate it to the other things you know (Schmidt & Sherman, 1984). Indeed, persuasive messages may be most effective when they present information that is well remembered, either because it fits with schema-based expectations or because it is novel and highly inconsistent with expectations. For example, the surgeon general might argue that "Marijuana is addictive," and this would probably fit into your conceptions of typical antidrug campaigns. The argument would then be stored in memory as part of a generic antidrug schema and might be recalled more readily (Schmidt & Sherman, 1984). If she claims, however, that "Marijuana protects against cancer," you would probably note that this is not a typical argument concerning drug use. You may be startled by the news about cancer because it does not fit your schema, and the novelty of this argument may make you attend to it and remember it. If opinions are based on recall of message content, then arguments consistent or highly inconsistent with your schema-based expectations might be most persuasive.

In sum, people differ in the way they organize information relevant to their opinions on certain topics, and this organization appears to affect message processing, especially yielding, and opinion change. It is relatively difficult to persuade people whose attitudes and beliefs are highly consistent and people who can remember a great deal of information and prior experiences related to their opinions. But characteristics of recipients affect influence through mechanisms other than information processing. Influence is part of social interaction, and recipient attributes may be important because they determine the rules and expectations for agreement with others. The next section of this chapter will consider the impact of characteristics like sex that regulate social influence.

Social Expectations for Influence: Are Women More Influenceable Than Men?

Upon initial acquaintance, the most obvious attributes of a person are physical. Our expectations of what others are like and our reactions to them are likely to be, at least initially, strongly affected by such attributes (Fiske & Taylor, 1991).

Social expectations about influence for people of varying age, race, sex, and attractiveness are apparent from stereotypes and cultural beliefs. For example, people are often thought to be especially impressionable and susceptible to influence attempts when young, and only after adolescence do they solidify their views. Younger people thus would be expected to be easier to influence than older ones. Likewise, less attractive people may be thought to worry more about social acceptance than attractive ones. Consequently, we might expect it to be easier to convince unattractive individuals to adopt a new opinion if a desirable reference group also holds that position. Only a few physical attributes of recipients have received much systematic attention from influence researchers (physical attractiveness, Chaiken, 1986; age, Krosnick & Alwin, 1989). There is, however, a considerable body of research on recipients' sex, and we will use this attribute to illustrate how social expectations can structure interaction and direct responses to influence attempts.

Males and females are frequently thought to differ in ease of influenceability. On television, the supposed naivete and gullibility of Edith, Lucy, Mary, Diane, or Mallory cause continuous alarm and exasperation for Archie, Ricky, Lou, Sam, or Alex, whereas the males are generally portrayed as being muleheaded and resistant to influence.[1] Does art imitate life? Various studies of the public's stereotypes have found that women, when compared with men, are perceived to be more easily influenced, more dependent, less aggressive, less dominant, and less able to act as leaders (Broverman, Vogel, Broverman, Clarkson, & Rosenkrantz, 1972; Spence, Helmreich, & Stapp, 1974; Taylor, Fiske, Etcoff, & Ruderman, 1978). These various sources of social stereotypes about sex, then, suggest that people believe women are relatively conforming, agreeable, and receptive to others' views, whereas men are relatively noncompliant and resistant to influence.

It is interesting to compare these stereotypic beliefs to experimental research on social influence. Although the majority of experimental studies of influence have reported no statistically significant sex difference, among those that have reported differences, almost all differences are in the direction of women being more influenceable than men (Maccoby & Jacklin, 1974; Eagly, 1978). Reviews of this research that have estimated the size of the sex difference have found an overall effect that, in statistical terms, is of small to moderate size (Cooper, 1979; Eagly & Carli, 1981).

It would be incorrect to conclude that, because of its size, the sex difference is trivial or unimportant in natural settings. Even effects that are small in an absolute sense may have practical importance. As Abelson (1985) has argued, in baseball, a batter's skill has only a small effect on any one batting performance (other factors like the particular pitch may be much more influential). Yet the importance of a player's skill to the team record becomes apparent when performances are cumulated over a season or a career. Similarly, even a small sex difference in influenceability can be important to men and women who work together over time.

The tendency for women to be more influenceable than men has also been found to vary with the social setting of the research. It appears to be largest in a particular context, that of group pressure conformity studies (Becker, 1986; Cooper, 1979; Eagly & Carli, 1981). In this setting, subjects are usually informed that other people in their experimental group hold a belief or attitude that is different from subjects' own positions. These other people have surveillance over subjects' responses; that is, they know (or appear to know) whether subjects conformed to their views. (See Chapter 8 by Kitayama and Burnstein for a discussion of these studies.)

A smaller sex difference has been obtained in the other settings in which psychologists have studied influence. Women appear only slightly more influenceable than men in conformity experiments not involving group pressure (that is, when the influence source would not be aware of subjects' stated opinions) and in persuasion experiments in which a communicator presents arguments supporting a position (Becker, 1986; Eagly & Carli, 1981).

Experimental research that has directly compared whether or not the group has surveillance over subjects' opinions has similarly found sex differences primarily when others are present. Women appear to be more influenceable than men primarily when they believe they are under others' surveillance (Eagly & Chrvala, 1986; Eagly, Wood, & Fishbaugh, 1981; Newton & Schulman, 1977). No significant sex differences emerged in these studies when subjects believed that their opinions would not be known to the rest of the group.

Why Are Women More Influenceable than Men?

Group pressure experiments differ from the other research settings in which influence has been studied because in group settings others are present to hear subjects' opinions. The presence of others is a clue about the origins of sex differences in influenceability.

Social Role Theory

One reason other people are important to the sex effect is because they introduce norms and expectations about the appropriate and likely influence behavior for women and men. Such expectations for sex differences in influence stem in part from the different social roles of men and women in American society (Berger, Wagner, & Zelditch, 1985; Eagly, 1987; Eagly & Wood, 1991). That is, our expectations of others are based largely on the social roles in which we encounter them; these expectations are communicated to others both verbally and nonverbally, and we tend to reinforce people when they meet our expectations. Thus, the high school nerd may act like a nerd because people have always expected him to do so. His peers are responsive to his awkwardness while overlooking any redeeming or interesting qualities, and he responds by becoming more consistently nerdy. Those same students who happen across him at their 10-year reunion may report with astonishment that he has turned into a profound and fascinating individual. Actually, they have not observed a transformation, just an individual whose current situation no longer makes him conform to such limited expectations.

From this perspective, sex differences in influence occur because men and women in our society have different social roles. We tend to believe that people possess attributes that fit the roles they fill. Men are more likely than women to be employed full time in work settings and to fill highly paid jobs of authority and status. As a result, men are more likely than women to be attributed the competent, dominant, and assertive characteristics that such positions seem to require (Eagly & Steffen, 1984; Eagly & Wood, 1982; Wood & Karten, 1986). Similarly, because women are more likely than men to fill the domestic roles of primary caretaker of children and full-time homemaker, women are ascribed attributes of agreeableness and providing support to others (Eagly & Steffen, 1984). Sex differences in influence result because people behave consistently with these role-related beliefs and expectations.

Social roles also contribute to sex differences through people's skills and attitudes. Your personal history of enacting social roles has given you a particular repertoire of abilities and values. If, in the past, you have tended to fill leadership positions (e.g., captain of sports teams, student body president), you are likely to possess the skills of influencing others and resisting others' attempts to direct and influence you. You are also likely to be comfortable with these behaviors. To the extent that men's roles provide these skills and attitudes more than women's roles, then men will resist influence more than women. On the other hand, if you have in the past typically filled positions in which you assist, support, and care for others (e.g., babysitter, nursing home worker), you are likely to know how to be agreeable and accept others' points of view, and you are likely to feel comfortable doing so. To the extent that women's roles, more than men's, provide this set of attitudes and abilities, women should be more influenceable than men.

According to a social role account, then, the sex difference in influenceability stems from the tendency for men and women to behave consistently with their gender roles, as well as from the different skills and attitudes that men and women have acquired from their past role-related experiences. In addition, social role theory recognizes that agreement may be a useful strategy for women and for people in subordinate positions to facilitate their later attempts at influence (Ridgeway, 1978; Shackelford, Wood, & Worchel, 1993). To understand why this is so, imagine that you want to convince your boss at work to adopt one of your ideas. You are not likely to be successful in demanding that a superior agree with you. This behavior is not expected from a subordinate (just as it is not necessarily part of expectations for women). It would raise questions about your motivation, not to mention the longevity of your job. A more effective strategy would be to bolster your case by convincing your boss that you are motivated by a concern for her and for the organization's welfare. One way to accomplish this would be to act friendly and agreeably. Thus, sex differences in influence may arise because women need to demonstrate their concern for others in order successfully to exert influence in the future. However, role theory is not the only account offered for sex differences in social behavior, and we consider these other explanations in the following sections.

Personalities of Women and Men

Psychologists have often explained sex differences in social behavior by arguing that different socialization pressures for boys and girls (e.g., interactions with parents, types of toys) result in sex differences in adults' personality traits and dispositions. It is perhaps through such processes that men in American society become oriented toward *agentic* (masculine) concerns, including self-assertion, self-expansion, and the urge to master, and women become oriented toward *communal* (feminine) concerns, including selflessness, concern for others, and desire to be at one with others (Bakan, 1966; Block, 1973).

Agentic and communal qualities might be linked to influenceability in a variety of ways (Eagly & Wood, 1985). For example, men's high level of agency includes dominance and assertiveness, attributes linked to resisting influence. Highly agentic, or masculine, individuals might be particularly difficult to influence. Furthermore, women's high level of communion involves concern for others' feelings, an attribute expressed through agreement with others. Highly communal, or feminine, individuals, then, might easily change their opinions.

Although sex-typed personality traits are intuitively plausible as an account of sex differences, they do not explain why the effect is largest in group pressure settings, in which others are present to hear the opinions given. Furthermore, research designed to test the personality account has obtained inconsistent support, with some studies finding a relation between amount of influence and masculinity or femininity as measured by personality scales (e.g., Bem, 1975) and others finding no relation (e.g., Eagly, Wood, & Fishbaugh, 1981; Falbo, 1977).

Other Features of Influence Studies

Several other factors have been suggested as possible sources of sex differences in influenceability. For example, the influence topic could generate sex differences. Topics can draw on men's interests and expertise more than women's (e.g., football, car mechanics) or may reflect women's interests and expertise more than men's (e.g., child care, nutrition). As you would expect, with male-oriented topics, men tend to be more resistant to influence than women (Sistrunk & McDavid, 1971). Although the topic is probably an important determinant of men's and women's influenceability in real-world settings, it does not explain why sex differences in influence appear in psychological research. Overall, the topics used in research do not appear to favor men's interests and expertise over women's, and consequently, the tendency for women to be more influenceable than men is not due to the type of topics researchers have featured in their studies (Eagly & Carli, 1981).

Other study attributes could contribute to apparent sex differences in psychological research. For example, Eagly and Carli (1981) noted that the majority of studies of sex differences in influenceability tended to have male authors, and male authors tended to obtain larger sex differences than female authors! In fact, for studies authored by women, no sex differences have been observed. Given that resistance to influence is a desirable characteristic, Eagly and Carli concluded that researchers have tended to generate or report data that are flattering to their own sex.

Exactly how authors' sex could affect study outcome is unclear. This effect is not necessarily intentional, as many subtle aspects of a study's design, implementation, or eventual reporting could be indirectly affected by researchers' sex. For example, at least for some studies, male researchers tended to use more stimulus items in their research, and thus their methods may have been more precise and accurate than those of female researchers (Becker, 1986). It is possible, then, that studies done by males tended to obtain a better (in this case larger) estimate of the sex difference because they employed better measures.

However, it seems unlikely that the sex difference obtained in laboratory research is solely due to experimental methods. The widespread belief in sex differences in influenceability in real-world settings is unlikely to be completely false. Stereotypes likely persist because they contain some kernel of truth. The kernel in this case is likely to be the different employment and domestic roles filled by men and women in American society.

In summary, women appear to be slightly more influenceable than men, and this sex difference is largest in a group context where other group members appear to be aware of the opinions given. According to a social role account, the sex difference in influence stems from the tendency for men and women to behave consistently with social expectations as well as from the different skills and attitudes that men and women have acquired from their past role-related experiences. In addition, we considered whether the sex difference is the result of socialization that instills in males personality traits linked to resisting persuasion and in females traits related to yielding. Finally, we considered whether attributes of research studies could be responsible, such as the tendency for most influence studies to be authored by men and the tendency for male researchers to find greater female influenceability.

A Final Word on Persons and Situations

In this chapter, we have reviewed an impressive amount of evidence indicating that people differ in how easily they can be influenced. Sometimes the relations between individual attributes and influence were complex because they varied with the situation. For example, low-self-esteem people should be easier to influence than high-self-esteem ones primarily when messages are easy to attend to and comprehend (that is, when both highs and lows can receive the information); opinion change is then a result of people with high self-esteem yielding less to others' views than those with low self-esteem. Furthermore, women are more influenceable than men primarily in group settings in which others know what opinions they state.

This dependence on situations is not an unusual occurrence. It is true that social behaviors such as influence are a function of both the kind of *person* one is and the kind of *situation* one is in. Although we recognize these many predictors of social behavior, our goal in the present chapter is to identify as clearly as possible the effects of individual differences on influence. As a final note, we present several strategies for thinking about social behavior that are likely to reveal these effects most clearly. That is, the effects of individual differences on influence are most likely to be apparent for certain types of persons, in certain types of situations, and for certain ways of measuring behavior (Snyder & Ickes, 1985). (See Chapter 4 by Fazio and Roskos-Ewoldsen for a similar approach to the relation between attitudes and behavior.)

Types of Persons

It seems that there are particular kinds of people whose behavior can best be predicted from individual attributes. One such group is those who rely on inner states, attributes, and attitudes to guide their actions. These individuals, labeled *low self-monitors* (Snyder, 1974, 1979), can be compared to *high self-monitors*, who tailor their behavior to fit what is most appropriate in a given situation.

The concept of self-monitoring (described in detail in Chapter 4) can help to anticipate when influence will be determined by people's dispositions and when it will be affected by situations. Because low self-monitors rely on internal dispositions when deciding how to act, opinion change should be a function of their personality traits, abilities, and the attitude-relevant information they possess. The opinions adopted by high self-monitors should be largely determined by the social situation they are in, and thus we should not have much success predicting influence from their dispositions. Indeed, because high self-monitors tailor their stated opinions to be consistent with social pressures, they are generally more likely than low self-monitors to change their opinions when others disagree with them (Rarick, Soldow, & Geizer, 1976; Snyder & DeBono, 1985; Snyder & Monson, 1975; for an exception, see Santee & Maslach, 1982).

Types of Situations

Our ability to predict influence from recipients' personal attributes also depends on the situation in which opinions are assessed. Highly structured situations provide clear guides to appropriate action and are likely to be perceived and evaluated in a similar manner by most people (Ickes, 1982; Mischel, 1977). Some structured situations generate a readiness to be influenced, whereas others invoke resistance to change. There are few people who could avoid buying Tupperware at the party held by a good friend in desperate financial circumstances (see Chapter 9 by Cial-dini). Individual differences in influence are not likely to be highly apparent in such a setting.

In unstructured settings that are ambiguous and offer few guides to behavior, influence is more likely to be directed by dispositions such as personality traits, abilities, and the extent and structure of attitude-relevant information in memory. During a lazy Saturday afternoon following payday, your generosity to a telephone solicitor requesting donations to an important charity may be largely determined by such personal attributes.

Ways to Measure Influence

Personality characteristics such as self-esteem are measured through very general questionnaires that tap a variety of aspects of one's identity. Persuasion and conformity, however, are typically measured much more specifically, often as a single response at a given point in time. It is a rule of thumb that two variables show the strongest relationship when they are assessed at a similar level of generality (Ajzen & Fishbein, 1977; Epstein, 1979; see also Chapter 4). Consequently, global traits like self-esteem will be most closely linked to influence if influence is similarly assessed in a general manner, across times and settings.

Consider Dennis the Menace and his neighbor, Mr. Wilson. Most people would agree that Mr. Wilson has a generally grouchy personality, yet Dennis seems unaware of Mr. Wilson's temperament as a determinant of his behavior. Thus, Dennis often reacts with surprise and misunderstanding when Mr. Wilson responds unfavorably to some prank. Dennis might find it easier to change Mr. Wilson's mind about children's games if he would acknowledge that grouchy personality. Indeed, the basic humor of this situation is that readers intuitively recognize that personality variables are important mediators of influence, but little boys do not. We know this because we have had many experiences with people like Mr. Wilson, but Dennis is individually evaluating each response rather than combining multiple observations. Likewise, in many research paradigms, the mediating effects of personality variables on influenceability are not apparent until a large number of observations have been made.

Note that incompatibility in measurement of individual differences and influence is not as much of a problem with topic-bound approaches as with the study of general dispositions (e.g., self-esteem). Measures of the extent and organization of attitude-relevant information correspond, at least in attitude topic, to the attitude that is assessed.

Conclusion

Clearly, people differ in how easily they are influenced. In this chapter, we considered two mechanisms by which individual differences affect influenceability. According to the Yale-McGuire model, recipient attributes affect influence because they direct reception of and yielding to persuasive appeals. Experimental research has demonstrated good support for the model with the personality trait of self-esteem. People low in self-esteem seem to be too preoccupied to receive messages, and people high in self-esteem appear to be too skeptical and independent to yield; thus, both groups are resistant to change. People of moderate self-esteem appear easiest to influence.

We next examined how the extent and structure of attitude-relevant information in memory affects yielding to persuasive appeals. In this approach, recipients use the specific information they possess on an attitude topic to evaluate the content of an appeal. Consistency between one's attitude and supporting beliefs and extensive working knowledge on the attitude topic are likely to provide the necessary information base to critically evaluate and resist all but the most cogently argued appeals.

We also considered whether influence varies with social expectations based on recipients' demographic attributes, like sex and age. In particular, the tendency for women to be easier to influence than men, especially when others will know what opinions they state, appears to be due to different expectations for men and women. The different roles of men and women in American society (i.e., men are more likely than women to be employed full time and to hold high-paying positions, whereas women are more likely than men to be homemakers and caretakers of children) generate expectations that men are likely to be assertive and resist influence, whereas women are likely to be agreeable and supportive of others' views. Sex differences result when people conform to these expectations.

Although we have separated our presentation of these two mechanisms by which recipient attributes affect influence, in reality, they combine to produce individual differences. We are most likely to be successful in predicting differences among recipients if we consider the variety of ways that attributes can affect influence—if we consider effects on message processing in addition to social expectations for agreement with others.

Note

1. For those of you who do not follow the syndicated sitcoms, this example refers to "All in the Family," "I Love Lucy," "The Mary Tyler Moore Show," "Cheers," and "Family Ties," respectively.

Acknowledgments

The authors would like to thank Shelly Chaiken, Alice Eagly, Sharon Shavitt, and Jeffry Simpson for their helpful comments on an earlier draft of the chapter. Preparation of this chapter was supported by a grant from the Rockefeller Foundation to Wendy Wood.

References

Abelson, R. P. (1985). A variance explanation paradox: When a little is a lot. *Psychological Bulletin, 97*, 129–133.

Ajzen, I., & Fishbein, M. (1977). Attitude-behavior relations: A theoretical analysis and review of empirical research. *Psychological Bulletin, 84*, 888–918.

Bakan, D. (1966). *The duality of human existence: An essay on psychology and religion.* Chicago: Rand McNally.

Becker, B. J. (1986). Influence again: Another look at studies of gender differences in social influence. In J. S. Hyde & M. Linn (Eds.), *The psychology of gender: Advances through meta-analysis* (pp. 178–209). Baltimore: Johns Hopkins University Press.

Bem, S. L. (1975). Sex-role adaptability: One consequence of psychological androgyny. *Journal of Personality and Social Psychology, 31*, 634–643.

Berger, J., Wagner, D. G., & Zelditch, M., Jr. (1985). Introduction: Expectation states theory: Review and assessment. In J. Berger & M. Zelditch (Eds.), *Status, rewards and influence* (pp. 1–72). San Francisco: Jossey-Bass.

Biek, M., Wood, W., Nations, C., & Chaiken, S. (1993). *Working knowledge, cognitive processing, and attitudes: On the determinants of bias.* Manuscript under editorial review.

Block, J. H. (1973). Conceptions of sex roles: Some cross-cultural and longitudinal perspectives. *American Psychologist, 28*, 512–526.

Bransford, J. D., & Johnson, M. K. (1972). Contextual prerequisites for understanding: Some investigations of comprehension and recall. *Journal of Verbal Learning and Verbal Behavior, 11*, 717–726.

Broverman, I. K., Vogel, S. R., Broverman, D. M., Clarkson, F. E., & Rosenkrantz, P. S. (1972). Sex-role stereotypes: A current appraisal. *Journal of Social Issue, 28*, 59–78.

Chaiken, S. (1982). *Affective-cognitive consistency, counterarguing, and persuasion.* Unpublished manuscript, Vanderbilt University, Nashville, Tennessee.

Chaiken, S. (1986). Physical appearance and social influence. In C. P. Herman, M. P. Zanna, & E. T. Higgins (Eds.), *Physical appearance and social behavior: The Ontario symposium* (Vol. 3). Hillsdale, NJ: Erlbaum.

Chaiken, S., Liberman, A., & Eagly, A. H. (1989). Heuristic and systematic information processing within and beyond the persuasion context. In J. S. Uleman & J. A. Bargh (Eds.), *Unintended thought* (pp. 212–252). New York: Guilford.

Chaiken, S., Pomerantz, E. M., & Giner-Sorolla, R. (in press). Structural consistency and attitude strength. In R. E. Petty & J. A. Krosnick (Eds.), *Attitude strength: Antecedents and consequences.* Hillsdale, NJ: Erlbaum.

Chaiken, S., & Yates, S. (1985). Affective-cognitive consistency and thought-induced attitude polarization. *Journal of Personality and Social Psychology, 49*, 1470–1481.

Converse, P. (1962). Information flow and the stability of partisan attitudes. *Public Opinion Quarterly, 26*, 578–599.

Cooper, H. M. (1979). Statistically combining independent studies: A meta-analysis of sex differences in conformity research. *Journal of Personality and Social Psychology, 37*, 131–146.

Cox, D. F., & Bauer, R. A. (1964). Self-confidence and persuasibility in women. *Public Opinion Quarterly, 28*, 453–466.

Eagly, A. H. (1978). Sex differences in influenceability. *Psychological Bulletin, 85*, 86–116.

Eagly, A. H. (1987). *Sex differences in social behavior: A social role interpretation.* Hillsdale, NJ: Erlbaum.

Eagly, A. H., & Carli, L. L. (1981). Sex of researchers and sex-typed communications as determinants of sex differences in influenceability: A meta-analysis of social influence studies. *Psychological Bulletin, 90*, 1–20.

Eagly, A. H., & Chaiken, S. (1993). *The psychology of attitudes.* Fort Worth, TX: Harcourt, Brace, & Jovanovich.

Eagly, A. H., & Chrvala, C. (1986). Sex differences in conformity: Status and gender-role interpretations. *Psychology of Women Quarterly, 10*, 203–220.

Eagly, A. H., & Steffen, V. J. (1984). Gender stereotypes stem from the distribution of men and women into social roles. *Journal of Personality and Social Psychology, 46*, 735–754.

Eagly, A. H., & Wood, W. (1982). Inferred sex differences in status as a determinant of gender stereotypes about social influence. *Journal of Personality and Social Psychology, 43*, 915–928.

Eagly, A. H., & Wood, W. (1985). Sex differences in influenceability: Stereotype vs. behavior. In V. E. O'Leary, R. K. Unger, & B. S. Wallston (Eds.), *Women, gender, and social psychology* (pp. 225–256). Hillsdale, NJ: Erlbaum.

Eagly, A. H., & Wood, W. (1991). Explaining sex differences in social behavior: A meta-analytic perspective. *Personality and Social Psychology Bulletin, 17*, 306–315.

Eagly, A. H., Wood, W., & Fishbaugh, L. (1981). Sex differences in conformity: Surveillance by the group as a determinant of male nonconformity. *Journal of Personality and Social Psychology, 40*, 384–394.

Epstein, S. (1979). The stability of behavior: I. On predicting most of the people much of the time. *Journal of Personality and Social Psychology, 37*, 1097–1126.

Falbo, T. (1977). Relationships between sex, sex role, and social influence. *Psychology of Women Quarterly, 2*, 62–72.

Fiske, S. T., & Taylor, S. E. (1991). *Social cognition* (2nd ed.). Reading, MA: Addison-Wesley.

Hovland, C. I., Janis, I. L., & Kelley, H. H. (1953). *Communication and persuasion*. New Haven, CT: Yale University Press.

Hovland, C. I., Lumsdaine, A. A., & Sheffield, F. D. (1949). *Experiments on mass communication*. Princeton, NJ: Princeton University Press.

Ickes, W. (1982). A basic paradigm for the study of personality, roles, and social behavior. In W. Ickes & E. S. Knowles (Eds.), *Personality, roles and social behavior* (pp. 305–341). New York: Springer-Verlag.

Janis, I. L., & Hovland, C. I. (1959). An overview of persuasibility research. In C. I. Hovland & I. L. Janis (Eds.), *Personality and persuasibility* (pp. 1–26). New Haven, CT: Yale University Press.

Krosnick, J. A., & Alwin, D. F. (1989). Aging and susceptibility to attitude change. *Journal of Personality and Social Psychology, 57*, 416–425.

Maccoby, E. E., & Jacklin, C. N. (1974). *The psychology of sex differences*. Stanford, CA: Stanford University Press.

McGuire, W. J. (1969a). Personality and susceptibility to social influence. In E. F. Borgatta & W. W. Lambert (Eds.), *Handbook of personality theory and research* (pp. 171–196). Chicago: Rand McNally.

McGuire, W. J. (1969b). The nature of attitudes and attitude change. In G. Lindzey & E. Aronson (Eds.), *Handbook of social psychology* (2nd ed., Vol. 3, pp. 136–314). Reading, MA: Addison-Wesley.

McGuire, W. J. (1985). Attitudes and attitude change. In G. Lindzey & E. Aronson (Eds.), *Handbook of social psychology* (3rd ed., Vol. 2, pp. 233–346). New York: Random House.

Mischel, W. (1977). The interaction of person and situation. In D. Magnusson & N. S. Endler (Eds.), *Personality at the crossroads: Current issues in interactional psychology* (pp. 333–352). Hillsdale, NJ: Erlbaum.

Newton, R. R., & Schulman, G. L. (1977). Sex and conformity: A new view. *Sex Roles, 3*, 511–521.

Norman, R. (1975). Affective-cognitive consistency, attitudes, conformity, and behavior. *Journal of Personality and Social Psychology, 32*, 83–91.

Petty, R. E., & Cacioppo, J. T. (1986). The elaboration likelihood model of persuasion. In L. Berkowitz (Ed.), *Advances in experimental social psychology* (Vol. 19, pp. 123–205). Orlando, FL: Academic Press.

Rarick, D. L., Soldow, G. F., & Geizer, R. S. (1976). Self-monitoring as a mediator of conformity. *Central States Speech Journal, 27*, 267–271.

Rhodes, N., & Wood, W. (1992). Self-esteem and intelligence affect influenceability: The mediating role of message reception. *Psychological Bulletin, 111*, 156–171.

Ridgeway, C. L. (1978). Conformity, group-oriented motivation, and status attainment in small groups. *Social Psychology, 41*, 175–188.

Ridgeway, C. L. (1982). Status in groups: The importance of motivation. *American Sociological Review, 47*, 76–88.

Rosenberg, M. J. (1960). A structural theory of attitude dynamics. *Public Opinion Quarterly, 24*, 319–341.

Rosenberg, M. J. (1968). Hedonism, inauthenticity, and other goads toward expansion of a consistency theory. In R. P. Abelson, E. Aronson,

W. J. McGuire, T. M. Newcomb, M. J. Rosenberg, & P. H. Tannenbaum (Eds.), *Theories of cognitive consistency: A sourcebook* (pp. 73–111). Chicago: Rand McNally.

Santee, R. T., & Maslach, C. (1982). To agree or not to agree: Personal dissent amid social pressure to conform. *Journal of Personality and Social Psychology, 42,* 690–700.

Schmidt, D. F., & Sherman, R. C. (1984). Memory for persuasive messages: A test of schema-copy-plus-tag-model. *Journal of Personality and Social Psychology, 47,* 17–25.

Shackelford S., Wood, W., & Worchel, S. (1993). *How can low-status group members influence others? Team players and attention-getters.* Manuscript submitted for publication.

Sistrunk, F., & McDavid, J. W. (1971). Sex variable in conformity behavior. *Journal of Personality and Social Psychology, 17,* 200–201.

Snyder, M. (1974). Self-monitoring of expressive behavior. *Journal o f Personality and Social Psychology, 30,* 526–537.

Snyder, M. (1979). Self-monitoring processes. In L. Berkowitz (Ed.), *Advances in experimental social psychology* (Vol. 12, pp. 85–128). New York: Academic Press.

Snyder, M., & DeBono, K. (1985). Appeals to image and claims about quality: Understanding the psychology of advertising. *Journal of Personality and Social Psychology, 49,* 586–597.

Snyder, M., & Ickes, W. (1985). Personality and social behavior. In G. Lindzey & E. Aronson (Eds.), *Handbook of social psychology* (3rd ed., Vol. 2, pp. 949–992). New York: Random House.

Snyder, M., & Monson, T. C. (1975). Persons, situations, and the control of social behavior. *Journal of Personality and Social Psychology, 32,* 637–644.

Spence, J. T., Helmreich, R. L., & Stapp, J. (1974). The Personal Attributes Questionnaire: A measure of sex-role stereotypes and masculinity-femininity. *JSAS: Catalog of Selected Documents in Psychology, 4,* 43 (ms. no. 617).

Taylor, S. E., Fiske, S. T., Etcoff, N. L., & Ruderman, A. J. (1978). Categorical and contextual bases of person memory and stereotyping. *Journal of Personality and Social Psychology, 36,* 778–793.

Wood, W. (1982). Retrieval of attitude-relevant information from memory: Effects on susceptibility to persuasion and on intrinsic motivation. *Journal of Personality and Social Psychology, 43,* 798–810.

Wood, W., & Kallgren, C. A. (1988). Communicator attributes and persuasion: A function of access to attitude-relevant information. *Personality and Social Psychology Bulletin, 14,* 172–182.

Wood, W., Kallgren, C. A., & Preisler, R. M. (1985). Access to attitude-relevant information in memory as a determinant of persuasion: The role of message attributes. *Journal of Experimental Social Psychology, 21,* 73–85.

Wood, W., & Karten, S. (1986). Sex differences in interaction style as a product of perceived sex differences in competence. *Journal of Personality and Social Psychology, 50,* 341–347.

Wood, W., & Rhodes, N. D. (1989). *Men's and women's status judgments in task performing groups.* Unpublished manuscript, Texas A&M University.

Wood, W., & Rhodes, N. D. (1992). Sex differences in interaction style in task groups. In C. Ridgeway (Eds.), *Gender, interaction, and inequality* (pp. 97–121). New York: Springer-Verlag.

Wood, W., Rhodes, N. D., & Biek, M. (in press). Working knowledge and attitude strength: An information-processing analysis. In R. E. Petty & J. Krosnick (Eds.), *Attitude strength: Antecedents and consequences.* Hillsdale, NJ: Erlbaum.

8

SOCIAL INFLUENCE, PERSUASION, AND GROUP DECISION MAKING

SHINOBU KITAYAMA
Kyoto University

EUGENE BURNSTEIN
University of Michigan

Introduction

Paul is an active member of a fraternity at a private college in the South. During the last few months, his fraternity has been accused of several alcohol-related incidents and is being closely monitored by the local police as well as the college administration. Paul does usually like to party and thinks that beer is a good thing to drink on such occasions. Because of these incidents, however, he has also begun to feel that the alcohol policy of his house might be too lenient. At the same time, he is acutely aware that a vast majority of his fraternity brothers are strongly opposed to tightening their alcohol policy. So he has never openly expressed his opinion on this matter to them.

The kind of situation that Paul faces in the above example is extremely common in everyday life. We live most of our lives in groups. We get ideas about what is right and wrong from what others in the group are saying and doing. Not only that, we also often go along with our group even when we really disagree at heart. At the same time, however, there are many occasions in which we firmly stand up for our opinions and beliefs, even though they conflict with those held by a majority of other members, resist influence from the group, assert our views, and try to persuade the others. And in many cases, we can and do, in fact, influence the course of action the group eventually takes. Thus, to understand persuasion in groups, we have to analyze not only how the individual is influenced by a group but also how he or she influences the group. The organization of the present chapter reflects this consideration.

The first theme of the chapter is *majority influence*, or conformity. Often, individuals change their behavior as a result of having been exposed to opinions, behaviors, or preferences of other individuals in the group. Paul's example above is a case in point. The source of social influence is a majority within the group (the other members of the house) and the recipient of influence is a minority (Paul himself). Keep in mind that influence can occur without any explicit communication. For example, just by observing how the other members behave, Paul probably can figure out what they think about restricting drinking, what are the consequences of agreeing or disagreeing with them on this issue, and the like. As a result of these observations, Paul may change his actions so that they conform with those of the majority, or he may refuse to conform.

No matter how pervasive and powerful conformity pressures may be, individuals are rarely passive recipients of influence from the majority. A minority can also influence the majority. For example, in Paul's case, if the issue of excessive drinking is important to him, and if he disagrees with the group, he may stand up and express his opinion in front of other house members. In other words, Paul may become an *active minority* and initiate innovative processes in the group. How can a minority influence a majority? Does minority influence work the same way or differently from majority influence? These questions will be the topic for the second section.

In the third section, we will shift gears and discuss persuasion in groups in more natural situations, namely, where members engage in face-to-face discussion. We will ask what social influence processes are at work under these conditions. Finally, we will discuss some pitfalls of group discussion and suggest possible ways to avoid these pitfalls.

Majority Influence

As Barbara Ehrenreich puts it, "The Jacobins of the multiculturalist movement, who are described derisively as P.C., or politically correct, are said to have launched a campus reign of terror against those who slip and innocently say 'freshman' instead of 'freshperson,' 'Indian' instead of 'Native American' or, may the Goddess forgive them, 'disabled' instead of 'differently abled' " (Ehrenreich, 1991, p. 84). This quote vividly illustrates that even though many of us think it silly to confuse verbal purity with a truly enlightened commitment to ethnic and cultural diversity, on many American college campuses today, we often cannot help but feel pressured to conform and use so-called politically correct terms and phrases (see Figure 8-1). Conformity pressure like this, however, has always existed as long as there have been human groups. Not surprisingly, research on this topic can also be

FIGURE 8-1   **A hapless college teacher encounters
the mandarins of political correctness.**

Source: Robert Neubecker.

traced back to the very first years of modern social psychology. Specifically, Sherif
(1935) and Asch (1951, 1956) used markedly contrasting procedures to address this
same topic, with vastly different results and theoretical implications.

Sherif: Social Influence When Physical Reality Is Ambiguous

Common sense suggests that social influence should be quite substantial when we
do not know what the "right" behavior really is. In these circumstances, our *public
behavior* will certainly be influenced by what other individuals say and do. Evidence suggests, however, that social influence can go even deeper, changing our
private beliefs and perceptions, as well. Sherif (1935) addressed this possibility
with ingenuity, using a perceptual illusion called the *autokinetic effect*.

  Imagine that we focus our attention on a pinpoint of light in an otherwise completely dark room. Typically, after several seconds, the light will appear to move
erratically. The movement is illusory, because the light source is actually stationary.
The illusion is due to the absence of any spatial frame of reference that helps locate
the light. (Remember that the room is completely dark.) Sherif had subjects simply
estimate the size of light movement in inches. When subjects made this judgment
alone, their judgment varied within some sizable range. Later, they came together
in groups of two or three and made their judgments aloud, one after the other. Discussion was forbidden. Initially, each member of the group stuck to the particular
estimate that he or she had made while judging alone, and, as a result, there was

considerable disagreement about the precise amount of movement. Over time, however, the judgments began to converge; people began to agree more and more so that eventually their judgments always fell within a rather narrow *common range*. Once this common range, or *group norm*, had been created, each person from then on reported perceiving a similar amount of movement. Interestingly, the subjects continued to respond in accordance with the group norm even when they made a judgment alone and in private, after having left the group. Thus, they were not just going along to avoid disagreement. Exposure to the judgments of others altered their frame of reference (standard) for estimating movement and, hence, their actual perception of movement in this situation. Moreover, they carried the new frame of reference with them and used it outside of the group. In short, the group norm was *internalized*.

Asch: Social Influence When Physical Reality Is Clear

The substantial amount of social influence observed in the Sherif study would seem reasonable because, after all, the stimulus was extremely ambiguous. We might predict, therefore, that once ambiguity is eliminated and the stimulus is clear cut, social influence should disappear. If physical reality is obvious, we should be capable of independent judgment and resist any social influence inconsistent with this reality. With the goal of studying *independence* from others in mind, therefore, Asch (1951, 1956) began a series of experiments. These experiments, however, turned out to be *the* most widely cited demonstrations of *conformity*.

Asch presented a standard line, along with two or three comparison lines, to a group of individuals. Members of the group were to announce, one at a time, which of the comparison lines was identical in length to the standard. This was repeated for many trials with different standard and comparison lines. In every instance, however, the correct answer was obvious; so when the same judgments were made in private, no one made an error. The size of the group varied from condition to condition and from experiment to experiment (see following), although typically, there were several members. Whatever its size, a group always contained only one naive subject, and the remaining individuals were accomplices of the experimenter who had been instructed ahead of time as to the judgments they were to make. The seating was prearranged so that the naive individual would always have to report his judgment next to last. By the time his turn came around, therefore, almost everybody else had made their opinion public. On one-third of the trials, the accomplices were correct and the naive person had no problem going along. On the other two-thirds, however, something mysterious happened in the eyes of the naive subject. All the other members in the group chose what to him was clearly the wrong comparison line.

To his surprise, Asch discovered an appreciable tendency to conform with the majority, even though the position taken by the majority was patently incorrect. On the average, the naive subject conformed with the incorrect majority on more than 30% of the trials. Further, more than 60% of the naive subjects made such a conformity response at least once during the experiment. Having realized the significance of the result, Asch quickly changed the objective of the study 180 degrees from independence to conformity. He thus contributed a classic method of studying majority influence.

Some Cognitive Processes at Work in the Asch Situation

Why does conformity occur, even in the face of undeniable physical reality? Keep in mind that, in the Asch situation, no verbal communication is allowed. Members cannot discuss their differences and argue why they think their judgment is correct. Thus, social influence or persuasion in this situation occurs with minimal social interaction, primarily *within* the mind of the recipient of the influence. Let us discuss some important factors implicated in this process.

Cognitive Conflict

To begin with, the very fact that the target stimulus is crystal clear may produce a high degree of cognitive conflict. Some researchers have argued that it is this conflict that induces a person to conform (Ross, Bierbrauer, & Hoffman, 1976). They reason that when physical reality is undeniably clear, we anticipate complete agreement among members. Therefore, upon discovering a unanimous yet seemingly incorrect majority, naive subjects must ask themselves why everyone else in the group is making what appears to them to be a clearly incorrect choice. It is very difficult to discount completely the possibility that the majority position might actually be correct. As a result, naive subjects begin to question their own sensory experience and may, instead, turn to the majority for the "correct" judgment. Another important source of ambiguity is an expectation held by naive subjects that since there is a clear physical reality, the majority expects that there will be no disagreement among group members. This in turn makes naive subjects apprehensive about what the majority will think of them if they violate this expectation. Such apprehension can also lead to a considerable pressure to agree with the majority.

Informational and Normative Influence

Another important determinant of conformity is the *goal* of the person who confronts an erroneous majority. Researchers have distinguished two general classes of goals. The first is *being correct*. That is to say, members may want to discover the correct solution to problems presented to them in a given situation. In the Asch situation, the very fact that a unanimous majority endorses one position may suggest that the position must be correct. Individuals then give up trusting their own senses and instead conform to the majority. When social influence occurs because the member wants to be correct, the influence is said to be *informational*. The second goal is *social approval*. Members want to feel liked and approved of by others. In the service of this desire, individuals may adjust their opinions to those of others; it is a tactic that enables them to gain approval or avoid rejection (see Chapter 9 by Cialdini in this volume). When social influence is mediated by the motive for social approval, it is said to be *normative*.

There seems to be a sizable component of normative social influence in the Asch situation. This has been suggested by subsequent experiments that demonstrate that conformity decreases dramatically once naive subjects can respond anonymously (Crutchfield, 1955; Deutsch & Gerard, 1955; see Allen, 1965, for a review). Quite interestingly, however, even in these conditions where complete anonymity is assured, some small yet reliable amount of conformity still remains, suggesting that some portion of the influence is informational. Finally, it must be noted that in the Sherif study discussed above, the influence was predominantly informational. This was indicated by the fact that contrary to Asch's subjects, those in Sherif's study continued to judge the light movement in accordance with the group norm even after the group itself had been disbanded.

Majority Size: The Critical Role of Perceptual Grouping

How many individuals does a majority need to have to produce a significant amount of conformity? Will a majority produce more conformity as its size increases? These issues, in fact, were addressed in Asch's original experiment, where the number of the accomplices was varied from 1 through 16 (1, 2, 3, 4, 8, and 16). The result was quite revealing. Conformity increased quite rapidly until the majority reached the size of 3 or 4 and, thereafter, leveled off. Thus, a majority of 8 or even 16 was no more effective than a majority of 3 or 4. This finding has been replicated by several other researchers (Gerard, Wilhelmy, & Conolley, 1968; Rosenberg, 1961; Wilder, 1977). In every instance, a rather small majority had as much power over the individual as did a quite large majority.

Why this is true is not entirely clear; but we shall offer one tentative interpretation along with some evidence for it. Following Wilder (1977), we think that when there are more than three or four individuals advocating the same position, these individuals are no longer perceived as separate individuals but rather as a *clique*—we pigeonhole them to form a single category like "those guys with a different point of view." Once individuals are packaged, the package functions as a *single* unit, virtually regardless of its size, resulting in no appreciable increase in conformity as its size increases. Support for this hypothesis comes from several experiments. In one study, Wilder (1977) found that individuals are influenced more by two *independent* groups of two people than by one group of four people. Similarly, three groups of two individuals were more influential than two groups of three individuals, which in turn were more influential than one group of six individuals. In short, it is easier to discount the opinions of others when we can perceive these individuals as belonging together, as being cliqueish or nonindependent judges.

A similar point was made by Kitayama, Burnstein, and Nelson (1987) within an Asch-type conformity situation. At the beginning of their study, twelve subjects were divided into two groups of six people on an entirely arbitrary basis. Subjects were then seated in individual cubicles and exchanged their views on a variety of issues by pressing a key on a computer keyboard in front of them. In fact, on several issues, the feedback about "others' opinions" had been prearranged so that each subject had to express his or her own opinion in fifth place after four "preceding persons" had expressed their opinions, which were uniformly extreme responses. Further, these four were either from a single group or from two different groups (two from one group and the remaining two from the other group). Subjects' response tended to move more in the direction of the majority position when the majority consisted of two groups of two individuals than when it consisted of one group of four individuals.

Minority Influence

Let us return to the case of Paul, the fraternity brother who thinks that a more strict alcohol policy is desirable. What if Paul publicly and consistently argues for his position, despite the fact that virtually everybody else in the fraternity strongly opposes such a policy? Most likely, other members will try to persuade Paul to change his opinion and conform; they may even threaten to ostracize him (Schachter, 1951). Nevertheless, suppose Paul still insists on vigorously expressing his belief in tighter regulation of alcohol in their house. How would the others respond to such a consistent, active minority?

In this section, we will review research on minority influence. Let us begin by distinguishing between two general effects of a minority.

Two Effects of an Active Minority

Liberating Effect

An important role that a minority can play in social influence was suggested by Asch in his original series of experiments. In these experiments, Asch showed that the influence of a majority can be greatly diminished if it is less than unanimous. In one of the experiments, each six-person group contained not only a majority but also a minority, that is, a single accomplice who had been instructed to respond correctly throughout. The minority member was always seated in the fourth position so that he announced his judgment just prior to the naive subject. In these conditions, conformity by the subject decreased dramatically. Recall that with a unanimous (and incorrect) majority, the naive subject conformed on more than 30% of the critical trials. When a single accomplice was instructed to defect from the majority and give a correct response, the naive subjects conformed with the majority on less than 6% of the trials.

It is evident that the presence of a small minority can greatly subvert the power of the majority (see Figure 8-2). The example of dissent frees members to express the correct opinion, as they would in the absence of an incorrect majority. A minority can *liberate* individuals from a unanimous majority for two reasons. First, a minority breaks the unanimity of a majority; and second, a minority can also provide social support for a naive subject's position. Note that although these two roles of liberating minorities often go together, they are theoretically distinct. For example, imagine a case in which the minority's position is quite different from

"Your Honor, on the first ballot the jury voted ten to two for conviction. For three emotionally charged hours, we discussed our points of difference. On the next ballot, it was seven to five for acquittal. Over the next several ballots, the vote seesawed back and forth. One juror became ill and was replaced by an alternate. By now, we had been in session for ten hours straight. Tempers were rising and some jurors were near the breaking point."

FIGURE 8-2   The presence of an active minority can make group members feel free to express their own opinions.

Source: Drawing by Dana Fradon; © 1986 The New Yorker Magazine, Inc.

that of the majority, as well as that of the naive subject. In this case, the minority breaks the unanimity of the majority but does not provide any support for the naive subject's position. Interestingly, in the perceptual judgment task examined by Asch, conformity was reduced by a minority that disagreed with both the naive subject and the majority as effectively as by a minority that agreed with the naive subject, that is, who both broke the unanimity *and* provided social support (Allen & Levine, 1969). It appears, therefore, that unanimity is the primary source of the power of a majority in the Asch situation.

Belief Conversion Effect

Besides the liberating effect, a minority can have another, equally significant effect. Under certain conditions, a minority can influence majority members' private beliefs even when the minority is publicly rejected or ignored. In other words, a minority can produce *conversion* in the private beliefs of majority members without any apparent influence on what they say overtly or publicly. Evidence tends to indicate that such a conversion effect produced by a minority is mediated by psychological processes somewhat different from those underlying majority influence or conformity. Although still controversial (see e.g., Latané & Wolf, 1981; Tanford & Penrod, 1984, for alternative views), this possibility is intriguing both theoretically and empirically and, in fact, has been actively pursued by a number of researchers since it was first proposed by a French social psychologist, Serge Moscovici (e.g., Moscovici & Faucheux, 1972).

Belief Conversion in Minority Influence

Several studies have demonstrated, in a situation analogous to Asch's, that a numerical minority can influence majority members' (i.e., naive subjects') judgments even though the minority's position is incorrect. In a typical experiment of this kind, Moscovici had five individuals name the color of a blue slide (e.g., Moscovici & Faucheux, 1972). As in the Asch experiment, the correct answer was very obvious. However, two of the five members were in fact accomplices of the experimenter and had been instructed to report consistently that the color was "green." When the percent of "green" responses made by the naive majority subjects was examined, they were found to occur on about 10% of the trials, thus demonstrating reliable minority influence. Interestingly, however, the minority influence completely vanished when the minority was not consistent, that is, when they made correct "blue" responses on some trials and incorrect "green" responses on the others. Based on findings such as these, Moscovici has suggested that *behavioral consistency* is a necessary condition for a minority to exert influence on a majority (see also Nemeth, Swedlund, & Kanki, 1974; Nemeth & Wachtler, 1974).

Why Consistency?

Earlier in this chapter, we suggested two sources of majority influence. First, informational influence occurs because the very fact that a large number of individuals agree on an issue suggests that this view must be correct. Second, normative influence takes place because individuals often want to be liked or accepted by the rest of the group, namely, the majority. Neither of these processes are likely when the source of influence is a numeric minority. Indeed, the fact that very few other people constitute the minority suggests that its position is likely to be *incorrect*. Further, individuals would presumably wish to be liked by more, rather than fewer, members, that is, by a majority of their group instead of a minority.

Moscovici (e.g., Moscovici & Faucheux, 1972) has proposed that, even under these circumstances, minorities can still exert an important influence on majorities but only if they are consistent in their behavioral style. If a minority consistently insists on its position, a majority will not be able to ignore the minority even though they still believe that the minority's position is incorrect. Also, members assume that a minority status is disadvantageous and that there is little incentive for the minority to insist on its position unless the minority sincerely believes that position. The inevitable inference, then, is that the minority members must be really and truly convinced that their position is correct (Kelley, 1973). As a consequence, the majority members will begin to think about possible perspectives and potential arguments that may cause the minority to believe so strongly in their position.

To illustrate, let us examine Paul's case again. In their attempt to make sense of Paul's deviant behavior, the other members of the fraternity (i.e., the majority) may begin generating arguments that would explain Paul's (the minority's) position. Naturally, these self-generated arguments would on the whole support his position. As a consequence, the members will start to see some reasonable points to what Paul has been saying, which they had not thought about before. Their private opinions may then gradually change. In short, minority influence is likely to be mediated by issue-relevant thoughts activated in members of the majority by the consistent, deviant behavior of a minority, and it is likely to induce private change of opinion. (See Chapter 6 by Petty et al. for a discussion of the persuasive effects of self-generated thoughts.)

Minority Influence versus Majority Influence

Moscovici (e.g., Moscovici & Faucheux, 1972) has argued that the cognitive processes involved in generating arguments to explain a deviant position occur primarily when the deviant is a minority in the group and that these processes are unlikely when a deviant position is taken by a majority (see Maass & Clark, 1984; Nemeth, 1986, for reviews). In the case of majority influence, several factors work in concert to reduce the likelihood that members will engage in issue-relevant thinking. First, a member may decide to conform publicly to the majority without thinking seriously or deeply about arguments explaining what may have caused the majority to take the position they did. As we noted earlier, conformity is often a tactic to gain approval from a majority (i.e., normative influence). If the concern for approval dominates one's decision to go along with others, then very few issue-relevant thoughts are likely to be generated. Further, belonging to the majority has some obvious advantages, such as higher status and power within the group. Recognition of these facts by naive individuals makes them uncertain whether the majority members hold to their position because they really believe it or because they benefit from belonging to the majority. We are much less likely to think that a member belongs to a minority because of the benefits this status confers. Thus, the credibility of the majority is more likely to be in doubt than that of a minority. All in all, then, when faced with a deviant position, individuals attend to the issue and attempt to understand the deviant perspective only if those holding this perspective constitute a minority, not a majority.

Support for this analysis comes from a recent experiment by Atsumi and Burnstein (1991). They examined whether the judgmental accuracy of a naive member is influenced more by an inaccurate majority or an inaccurate minority. Subjects in the experiment participated in groups of six. Each subject was seated in front of a computer screen, on which a 10×10 matrix was displayed. Some of the 100 slots in the matrix were filled with circles, and the remaining were not filled. Subjects' task was to judge whether and to what extent the filled slots exceeded 50% of the total slots. Atsumi and Burnstein reasoned that the accuracy in this judgment should increase when individuals pay more attention to the stimulus pattern, whereas it should decrease if they pay less attention. Each participant observed the responses allegedly made by the other members *before* the participant made his or her own judgment. In fact, this information about the others' judgments had been rigged so that on some trials, all five of the others' judgments were incorrect (majority condition), whereas on some trials, only two of them were incorrect (minority condition).

These researchers found that the accuracy of judgments increased in the minority condition but decreased in the majority condition. Their result clearly supports the hypothesis that members should pay more attention to the issue in question when a deviant position is taken by a minority than when the identical position is taken by a majority. Notice also that this experiment suggests a little dissent in a group is beneficial. It induces more critical evaluation of the issue and, as a consequence, makes for a more accurate group decision.

Additional and interesting support for the hypothesis that individuals attempt to understand a minority position rather than a majority position comes from a study by Maass and Clark (1983). In a group discussion about gay rights, individuals were more likely to agree with a majority position when their opinions had to be expressed in public than when they had to be expressed in private, but they were more likely to agree with a minority position when their opinions could be expressed in private rather than in public (see also Nemeth & Wachtler, 1974; Maass & Clark, 1984; Nemeth, 1986, for reviews). Thus, majority influence results mostly in public compliance without private acceptance. Minority influence, however, can lead to private acceptance in the absence of any noticeable influence in public.

The Active Minority and Social Change

All in all, there is considerable evidence that minorities can influence majorities by inducing issue-relevant thought congruent with the minority position. Having said this, however, we hasten to point out that it still is fairly rare that minorities have substantial impacts on majorities in everyday life. For example, Kalven and Zeisel (1966; cited in Nemeth, 1986, p. 23) analyzed 225 juries and found that the majority position on the first ballot became the final verdict in over 85% of the cases.

Perhaps this should not come as any surprise. After all, there are many hurdles to be cleared before minorities can produce significant change in both the private beliefs and the public behaviors of majorities. To begin with, it may take considerable time for minority members to make majority members *notice* as well as think about their deviant position. And supposing that the minority is successful in getting the majority to examine its position, this in no way guarantees that the majority will come up with cogent arguments that support the minority position.

Even in the best of circumstances, when the majority members do come up with relevant arguments in favor of the minority position, there still exists another major hurdle. The minority will have to overcome *pluralistic ignorance*.

Imagine that you are a member of the fraternity where Paul and his brothers are discussing their alcohol policy. Further, suppose that you have been convinced by Paul, in private, that it is necessary to have a more strict alcohol policy. Even if you are so convinced, you may not express your opinion because you *think* that other fraternity members are still opposed to such a position. Now, what if the other members, one by one, have also been persuaded by Paul so that virtually everyone in the group agrees with Paul in private? Will anything happen? Maybe not—for everyone believes that everyone else is still opposed to a strict alcohol policy. When, as in this case, people behave in the same way based on a wrong yet widely shared belief, the phenomenon is called *pluralistic ignorance*. If everybody publicly maintains their old position, breaking the consensus can be quite difficult even when all of them have been privately converted to a minority position.

Group Discussion

So far, we have discussed majority influence and minority influence separately. In real life, of course, these two forms of influence are mutual and simultaneous. Indeed, group discussion, the typical medium of influence in groups, has certain characteristics that cannot be fully captured when the interaction is divided into majority influence and minority influence. We will now turn to these more dynamic characteristics of group discussion (see Figure 8-3).

Group-Induced Opinion Shift

The Risky Shift
Imagine a college senior who is very eager to pursue graduate study in chemistry leading to the Doctor of Philosophy degree. He has been accepted by both University X and University Y. University X has a worldwide reputation for excellence in chemistry. While a degree from University X would signify outstanding training in this field, the standards are so rigorous that only a fraction of the degree candidates actually receive the degree. University Y, on the other hand, has much less of a reputation in chemistry, but almost everyone admitted is awarded the Doctor of Philosophy degree, though the degree has much less prestige than the corresponding degree from University X.

In many everyday situations, an attractive course of action often entails greater risk than a less attractive course of action. Thus, a dilemma arises: Should we take a chance and go for it, or should we be more cautious? These dilemmas can be highly dramatic, as when the president of a nation and his or her advisers formulate their policies in international and domestic crises; or more mundane but still important, as when corporate managers evaluate the pros and cons of their investment plans. Having a group discussion in these circumstances may make perfect sense, especially when the stakes involved are very high.

Because group decisions require consensus and compromise, one might expect them to be more conservative, prudent, and cautious than individual decisions. In 1961, however, Stoner reported an effect that challenged this naive belief. He dis-

"I understand Mr. Gunderson has an idea he'd like to toss in the hopper."

FIGURE 8-3   Intimidation in group discussion

Source: Drawing by Saxon; © 1986 The New Yorker Magazine, Inc.

covered that individual opinions become *riskier* after group discussion. In the next 20 years or so, there was an explosion of studies that tried to understand this phenomenon.

Group Polarization

Once researchers began studying the *risky shift*, it gradually became clear, somewhat ironically, that *risky* was a sort of misnomer. Their findings indicated that group discussion sometimes does produce more cautious decisions than those made by individuals prior to discussion. From a number of subsequent studies, a fairly simple rule of thumb emerged in predicting which shift would occur in group discussion: Discussion leads members to make more extreme decisions in the direction toward which they were initially inclined. For example, if, on the whole, members favor a risky course in private prior to discussion, they will choose an even riskier option after discussion; however, if, on the whole, they initially favor a cautious course, discussion will lead them to become even more cautious. Thus, the initial risky shift effect was a special case of a more general effect of group discussion, namely, that discussion produces opinions that are more extreme than those held by the members before they entered into the discussion.

Furthermore, some researchers have demonstrated an analogous shift of opinions through group discussion with a wide variety of topics unrelated to risk. Moscovici and Zavalloni (1969), for example, found that French university students who initially disapproved of U.S. foreign policy or who initially admired the policies of General DeGaulle evidenced even greater disapproval or admiration, respectively, after group discussion of these issues (see Doise, 1969, as well as reviews by Isenberg, 1986, and Myers & Lamm, 1976). Again, the rule of thumb is that group discussion induces more extreme opinions or beliefs. In other words, group discussion typically *polarizes* individuals' positions. These findings, as a whole, now constitute the phenomenon referred to as *group polarization*.

Theories of Group Polarization

How can group polarization be explained? A number of possibilities have been examined in the past 30 years. Here we will focus on the two that have received the most research attention: social comparison theory and persuasive argument theory. There are some close connections between these theories and some of the theoretical ideas we examined earlier in this chapter. On the one hand, we have social comparison theory, which assumes that individuals shift their opinions so as to gain approval or to be accepted by other group members. This theory therefore says, basically, that group polarization is due to *normative* influence. On the other hand, persuasive argument theory holds that group polarization is a necessary consequence of the argumentation that occurs in group discussion. This theory therefore emphasizes the role of issue-relevant thinking and views group polarization as due to *informational* influence.

Social Comparison

How can a concern about social approval lead to polarization? The earliest answer appeared in an analysis by Roger Brown (1965). He assumed that relatively extreme opinions are socially approved and that people who present themselves in this fashion are liked. Which extreme happens to be the socially approved one depends on what the values actually are. Brown argued that, at least in Western culture, a greater value seems to be placed on riskiness in such domains as games, careers, and business, whereas in such domains as health, family, and loved ones, prudence is more valued. According to this theory, members constantly compare their own positions with the positions of others in the group and strive to present themselves as at least as extreme as the others—so comes the name, *social comparison* (see also Mackie, 1986, for another more recent version of normative influence in group polarization).

One seemingly straightforward implication of social comparison theory is that group polarization should occur even when one only knows other members' choices. No discussion should be necessary. This in fact turns out to be the case (Sanders & Baron, 1977; Goethals & Zanna, 1979). However, the amount of polarization under these conditions is substantially smaller than in more naturalistic conditions in which actual discussion takes place. Thus, it is unlikely that social comparison is the only mechanism underlying group polarization.

Persuasive Argument

The other important theory of group polarization assumes that it is issue-relevant thoughts exchanged during discussion that lead to opinion polarization (Burnstein, 1982; Burnstein & Vinokur, 1977). According to the theory, on any given issue, there is a pool of arguments available in the culture, some of which favor one position and others of which favor the alternative position. These arguments, however, are not always shared; any given person usually thinks of only some of these arguments. Through group discussion, initially unshared arguments are exchanged and become widely available. And it is these arguments that are newly gained in discussion that lead to polarization.

This theory explains why group discussion polarizes opinions in a popular direction—one that most members were leaning toward prior to discussion. Such a position is popular precisely because, within the culture, arguments that favor that position are more numerous and more persuasive than those that favor the alternative position (Vinokur & Burnstein, 1974, 1978; see also Myers & Lamm, 1976). In discussion, members are likely to discover more and better reasons for having made the choices they did and, hence, polarize their positions.

Groupthink

Late in the Eisenhower administration the CIA concocted a plan to send 1,400 trained exiles into Cuba to overthrow Fidel Castro. When the Kennedy administration took over, the plan was presented to the president and his advisers. Some of the latter individuals had deep misgiving about the plan. They knew, however, that Kennedy wanted an operation of this kind. As a result, when as a group they decided to go ahead with the CIA plan, none of them gave voice to their misgivings. It turned out to be a fiasco. Afterward they lamented: "How could we have been so stupid?"

The research we have reviewed thus far is based mostly on laboratory experiments. One might ask, therefore, whether the phenomena and theoretical principles identified in this work have any relevance to more naturalistic groups. In his seminal work on group decision making, Janis (1971) showed that a number of psychological factors, including those we have discussed, can have some very powerful consequences in the real world. Specifically, these factors conspire to create a phenomenon called *groupthink*, which causes defective group decisions. In this section, we will discuss some pitfalls of group discussion that have made history, such as the ones exemplified by the Kennedy administration's infamous decision to invade Cuba in 1961, and suggest possible ways of avoiding these pitfalls.

Groupthink occurs when members of a cohesive group have a strong desire to achieve and maintain consensus and unity. This tendency toward concurrence seeking overrides the group's realistic appraisals of their alternatives. As a result, the group decision has a good chance of being defective. When the members' need to agree becomes excessive, they tend to generate arguments that allow the group as a whole to rationalize their preexisting positions. Dissent is not welcome. The members become extremely reluctant to communicate disagreements with what they perceive to be the established consensus. This reluctance to openly disagree, deriving from each individual's desire to secure social approval, leads to an illusory confidence in the group decision and to the unwarranted belief that the decision is universally accepted, that it has the status of a group norm, and that, as such, it is inviolable. In groupthink, the group itself becomes sacrosanct. In Janis's own words, there arise both an "unquestioned belief in the group's morality" and an "illusion of unanimity" so that the issues raised and the arguments made tend to be detached from the outside realities.

Janis demonstrated that the tendency toward groupthink can be seen in well-known policy decisions made by the nation's highest officials. He analyzed and compared several good and bad policy decisions made by U.S. presidents and their advisers. Drawing on historical documents, Janis concluded that the tendency toward groupthink has been the cause of numerous blunders in several administrations. As mentioned earlier, one well-known instance occurred during the Kennedy administration when the president and his advisers blindly adopted a jerry-rigged plan to invade Cuba. Janis observed virtually every symptom of groupthink among cabinet members of the Kennedy administration during their discussion of the invasion plan. For example, one cabinet member at that time, Arthur Schlesinger (1965), frankly admitted at a later date that "I can only explain my failure to do more than raise a few timid questions by reporting that one's impulse to blow the whistle on this nonsense was *simply undone by the circumstances of the discussion*" (p. 255; emphasis added). According to Janis, Schlesinger greatly valued his membership in this very powerful and prestigious group and imposed *self-censorship* in order not only to maintain consensus in the group but also, in the long run, to avoid rejection by other cabinet members as well as by the president himself.

A later instance of groupthink can be found in the decision to escalate the Vietnam War, taken in a series of meetings from 1965 to 1970 by the Johnson administration. In his recent memoirs, Clark Clifford, a private adviser to President Johnson during the escalation in Vietnam, recounted that, on one occasion, when he tried to raise doubts about the president's decision to renew bombing, the secretary of state, Dean Rusk, quickly interrupted and "immediately shifted the discussion to other matters" (Clifford, 1991, p. 63). Rusk, in this example, volunteered to protect the president from potential dissent. Janis called such an individual a *mind guard*. A mind guard protects a leader from a potential threat to his positions, arguments, and beliefs, just as a body guard protects him from a physical assault.

The self-restraint exercised by Schlesinger and the mind-guard role assumed by Rusk are subtle yet extremely powerful means to secure group consensus. At the same time, these behaviors reduce the likelihood that external reality is appraised in a balanced and comprehensive fashion. Thus, they are a precursor of defective group decisions.

Remedies for Groupthink

What can prevent groups from falling prey to groupthink? Janis has suggested several possibilities. First, it is important to bring in outside experts who have no vested interest in the group in order to present a broad range of ideas and to have members of the group debate alternative positions with the outsiders. Second, the leader must establish a norm that encourages the critical examination of all possible courses of action. Third, the leader must remain impartial and avoid publicly stating his or her view during discussion.

To this list, we may add a few more. Hierarchical structure is a fact of life. In real groups, differences in power are salient to members. This leads inevitably to a heightened need for social approval and acceptance among subordinates. Because the need for approval and the desire for acceptance are major conditions for groupthink, procedures that make hierarchy and social approval less salient should reduce the likelihood of groupthink. To begin with, it is important for leaders not to make their approval contingent on remarks made by other members in discussion. Instead, leaders have to make it clear that the members have their support and trust *regardless of the position taken by them*. In order to demonstrate that support and trust are nonconditional, the leader must give evidence of it to subordinates, not only in task settings but also in more informal, nonwork domains. In this way, a concern for social approval may cease to be a major source of bias when critical decisions are made. A further possibility, noted by Janis, as well, is to form subgroups or subcommittees that have no formal leader in order to discuss critical issues before they are raised as formal matters in the larger group. In nonhierarchical subgroups of this kind, social approval is likely to be only a minor concern. All of this is in the service of unbiased and thorough argumentation in the group, without which the possibility of groupthink always looms.

Summary

In this chapter, we have reviewed a few lines of research that are fundamental to our understanding of persuasive processes in groups. A major distinction is made between persuasion produced by a majority and that produced by a minority. It was shown that different theoretical terms are required to describe these two forms of social influence. In a nutshell, majority influence generally results in public compliance without necessarily producing private acceptance. Minority influence, however, usually entails private acceptance without necessarily producing any public sign of acceptance. Finally, factors relevant in our understanding of majority and minority influence are also closely implicated in more naturalistic group discussions; they operate in concert to produce such intriguing phenomena as group polarization and groupthink.

References

Allen, V. L. (1965). Situational factors in conformity. In L. Berkowitz (Ed.), *Advances in experimental social psychology* (Vol. 2, pp. 133–170). New York: Academic Press.

Allen, V. L., & Levine, J. M. (1969). Consensus and conformity. *Journal of Experimental Social Psychology, 5*, 389–399.

Asch, S. E. (1951). Effects of group pressure upon the modification and distortion of judgments. In H. Guetzkow (Ed.), *Groups, leadership, and men* (pp. 177–190). Pittsburgh, PA: Carnegie Press.

Asch, S. E. (1956). Studies of independence and submission to group pressure: I. A minority of one against a unanimous majority. *Psychological Monograph, 70*, No. 9 (Whole No. 416).

Atsumi, T., & Burnstein, E. (1991). Is minority influence different from majority influence? Unpublished manuscript, University of Michigan.

Brown, R. (1965). *Social psychology* (1st ed.). New York: Free Press.

Burnstein, E. (1982). Persuasion as argument processing. In H. Brandstatter, J. H. David, & G. Stocker-Dreichgauer (Eds.), *Group decision making* (pp. 103–124). London: Academic Press.

Burnstein, E., & Vinokur, A. (1977). Persuasive arguments and social comparison as determinants of attitude polarization. *Journal of Experimental Social Psychology, 13*, 315–332.

Clifford, C. (1991, May 20). Serving the president: The Vietnam years. *The New Yorker.*

Crutchfield, R. A. (1955). Conformity and character. *American Psychologist, 10*, 191–198.

Deutsch, M., & Gerard, H. B. (1955). A study of normative and informational social influences upon individual judgment. *Journal of Abnormal and Social Psychology, 51*, 626–636.

Doise, W. (1969). Intergroup relations and polarization of individual and collective judgments. *Journal of Personality and Social Psychology, 12*, 136–143.

Ehrenreich, B. (1991, April 8). Teach diversity—with a smile. *Time*, p. 84.

Gerard, H. B., Wilhelmy, R. A., & Conolley, E. S. (1968). Conformity and group size. *Journal of Personality and Social Psychology, 8*, 79–82.

Goethals, G. R., & Zanna, M. P. (1979). The role of social comparison in choice shifts. *Journal of Personality and Social Psychology, 37*, 1469–1476.

Isenberg, D. J. (1986). Group polarization: A critical review and meta-analysis. *Journal of Personality and Social Psychology, 50*, 1141–1151.

Janis, I. L. (1971). *Victims of groupthink.* Boston: Houghton Mifflin.

Kalven, H., Jr., & Zeisel, H. (1966). *The American jury.* Boston: Little, Brown.

Kelley, H. H. (1973). The processes of causal attribution. *American Psychologist, 28*, 107–128.

Kitayama, S., Burnstein, E., & Nelson, T. (1987). Effects of thinking time and group composition of a majority on social influence. Paper presented at the annual meeting of the American Psychological Association, New York, NY.

Latané, B., & Wolf, S. (1981). The social impact of majorities and minorities. *Psychological Review, 88*, 438–453.

Maass, A., & Clark, R. D., III. (1983). Internalization versus compliance: Differential processes underlying minority influence and conformity. *European Journal of Social Psychology, 13*, 197–215.

Maass, A., & Clark, R. D., III. (1984). The hidden impact of minorities: Fifteen years of minorities influence research. *Psychological Bulletin, 95*, 428–450.

Mackie, D. M. (1986). Social identification effects in group polarization. *Journal of Personality and Social Psychology, 50*, 720–728.

Moscovici, S., & Faucheux, C. (1972). Social influence, conforming bias, and the study of active minorities. In L. Berkowitz (Ed.), *Advances in experimental social psychology* (Vol. 6, pp. 149–202). New York: Academic Press.

Moscovici, S., & Zavalloni, M. (1969). The group as a polarizer of attitudes. *Journal of Personality and Social Psychology, 12*, 125–135.

Myers, D. G., & Lamm, H. (1976). The group polarization phenomenon. *Psychological Bulletin, 83,* 602–627.

Nemeth, C. (1986). Differential contributions of majority and minority influence. *Psychological Review, 93,* 23–32.

Nemeth, C., Swedlund, M., & Kanki, G. (1974). Patterning of the minority's responses and their influence on the majority. *European Journal of Social Psychology, 4,* 53–64.

Nemeth, C., & Wachtler, J. (1974). Creating the perceptions of consistency and confidence: A necessary condition for minority influence. *Sociometry, 37,* 529–540.

Rosenberg, L. A. (1961). Group size, prior experience, and conformity. *Journal of Abnormal and Social Psychology, 63,* 436–437.

Ross, L., Bierbrauer, G., & Hoffman, S. (1976). The role of attribution processes in conformity and dissent: Revising the Asch situation. *American Psychologist, 31,* 148–157.

Sanders, G., & Baron, R. S. (1977). Is social comparison irrelevant for producing choice shifts? *Journal of Experimental Social Psychology, 13,* 303–314.

Schachter, S. (1951). Deviation, rejection and communication. *Journal of Abnormal and Social Psychology, 46,* 190–207.

Schlesinger, A. M., Jr. (1965). *A thousand days.* Boston: Houghton Mifflin.

Sherif, M. (1935). *The psychology of social norms.* New York: Harper & Row.

Stoner, J. A. F. (1961). A comparison of individual and group decision involving risk. Unpublished masters thesis, Massachusetts Institute of Technology (Cited by D. G. Marguis in Individual responsibility and group decisions involving risk. *Industrial Management Review, 3,* 8–23.

Tanford, S., & Penrod, S. (1984). Social influence model: A formal integration of research on majority and minority influence processes. *Psychological Bulletin, 95,* 189–225.

Vinokur, A., & Burnstein, E. (1974). The effects of partially shared persuasive arguments in group-induced shifts: A group problem solving approach. *Journal of Personality and Social Psychology, 29,* 305–315.

Vinokur, A., & Burnstein, E. (1978). Depolarization of attitudes in groups. *Journal of Personality and Social Psychology, 36,* 872–885.

Wilder, D. A. (1977). Perception of groups, size of opposition, and social influence. *Journal of Experimental Social Psychology, 13,* 253–268.

9

INTERPERSONAL INFLUENCE

ROBERT B. CIALDINI
Arizona State University

Have you ever been tricked into saying yes? Ever felt trapped into buying something you didn't really want or contributing to some cause you had hardly heard of? And have you ever wished you understood why you acted in this way so that you could withstand these clever ploys in the future?

Yes? Well, then, it's clear to me that this little chapter I have here is perfect for you. It contains all kinds of valuable information on the most powerful psychological pressures that get us to say yes to requests. And it is chock full of new, improved evidence from research showing exactly how and why these pressures work on us the way they do. What's more, because I like you (and I genuinely do like you), I am going to throw in—at no extra cost—a list of references to which you can go to learn more about this fascinating topic you've already told me holds great interest for you. So, if you don't mind, I'll just step right in and show you this chapter that, I think you'll agree, is destined to change your life for the better.

The scientific study of the interpersonal influence process has been with us for nearly half a century, beginning with the government public information and persuasion programs of World War II (e.g., Hovland, Lumsdaine, & Sheffield, 1949). Since that time, numerous social scientists have investigated the ways in which one individual can influence another individual's attitudes, beliefs, perceptions, or behaviors. For the past 15 years, I have been a fascinated participant in the endeavor, concentrating primarily on the major factors that bring about behavior change. More specifically, I have explored a certain type of behavior change—*com-*

pliance, which can be defined as action that is taken only because it has been requested. The process of generating compliance, then, refers to the process of getting others to say yes to a request. In other words, it is the science of getting what you ask for.

When I first undertook to research compliance, it was (1) to determine the most powerful influences on our everyday decisions to say yes to a request and (2) to understand why these powerful influences work so successfully. Very quickly, a critical question arose: How does one determine which are the most powerful compliance principles and tactics? After a while, an answer struck me: By observing systematically what the commercial compliance professionals do—the people who have been using these principles and tactics on me all my life.

The Evolution of Powerful Compliance Principles Within Compliance Professions

Who are the commercial compliance professionals, and why should we study their actions for clues to the factors that influence everyday compliance decisions? *Compliance professionals* can be defined as those individuals whose business or financial well-being is dependent on their ability to induce compliance (e.g., salespeople, fundraisers, advertisers, political lobbyists, cult recruiters, con artists). With this definition in place, one can begin to recognize why the regular and widespread practices of these professionals would be noteworthy indicators of the powerful influences on the compliance process: A law not unlike that of natural selection assures it. That is, because the livelihoods of commercial compliance professionals depend on the effectiveness of their procedures, those professionals who use procedures that work well to elicit compliance responses will survive and flourish. Further, they will pass these successful procedures on (somewhat like genes) to succeeding generations (e.g., trainees). However, those practitioners who use unsuccessful compliance procedures either will drop them or will quickly go out of business; in either case, the procedures themselves will not be passed on to newer generations.

Several years ago, I resolved to become a careful observer of commercial compliance pros. Accordingly, I took training or employment in a host of compliance professions, keeping my true identity and purposes unknown to those around me.[1] In this fashion, it was possible to learn which compliance procedures were being used and taught across an array of merchandising, advertising, direct sales, promotion, and fundraising concerns. These firsthand experiences were supplemented with information from other sources, such as instructional materials (e.g., sales-training texts, handbooks on lobbying techniques) and personal interviews with especially successful practitioners. In the process, I looked for overarching compliance principles, that is, those principles that (a) occurred in a multitude of versions, (b) appeared across the range of compliance professions, (c) were employable by the greatest number of compliance practitioners, and (d) had been successfully used historically.

The Principles

Which were the pervasive principles of influence that emerged from this analysis? Six stood out from the rest: reciprocity, social validation, commitment/consistency, friendship/liking, scarcity, and authority. A full account of the origins, workings, and prevalence of the six principles is available elsewhere (Cialdini, 1988). However, the material presented in the following sections offers a summary of the results of my investigations. It is organized around the six social psychological principles that appeared from my evidence to be most implicated in naturally occurring compliance.[2] The implications for compliance that come from each principle are also discussed, as are the common tactics that activate the principles. Additionally, the treatment of each principle includes an attempt to offer experimental data on the relevant hows and whys of the compliance process.

Reciprocity

According to the sociologist Alvin Gouldner (1960), who made an extensive review of the subject, every human society trains its members to live by the rule for reciprocity, which obligates people to give back the form of behavior they have received. So, gifts are to be met with return gifts, favors with return favors, benefits with return benefits, and so on. It is this sense of obligation to give back to those who have given first that forms a stimulus for compliance. People tend to say yes when they feel obligated to a requester who has previously provided them with some service or concession. To do otherwise would be to risk being labeled as a moocher or taker or ingrate—labels everyone wishes to avoid.

Sometimes the effects of the rule for reciprocity are so great that we find people performing acts that under no other circumstances would have occurred, except for an existing obligation to repay. For instance, recently the Red Cross of Ethiopia—a country that can fairly lay claim to the greatest privation, suffering, and need in the world—donated $5,000 to the victims of the 1985 earthquake in Mexico City. When stunned reporters asked why, the answer came back clearly: Because in 1935, when Italy invaded Ethiopia, Mexico had sent aid. The rule for reciprocity and its attendant sense of obligation can be as forceful, elemental, and long lasting as that.

A widely shared feeling of future obligation made an enormous difference in human social evolution because it meant that one person could give something (e.g., food, energy, care) to another with confidence that it was not being lost. For the first time in evolutionary history, one individual could give away any of a variety of resources without actually giving them away. Thus, a person could provide help, gifts, defense, or trade goods to others in the group knowing that, when the time came, he or she could count on their repayment. Sophisticated and coordinated systems of gift giving, defense, and trade became possible, bringing immense benefit to the societies that possessed them. With such clearly adaptive consequences for the culture, it is not surprising that the norm for reciprocation is so deeply implanted in us by the process of socialization we all undergo.

A reciprocation principle for compliance can be worded as follows: *One should be more willing to comply with a request from someone who has previously provided a favor or concession.* Under this general principle, then, people will sometimes be willing to return a favor with a larger favor (e.g., Regan, 1971). A number of sales and fundraising tactics use this factor to their own advantage. The compliance professional initially gives something to the target person, thereby causing the target to be more likely to give something in return. Often, this "something in return" is the target person's compliance.

The unsolicited gift, accompanied by a request for a donation, is a commonly used technique that employs the norm for reciprocation. One example experienced by many people is the Hare Krishna solicitor who gives the unwary passerby a book or a flower and then asks for a donation. Other organizations send free gifts through the mail; legitimate and less-than-legitimate missionary and disabled veterans organizations often employ this highly effective device. These organizations count on the fact that most people will not go to the trouble of returning the gift and will feel uncomfortable about keeping it without reciprocating in some way. The organizations also count on the willingness of people to send a contribution that is larger than the cost of the gift they received.

Retail stores and services also make use of the powerful social pressure for reciprocation in their sales techniques. It is not uncommon to find exterminating companies that offer free home inspections. These companies bargain on the fact that, once confronted with the knowledge that a home is infested with termites, the consumer will not delay action until he or she has done some comparison shopping. A customer who feels indebted to a particular company will buy its services to repay the favor of a free examination. Certain companies, knowing that the customer is unlikely to comparison shop, have been known to raise the quoted price of extermination above normal for those who have requested a free inspection.

Reciprocal Concessions

A variation of the norm for reciprocation of favors is that for reciprocation of concessions. A reciprocal concessions procedure (or *door-in-the-face technique*) for inducing compliance has been documented by Cialdini, Vincent, Lewis, Catalan, Wheeler, and Darby (1975). A requester uses this procedure by beginning with an extreme request that is nearly always rejected and then retreating to a more moderate favor—the one the requester had in mind from the outset. In doing so, the requester hopes that the retreat from extreme to moderate request will spur the target person to make a reciprocal concession—by moving from initial rejection of the larger favor to acceptance of the smaller one (see Figure 9-1). This reciprocal concessions strategy has been successfully used in fundraising contexts where, after refusing a larger request for donations, people are substantially more likely than before to give an average-size contribution (e.g., Reingen, 1978).

Cialdini and Ascani (1976) also used this technique in soliciting blood donors. They first requested a person's involvement in a long-term donor program. When

FIGURE 9-1 The door-in-the-face technique—sequence is everything

Source: Reprinted with special permission of King Features Syndicate.

that request was refused, the solicitor made a smaller request for a one-time dona-tion. This pattern of a large request (that is refused) followed by a smaller request significantly increased compliance with the smaller request, as compared to a con-trol condition of people who were asked only to perform the smaller, one-time favor (50% versus 32% compliance rate).

Of special interest to college students is evidence that the door-in-the-face tech-nique can greatly increase a university professor's willingness to spend time help-ing a student (Harari, Mohr, & Hosey, 1980). In that study, only 59% of faculty members were willing to spend "15–20 minutes" to meet with a student on an issue of interest to the student when that was the only request the student made. However, significantly more faculty (78%) were willing to agree to that same request if they had first refused the student's request to spend "2 hours a week for the rest of the semester" meeting with the student.

Related to the door-in-the-face technique but somewhat different from it is the *that's-not-all technique* investigated by Burger (1986) and frequently used by sales operators (see Figure 9-2). An important procedural difference between the two tech-niques is that, in the that's-not-all tactic, the target person does not turn down the first offer before a better, second offer is provided. After making the first offer but before the target can respond, the requester betters the deal with an additional item or a price reduction. Burger (1986) found this approach to be useful in selling more cup-cakes during a campus bake sale. One reason, but not the only reason, that this tech-nique works appears to be the target person's desire to reciprocate for the better deal.

Social Validation

The principle of social validation states that one means we use to determine what is correct is to find out what other people think is correct (see Chapter 8 by Kitayama and Burnstein). Thus, we view a behavior as more correct in a given sit-uation to the degree that we see others performing it. Whether the question is what to do with an empty popcorn box in a theater, how fast to drive on a certain stretch

"How much would you pay for all the secrets of the universe? Wait, don't answer yet. You also get this six-quart covered combination spaghetti pot and clam steamer. Now how much would you pay?"

FIGURE 9-2   The that's-not-all technique

Source: Drawing by Maslin; © 1981 The New Yorker Magazine, Inc.

of highway, or how to eat the chicken at a dinner party, the actions of those around us will importantly define the answer.

The tendency to see an action as more appropriate when others are doing it normally works quite well. As a rule, we will make many fewer mistakes by acting in accord with social evidence than contrary to it. Usually, when a lot of people are doing something, it is the right thing to do. That is why the more people who are performing a behavior, the stronger is our likelihood of doing it, too. Anyone who doubts that the seeming appropriateness of an action is importantly influenced by the number of others performing it might try a small experiment. Stand on a busy sidewalk, pick an empty spot in the sky or on a tall building, and stare at it for a full minute. Very little will happen around you during that time—most people will walk past without glancing up, and virtually no one will stop to stare with you. Now, on the next day, go to the same place and bring along four friends to look upward, too. Within 60 seconds, a crowd of passersby will have stopped to crane their necks skyward with the group. For those pedestrians who do not join you, the pressure to look up at least briefly will be nearly irresistible; if the results of your experiment are like those of one performed by three New York social psychologists, you and your friends will cause 80% of all passersby to lift their gazes to your empty spot (Milgram, Bickman, & Berkowitz, 1969).

In addition to the *number* of others, the *similarity* of those others to us plays an important role in determining how we will see the correctness of an action (Festinger, 1954). Powerful modeling effects of similar others have been found in such diverse activities as altruism (e.g., Hornstein, Fisch, & Holmes, 1968), paint store purchases (Brock, 1965), and suicides (Phillips, 1974). In each case, the more similar an observer was to someone taking an action, the more likely it was that the observer would follow suit.

The social validation rule for compliance can be stated as follows: *One should be more willing to comply with a request for behavior if it is consistent with what similar others are thinking or doing.* Our tendency to assume that an action is more correct if others are doing it is exploited in a variety of settings. Bartenders often "salt" their tip jars with a few dollar bills at the beginning of the evening to simulate tips left by prior customers and, thereby, to give the impression that tipping with folding money is proper barroom behavior. Church ushers sometimes prime collection baskets for the same reason and with the same positive effect on proceeds. Evangelical preachers are known to seed their audiences with "ringers," who are rehearsed to come forward at a specified time to give witness and donations. For example, an Arizona State University research team that infiltrated the Billy Graham organization reported on such advance preparations prior to one of his Crusade visits. "By the time Graham arrives in town and makes his altar call, an army of 6,000 await with instructions on when to come forth at varying intervals to create the impression of spontaneous mass outpouring" (Altheide & Johnson, 1977). Advertisers love to inform us when a product is the "fastest growing" or "largest selling" because they do not have to convince us directly that the product is good; they need only say that many others think so, which seems proof enough. The producers of charity telethons devote inordinate amounts of time to the incessant listing of viewers who have already pledged contributions. The message being communicated to the holdouts is clear: Look at all the people who have decided to give; it *must* be the correct thing to do.

Among the multitude of clever ways that compliance professionals have managed to commission the principle of social validation in their behalf, two have been specifically investigated as compliance techniques by social scientists. The first, called the *list technique*, involves asking for a request only after the target person has been shown a list of similar others who have already complied. Reingen (1982) conducted several experiments in which college students or homeowners were asked to donate money or blood to a charitable cause. Those individuals who were initially shown a list of similar others who had already complied were significantly more likely to comply themselves. What's more, the longer the list, the greater was the effect.

A second social validation–based compliance technique to undergo controlled investigation is the *social labeling technique*. Here, the target person is informed that certain others have labeled him or her in a specific way. Later, the target person is found to be more willing to comply with requests that are in keeping with that label. Perhaps the clearest such labeling effect comes from a study by Kraut (1973). One week after being labeled as charitable people, New Haven, Connecticut, homeowners gave more money to a canvasser from the Multiple Sclerosis Association than those who had not been so labeled earlier. Other studies have confirmed the effectiveness of the labeling technique among both adults (Swinyard & Ray, 1977) and children (Grusec & Redler, 1980; Miller, Brickman, & Bolen, 1975).

Commitment/Consistency

"Consistency is the hobgoblin of little minds." Or, at least, so goes a frequently heard quotation attributed to Ralph Waldo Emerson. But what a very odd thing to say. Looking around today, just the reverse appears to be the case. It seems that those among us who are *inconsistent* are the ones thought to be intellectually limited. The woman who changes her mind again and again is considered flighty or scatterbrained. The man whose opinions can be easily influenced is viewed as indecisive and weak willed. The person whose beliefs, words, and deeds do not match is seen as confused, at best. And disjointed behavior is regarded as a key symptom of mental illness.

Quite contrary to what Emerson seems to have suggested, consistency is normally associated with intellectual strength. A high degree of consistency is at the heart of logic, rationality, stability, and even honesty. Certainly, good consistency within one's thoughts, words, and actions is highly valued in American society. And well it should be. It provides us with a reasonable and adaptive orientation to the world. Most of the time, we will be better off if our approach to things is well laced with consistency.

Social psychologists have long understood the strength of the consistency principle to direct human action. Prominent theorists like Leon Festinger (1957), Fritz Heider (1958), and Theodore Newcomb (1953) have viewed the desire for consistency as a prime motivator of our behavior. (One important example is cognitive dissonance theory, described by Cooper and Scher in Chapter 5.) More recently, other theorists (e.g., Baumeister, 1982; Tedeschi, 1981) have recognized that the desire to *appear* consistent exerts considerable influence over our behavior, as well. If we grant that the power of consistency is formidable in directing human action, an important practical question immediately arises: How is that force engaged? Social psychologists think they know the answer—commitment. If I can get you to make a commitment (that is, to take a stand, to go on record), I will have set the stage for your consistency with that earlier commitment. Once a stand has been taken, there is a natural tendency to behave in ways that are stubbornly consistent with the stand (Deutsch & Gerard, 1955; Kiesler, 1971).

A commitment/consistency principle for compliance can be worded as follows: *After committing oneself to a position, one should be more willing to comply with requests for behaviors that are consistent with that position.* Any of a variety of strategies may be used to generate the crucial instigating commitment. One such strategy is called the *four-walls technique* (see Figure 9-3). It was the one I used at the

FIGURE 9-3   The four-walls technique

Source: U.S. ACRES reprinted by permission of UFS, Inc.

outset of this chapter in a spoofing attempt to draw your interest. As far as I know, it has never been experimentally investigated. Yet it is a frequent practice of door-to-door salespeople, who use it primarily to gain permission to enter a customer's home. I first encountered it while training as an encyclopedia salesperson. The technique consists of asking several questions to which the customer will be very likely to answer yes. To be consistent with the previous answers, the customer must then say yes to the crucial final question. In the encyclopedia sales situation I infiltrated, the technique proceeded as follows:

> *First wall*—"Do you feel that a good education is important to your children?"
>
> *Second wall*—"Do you think that a child who does his or her homework well will get a better education?"
>
> *Third wall*—"Don't you agree that a good set of reference books will help a child do well on homework assignments?"
>
> *Fourth wall*—"Well, then, it sounds like you'll want to hear about this fine set of encyclopedias I have to offer at an excellent price. May I come in?"

A similar start-small procedure is embodied in the much more researched *foot-in-the-door technique* (Freedman & Fraser, 1966). A solicitor using this technique will first ask for a small favor that is virtually certain to be granted. The initial compliance is then followed by a request for a larger, *related* favor. It has been found repeatedly that people who have agreed to the initial, small favor are more willing to do the larger one (see Beaman et al., 1983, for a review), seemingly to be consistent with the implication of the initial action. For instance, homeowners who had agreed to accept and wear a small lapel pin promoting a local charity were, as a consequence, more likely to contribute money to that charity when canvassed during a subsequent donation drive (Pliner, Hart, Kohl, & Saari, 1974).

Freedman and Fraser (1966) have argued that the foot-in-the-door technique is successful because performance of the initially requested action causes individuals to see themselves as possessing certain traits. For example, in the Pliner et al. (1974) study, after taking and wearing the charity pin, subjects would be expected to see themselves as favorable toward charitable causes, especially this particular one. Later, when asked to perform the larger, related favor of contributing to that charity, subjects would be more willing to do so to be consistent with the charitable trait they had assigned to themselves. Recent support for this interpretation comes from a study showing that children are not influenced by the foot-in-the-door technique until they are old enough to understand the idea of a stable personality trait (around six to seven years). Once children are old enough to understand the meaning of a stable trait, the foot-in-the-door tactic becomes effective, especially among those children who prefer consistency in behavior (Eisenberg, Cialdini, McCreath, & Shell, 1986).

Other more unsavory techniques induce a commitment to an item and then remove the inducements that generated the commitment. Remarkably, the commitment frequently remains. For example, the *bait-and-switch procedure* is used by some retailers who may advertise certain merchandise (e.g., a room of furniture) at a special low price. When the customer arrives to take advantage of the special, he or she finds the merchandise to be of low quality or sold out. However, because customers have by now made an active commitment to getting new furniture at that particular store, they are more willing to agree to examine and, consequently, to buy alternate merchandise there.

A similar strategy is employed by car dealers in the *low-ball technique*, which proceeds by obtaining a commitment to an action and *then* increasing the costs of performing the action. The automobile salesperson who "throws the low-ball" induces the customer to decide to buy a particular model car by offering a low price on the car or an inflated one on the customer's trade-in. After the decision has been made (and, at times, after the commitment is enhanced by allowing the customer to arrange financing, take the car home overnight, etc.), something happens to remove the reason the customer decided to buy. Perhaps a price calculation error is found, or the used car assessor disallows the inflated trade-in figure. By this time, though, many customers have experienced an internal commitment to that specific automobile and proceed with the purchase.

Experimental research has documented the effectiveness of this tactic in settings beyond automobile sales. For example, in one study by Cialdini, Cacioppo, Bassett, and Miller (1978), the low-ball procedure was directed at college students who were told of a 7:00 A.M. starting time only after they had agreed to be in a psychology experiment. Upon then learning of the starting time and being given the chance to cancel, these individuals remained more willing to make an appointment to participate than individuals who had heard of the 7:00 A.M. time from the outset; further, virtually all of the low-ball subjects who agreed to participate appeared for the study as promised. Cialdini et al. (1978) interpreted these results in terms of subjects' desire for consistency with their earlier verbal commitment. Additional research indicated that the tactic is effective primarily when used by a single requester (Burger & Petty, 1981) and when the initial commitment is freely made (Cialdini et al., 1978).

One thing that these procedures (and others like them) have in common is the establishment of an earlier commitment that is consistent with a later action desired by the compliance professional. The need for consistency then takes over to compel performance of the desired behavior. However, not all types of these earlier commitments are equally effective. There is research evidence suggesting that certain types of commitments lead to consistent future responding. The present context does not allow sufficient space for a thorough discussion of that evidence. Nonetheless, I would argue that a fair summary of the research literature is that a commitment is most likely to produce consistent future behavior to the extent that it is active (Bem, 1967), effortful (Aronson & Mills, 1959), public (Deutsch & Gerard, 1955), and viewed as internally motivated (i.e., uncoerced, Freedman, 1965).

Another approach to employing the commitment/consistency principle also has popularity among commercial compliance professionals. Rather than inducing a new commitment to their product or service, many practitioners point out existing commitments within potential customers that are consistent with the product or service being offered. In this way, desirable existing commitments are made more visible to the customer, and the strain for consistency is allowed to direct behavior accordingly. For example, insurance agents are frequently taught to stress to new homeowners that the purchase of a $100,000 house reflects an enormous personal commitment to one's home and the well-being of one's family. Consequently, they argue, it would only be consistent with such a commitment to home and family to purchase home and life insurance in amounts that befit the size of this commitment.

Research of various kinds indicates that this sort of sensitization to commitments and to consequent inconsistencies can be effective in producing belief and attitude change. One impressive program of work in this regard comes from Milton Rokeach (1973). Recently, Ball-Rokeach, Rokeach, and Grube (1984) demonstrated long-term behavioral effects from a television program that focused viewers on their personal commitments to certain deep-seated values (e.g., freedom, equality), on the one hand, and their current beliefs and behaviors, on the other. Not only did uninterrupted viewers of this single program demonstrate enhanced commitment to these values, but they were significantly more likely to donate money to support causes consistent with the values two to three months after the program had aired.

A more manipulative tactic than merely focusing people on their existing values is to put them in a situation where to refuse a specific request would be inconsistent with a value that people wish to be known as possessing. One such tactic is the *legitimization-of-paltry-favors* (or *even-a-penny-would-help*) *technique*. Most people prefer to behave in ways that are consistent with a view of themselves as helpful, charitable individuals. Consequently, a fundraiser who makes a request that legitimizes a paltry amount of aid ("Could you give a contribution? Even a penny would help") makes it difficult for a target to refuse to give at all; to do so risks appearing to be a very unhelpful person. Notice that this procedure does not specifically request a trivial sum; that would probably lead to a profusion of pennies and a small total take. Instead, the request simply makes a miniscule form of aid acceptable, thereby reducing the target's ability to give nothing and still remain consistent with the desirable image of a helpful individual. After all, how could a person remain committed to a helpful image after refusing to contribute when "even a penny would help"?

Experimental research done to validate the effectiveness of the technique has shown it to be successful in increasing the percentage of charity contributors (Brockner et al., 1984; Cialdini & Schroeder, 1976; Reeves, Macolini, & Martin, 1987; Reingen, 1978; Weyant, 1984). What's more, in each of these studies, the even-a-penny procedure proved profitable because subjects did not actually give a penny but provided the donation amount typically given to charities. Thus, the legitimization-of-paltry-favors approach appears to work by getting more people to agree to give (so as to be consistent with a helpful image); but the decision of how much to give is left unaffected by the mention of a paltry amount. The consequence is increased proceeds.

Friendship/Liking

A fact of social interaction that each of us can attest to is that people are more favorably inclined toward the needs of those they know and like. Consequently, a friendship/liking principle for compliance can be worded as follows: *One should be more willing to comply with the requests of friends or other liked individuals.*

The clearest illustration I know of the professional exploitation of the friendship/liking rule is the Tupperware home party. The power of the Tupperware party comes from a particular arrangement that trades on the friendship/liking rule. Despite the entertaining and persuasive salesmanship of the Tupperware representative, the true request to purchase the product does not come from this stranger; it comes from a friend to every woman in the room. Oh, the Tupperware representative may physically ask for each party-goer's order all right, but the more psychologically compelling requester is a housewife sitting off to one side, smiling, chatting, and serving refreshments. She is the party hostess, who has called her friends together for the demonstration in her home and who, everyone knows, makes a profit from each piece sold at her party.

Simple. By providing the hostess with a percentage of the take, the Tupperware company arranges for their customers to buy from and for a friend, rather than an unknown salesperson. In this way, the attraction, the warmth, the security, and the obligation of friendship are brought to bear on the sales setting. The results have been remarkable. It was recently estimated that Tupperware sales exceed a million dollars a day.

With so irresistible an ally as the friendship/liking rule operating, there is little wonder that the company has abandoned retail sales outlets and has pushed the home party concept such that now, a Tupperware party starts somewhere in the world every 10 seconds. But, of course, all sorts of other compliance professionals recognize the pressure to say yes to someone we know and like (see Figure 9-4). Take, for instance, the large number of charity organizations who recruit volunteers to canvass for donations close to their own homes. They understand perfectly

"*Louise, there's a gentleman here who says that you and he were in love in 1962 but you drifted apart and now he's come back in the hope that we might order a set of encyclopedias.*"

FIGURE 9-4   The liking/friendship rule

Source: Drawing by Handelsman; © 1982 The New Yorker Magazine, Inc.

how much more difficult it is for us to turn down a charity request when it comes from a friend or neighbor.

The use by compliance practitioners of the liking bond between friends tells us much about the power of the friendship/liking rule to produce assent. Still more informative in this regard is that such professionals seek to benefit from the rule even when already formed friendships are not present for them to employ. Under these circumstances, the professionals' compliance strategy is quite direct: They first get us to like *them*. But how do they do it? It turns out that the tactics that practitioners use to generate liking cluster around certain factors that also have been shown by controlled research to increase liking.

Physical Attractiveness

Although it is generally acknowledged that good-looking people have an advantage in social interaction, recent findings indicate that we may have sorely underestimated the size and reach of that advantage. There appears to be a positive reaction to good physical appearance that generalizes to such favorable trait perceptions as talent, kindness, honesty, and intelligence (e.g., Dion, Berscheid, & Walster, 1972; Rich, 1975). As a consequence, attractive individuals are more persuasive both in terms of changing attitudes (Chaiken, 1979) and getting what they request (Benson, Karabenic, & Lerner, 1976).

For instance, a study of the 1974 Canadian Federal elections found that attractive candidates received more than two and one-half times the votes of unattractive ones (Efran & Patterson, 1976). Equally impressive results seem to be obtained in the judicial system. In a Pennsylvania study, researchers rated the physical attractiveness of 74 separate male defendants at the start of their criminal trials. When much later, the researchers checked the results of these cases via court records, they found that the better-looking men received significantly lighter sentences. In fact, the attractive defendants were twice as likely to avoid incarceration as the unattractive defendants (Stewart, 1980). When viewed in the light of such powerful effects, it is not surprising that extremely attractive models are employed to promote products and services, that sales trainers frequently include appearance and grooming tips in their presentations, nor that, commonly, con men are handsome and con women pretty.

Similarity

We like people who are similar to us (Byrne, 1971). This fact seems to hold true whether the similarity occurs in the area of opinions, personality traits, background, or lifestyle. Consequently, those who wish to be liked in order to increase our compliance can accomplish that purpose by appearing similar to us in any of a wide variety of ways.

Dress is a good example. Several studies have demonstrated that we are more likely to help those who dress like us. In one study, done in the early 1970s when young people tended to dress either in "hippie" or "straight" fashion, experimenters donned hippie or straight attire and asked college students on campus for a dime to make a phone call. When the experimenter was dressed the same as the student, the request was granted in over two-thirds of the instances; but when the student and requester were dissimilarly dressed, a dime was provided less than half of the time (Emswiller, Deaux, & Willits, 1971). Another experiment shows how automatic our positive response to similar others can be. Marchers in an antiwar demonstration were not only found to be more likely to sign the petition of a similarly dressed requester but to do so without bothering to read it first (Suedfeld, Bochner, & Matas, 1971).

Compliments

Praise and other forms of positive estimation also stimulate liking (e.g., Byrne & Rhamey, 1965). The actor McLean Stevenson once described how his wife tricked him into marriage: "She said she liked me." Although designed for a laugh, the remark is as much instructive as humorous. The simple information that someone fancies us can be a bewitchingly effective device for producing return liking and willing compliance. Although there are limits to our gullibility—especially when we can be sure that the flatterer's intent is manipulative (Jones & Wortman, 1973)— we tend as a rule to believe praise and to like those who provide it.

Evidence for the power of praise on liking comes from a study (Drachman, deCarufel, & Insko, 1978) in which men received personal comments from someone who needed a favor from them. Some of the men got only positive comments, some got only negative comments, and some got a mixture of good and bad. There were three interesting findings. First, the evaluator who offered only praise was liked the best. Second, this was so even though the men fully realized that the flatterer stood to gain from their liking of him. Finally, unlike the other types of comments, pure praise did not have to be accurate to work. Compliments produced just as much liking for the flatterer when they were untrue as when they were true.

It is for such reasons that direct salespeople are educated in the art of praise. A potential customer's home, clothes, car, taste, and the like are all frequent targets for compliments.

Cooperation

Cooperation is another factor that has been shown to enhance positive feelings and behavior (cf. Aronson, Bridgeman, & Geffner, 1978; Cook, 1978). Those who cooperate toward the achievement of a common goal are more favorable and helpful to each other as a consequence. That is why compliance professionals often strive to be perceived as cooperating partners with a target person. Automobile sales managers frequently set themselves as "villains" so that the salesperson can "do battle" on the customer's behalf. The cooperative, pulling together kind of relationship that is consequently produced between the salesperson and customer naturally leads to a desirable form of liking that promotes sales.

Scarcity

Opportunities seem more valuable to us when they are less available. Interestingly, this is often true even when the opportunity holds little attraction for us on its own merits. Take as evidence the experience of Florida State University students who, like most undergraduates, rated themselves dissatisfied with the quality of their campus cafeteria food. Nine days later, they had changed their minds, rating that food significantly better than they had before. It is instructive that no actual improvement in food service had occurred between the two ratings. Instead, on the day of the second rating, the students had learned that, because of a fire, they could not eat at the cafeteria for two weeks (West, 1975).

Collectors of everything from baseball cards to antiques are keenly aware of the influence of scarcity in determining the worth of an item. As a rule, if it is rare or becoming rare, it is more valuable. Especially enlightening as to the importance of scarcity in the collectibles market is the phenomenon of the "precious mistake."

Flawed items—a blurred stamp or double-struck coin—are sometimes the most valued of all. Thus, a stamp carrying a three-eyed likeness of George Washington is anatomically incorrect, aesthetically unappealing, and yet highly sought after. There is instructive irony here: Imperfections that would otherwise make for rubbish make for prized possessions when they bring along an abiding scarcity.

There appear to be two major sources of the power of scarcity. First, because we know that the things that are difficult to possess are typically better than those that are easy to possess, we can often use an item's availability to help us quickly and correctly decide on its quality. Thus, one reason for the potency of scarcity is that, by assessing it, we can get a shortcut indication of an item's value.

In addition, there is a unique, secondary source of power within scarcity: As the things we can have become less available, we lose freedoms; and we *hate* to lose the freedoms we already have. This desire to preserve our established prerogatives is the centerpiece of *psychological reactance theory* (Brehm, 1966; Brehm & Brehm, 1981), developed to explain the human response to diminishing personal control. According to the theory, whenever our freedoms are limited or threatened, the need to retain them makes us want them (as well as the goods and services associated with them) significantly more than we did before. So, when increasing scarcity—or anything else—interferes with our prior access to some item, we will *react against* the interference by wanting and trying to possess the item more than before.

One naturally occurring example of the consequences of increased scarcity can be seen in the outcome of a decision by county officials in Miami to ban the use and possession of phosphate detergents. Spurred by the tendency to want what they could no longer have, the majority of Miami consumers came to see phosphate cleaners as better products than before. Compared to Tampa residents, who were not affected by the Miami ordinance, the citizens of Miami rated phosphate detergents as gentler, more effective in cold water, better whiteners and fresheners, more powerful on stains, and so on. After passage of the law, they had even come to believe that phosphate detergents poured easier than the Tampa consumers believed (Mazis, 1975).

This sort of response is typical of individuals who have lost an established freedom and is crucial to an understanding of how psychological reactance and scarcity work on us. When our freedom to have something is limited, the item becomes less available, and we experience an increased desire for it. However, we rarely recognize that psychological reactance has caused us to want the item more; all we know is that we *want* it. Still, we need to make sense of our desire for the item, so we begin to assign it positive qualities to justify the desire. After all, it is natural to suppose that, if one feels drawn to something, it is because of the merit of the thing. In the case of the Miami antiphosphate law—and in other instances of newly restricted availability—that is a faulty supposition. Phosphate detergents clean, whiten, and pour no better after they are banned than before. We just assume they do because we find that we desire them more.

Other research has suggested that, in addition to commodities, limited access to information makes the information more desirable—and more influential

(Brock, 1968). A recent test of Brock's thinking by one of my students found good support in a business setting. Wholesale beef buyers, who were told of an impending imported beef shortage, purchased significantly more beef when they were informed that the shortage information came from certain "exclusive" contacts that the importer had (Knishinsky, 1982). Apparently, the fact that the news was itself scarce made it more valued and persuasive.

A scarcity principle for compliance can be worded as follows: *One should try to secure those opportunities that are scarce or dwindling.* With scarcity operating powerfully on the worth assigned to things, it should not be surprising that compliance professionals have a variety of techniques designed to convert this power to compliance. Probably the most frequently such used technique I witnessed was the *limited-number tactic* in which the customer is informed that membership opportunities, products, or services exist in a limited supply that cannot be guaranteed to last for long. In some instances I observed, the limited-number information was true; in others, it was not. In each case, however, the intent was to convince prospects of an item's scarcity and thereby increase its immediate worth in their eyes. At one appliance store where I worked, it was not uncommon for salespeople to raise the value of a particular sale item for a customer by announcing that "The last one has just been sold, and I'm sure we have no more in the back; however, I can check with our other store, and if I can get it for you at the sale price, would you like to buy it?" In this way, customers were induced to make a commitment at a time when the scarcity principle would render the merchandise most attractive. Many of the customers agreed eagerly and were uniformly pleased (even relieved) when the salesperson invariably reported that, yes, the other store location still had one in stock.

Related to the limited-number tactic is the *deadline technique* in which an official time limit is placed on the customer's opportunity to get what is being offered. Newspaper ads abound with admonitions to the customer regarding the folly of delay: "Last three days." "Limited time offer." "One week only sale." One rather single-minded movie advertiser managed to load three separate appeals to the scarcity principle into just five words of copy in a newspaper ad I recently saw. It read, "Exclusive, limited engagement, ends soon."

The purest form of a decision deadline—right now—occurs in a variant of the deadline technique in which customers are told that, unless they make an immediate purchase decision, they will have to buy the item at a higher price or they will not be able to purchase it at all. I found this tactic used in numerous compliance settings. A large child photography company urged parents to buy as many poses and copies as they could afford because "Stocking limitations force us to burn the unsold pictures of your children within 24 hours." A prospective health club member or automobile buyer might learn that the deal offered by the salesperson is good for that one time; should the customer leave the premises, the deal is off. One home vacuum cleaner sales company instructed me as a trainee to claim to prospects that "I have so many other people to see that I have the time to visit a family only once. It's company policy that even if you decide later that you want this machine, I can't come back and sell it to you." For anyone who thought about it carefully, this was nonsense; the company and its representatives are in the business of making sales, and any customer who called for another visit would be accommodated gladly. The real purpose of the can't-come-back-again claim was to evoke the scarcity rule for compliance.

Authority

Legitimately constituted authorities are extremely influential persons (e.g., Aronson, Turner, & Carlsmith, 1963; Milgram, 1974). Whether they have acquired their positions through knowledge, talent, or fortune, their positions bespeak of superior information and power. For each of us, this has always been the case. Early on, these people (e.g., parents, teachers) knew more than we did, and we found that taking their advice proved beneficial—partly because of their greater wisdom and partly because they controlled our rewards and punishments. As adults, the authority figures have changed to employers, judges, police officers, and the like, but the benefits associated with doing as they say have not changed. For most people, then, conforming to the dictates of authority figures produces genuine practical advantages. Consequently, it makes great sense to comply with the wishes of properly constituted authorities. It makes so much sense, in fact, that people often do so when it makes no sense at all.

Take, for example, the strange case of the "rectal earache" reported by two professors of pharmacy, Michael Cohen and Neil Davis (1981). A physician ordered eardrops to be administered to the right ear of a patient suffering pain and infection there. But instead of writing out completely the location "right ear" on the prescription, the doctor abbreviated it so that the instructions read "Place in R ear." Upon receiving the prescription, the duty nurse promptly put the required number of eardrops into the patient's anus. Obviously, rectal treatment of an earache made no sense. Yet neither the patient nor the nurse questioned it.

An authority principle for compliance can be worded as follows: *One should be more willing to follow the suggestions of someone who is a legitimate authority.* Authorities may be seen as falling into two categories: authorities with regard to the specific situation and more general authorities. Compliance practitioners employ techniques that seek to benefit from the power invested in authority figures of both types.

In the case of authority relevant to a specific situation, we can note how often advertisers inform their audiences of the level of expertise of product manufacturers (e.g., "Fashionable Men's Clothiers since 1841." "Babies are our business, our only business."). (Chapter 6 by Petty, et al. describes when tactics involving expertise are most likely to be effective.) At times, the expertise associated with a product has been more symbolic than substantive, for instance, when actors in television commercials wear physician's white coats to recommend a product. In one famous Sanka commercial, the actor involved, Robert Young, did not need a white coat, as his prior identity as television doctor, Marcus Welby, M.D., provided the medical connection.

It is instructive that the mere symbols of a physician's expertise and authority are enough to trip the mechanism that governs authority influence. One of the most prominent of these symbols, the bare title "Dr.," has been shown to be devastatingly effective as a compliance device among trained hospital personnel. In what may be the most frightening study I know, a group of physicians and nurses conducted an experiment that documented the dangerous degree of blind obedience that hospital nurses accorded to an individual whom they had never met but who had claimed in a phone call to be a doctor (Hofling, Brotzman, Dalrymple, Graves, & Pierce, 1966). Ninety-five percent of those nurses were willing to administer an unsafe level of a drug merely because that caller requested it.

In the case of influence that generalizes outside of a specific situation, the impact of authority (real and symbolic) appears equally impressive. For instance, Bickman (1974) found that, when wearing a security guard's uniform, a requester could produce more compliance with requests (e.g., to pick up a paper bag on the street, to stand on the other side of a bus stop sign) that were irrelevant to a security guard's domain of authority. Less blatant in its connotation than a uniform but nonetheless effective is another kind of attire that has traditionally indicated authority status in our culture—the well-tailored business suit. It also can mediate influence. Take as evidence the results of a study by Lefkowitz, Blake, and Mouton (1955), who found that three and one-half times as many people were willing to follow a jaywalker into traffic when he wore a suit and tie versus a work shirt and trousers.

Con artists frequently make use of the influence inherent in authority attire. For example, a gambit called the *bank examiner scheme* depends heavily on the automatic deference most people assign to authority figures or those merely dressed as such. Using the two uniforms of authority we have already mentioned, a business suit and a guard's outfit, the con begins when a man dressed in a conservative three-piece business suit appears at the home of a likely victim and identifies himself as an official of the victim's bank. The victim is told of suspected irregularities in the transactions handled by one particular teller and is asked to help trap the teller by drawing out all of his or her savings at the teller's window. In this way, the examiner can catch the teller redhanded in any wrongdoing. After cooperating, the victim is to give the money to a uniformed bank guard waiting outside, who will then return it to the proper account. Often, the appearance of the bank examiner and uniformed guard are so impressive that the victim never thinks to check on their authenticity and proceeds with the requested action, never to see the money or those two individuals again.

Summary

At the outset of this chapter, it was suggested that an important question for anyone interested in understanding, resisting, or harnessing the process of interpersonal influence is, Which are the most powerful principles that motivate us to comply with another's request? It was also suggested that one way to assess such power would be to examine the practices of commercial compliance professionals for their pervasiveness. That is, if compliance practitioners made widespread use of certain principles, this would be evidence for the natural power of these principles to affect everyday compliance.

Six psychological principles emerged as the most popular in the repertoires of the compliance pros: reciprocity, social validation, commitment/consistency, friendship/liking, scarcity, and authority. Close examination of the principles revealed broad professional usage that could be validated and explained by controlled, experimental research. As with most research projects, additional work needs to be done before we can have high levels of confidence in the conclusions. Until that time, however, my own best guess is that these six principles engage central features of the human condition in the process of motivating us to say yes.

Notes

1. In certain cases, a highly placed individual within an organization was informed of my research and cooperated both to conceal my identity and to arrange for a proper placement. In most instances, however, I remained incognito to all in an organization throughout my association with it. On leaving an organization, I gave a full revelation of my intent and identity, along with a promise that I would protect the organization's anonymity.

2. It should be noted that evidence for the pervasiveness of a seventh principle, material self-interest, was also abundant. Practitioners of all sorts frequently appeal to the desire to maximize one's material benefits and minimize one's material costs in their campaigns for compliance. However, I did not treat this principle in separate detail, as I considered it a motivational given and less interesting as a consequence.

Acknowledgment

Portions of this chapter were adapted from the author's book *Influence: Science and Practice* (New York: Harper/Collins, 1988).

References

Altheide, D. L., & Johnson, J. M. (1977). Counting souls: A study of counseling at evangelical crusades. *Pacific Sociological Review, 20,* 323–348.

Aronson, E., & Mills, J. (1959). The effect of severity of initiation on liking for a group. *Journal of Abnormal and Social Psychology, 59,* 177–181.

Aronson, E., Bridgeman, D. L., & Geffner, R. (1978). The effects of a cooperative classroom structure on students' behavior and attitudes. In D. Bar-Tal & L. Saxe (Eds.), *Social psychology of education: Theory and research.* New York: Halstead Press.

Aronson, E., Turner, J. A., & Carlsmith, J. M. (1963). Communicator credibility and communication discrepancy as a determinant of opinion change. *Journal of Abnormal and Social Psychology, 67,* 31–36.

Ball-Rokeach, S., Rokeach, M., & Grube, J. W. (1984). *The great American values test.* New York: Free Press.

Baumeister, R. F. (1982). A self-presentational view

of social phenomena. *Psychological Bulletin, 91,* 3–26.

Beaman, A. L., Cole, C. M., Preston, M., Klentz, B., & Steblay, N. H. (1983). A meta-analysis of fifteen years of foot-in-the-door research. *Personality and Social Psychology Bulletin, 9,* 181–196.

Bem, D. J. (1967). Self-perception: An alternative interpretation of cognitive dissonance phenomena. *Psychological Review, 74,* 183–200.

Benson, P. L., Karabenic, S. A., & Lerner, R. A. (1976). Pretty pleases: The effects of physical attractiveness on race, sex, and receiving help. *Journal of Experimental Social Psychology, 12,* 409–415.

Bickman, L. (1974). The social power of a uniform. *Journal of Applied Social Psychology, 4,* 47–61.

Brehm, J. (1966). *A theory of psychological reactance.* New York: Academic Press.

Brehm, S. S., & Brehm, J. (1981). *Psychological reactance.* New York: Academic Press.

Brock, T. C. (1965). Communicator-recipient similarity and decision change. *Journal of Personality and Social Psychology, 1,* 650–654.

Brock, T. C. (1968). Implications of commodity theory for value change. In A. G. Greenwald, T. C. Brock, & T. M. Ostrom (Eds.), *Psychological foundations of attitudes* (pp. 243–276). New York: Academic Press.

Brockner, J., Guzzi, B., Kane, J., Levine, E., & Shaplen, K. (1984). Organizational fundraising: Further evidence on the effects of legitimizing small donations. *Journal of Consumer Research, 11,* 611–614.

Burger, J. M. (1986). Increasing compliance by improving the deal: The that's-not-all technique. *Journal of Personality and Social Psychology, 51,* 277–283.

Burger, J. M., & Petty, R. E. (1981). The low-ball technique: Task or person commitment? *Journal of Personality and Social Psychology, 40,* 492–500.

Byrne, D. (1971). *The attraction paradigm.* New York: Academic Press.

Byrne, D., & Rhamey, R. (1965). Magnitude of positive and negative reinforcements as a determinant of attraction. *Journal of Personality and Social Psychology, 2,* 884–889.

Chaiken, S. (1979). Communicator physical attractiveness and persuasion. *Journal of Personality and Social Psychology, 37,* 1387–1397.

Cialdini, R. B. (1988). *Influence: Science and practice.* New York: Harper/Collins.

Cialdini, R. B., & Ascani, K. (1976). Test of a concession procedure for inducing verbal, behavioral, and further compliance with a request to give blood. *Journal of Applied Psychology, 61,* 295–300.

Cialdini, R. B., Cacioppo, J. T., Bassett, R., & Miller, J. A. (1978). Low-ball procedure for producing compliance: Commitment then cost. *Journal of Personality and Social Psychology, 36,* 463–476.

Cialdini, R. B., & Schroeder, D. A. (1976). Increasing compliance by legitimizing paltry contributions: When even a penny helps. *Journal of Personality and Social Psychology, 34,* 599–604.

Cialdini, R. B., Vincent, J. E., Lewis, S. K., Catalan, J., Wheeler, D., & Darby, B. L. (1975). Reciprocal concessions procedure for inducing compliance: The door-in-the-face technique. *Journal of Personality and Social Psychology, 31,* 206–215.

Cohen, M., & Davis, N. (1981). *Medication errors: Causes and prevention.* Philadelphia, PA: G. F. Stickley.

Cook, S. W. (1978). Interpersonal and attitudinal outcomes in cooperating interracial groups. *Journal of Research and Development in Education, 12,* 28–38.

Deutsch, M., & Gerard, H. B. (1955). A study of normative and individual judgments. *Journal of Abnormal and Social Psychology, 51,* 629–636.

Dion, K., Berscheid, E., & Walster, E. (1972). What is beautiful is good. *Journal of Personality and Social Psychology, 24,* 285–290.

Drachman, D., deCarufel, A., & Insko, C. A. (1978). The extra-credit effect in interpersonal attraction. *Journal of Experimental Social Psychology, 14,* 458–467.

Efran, M. G., & Patterson, E. W. J. (1976). *The politics of appearance.* Unpublished manuscript, University of Toronto.

Eisenberg, N., Cialdini, R. B., McCreath, H., & Shell, R. (1986). *Consistency based compliance: When and why do children become vulnerable?* Unpublished manuscript, Arizona State University.

Emswiller, T., Deaux, K., & Willits, J. E. (1971).

Similarity, sex, and requests for small favors. *Journal of Applied Social Psychology, 1*, 284–291.

Festinger, L. (1954). A theory of social comparison processes. *Human Relations, 2*, 117–140.

Festinger, L. (1957). *A theory of cognitive dissonance.* Stanford, CA: Stanford University Press.

Freedman, J. L. (1965). Long-term behavioral effects of cognitive dissonance. *Journal of Experimental Social Psychology, 1*, 145–155.

Freedman, J. L., & Fraser, S. C. (1966). Compliance without pressure: The foot-in-the-door technique. *Journal of Personality and Social Psychology, 4*, 195–203.

Gouldner, A. W. (1960). The norm of reciprocity. *American Sociological Review, 25*, 161–178.

Grusec, J. E., & Redler, E. (1980). Attribution, reinforcement, and altruism: A developmental analysis. *Developmental Psychology, 16*, 525–534.

Harari, H., Mohr, D., & Hosey, K. (1980). Faculty helpfulness to students: A comparison of compliance techniques. *Personality and Social Psychology Bulletin, 6*, 373–377.

Heider, F. (1958). *The psychology of interpersonal relations.* New York: Wiley.

Hofling, C. K., Brotzman, E., Dalrymple, S., Graves, N., & Pierce, C. M. (1966). An experimental study in nurse-physician relationships. *Journal of Nervous and Mental Disease, 143*, 177–180.

Hornstein, H. A., Fisch, E., & Holmes, M. (1968). Influence of model's feeling about his behavior and his relevance as a comparison other on observer's helping behavior. *Journal of Personality and Social Psychology, 10*, 222–226.

Hovland, C. I., Lumsdaine, A. A., & Sheffield, F. D. (1949). *Studies in social psychology in World War II* (Vol. 3). Princeton, NJ: Princeton University Press.

Jones, E. E., & Wortman, C. (1973). *Ingratiation: An attributional approach.* Morristown, NJ: General Learning Press.

Kiesler, C. A. (1971). *The psychology of commitment: Experiments linking behavior to belief.* San Diego, CA: Academic Press.

Knishinsky, A. (1982). *The effects of scarcity of material and exclusivity of information on industrial buyer perceived risk in provoking purchase decisions.* Doctoral Dissertation, Arizona State University.

Kraut, R. E. (1973). The effects of social labeling on giving to charity. *Journal of Experimental Social Psychology, 9*, 551–562.

Lefkowitz, M., Blake, R. R., & Mouton, J. S. (1955). Status factors in pedestrian violation of traffic signals. *Journal of Abnormal and Social Psychology, 51*, 704–706.

Mazis, M. B. (1975). Antipollution measures and psychological reactance theory: A field experiment. *Journal of Personality and Social Psychology, 31*, 654–666.

Milgram, S. (1974). *Obedience to authority.* New York: Harper.

Milgram, S., Bickman, L., & Berkowitz, O. (1969). Note on the drawing power of crowds of different size. *Journal of Personality and Social Psychology, 13*, 79–82.

Miller, R. L., Brickman, P., & Bolen, D. (1975). Attribution versus persuasion as a means for modifying behavior. *Journal of Personality and Social Psychology, 31*, 430–441.

Newcomb, T. M. (1953). An approach to the study of communicative acts. *Psychological Review, 60*, 393–404.

Phillips, D. P. (1974). The influence of suggestion on suicide: Substantive and theoretical implications of the Werther effect. *American Sociological Review, 39*, 340–354.

Pliner, P. H., Hart, H., Kohl, J., & Saari, D. (1974). Compliance without pressure: Some further data on the foot-in-the-door technique. *Journal of Experimental Social Psychology, 10*, 17–22.

Reeves, R. A., Macolini, R. M., & Martin, R. C. (1987). Legitimizing paltry contributions: On-the-spot vs mail-in requests. *Journal of Applied Social Psychology, 17*, 731–738.

Regan, D. T. (1971). Effects of a favor and liking on compliance. *Journal of Experimental Social Psychology, 7*, 627–639.

Reingen, D. H. (1978). On inducing compliance with requests. *Journal of Consumer Research, 5*, 96–102.

Reingen, D. H. (1982). Test of a list procedure for inducing compliance with a request to donate money. *Journal of Applied Psychology, 67*, 110–118.

Rich, J. (1975). Effects of children's physical attractiveness on teacher's evaluations. *Journal of Educational Psychology, 67*, 599–607.

Rokeach, M. (1973). *The nature of human values.* New York: Free Press.

Stewart, J. E. (1980). Defendant's attractiveness as a factor in the outcome of trials. *Journal of Applied Social Psychology, 10,* 348–361.

Suedfeld, P., Bochner, S., & Matas, C. (1971). Petitioner's attire and petition signing by peace demonstrators: A field experiment. *Journal of Applied Social Psychology, 1,* 278–283.

Swinyard, W. R., & Ray, M. L. (1977). Advertising-selling interactions: An attribution experiment. *Journal of Marketing Research, 4,* 509–516.

Tedeschi, J. T. (Ed.). (1981). *Impression management theory and social psychological research.* New York: Academic Press.

West, S. G. (1975). Increasing the attractiveness of cafeteria food: A reactance theory perspective. *Journal of Applied Psychology, 60,* 656–658.

Weyant, J. M. (1984). Applying social psychology to induce charitable donations. *Journal of Applied Social Psychology, 14,* 441–447.

10

PERSUASION AND HEALTH ATTITUDES

HOWARD LEVENTHAL
Rutgers University

LINDA CAMERON
St. Joseph's University

The Nature of the Persuasion Problem

What comes to mind when you think about health and persuasion? A decade or more ago, this question would have directed your thoughts to media messages about issues such as the link between blood pressure and heart disease or that between fluoridation and tooth decay. Today, however, it is very likely that your response centers on the prevention and control of AIDS (acquired immune deficiency syndrome), the most predominant health concern in the nation. Reports and messages about AIDS appear daily in our newspapers, magazines, television programs, even our conversations with family and friends. Unfortunately, many of these messages have been constructed in such a way that they have generated misconceptions about the disease that have fueled widespread panic and fear about AIDS and people with AIDS. As a result, health professionals are faced not only with the problem of persuading people to adopt lifestyles that will help in the control of the disease but also with the problem of alleviating the nationwide AIDS hysteria caused by its misrepresentations (see Figure 10-1).

Because AIDS is a relatively new health problem, there has not been time to conduct investigations on how most effectively to change AIDS-related attitudes and lifestyle behaviors. Fortunately, a great deal has been learned about health persuasion through approaches to other health problems, such as campaigns to stop cigarette smoking, media programs on cardiovascular disease, and studies on

Doonesbury

FIGURE 10-1   Misconceptions about AIDS have fueled widespread hysteria.

enhancing the effectiveness of doctors' instructions to control hypertension. We believe that these past findings can be used to prevent more effectively the spread of the AIDS virus, as well as the unfortunate mistreatment of people with AIDS, and heightened fear resulting from its misrepresentations. In fact, we believe that this research on health messages is relevant to virtually all types of persuasion efforts, as these messages involve the basic features of the persuasion process common to all areas of attitude change.

Persuasive communications, whether about health, politics, or laundry detergent, all share five specific features:

1. A specific *goal*, or issue (e.g., practicing "safe sex" to prevent AIDS)
2. A *source*, or communicator (e.g., a celebrated radio counselor)
3. A *message* (e.g., the statements about safe sex and AIDS)
4. A *channel* or medium on which to transmit the communication (e.g., a magazine advertisement)
5. A *recipient* (e.g., the magazine reader)

Of course, aspects of the issue, source, message, media, and recipients will vary from one communication to another, leading to successful persuasion on some occasions and failure on others (see Chapter 6).

The great variation of these features across media campaigns and other persuasion attempts often makes it difficult, if not impossible, to tell what is responsible for success or failure. The confusion creates a strong temptation to proclaim one or another as a pat solution to the communication problem. People may assert that the way to overcome the AIDS problem is to have well-known celebrities deliver messages about safe-sex practices over television, to use peer rather than adult communicators in the high school classroom, or to use threatening messages that arouse high levels of fear.

The solutions are rarely so simple, however, because source, message, and recipient factors frequently interact and affect one another. For example, it may seem reasonable to assume that a very strong, fear-provoking message will always lead to more persuasion than a message generating little or no fear. Yet, as we will discuss later, research indicates that a highly threatening message will often be no better than a message generating low levels of fear.

Moreover, the media are filled with conflicting messages (see Figure 10-2). The same television channels that broadcast public service messages about condoms as a means of reducing the risk of contracting AIDS also broadcast images of sexually alluring figures, flashy dress, and expensive cars advertising a lifestyle of impulse and self-indulgence—hardly the restraint required for safe sex!

We believe that an understanding of the effects of various communication factors, including conflicting messages, can only be achieved through systematic, carefully designed studies that generate and test hypotheses based upon an underlying theoretical framework. If we ignore theory, no amount of data will replace confusion with orderly patterns.

The Name of the Game Is Behavior Change

The goal of this chapter is to discuss the features of the persuasion problem that are common to health topics in general and then to relate these features to the problem of AIDS. We begin by briefly describing two basic areas of health persuasion: disease prevention and compliance to treatment regimens. We will then lay out a sequence of steps in the communication process that is critical for the ultimate goal of health persuasion: behavior change! Next, we will examine the two major types of theoretical models, learning models and cognitive-decision models, which have influenced investigators studying health persuasion. These models are important because they attempt to tell us *how* persuasion occurs.

Two Goals of Health Persuasion

Two main goals of health persuasion are (1) the *prevention* of disease and (2) *compliance* with treatment. Communications aimed at illness prevention attempt to persuade the individual to behave in a manner that will ward off or block future disease threats. Thus, the goal is to prompt *action* with respect to something that may or may not happen by people who may or may not be concerned with the threat. *Action* is also the key in compliance to prescribed treatment for an existing illness; a treatment cannot cure a disease if it is not used. As we shall see, however, basic differences in the behaviors required for effective disease prevention and the actions needed for compliance to treatments require different types of persuasive communications.

Enhancing the Prevention of Illness
Issues involving the prevention of illness are extraordinarily varied. They range from relatively simple actions, such as getting tetanus vaccines or using seatbelts,

Before you eat another bite, think about how saturated fat can raise your blood cholesterol. Then think about how high blood cholesterol can clog up your arteries. Then think about heart attack. Enough to ruin your appetite?

American Heart Association

WE'RE FIGHTING FOR YOUR LIFE

This space provided as a public service.

FIGURE 10-2 We wish we could show you the ad for "beef and cheese" sandwiches and fries that appeared right next to this public service ad in a major college newspaper—but the fast-food company that ran it didn't want us to! Commercial ads and public service ads often send conflicting messages about health values.

Source: Reproduced with permission. © Public Service Announcement: "Have You Ever Wondered What All That Fat Is Doing To Your Arteries?" Copyright American Heart Association. Additional permission from *The Daily Illini,* University of Illinois.

to more complex behaviors, such as smoking cessation or changing sexual practices to prevent AIDS.

Despite their variety, common threads exist among these issues that impact on the success of persuasion attempts. Potentially important features of preventive actions include the length of time and cost that these actions entail. Lifestyle changes involving complex, long-term commitments and deprivations may require different persuasion strategies than relatively easy, short-term, and inexpensive actions such as inoculations (Janis, 1982).

The visibility of the rewards for taking recommended actions is another important factor for most prevention behaviors. If the health benefits are remote, probabilistic, and abstract, as with quitting smoking, it is not surprising to find that many people are highly motivated and adhere to recommendations only while in prevention or treatment programs but fail to do so six months to a year later. The treatment program not only stresses the potential outcomes of smoking cessation but provides immediate social reinforcement for these behaviors. Once the program ends, so does the salience of the long-term rewards and the substantial social reinforcement.

The Importance of Compliance

The rise of chronic and incurable diseases has led to increased recognition of the importance of compliance to medical regimens. As with preventive actions, compliance behaviors vary greatly by treatment regimen, and they, too, can be compared on the basis of critical features. Treatments are often simple and short lived for infectious diseases, such as taking medication for a week to eliminate an inner-ear infection. However, in the absence of simple cures, the treatments for chronic illnesses make increasingly heavy demands on behavioral compliance and may require lifelong adherence to what is often a stressful medical regimen. For example, surgery and chemotherapy for cancers are threatening, painful, and disruptive of daily life over a period of weeks and months. Similarly, the control of diabetes often requires lifelong commitment to diet restrictions and weight regulation.

Compliance behaviors also vary in the degree to which they provide feedback on their effectiveness in battling disease and related symptoms. For example, careful use of medication will usually produce fairly immediate changes in the Parkinson patient's ability to move and walk. The proper use of hypertension medication, on the other hand, will generally not produce any noticeable change in one's experience of symptoms because the disease itself is virtually asymptomatic; that is, there are no perceptible signs of hypertension. Similarly, controlling blood sugar will eliminate some of the more immediate consequences of hyperglycemia, such as thirst and excessive urination, but diabetics may be discouraged from insulin use when they notice a reduction in the good or euphoric sensations that often accompany hyperglycemia (Gonder-Frederick, Cox, Bobbitt, & Pennebaker, 1989).

Overall, it would appear that the rewards for compliance may be more immediate and somewhat less abstract than those for preventive actions. Still, despite the possibility of immediate feedback, studies show that anywhere from 20% to 90% of patients fail to adhere to prescribed treatment regimens (Haynes, Taylor, &

Sackett, 1979)! In many instances, adherence is low for relatively mindless reasons. People forget to buy, inadvertently lose, or simply forget to take their medications. In other cases, compliance is low because of conscious decisions and deliberate action. For example, people may refuse to take medications because they are too expensive, too strong, make them feel bad, or do not make them feel better and therefore seem to be ineffective.

Common Objectives of Prevention and Compliance Messages

Persuasive efforts to enhance disease prevention and those involving treatment compliance share three broad objectives. First, the message must *motivate* the recipient. That is, the message must convince the recipient that the issue is important, that its position is correct, and that the problem depicted in the message is directly relevant to him or her. These motivational effects are essential to establishing a desire for action. Many communications may accomplish only part of this task. For example, a persuasion attempt may convince the recipient of the importance of an issue and the accuracy of the message while failing to make the issue seem personally relevant. (The important role of perceived personal relevance in persuasion is discussed by Petty et al. in Chapter 6.)

Second, as we stated previously, the ultimate objective of these health communications is *behavior* change. For example, the prevention of cancer and coronary disease requires persuading people to quit smoking, reduce dietary fat intake, and increase fiber in the diet (Greenwald & Sondik, 1986). While some other types of communications are simply designed to draw attention to an issue or to change attitudes, a health communication is likely to be deemed a failure if it does not lead to action!

Third, our messages need to consider *long-term* as well as *short-term* behavior change. Whether we examine the multitude of studies on smoking cessation, weight loss, adherence to medication for controlling hypertension, or regular insulin use to control diabetes, there is one finding on which there is virtually unanimous agreement: It is extremely difficult to sustain adherence to a behavioral program for periods greater than six months to a year. While it is not uncommon for 80% to 100% of people to adhere to a preventive or treatment behavior during the early stages of a program, this figure will usually drop to 35% participation rates by six months and 25% by a year (Leventhal, Zimmerman, & Gutmann, 1984).

The difficulty in sustaining long-term behavioral control is a complex issue that has significant implications for the problem of controlling illnesses, including the spread of AIDS. AIDS prevention essentially demands the consistent, lifelong practice of safe sexual behaviors and the avoidance of infection when satisfying drug addiction. We need to know how to construct persuasion attempts in order effectively to induce long-term behavior control and sustained motivation. We will now consider research findings concerning how to construct effective health communications.

The Process of Health Communication

Thus far, we have noted that the two primary goals of health persuasion are disease prevention and treatment compliance and that the three critical objectives for health messages are generating motivation, changing behavior, and maintaining behavioral change. We now turn our attention to the *process* of change. Specifically, how do persuasive messages accomplish these goals? If we can improve our understanding of this communication process, we can do a better job in the practice of persuasion.

The Steps to Communication

To understand how communications can succeed and/or fail, it is helpful to break the communication process into a series of steps. This approach was central to persuasion research carried out by some of the early investigators of attitude development and change (McGuire, 1968). They identified six steps in the communication process:

1. *Exposure*
2. *Attention* to message content
3. *Comprehension* of the content
4. *Retention* of the content in memory
5. *Acceptance* (i.e., attitude change)
6. *Action* (i.e., behavior change)

(See Chapter 7 by Wood and Stagner.)

The application of this relatively simple sequence of steps to health communications in a variety of settings reveals interesting and sometimes surprising findings. For example, *exposure* to the message was taken for granted in early studies of adherence to treatment regimens, because treatments are usually prescribed by the physician in face-to-face encounters with the patient: One might think exposure would be ensured. Unexpectedly, several researchers have found otherwise. In one such study, Bonnie Svarstad (1976) observed interactions of hypertension patients and doctors during routine appointments. After listening to a number of these encounters, she realized that physicians often failed to give instructions on when or how often to take antihypertensive medication. Moreover, when physicians gave such information, it was done in so incomplete or technical a manner that she, a highly educated observer, was often unable to understand what they were asking patients to do!

There is more to exposure, however, than giving the message: How it is given and when it is given can have dramatic effects on the success of communication. The *how* factors include various expressive cues, such as an abrupt, cold manner versus a warm and friendly one. Data show that a patient's adherence is better when a complete and clear message is given by a friendly physician who expresses interest in her patient (Svarstad, 1976). The *when* factors include organizational aspects of the persuasive message, such as whether instructions for a treatment regimen (e.g., taking medication) are given before or after giving the diagnosis. Surprisingly, research indicates that adherence is often better if instructions are given before the diagnosis. When instructions are given afterward, patients seem less able to absorb the treatment information because they are preoccupied with the implications of the diagnosis for their current and future life (Ley, 1977). This seems especially likely when the diagnosis implies a potentially life-threatening, difficult to treat disease, such as diabetes or kidney disease.

Exposure will produce few gains in adherence for disease prevention or treatment, however, if the recipient is not motivated to *attend* to the message. Investigators who have been developing antismoking programs for schoolchildren have suggested that the messages most likely to capture attention will appeal to multiple rather than single needs. For example, messages that focus on enhancement of self-image, quality of life, gains in social standing, *and* good health will be more likely to attract attention than messages focusing solely on improvement of health (Flay & Cook, 1981). It also appears that attention to health themes is enhanced by messages that are vivid, novel, and entertaining. A television commercial focusing on the statistical relationships of seatbelt use and accident deaths will not attract as much attention as one in which seatbelt test dummies sing and dance about seatbelt use.

The third and fourth steps, *comprehension* and *retention*, have been shown to be dependent upon message clarity and organization. For example, doctors participating in one study were instructed first to give a simple outline of what they were going to say before giving the patient the diagnosis and treatment (e.g., "I'm going to tell you what it seems to be, then what it will do to you, then what probably caused it, and finally what to do about it") and to repeat each point in the outline before giving the information in that area. Organizing information in this way led to substantial increases in patients' comprehension, improved retention of the information in memory, *and* improved compliance with recommended treatments.

Because behavior change is the goal, *acceptance* of a health message requires believing a danger is relevant to oneself. For example, messages emphasizing the risks of contracting AIDS through unprotected sexual activity must persuade the individual that these risks are personally relevant. People, particularly adolescents, frequently harbor misconceptions that only homosexuals and drug addicts, particularly the older members of these social groups, are vulnerable to AIDS. Yet the fact remains that heterosexuals engaging in unprotected intercourse are still at a distinct risk for contracting the disease. AIDS prevention attempts must therefore make explicit the recipient's vulnerability to the virus.

Appealing to values of special relevance to the recipient may also enhance acceptance. An antismoking message could have a critical impact on an audience of young, pregnant women by appealing to the desire for a healthy baby. For an audience with a religious commitment, antismoking messages could cite data linking smoking to a variety of immoral behaviors. In sum, acceptance can be enhanced by linking ideas to existent attitudes and values.

The sixth and final step, *action*, requires special consideration, as it is clear that messages may change attitudes yet fail to change behavior (see Chapter 4 by Fazio and Roskos-Ewoldsen). If a message is to influence behavior, it must specify which behaviors are to be taken to avoid or reduce the threat, and it must provide suggestions or models for performance. For example, a newspaper article may persuade a person that excessive dietary fat poses a genuine, personal threat of heart disease, but the person may have few if any ideas as to ways of reducing fat in his diet. To act on this belief, he needs to know which foods are high in fat and which ways of preparing foods will maintain the low-fat diet. Moreover, he may need detailed suggestions on planning and practicing specific actions, such as how to develop and prepare low-fat menus, in order to perform these acts at the right time and place.

The Process of Changing Health Attitudes and Behaviors

Practitioners, public health officials, doctors, and nurses generally prefer practical or technical answers to questions such as, How can we change health attitudes and health behavior? They want to know what to do and say to get people to stop smoking, to take medications, and to adopt safe sexual practices. Rather than a discourse on theory, they want to know whether they should "hit 'em hard" with a fear message or smile when they talk.

In contrast, the theoretically minded investigator typically prefers a more abstract answer. The theorist wants to know about underlying mental processes that suggest a number of different communication techniques, each of which would be effective in different situations and with different people. The investigator realizes that, given the wide variety of situations and audiences, no single technique may be suitable for all places at all times. If we know enough about the specific circumstances of the recommended behavior (e.g., its complexity and for how long it must be done), the communication setting (e.g., how will the message be delivered), and the recipient (e.g., what the recipient expects), we should be able to use theory to make specific suggestions as to technique. As many social psychologists proclaim, "There is nothing so practical as a good theory."

With that said, we shall look at the two broad classes of theories of health persuasion—behavioral learning approaches and decision approaches—to gain further insight into how to influence health beliefs and, ultimately, change health behaviors. Behavioral learning theories propose that health behaviors are acquired through positive reinforcement; rewarding health behaviors and attitudes leads to adoption of these attitudes and actions. Decision theories, on the other hand, view health behaviors as determined by beliefs about the personal relevance or meaning of health threats and beliefs about available protective actions.

Behavioral Learning Approaches to Health Persuasion

The Fear Drive Model

The most influential behavioral learning theory of health persuasion has been the *fear drive model*. According to this model, changes in health beliefs and behaviors are learned when a threatening message arouses fear and the decision to take the recommended health action reduces this distress. In effect, engaging in (or deciding to engage in) the promoted health behavior provides relief, and this positive change in emotional arousal reinforces the decision or action. This reinforcement process leads to learning the healthy action, in that it increases the likelihood that the action will be taken in future, similar situations.

Some of the initial studies of health persuasion, conducted over two decades ago by the senior author and his colleagues, were based on this fear drive model. The goal of these studies was to understand how fear induced by a health threat would affect the learning of attitudes and behaviors to control the threat. In one study, we attempted to persuade a group of college students to take vaccines to protect themselves against tetanus (Leventhal, Singer, & Jones, 1965). This preventive action is quite important, as uninoculated individuals can easily contract tetanus through such simple accidents as stepping on a rusty nail. To study the effects of fear on health persuasion, we divided undergraduates into four groups. Two of these groups received a highly threatening message indicating that tetanus bacilli were everywhere in the individual's everyday environment, even under one's fingernails. The message also vividly described a case history of a tetanus patient who experienced horrific symptoms (such as muscular contractions that led to severe biting of the tongue) and ultimately died. Color photographs depicting consequences of the disease and its treatment, such as one illustrating a tracheotomy, were also included.

The other two groups were exposed to messages that presented essentially the same content in a far less threatening way. The text was technical and impersonal, and the case history description and color photographs were nonthreatening (e.g., it was said that muscular spasms could be controlled by protective steps and that the patient survived). After presentation of the high- or low-threat material, a recommendation was given to all four groups to start a series of tetanus inoculations or to obtain a booster shot, whichever was needed, at the student health service.

The logic behind the manipulation of the threat content was simple: It was assumed that the threatening content would provoke fear, which would *motivate* the recipient to form and rehearse a mental plan for the protective action and that creating and acting on such a plan would make the individual feel less frightened. We believed that the reduction of fear would automatically lead to the *learning* or reinforcement of these protective reactions.

The second major factor varied in this study was the inclusion of a *specific plan for action* for one of the high-threat groups and one of the low-threat groups. Each participant receiving the plan was asked to review his or her daily class schedule and plan a specific time for action. Participants were to find times in their schedules where they would be near the health service so that taking their tetanus shots could be fitted into their daily routines. The participants in the other high- and low-fear groups did not go through this planning schedule.

The results of this study were straightforward. First, subjects exposed to the high-threat messages reported more fear and looked more fearful than those receiving the low-threat messages. A second and more important finding is that recipients of high-threat messages expressed more favorable attitudes and intentions toward getting the vaccines after receiving the tetanus communications but were no more likely actually to get the tetanus shots than subjects exposed to low-threat messages. The third finding was that individuals who were most likely to take inoculations in the months following the study were the ones exposed to either a high- or low-threat message *and* to the action plan.

In short, while the high-threat message created more favorable attitudes and intentions towards tetanus vaccines, it did not lead to prevention behavior unless it was coupled with a specific action plan. But while the high- or low-threat communications were equally effective in increasing prevention behavior when a plan accompanied the threat messages, the plan alone was ineffective in changing attitudes and/or behavior. Thus, while the plan information was critical for the transition from the step of acceptance to that of action, its effectiveness in producing the transition was dependent upon the presence of a prior, motivational message. Moreover, the findings suggest that the message need not be highly threatening to promote action: A low-threat message that produces moderate levels of motivation may work just as well as a high-threat message in increasing health protective behavior (see Figure 10-3).

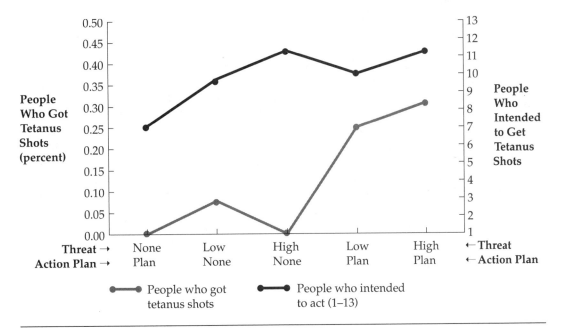

FIGURE 10-3 **The effects of fear and plan messages on intentions to get and actually getting tetanus shots. The percentage of individuals who got tetanus shots (scale on left) is high for both "high" and "low" fear messages *with* an action plan. Note the different pattern for individuals who intended to act (scale on right). Intentions are lowest in the absence of both a fear message and a plan ("none" condition), highest in the two "high" fear groups (both the group with and the group without a plan), and lower in the "low" fear groups.**

The Need to Learn the Skills Required for Health Action

Numerous fear studies on the effectiveness of threatening messages made clear that a substantial gap exists between the favorable intentions induced by threat and taking action to minimize the threat. If a message is to induce action, it must provide a specific action plan in which the behavior is clearly described, related to the individual's daily schedule, and rehearsed. This is clearly seen in behavioral learning studies on the cessation and prevention of smoking. Effective therapies must not only reinforce positive actions, but they must communicate specific plans and strategies for maintaining the newly learned behavior.

For example, in a recent series of studies, Tim Baker and his colleagues (Brandon, Zelman, & Baker, 1987) have used rapid smoking (smokers go for a day without cigarettes and then smoke a cigarette, puffing on signal at six-second intervals) to develop an aversive response to cigarettes. This communication technique is designed to condition a fear-disgust response to the cigarette, so that the participants learn to avoid cigarettes. While these smokers have already indicated high intentions to quit smoking by joining the program, their strong cravings to engage in the pleasurable experience of smoking undermine their more abstract desires to stop smoking. The new aversion to cigarettes fortifies motivation to quit smoking by reducing the opposing motivation to smoke.

Here, too, however, the enhanced motivation to avoid cigarettes induced by rapid smoking is not enough: To maintain a nonsmoking status, rapid smoking must be combined with an intensive counseling program on how to remain a nonsmoker. The messages in the counseling sessions are designed to give the participants specific behavior strategies for dealing with temptations to smoke. In particular, participants are asked to define a precise time for quitting and to set a goal for going without cigarettes. They learn to identify internal changes that may provoke the urge to smoke, such as distress due to withdrawal, symptoms that may be erroneously interpreted as evidence that *not* smoking is unhealthy (e.g., many heavy smokers cough up phlegm as the cilia in their lungs return to life), and weight gain (ex-smokers tend to gain weight, although the amount is usually limited to about five pounds). Participants also identify social cues that may provoke urges to smoke, such as boredom, stimulating social gatherings in which smoking is common, life stresses, and so on. Not only do participants learn how to identify these internal and external cues; they also formulate and rehearse coping skills to interrupt and control these urges as soon as they are experienced and to deal with these urges should they persist.

The counseling messages also focus on coping strategies to be used if one relapses and smokes. As Marlatt and Gordon (1980) have indicated, it is critical that participants acquire the ability to cope with feelings of regret, distress, and self-blame if one violates the no-smoke rule. Failure to manage these feelings will lead the ex-smoker to return to high levels of smoking and to be far more reluctant to try to quit and far less confident of success.

These studies have found that the combination of aversion therapy and counseling on strategies to remain a nonsmoker can ensure that 40% to 50% will quit smoking for two years. This is substantially superior to the 15% to 25% success rates for a six-month period obtained by prior studies that failed to include both motivational and action-focused components in their therapeutic communications.

Skills Communications in Smoking Prevention

The enormous effort involved in communicating and persuading adult smokers to quit has prompted public health officials to launch widescale campaigns for the prevention of smoking in schoolchildren. It seems better to prevent the development of an addictive habit than to try to break it after it is acquired. Nearly 200 antismoking programs were conducted in schools in the United States, Canada, and Scotland between 1950 and 1978: Virtually none induced reductions in smoking rates for more than one year. However, more recent studies have utilized a variety of antismoking messages designed to motivate and teach specific preventive skills. For example, videotaped training sessions have been developed to teach various ways to resist peer pressure to smoke, without sacrificing friendships (Biglan et al., 1987).

The broadest approach to skills communication is seen in the *life-skills* training programs (Botvin & Wills, 1980). In addition to providing strategies to avoid smoking, these programs present messages to generate skills for handling stress. Supposedly, improvement in the management of daily life situations reduces the failure-induced anxiety and distress that produce the urge to smoke. While there is reason to believe the skills-based approach to antismoking persuasion will produce positive benefits by reducing adolescent smoking, a careful review of these studies suggests these benefits are both small and uncertain (Flay, 1985). Modest reductions in the number of children trying cigarettes and becoming regular smokers have been reported in some studies, but there were no signs of reductions in some of the largest and most carefully designed programs. Thus, the jury is still out on the cost effectiveness of school-based antismoking programs as they are now conceived. If we change our theoretical conceptualization of the development of smoking and focus more closely on the motivational aspects of the problem, we may find new ways of developing effective messages for protection.

Decision Approaches to Health Persuasion

The decision theories of health persuasion can be divided into two camps: (1) those that make use of formal decision models entailing rational *cost-benefit analyses* of health behavior and (2) self-regulatory models that focus on the ways in which more commonsensical attitudes about health threats interact with emotions to motivate health actions. The rational decision models focus on the logical assessment of information, whereas the self-regulatory models view decisions as based on intuitions and emotions, as well as more reasoned beliefs. Because both approaches emphasize cognition and thought, they have often been less attentive than learning (reinforcement) models to the acquisition of the skills needed for performing preventive and compliance behaviors.

Rational Decision Models

Formal decision models assume that reactions to a health message are based upon estimates of personal vulnerability to the health threat as well as beliefs about the severity of the health problem. Beliefs that one is likely to experience the health problem as well as perceptions that the health problem would create severe consequences will motivate decisions to take protective action. In addition, these decisions to adopt health-protective behaviors are also believed to be based on the individual's perceptions about the difficulty and aversiveness of the recommended action and about how effective the action will be in preventing the health problem. These health beliefs about vulnerability, severity, costs in terms of the resources needed to take the recommended action, and benefits in taking action will determine whether or not the individual will act in accordance with the persuasion message (Becker & Maiman, 1975) (see Figure 10-4).

An example can help make these ideas concrete. Consider the case of a young woman who is a smoker and is of childbearing age. Let us assume she has been exposed to official public health statistics and messages that make her realize that she is vulnerable to lung cancer and that there is a strong likelihood of death if she contracts it. While these beliefs may generate motivation to quit and emotional conflict about her continued smoking, she may still fail to quit. Her reasons for resisting change may include the conviction that she will lose certain benefits of smoking; she may feel that smoking relaxes her and helps her cope with life's daily stresses. Her knowledge that she has tried to quit twice before and failed to do so may be an added barrier to change. Let us assume next that she decides to have a child and that her obstetrician, husband, and friends have told her that smoking could harm her infant. She will now realize that her family and friends would be horrified and angry with her, and she would never forgive herself, if she smoked

BLOOM COUNTY   by Berke Breathed

FIGURE 10-4   Perceptions of personal vulnerability to a health threat can strongly affect behavior.

Source: © 1993, The Washington Post Writers Group. Reprinted with permission.

while pregnant and her baby had a birth defect. She may then entertain the additional advantages of quitting smoking—such as getting rid of her hacking cough, the smell of smoke that permeates her clothes and house, and so on—and decide to quit. Her decision on whether to quit smoking will be based on some process involving a weighing of both social norms and personal advantages and disadvantages of "kicking the habit" (Ajzen, 1988; Fishbein & Ajzen, 1975; see Chapter 4 for a discussion of this model).

Studies that have examined the impact of information about the dire consequences of ignoring health threats have found that persuasive messages emphasizing immediate rather than long-term consequences of a risky behavior have more influence on attitudes and behavior. For example, adolescents will often continue to smoke cigarettes in spite of knowing of the increased risk of heart disease and cancer because these risks are relatively distant consequences of the current behavior. However, they may be influenced by evidence of immediate, short-term effects, such as a hacking cough or reduced performance in athletic events.

It also appears that persuasive messages will elicit behavior change only when the individual believes that he or she can effectively perform the behavior. A study on dieting attempts and weight loss demonstrates the importance of one's perceived ability and control (Schifter & Ajzen, 1985). In this study, college women were asked about their attitudes and intentions toward losing weight and the degree to which they believed they *could* reduce their weight in the next six weeks. The amount of weight lost by the end of the next six weeks was then measured. It was found that both attitudes about weight loss and perceived ability to lose weight were correlated with actual weight reduction. However, perception of ability to lose weight was the *best* predictor of weight loss. Those women who believed they could lose weight were more successful in actually losing weight.

In summary, the use of rational decision models to analyze persuasive health messages has increased our understanding of how features of a health message affect attitude and behavior change. However, these models do not seem to capture all of the thoughts and feelings that impact on our health behavior decisions. Many researchers in the field of health psychology have therefore turned to models that deal not only with the rationality involved in health decisions but with the more intuitive and emotional impulses that guide our health behavior. We will now consider these self-regulation models of health behavior.

Self-Regulation in a Commonsense Environment

Suppose you were diagnosed as having hypertension and given medication to take every day. While you know that the medication will control your high blood pressure, your "gut-level" reaction may be that there is no point in taking it because you feel just fine. Or suppose that during a stressful day at work, you experience a symptom that does not to your knowledge match any illness. You may think to yourself, Why go to a doctor? It's just stress, and he or she won't be able to do anything about it.

We have all experienced situations where we have based our health decisions and behavior more upon intuition and gut-level beliefs than upon logic and rational thinking. Such gut-level reasoning may affect the perceived meaning or interpretation of persuasive health messages, their acceptance, and their impact upon behavior. Self-regulation theories attempt to consider these intuitive, commonsense attitudes about illness along with more rational, logical thinking in the hope that consideration of both the intuitive aspects and the rational aspects of illness attitudes and thinking will help us better understand persuasion.

Leventhal's self-regulatory model of illness behavior (Leventhal, Meyer, & Nerenz, 1980; Leventhal & Cameron, 1987) emphasizes that we must understand how an individual perceives a health threat in order to change his or her attitudes and behavior. That is, we must understand both the logical, rational attitudes and the more intuitive beliefs about a health threat, as these commonsense beliefs guide the individual's responses to messages about illness.

It pays to pause for a moment and examine what is meant by the expression *commonsense belief*. Commonsense beliefs refer to what you know from what you see, hear, and feel every day of your life: that tables are solid; that what goes up must come down; that the sun rises and sets. But every one of these commonsense beliefs is inaccurate: Solids, including tables, are mainly empty space; when an object goes up far enough, it will stay up; the sun does not rise and set, but rather the earth turns. Each of these commonsense rules is wrong because it fails to state how things truly work. Yet each is a useful description of our general, everyday experiences. Similarly, the commonsense belief that one feels pain and other symptoms when ill describes much of our typical experiences of acute, infectious conditions, such as the common cold. However, this rule is not valid for many disease conditions. Given that these commonsense rules guide our behavior, we will be at risk whenever the rule and the disease process are at variance with one another.

For example, it has been found that many individuals with hypertension believe that there are specific symptoms of this disease, such as headaches and dizziness. In fact, they may hold onto these beliefs, even when their doctor has told them that hypertension is an asymptomatic disease! Because commonsense beliefs are a natural guide to behavior, these patients will often use their symptoms as guides to taking their hypertension medicine: If they do not experience symptoms, they will stop taking their medication. It is therefore important to understand the individual's personal beliefs of an illness and to understand the impact of intuition and emotion on health decisions.

Let us consider the psychological situation of two women, both of whom are objectively healthy yet both of whom believe they have a high probability of contracting breast cancer. One *feels* healthy and fine: She is active and alert and involved in her everyday life. The second feels tired, has pains in her back, and is generally worn out. We have found that women who are feeling vulnerable *and* who are experiencing symptoms, like the second woman above, will also express considerable worry about cancer, while those with high-vulnerability beliefs and few symptoms will not (Easterling & Leventhal, 1989). In effect, worry seems to depend upon both the abstract belief that one is vulnerable and the presence of symptoms, even though none of the symptoms are actually symptoms of cancer. Indeed, the woman who believes herself vulnerable to cancer and is asymptomatic appears to be no more likely to worry about cancer than the woman who thinks her chances of getting breast cancer are very low. Now, the question is, Would these two women differ in their response to a message urging them to get a check-up for cancer or to engage in some form of cancer-preventive behavior, such as dietary change, or taking hormones on a daily basis (see Figure 10-5)?

We do not know enough to give a simple answer to this question. What we do know suggests that individuals typically view cancer as a chronic and immutable condition, and the intense worry experienced by a woman who holds these beliefs, feels vulnerable, and is symptomatic might destroy any hope that her cancer is controllable: Worry may confirm her *cognitive* suspicions that she cannot protect herself against this intractable disease. If a message about cancer prevention stimulates worry in such a woman, the worry might provoke a sense of resignation and

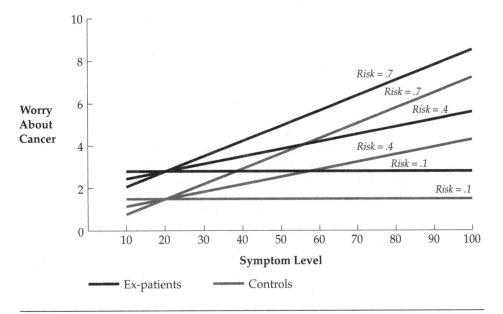

FIGURE 10-5   Worry about cancer is a product of the perceived probability of getting cancer, or perceived risk (lines are entered for 1, 4, and 7 out of 10 chances of getting cancer) and the presence of somatic sensations (noncancer symptoms). Solid lines represent former breast cancer patients, and dashed lines represent controls (close friends who did not have cancer). Worry about cancer does not increase with increases in the number of somatic sensations when perceived risk is very low (0 or 1 in 10), but worry increases rapidly with increases in the number of somatic sensations when perceived risk is high (e.g., 7 in 10). Neither perceived risk nor somatic sensations alone is sufficient to create worry.

Source: From "The Contribution of Concrete Cognition to Emotion: Neutral Symptoms as Elicitors of Worry About Cancer" by D. Easterling and H. Leventhal, 1989, *Journal of Applied Psychology, 74*, 787–796. Copyright 1989 by the American Psychological Association. Reprinted by permission.

defeat and convince her that she cannot protect herself. Hence, she will fail to act preventively.

A recent study by Gintner and his associates (Gintner, Rectanus, Accord, & Parker, 1987) suggests that a message might succeed in generating action for individuals with high-vulnerability beliefs if it avoids discussing the threatening aspects of the disease that might induce worry and emphasizes instead feelings of wellness as benefits to taking preventive actions. The study found that individuals who had a parent with hypertension (i.e., people who are vulnerable to this disease) were more than twice as likely to attend a blood pressure screening if they read a message emphasizing the value of acting to maintain feelings of vigor and well-being rather than a message emphasizing the severe consequences of the illness. Apparently, an illness-oriented message that is very threatening may leave some individuals feeling hopeless about protecting themselves. As a consequence, they may prefer to avoid thinking about or acting on the threat altogether in an effort to keep from being frightened.

Wellness-oriented information is more effective because it minimizes threat associations, it has a more optimistic focus, and it encourages individuals to use regularly occurring sensations of well-being rather than symptoms as cues to action (Gintner et al., 1987). Moreover, wellness messages may also stimulate a wider range of goals for health action, such as looking more attractive, feeling better, and gaining social approval for weight control, in comparison to most threat messages that stress the single motive of avoiding illness. However, a properly framed threat message may facilitate health persuasion when *inaction* is seen as the source of danger, that is, when not taking recommended action is seen as the source of uncertainty, anxiety, and loss of control over health outcomes. Translated to the cancer case, we may want to tell women that failing to conduct breast self-examinations or failing to eat a high-fiber diet will leave them at risk for illness and leave them feeling worried and distressed (Meyerowitz & Chaiken, 1987).

We can see, then, that the behavioral response evoked by a health message depends not only on the perceived validity of its information but also on thoughts and images generated when the recipient interprets the message. This new set of thoughts may provoke feelings of fear and loss of hope or competence that deter action *or* may stimulate action by creating the view that inaction will lead to danger, fear, and loss of hope.

Do the hypotheses and findings described above have implications for generating communication programs and strategies to control the spread of AIDS? Messages that merely attempt to generate fear and worry within the recipients will often provoke feelings of resignation and defeat, and the recipients may try to ignore the information in order to reduce their worry. A better approach would be to construct more optimistic messages that provide accurate information on AIDS and its transmission, specify effective strategies for adopting safe-sex and drug use practices, and stress how the use of these practices can reduce worry and therefore lead to more pleasurable experiences.

Of course, AIDS is yet more complex. The protective actions demand mutual participation, and it may not be easy to motivate or provide the skills needed to control sexual and/or drug-using partners. Can a woman living with and dependent upon an intravenous (IV) drug user insist on safe sex? To do so, she may have to persuade her partner that he is vulnerable to AIDS and must therefore practice safe sex, which may seem less pleasurable than their usual practices. If he is already ill, can she persuade him to protect her if he is angry about his forthcoming death and wants to take her to the grave? Can she risk losing her means of support and protection in a relatively hostile environment? Can she manage his wrath? Our models of health behavior have yet to be sufficiently developed to address these complex social questions.

Issues in Health Persuasion Not Covered by the Models

Our review of health persuasion has focused on message *content* because message factors have been the focus of most of the theoretical models. However, factors regarding the channel, source, and receiver are also of special concern to health persuasion. We will examine these characteristics briefly in the next three sections.

Characteristics of the Channel, or Medium

The two major channels for health communications in our society are (1) *one-to-one interactions* with a health advisor, such as that between a doctor and a patient, and (2) *mass media appeals*, such as television commercials, printed ads for over-the-counter medications, and articles on health appearing in newspapers and magazines. Both channels have their advantages and limitations.

The individualized nature of the one-to-one relationship increases the chances that a health message will be received and allows a health advisor to tailor the message to the recipient's health risks and beliefs about these risks. Thus, individualized communication is potentially more effective in changing attitudes and behavior because it provides the opportunity to translate abstract, population based data into personal realities. For example, a doctor can tailor the probabilities of heart disease messages for smokers into a personal message, such as "Given *your* family history and *your* current health status, smoking poses a serious risk of cardiac death." These types of persuasion messages have a personal relevance missing in media appeals targeted to an entire population.

In addition, person-to-person encounters are typically a consequence of the individual's concern for his or her health; the individual is often already motivated to acquire and use health-related information. This is generally not the case among most recipients of mass media health appeals. Finally, if the doctor-patient relationship is a continuing one, the meeting will be followed up by additional appointments, allowing the physician to gain repeated assessments of the patient's health status, give repeated and revised advice on reducing illness or disease risk, and monitor the patient's compliance. The implication, of course, is that the patient will have to account for his or her compliance or lack thereof.

The major shortcoming of this person-to-person channel is that it is likely to be limited to individuals who are already concerned about their health and may ignore those most in need of information and changes in behavior. In addition, there is a tendency for practitioners to ignore health issues related to primary prevention, such as wearing seatbelts, avoiding dangerous recreational drugs, or preventing exposure to the AIDS virus. Instead, most visits tend to deal with secondary prevention (i.e., behaviors that minimize illness through early detection and treatment) or tertiary prevention (i.e., behaviors that control the complications of illness). Moreover, these interactions are typically few and far between. Individuals may go for years without seeing their physicians, and reminders about particular health actions such as breast self-examinations or proper nutritional habits may not be provided with enough frequency.

Mass media, on the other hand, are able to fill in where doctor-patient interactions leave off. They are much more effective at reaching individuals who are either unaware of the existence of a specific health problem and/or unaware of their personal risk for the health threat. Television commercials are often used solely to sensitize viewers to health issues in the hope that they will then attend to other information that will induce behavior change. For example, community-based coronary disease–prevention programs often use television spots to sensitize viewers to health issues with the hope that these spots will increase attention to other sources of information, such as the list of contents on food packages or literature on antismoking programs. Mass media persuasion messages can also be aired or promoted frequently, via multiple channels (i.e., television, radio, billboards, etc.) and using multiple sources. They are particularly appropriate for illness-prevention issues, which are the primary behaviors that the interactions with health specialists tend to ignore. Indeed, media may garner enormous and unexpected influence over preventive health behaviors, such as diet and exercise, in relation to that provided by health practitioners, who are often seen to be indifferent or lacking expertise in these areas.

On the other hand, media-based interventions are limited in several respects. First, they are less able to change beliefs or behavior than they are to reinforce existing attitudes and habits (Budd & McCron, 1981). This is partly because the short amount of time or space in television and magazine ads does not allow room for thorough arguments. For example, a magazine advertisement about the dangers of cocaine abuse may reinforce the fears of a concerned parent who already thinks cocaine is dangerous and be ignored by a cocaine user who prefers to think that cocaine is safe and not addictive.

The second limitation of media-based messages is they are typically less persuasive when trying to change attitudes regarding well-established health practices, especially where people have substantial (and often inaccurate) private experience that appears to be inconsistent with the media message (Budd & McCron, 1981). For example, a short but vivid commercial about the dangers of marijuana may be more readily accepted by a person who has just recently begun to experiment with the drug than by a longtime user who has ample experience with the drug and has never noticed any deleterious effects. Again, media appeals usually have too little space to develop comprehensive arguments, which makes it easier for individuals of opposing viewpoints to reject the message as written by an uninformed or biased group of individuals.

Third, media appeals may fail to reach the audience to whom they are directed (Flay, DiTecco, & Schlegal, 1980). For example, a program on AIDS broadcast over public television may have bypassed key audiences because those most susceptible to AIDS and most in need of information may be less likely to view television and the least likely to view public television.

A fourth limitation of media appeals is the difficulty in evaluating the impact of a mass media program. It is often impossible to observe the responses of the audience to a media campaign. For example, it is difficult to assess whether the warnings on cigarette packages actually impact on either people's attitudes about smoking or their smoking behavior.

Finally, mass media programs are often in competition with other programs and commercials that present conflicting viewpoints (Lau, Kane, Berry, Ware, & Ray, 1980). Programs advocating healthy diets may be followed by commercials for cholesterol-laden desserts or fast foods. While commercials for Alcoholics Anonymous are being broadcast, billboards and magazine ads may project a sexy, stylish image of drinking alcoholic beverages. There seems to be a pervasive contradiction in health values in American society, with social values of proper diet, not smoking, avoiding alcohol and drugs, and exercise being advocated on the very same channels carrying advertisements for and showing film characters indulging in health vices. Although moderation is often the answer for such issues as drinking, eating rich or sugary foods, and exercise, media shows typically fail to deliver this message. Moreover, the manufacturers of such products as alcohol or unhealthy foods rarely stress moderation or suggest just how much is "enough."

One may be tempted to ask, Which is more effective, private interactions or mass media? Clearly, there are situations in which a face-to-face interaction with a health advisor is necessary (i.e., for issues concerning compliance with medication instructions or treatment regimens). On the other hand, mass appeals are certainly more far reaching than attempts to change attitudes and behaviors on an individualized level. And for health problems that are clearly public, such as the control of AIDS, mass media programs have an especially important role to play. For example, mass media campaigns on AIDS prevention appear to be the most effective means to:

1. Bring the issue to national awareness
2. Educate the public about the cause and spread of AIDS in order to quell the widespread fear of contact with people with AIDS
3. Provide information about specific ways of avoiding the health hazard
4. Create a norm or sense of public acceptance for preventive sexual behaviors, thereby reinforcing such behaviors for those who are doing them (see Figure 10-6)

In summary, the complex behavioral changes called for in medical treatments and dramatic lifestyle changes, such as smoking cessation or weight loss, may

HE LOVES ME.

HE LOVES ME NOT.

Love the one you're with and use condoms.
Condoms help prevent the spread of AIDS.
To you. And your lover. To know more about
condoms and AIDS, call the Madison AIDS
Support Network at 255-1711.

Condoms. They're a way of life.

FIGURE 10-6   Mass media campaigns play an important role in AIDS prevention.

Source: Reprinted with permission of Planned Parenthood of Wisconsin, Madison Advertising Federation, and Madison Newspapers, Inc.

require face-to-face interactions and training to establish these changes. The combination of mass media and face-to-face persuasion attempts, however, may prove to be the most effective way of creating, reinforcing, and *maintaining* these difficult healthful actions.

Characteristics of the Source

Health Advisor-Patient Interactions

A great deal of attention has been given to how characteristics of the practitioner can enhance information acceptance and ensure attitude and behavior change. The practitioner who displays warmth, friendliness, concern, and interest in patients will be much more successful in persuading them to adopt recommended behaviors (Leventhal, Zimmerman, & Gutmann, 1984). However, friendliness does not seem to be the most effective persuasion technique within the patient-practitioner interaction. More effective influence strategies used by doctors include attempts to justify the prescribed treatment (explaining how it will be effective in treating the problem) and placing emphasis on treatment instructions. Both strategies have been found almost to double rates of compliance with medication prescriptions (Svarstad, 1976).

Source Characteristics at the Mass Communication Level

While the trustworthiness and expertise of a message source undoubtedly impacts on attitude and behavior change in face-to-face interactions, source credibility is particularly important at the mass communication level. Indeed, credibility is often built in for the face-to-face relationship, as the patient typically has chosen to interact with the health advisor on the basis of his or her expertise. In contrast, the credibility of the source at the mass communication level is determined by the mass media program coordinators.

One must keep in mind, however, that *credibility* and *popularity* may have different effects. Clearly, individuals are more likely to attend to a persuasion appeal if the source is particularly credible and/or popular. In fact, people may pay more attention to an advertisement (e.g., about avoiding drugs) if the source is a celebrity (e.g., the First Lady of the United States or a rock star) than a source of high credibility (e.g., a representative from the American Medical Association). But while a celebrity may be more able to focus audience attention on an issue, a celebrity may be no better than an unknown expert in achieving attitude and behavior change. Some commercial producers have come up with clever solutions to the problem of celebrity versus credibility power. For example, a recent advertisement for a brand of aspirin used a well-known actor who played the role of a physician on a popular television series but who actually had no medical expertise whatsoever! (See also Chapter 9 by Cialdini.)

The source's similarity to the receiver can also impact on credibility for health issues where the similarity implies common problems and values. For example, pregnant women were more likely to use a rooming-in service (i.e., to keep their newborns with them rather than in the hospital nursery) when the recommenda-tion was delivered by a pregnant communicator and by a communicator of similar ethnic background (Mazen & Leventhal, 1972). Ethnic similarity was also impor-tant for the acceptance of persuasion messages about breast feeding. Findings such as these would lead one to expect that a message recommending that one "Just say no" to drugs would be more persuasive coming from a teenager than an adult; the younger source would likely be perceived as more knowledgeable of the compet-ing social pressures to take drugs and more credible as a source for ways of saying "No" (Shelton & Rogers, 1981).

It is easy to imagine that these advantages would hold for messages on safe sex and/or using clean needles. Homosexuals, partners of drug users, and intravenous drug users would be more persuasive and more likely to be listened to than out-siders to these local cultures. We can assume that a discussion of AIDS prevention by a source who shares the recipient's environment and personal characteristics will convey the notion that these ideas are in the best interest of the recipient's own social and personal needs. Thus, similarity should enhance both acceptance and action.

Finally, mass media messages will be more effective if they are delivered by a variety of sources (Flay & Cook, 1981). Clearly, using several credible speakers to deliver a health message will give the impression of consensus on the issue. (See Chapter 8 by Kitayama and Burnstein for ways to use multiple sources effectively.)

Characteristics of the Receiver

We suspect that a number of individual factors play a critical role in the conversion of attitudes and intentions to behavior change. The frightening content in health communications, such as implications of death and disfigurement or of painful treatment procedures, may be particularly likely to lead to a sense of hopelessness for individuals lacking confidence in their ability to solve problems and/or control their feelings. The fear-inducing images of a health warning often seem to affect such persons who have low self-esteem by further convincing them of their incom-petence.

There are also several individual factors that affect the degree to which a health message is perceived as personally relevant to the recipient. As we discussed ear-lier in the chapter, an individual is unlikely to accept and adopt a health behavior if it does not seem necessary or advantageous to do so, at least at that point in time. Indeed, there is abundant evidence showing that as people get older (and wiser?) they are increasingly open to health messages, because many illnesses seem more probable and, therefore, prevention behaviors appear to be more relevant to them.

A recent study demonstrates how the age of the recipient, and therefore the personal relevance of the issue, determines the success of various health persua-sion messages about osteoporosis (Rook, 1986). Information about the disease was presented in either a vivid manner (i.e., with a description of the experiences of a specific person with osteoporosis) or an abstract manner (i.e., with reference to women in general) to either premenopausal or postmenopausal women. Among the premenopausal women, for whom the message was of less relevance, the vivid version induced higher motivations to take calcium supplements and to exercise frequently than did the abstract version. This is in line with general expectations that vividly presented messages have enhanced persuasibility because they are comprehended and remembered more easily and are more emotionally arousing (Taylor & Thompson, 1982). However, among the postmenopausal women, for whom the message was of high relevance, the two types of messages were equally persuasive. Presumably, the high personal relevance of the health threat made them highly receptive to either vivid or abstract information.

Many persuasion efforts attempting to educate and change attitudes about AIDS and sexual precautions may also seem to be of low personal relevance, depending on the recipient's age. Consider, for example, the AIDS materials given in the primary and secondary schools to children and adolescents who are not sexually active and may not foresee themselves as being so in the near future. As with information about contraception in general, messages about sexual behavior may be ignored or quickly forgotten by students who are not sexually active.

The findings from the study on message vividness, relevance, and osteoporosis prevention behaviors suggest that AIDS-related persuasion attempts should use graphic messages that highlight the relevance of the material to the individual recipient. Vivid and dramatic presentations would be more likely to attract attention and may be more easily recalled years after message exposure, when the recipient needs to make choices about sexual activity. Recall, persuasion, and action are most likely, however, if the message has been attached to a personally meaningful theme. For example, by drawing clear analogies between prior experiences in which the child's impulsive behavior led to unpleasant outcomes, one might establish better recall and wariness of the impulsive actions associated with the risk of AIDS. This type of AIDS-prevention message may hit home with a very young audience for whom its sexual content is otherwise premature.

Resistance to smoking has been achieved in a similar manner. The very same antismoking message produced a fourfold improvement in resistance to starting smoking by linking the content of the antismoking message to prior life episodes. To do this, youngsters in the audience were asked to recall times in which they got into trouble because they ignored warning signs or because they were showing off. The antismoking message developed these very same themes for smoking and the linkage was clearly drawn in the discussion session following exposure to the media program (Leventhal, Baker, Brandon, & Fleming, 1989).

Characteristics of the Social Environment

Persuasion and behavior change are not purely individual matters. On the contrary, many decisions regarding health-relevant behaviors are heavily influenced by the social environment. Peer pressure, social support, social norms, and the health-related behaviors of other group members can all either promote or inhibit the individual from taking an action that risks his or her health (Flay, 1985; Fishbein & Ajzen, 1975). For example, a smoker who is trying to quit the habit may end up smoking if other group members are enjoying cigarettes and/or cajole this person into smoking. In contrast, a person attempting to quit smoking but who experiences strong urges to smoke may successfully resist the temptation, at least over the short term, when friends or family members offer encouragement and support.

The adoption and maintenance of healthy behaviors also rely on whether the individual's social environment provides opportunities to express these new attitudes and perform these new behaviors, with reinforcement for doing so (Flay, 1985). The success of support groups such as Alcoholics Anonymous and Weight Watchers may be partially due to the fact that they provide just this kind of environment for their members.

To enhance the impact of social support on behavior change, persuasion attempts should include messages tailored to significant family members and friends as well as messages for the target individual. For example, smoking cessation programs should not only deal with the individual but train family and friends in how to help the individual. Of the few programs that have succeeded in altering smoking, diet, and drug behaviors over a long period of time, many have included attempts to change the attitudes and behaviors of others so as to make the social environment more supportive and involved (Altman & King, 1986). Mass media appeals may also be able to implement behavior change by including efforts to change the attitudes and involvement of persons close to a target individual. More and more, drug commercials are instructing viewers, "If someone you know needs help, call or write for information on how to help."

Social norms and influences can be critical factors in promoting precautionary sexual practices because these behaviors are inherently social. In the absence of effective education, individuals in newly formed relationships may feel inhibited to suggest safe sexual practices for fear of insulting and/or losing their partner. They may not know how to bring up the subject or else decide that it must not be important since the partner does not bring up the topic. Many appeals for AIDS prevention are beginning to suggest strategies for initiating a discussion about precautionary sexual behaviors with one's partner and encourage viewers to try *role-playing*, or practicing these strategies with friends who can provide reinforcement, encouragement, and suggestions.

Conclusion

We have covered a wide range of social and individual processes that, under ideal circumstances, may act in concert to promote effective health behavior for one or more specific issues, such as smoking reduction and AIDS control. The central issue is when and how to apply specific procedures to achieve desirable health objectives. As you can imagine, this is no easy task. Although the theoretical models we have reviewed are useful tools for the analysis of problems in health persuasion, they lack detail and precision and do not cover the full range of factors that impact upon the wide range of health actions targeted by health messages. In addition, the empirical evidence is sketchy; there is virtually no evidence whatsoever for issues such as the best match of communication content to the personality and needs of specific individuals.

A Program to Control AIDS

We can quickly summarize both what is known and what gaps remain in our knowledge by considering what we can do to control the AIDS epidemic. An examination of the biomedical and epidemiological evidence would be the necessary first step in this speculative exercise. The first question is, How is AIDS spread? More specifically, What behaviors are responsible for this spread? The next question is, What population groups are vulnerable to this spread? That is, What groups are engaging in risk behaviors? Answers to these questions establish the goals and target groups for a communication campaign to protect the public.

Research to date indicates that the AIDS virus is spread through behaviors involving shared bodily fluids, typically through sexual intercourse and through needle sharing by intravenous drug users. The populations most at risk today are therefore sexually active individuals, particularly homosexual males, and intravenous drug addicts. These conclusions about risk behaviors and target populations are appropriate for *American culture at this point in time*. However, population susceptibility can and does vary, and tomorrow's AIDS problem in the United States may be different than that today.

Having defined the most currently vulnerable groups, we then need to determine which behavioral practices can most readily be changed to block the spread of the disease. Once this has been determined, the question is how best to communicate the need for change to the target groups. Specifically, how can we best communicate the risk of AIDS and ways of protecting oneself against AIDS to homosexual males and drug users? What can we say to make them aware of the threat, allow them to realize their personal vulnerability, and lead them to believe that they can indeed benefit by making appropriate behavioral changes?

Success in controlling AIDS appears at hand in many factions of the homosexual population. While information on AIDS and its spread may have been suppressed for two or three years, homosexual males, as consumers of media and members of a community with reasonably well-organized channels of communication, are now very much aware of the behaviors that lead to the spread of AIDS and have begun to change their sexual practices. But can more be done in the behavioral arena to check the spread of AIDS in this population? One suspects that the media have played their part. Reinforced by direct contact with AIDS victims, changes have occurred in specific practices and in homosexual lifestyles for those individuals unwilling to sacrifice their lives for momentary pleasures.

Drug users are a still more difficult target. Unorganized as a group and out of touch with society's communication channels, they may not recognize the threat. Moreover, their daily diet of misery and death may lead them to attribute misfortune to more salient causes, and they may fail to see AIDS as an especially serious threat. In short, it may be difficult to represent the threat of AIDS as a part of the drug user's world. Moreover, the most effective protection against AIDS, cessation of drug use, entails giving up a major, if not the only, source of relief and excitement in otherwise painful lives.

The difficulty of preventing AIDS among the risk-taking homosexual population and drug users may encourage the development of primary prevention programs among teenagers. Would it not make sense to teach safe-sex practices and drug avoidance to teens? In addition to reaching current and future homosexual partners and drug users, these programs would also educate current and future heterosexual partners. This group is currently less likely to acquire AIDS, but their estimated vulnerability may very well increase dramatically in the next decade. At the very least, these programs would provide this group with accurate information about the disease and help to decrease the panic and hysteria about AIDS and the people who contract it.

Although AIDS-prevention programs in the schools will effectively reach captive audiences of adolescents who are generally open to persuasive messages, the major barrier may be trying to convince them that AIDS is indeed a personal health threat. For the adolescent girl whose experimentation with sex is restricted to a local peer group, AIDS may seem part of another world. Her naive eyes do not see IV drug users, bisexuals, or promiscuous males among her friends, including those with whom she may first initiate sexual activity. They are all "part of the gang." But no one knows the complete history of each member of this informal gang, the risks taken on trips, the needs that drive one momentarily from safe to high-risk actions. Research to date suggests that the most effective persuasion attempts for adolescents would include vivid messages about AIDS transmission that also emphasize specific behavior strategies and social norms advocating safe sex and the avoidance of intravenous drugs. However, it is clear that more needs to be done to increase wariness of that which is regarded as safe (see, for example, the AIDS message presented in Chapter 1, p. 11).

While AIDS prevention poses a particularly difficult problem, several intervention programs have demonstrated encouraging levels of success in reducing risky behaviors and, in turn, lowering the number of new cases of human immunodeficiency virus (HIV) infection. One of the most successful campaigns was targeted at reducing the risky sexual practices among gay and bisexual men in San Francisco (McKusick, Conant, & Coates, 1985). The program combined mass communication attempts with more individualized intervention services to inform the gay population and to promote change in risky sexual practices. At the mass communication level, information about AIDS was disseminated throughout the community by way of media messages, town meetings, workshops, and seminars. These public messages gave explicit information about behaviors that put individuals at risk, thereby promoting realistic vulnerability appraisals and safer sexual practices. Individual health education and counseling were made available at HIV-testing sites and through phone information services, so that those identifying themselves as being at risk could receive communications tailored to their particular needs and concerns.

Moreover, the campaign placed a heavy focus on changing community norms about AIDS and safe sexual activities. The gay community was recruited to be actively involved in all phases of the prevention campaign and served as sources for persuasion messages and educational services. Positive social values about AIDS prevention were also fostered at workshops through structured discussions about how each participant might become personally involved in fighting the spread of AIDS (Communication Technologies, 1987). These communication efforts induced a significant shift in community norms so that low-risk sexual behaviors were valued and AIDS prevention became a unifying cause.

As a result of this extensive campaign, the number of new HIV infections among gay and bisexual men in San Francisco has been substantially reduced (Winkelstein, Samuel, Padian, Wiley, Lang, Anderson, & Levy, 1987). Moreover, recent studies report that gay males in San Francisco are far less likely to engage in risky sexual activity than men in other parts of the country (Coates, Stall, & Hoff, 1988).

The overwhelming success of the San Francisco prevention model, which has been adopted by other cities across the United States, gives new hope that the instigation of similar persuasion efforts can help curb the spread of AIDS. The campaign seems to have worked because it not only distributed information about AIDS but also provided services to help people change their risky behaviors and adopted strategies to change the group norms about AIDS and protective sexual practices. This campaign model can easily be revised for AIDS-prevention programs among other population groups, such as adolescents, heterosexuals with multiple partners, and intravenous drug users.

The success rates of the San Francisco campaign and similar programs are encouraging, but it is clear that our ability to control the spread of AIDS is far from adequate. The control of AIDS through behavioral-prevention efforts rests on the profound problem of understanding how our audience, in their environment, understands the topic of communication and how their understanding will shape their perception of our messages. It is our hope that future research efforts will cast more light on these mysteries of the persuasion process and will allow us more effectively to promote healthy attitudes and behaviors.

References

Ajzen, I. (1988). *Attitudes, personality, and behavior.* Chicago: Dorsey Press.

Altman, D. G., & King, A. C. (1986). Approaches to compliance in primary prevention. *The Journal of Compliance in Health Care, 1,* 55–73.

Becker, M. H., & Maiman, L. A. (1975). Sociobehavioral determinants of compliance with health and medical care recommendations. *Health Care, 13,* 10–24.

Biglan, A., Glasgow, R., Ary, D. Thompson, R., Severson, H., Lichtenstein, E., Weissman, W.,

Faller, C., & Gallison, C. (1987). How generalizable are the effects of smoking prevention programs?: Refusal skills training and parent messages in a teacher-administered program. *Journal of Behavioral Medicine, 10*(6), 613–628.

Botvin, G. J., & Wills, T. (1980). Preventing the onset of cigarette smoking through life skills and training. *Preventive Medicine, 9,* 135–143.

Brandon, T. H., Zelman, D. C., & Baker, T. B. (1987). Effect of maintenance sessions on smoking relapse: Delaying the inevitable?

Journal of Consulting and Clinical Psychology,
55, 780–782.

Budd, J., & McCron, R. (1981). Health education and the mass media: Past, present, and potential. In D. S. Leather, G. B. Hastings, & J. K. Davies (Eds.), *Health education and the media* (pp. 33–43). New York: Pergamon Press.

Coates, T. J., Stall, R. D., & Hoff, C. C. (1988). *Changes in sexual behavior of gay and bisexual men since the beginning of the AIDS epidemic.* Washington, DC: U.S. Congress, Office of Technology Assessment.

Communication Technologies, Inc. (1987). *A report on designing an effective AIDS prevention campaign strategy for San Francisco: Results from the fourth probability sample of an urban gay male community.* Unpublished manuscript. (Available from Communications Technologies, Inc., 260 California Street, San Francisco, CA 94111.)

Easterling, D., & Leventhal, H. (1989). The contribution of concrete cognition to emotion: Neutral symptoms as elicitors of worry about cancer. *Journal of Applied Psychology, 74,* 787–796.

Fishbein, M., & Ajzen, I. (1975). *Beliefs, attitude, intention, and behavior: An introduction to theory and research.* Reading, MA: Addison-Wesley.

Flay, B. R. (1985). Psychosocial approaches to smoking prevention: A review of the findings. *Health Psychology, 4*(5), 449–488.

Flay, B. R., & Cook, T. D. (1981). The evaluation of media-based prevention campaigns. In R. R. Rice & W. Paisley (Eds.), *Public communication campaigns.* Beverly Hills, CA: Sage.

Flay, B. R., DiTecco, D., & Schlegal, R. P. (1980). Mass media in health promotion: An analysis using an extended information-processing model. *Health Education Quarterly, 7*(2), 127–147.

Gintner, G., Rectanus, E., Accord, K., & Parker, B. (1987). Parental history of hypertension and screening attendance: Effects of wellness appeal versus threat appeal. *Health Psychology, 6,* 431–444.

Gonder-Frederick, L. A., Cox, D. J., Bobbitt, S. A., & Pennebaker, J. W. (1989). Mood changes associated with blood glucose fluctuations in insulin-dependent mellitus. *Health Psychology, 8*(1), 45–59.

Greenwald, P., & Sondik, E. J. (1986). *Cancer control objectives for the nation: 1985–2000.* NCI Research Monograph No. 2. A Publication of the National Cancer Institute, pp. 1–105.

Haynes, R. B., Taylor, D. W., & Sackett, D. L. (Eds.). (1979). *Compliance in health care.* Baltimore: Johns Hopkins University Press.

Janis, I. L. (1982). *Stress, attitudes, and decisions: Selected works.* New York: Praeger.

Lau, R., Kane, R. L., Berry, S., Ware, J., & Ray, D. (1980). Channeling health: A review of the evaluation of televised health campaigns. *Health Education Quarterly, 7*(1), 56–89.

Leventhal, H., Baker, T., Brandon, T., & Fleming, R. (1989). Intervening and preventing cigarette smoking. In T. Ney & A. Gale (Eds.), *Smoking and human behavior* (pp. 313–336). Oxford, England: John Wiley & Sons.

Leventhal, H., & Cameron, L. (1987). Behavioral theories and the problem of compliance. *Patient Education and Counseling, 10,* 117–138.

Leventhal, H., Meyer, D., & Nerenz, D. (1980). The common sense representation of illness danger. In S. Rachman (Ed.), *Medical psychology* (Vol. II, pp. 7–30). New York: Pergamon Press.

Leventhal, H., Singer, R., & Jones, S. (1965). Effects of fear and specificity of recommendations upon attitudes and behavior. *Journal of Personality and Social Psychology, 2,* 20–29.

Leventhal, H., Zimmerman, R., & Gutmann, M. (1984). Compliance: A self-regulation perspective. In W. D. Gentry (Ed.), *Handbook of behavioral medicine* (pp. 369–436). New York: Guilford Press.

Ley, P. (1977). Psychological studies of doctor-patient communication. In S. Rachman (Ed.), *Contributions to medical psychology* (pp. 9–42). Oxford, England: Pergamon Press.

Marlatt, G. A., & Gordon, J. R. (1980). Determinants of relapse: Implications for the maintenance of behavior change. In P. O. Davidson & S. M. Davidson (Eds.), *Behavioral medicine: Changing health lifestyles* (pp. 410–452). New York: Brunner/Mazel.

Mazen, R., & Leventhal, H. (1972). The influence of communicator-recipient similarity upon the beliefs of pregnant women. *Journal of Experimental Social Psychology, 8,* 289–302.

McGuire, W. J. (1968). Personality and susceptibility to social influence. In E. Borgotta & W. Lambert (Eds.), *Handbook of personality theory and research*. Chicago: Rand McNally.

McKusick, L., Conant, M., & Coates, T. J. (1985). The AIDS epidemic: A model for developing intervention strategies for reducing high-risk behavior in gay men. *Sexually Transmitted Diseases, 12*, 229–234.

Meyer, D., Leventhal, H., & Gutmann, M. (1985). Common sense models of illness: The example of hypertension. *Health Psychology, 4*(2), 115–135.

Meyerowitz, B. E., & Chaiken, S. (1987). The effect of message framing on breast self-examination attitudes, intentions, and behavior. *Journal of Personality and Social Psychology, 52*(3), 500–510.

Rook, K. S. (1986). Encouraging preventive behavior for distant and proximal health threats: Effects of vivid versus abstract information. *Journal of Gerontology, 41*, 526–534.

Rosenstock, I. (1966). Why people use health services. *Milbank Memorial Fund Quarterly, 44*, 94–124.

Schifter, D. B., & Ajzen, I. (1985). Intention, perceived control, and weight loss: An application of the theory of planned behavior. *Journal of Personality and Social Psychology, 49*, 843–851.

Shelton, M. L., & Rogers, R. W. (1981). Fear-arousing and empathy arousing appeals to help: The pathos of persuasion. *Journal of Applied Social Psychology, 4*, 366–378.

Svarstad, B. (1976). Physician-patient communication and patient conformity with medical advice. In D. Mechanic (Ed.), *The growth of bureaucratic medicine*. New York: John Wiley & Sons.

Taylor, S. E., & Thompson, S. C. (1982). Stalking the elusive "vividness" effect. *Psychological Review, 89*, 155–181.

Tiffany, S. T., Martin, E. M., & Baker, T. B. (1986). Treatments for cigarette smoking: An evaluation of the contributions of aversion and counseling procedures. *Behavior Research and Therapy, 24*, 437–452.

Winkelstein, W., Samuel, M., Padian, N., Wiley, J. A., Lang, W., Anderson, R. E., & Levy, J. (1987). Reduction in human immunodeficiency virus transmission among homosexual/bisexual men: 1982–1986. *American Journal of Public Health, 76*, 685–689.

11

MASS MEDIA AND POLITICAL PERSUASION

DAVID O. SEARS
University of California, Los Angeles

RICK KOSTERMAN
University of Washington

On Halloween Eve of 1938, a radio program of Spanish music was interrupted by a special news bulletin reporting strange explosions on the planet Mars. Sometime later, the music was interrupted again with a live report from Grover's Mill, New Jersey, where a "huge cylinder" had struck the earth "with a terrific force" (Koch, 1967) (see Figure 11-1). The reporter went on to describe a large, glistening, tentacled creature with serpentlike eyes emerging from the top of the cylinder. Soon, the "vanguard of an invading army from Mars" had overrun New Jersey, and New Yorkers were being urged to evacuate.

In his study of the effects of this broadcast, Hadley Cantril (1952) found that hundreds of thousands of Americans believed that this was a legitimate newscast and that the earth was actually being invaded by Martian monsters. They were "panic stricken. . . . Probably never before have so many people in all walks of life and in all parts of the country become so suddenly and so intensely disturbed" (Cantril, 1952, p. 198).

The growth of the electronic media early in this century led to a previously unimagined level of mass communication. By the 1930s, radio broadcasts were widely available in homes and public places throughout the Western world. In addition, talking movies, with accompanying newsreels, had become a source of mass entertainment. For the first time, propagandists could reach huge masses of people not merely through the printed word but through audio and visual channels alike. It was a cultural change as revolutionary as that instigated by the inven-

FIGURE 11-1 William Dock, of Grover's Mill, New Jersey, stands ready with his trusty shotgun to ward off the attack of the strange creatures from Mars who had supposedly invaded his hometown on Halloween Eve, 1938. The only invasion taking place, however, was that instigated by the imagination of Orson Welles. His very realistic radio broadcast of "War of the Worlds" threw the entire nation into a panic.

Source: UPI/Bettmann Newsphotos.

tion of the printing press but vastly more widespread, since it reached far beyond the literate few into the great mass of the citizenry. And the immediacy and vividness of the audio and visual presence added a dimension of realism far beyond even the most "yellow" printed journalism.

Orson Welles's famous "War of the Worlds" radio broadcast in 1938 seemed to confirm the worst for what had become a growing sense of uneasiness with this media saturation.

The massive effect of this single radio broadcast well illustrates the first phase of social scientists' perspectives on media effects. Later, we will see that this perspective has evolved a great deal: first, into the view that the media in fact have only minimal persuasive impact and finally, into an era of renewed respect for the media's effect, given the right circumstances.

Phase One: The Great Propaganda Scare

The seeming gullibility of the public, combined with unwavering intrusion of the electronic media into the very heart of the masses, horrified social scientists. And this horror was intensified by the rise of the great charismatic political leaders of the day, especially Hitler and his so-called propaganda minister, Joseph Goebbels, and their counterparts at home, such as Huey Long, the populist politician from Louisiana, and Father Charles Coughlin, the right-wing Catholic priest who had a very popular weekly radio program in the 1930s. Father Coughlin was a particularly alarming example, given his captivating sermonlike appeals that subtly digressed into anti-Semitic tirades. Franklin Roosevelt's fireside chats and Winston Churchill's radio broadcasts, rallying the British people from near defeat early in World War II, seemed to give even further evidence of radio's great power. But among the most frightening spectacles were the great Nuremberg rallies held by the Nazi party and the movies of them, such as Leni Riefenstahl's *Triumph of the Will* (see Figure 11-2). This showed hundreds of thousands of robotlike followers, chanting, singing and marching, seeming to be puppets in the Nazi leaders' hands.

The views of mob psychology that LeBon and Freud made popular among intellectuals suddenly seemed prophetic. LeBon (1896) had contended that people in crowds feel free to gratify their savage and destructive instincts. Freud (1922), extending this notion, emphasized the role of the group leader; the bonds between group members essentially depended on their common bonds with the leader. With the rise of mass audiences and of fascism, this mob psychology analysis was transformed by Kornhauser (1959) into a *mass society* analysis. He contended that modernization and industrialization led to the breakdown of primary-group ties, and the psychic void created by the loss of these ties was filled by the unstable, volatile swings of the masses from one extreme to another. The mass media presumably provided an important mechanism by which the masses could be manipulated.

Social scientists responded to this scare by closely examining the rhetoric of some of the most articulate propagandists of the day and describing the psychological dynamics behind their effectiveness. One product of this was a comprehensive list of *the principles of propaganda*, an enumeration of the persuasive methods used by these orators to win unsuspecting listeners over to their cause (e.g., Doob, 1935). The Institute for Propaganda Analysis, formed by a legion of the era's most prominent, liberal academic social scientists, put out regular newsletters as well as detailed exposés of the propagandistic devices employed by such speakers as Father Coughlin (e.g., Institute, 1939). Their method consisted of detailed analyses of the contents of speeches in which they systematically scrutinized "the tricks of the trade" used in propaganda. Hence, their analysis of Father Coughlin's speeches—typically riddled with anti-Semitic remarks and superpatriotic rallying cries to halt the moral decay of the nation—rested on seven tricks, such as *name-calling* (giving an idea a bad label), *testimonial* (attributing an idea to a trustworthy or evil source), and *bandwagon* (everyone believes it). They attempted to mark the

FIGURE 11-2   Leni Riefenstahl's movie *Triumph of the Will* (1934) depicted hundreds of thousands of highly disciplined German soldiers marching and chanting to the command of Adolf Hitler. This movie and others like it brought home to many Americans the awesome threat of Nazi Germany prior to World War II.

Source: *Triumph of the Will* is in the public domain. For distribution information, contact Video Yesteryear, Sandy Hook, CT, 06482.

use of these tricks in the texts of propagandistic messages; for example, their analysis of Coughlin's propaganda concludes with a 20-page quotation and includes about 330 symbols identifying his use of such tricks.

The conclusions reached by these intellectual critics of the late 1930s depended on three key assumptions. First, they were convinced that such mass political propaganda was in itself highly persuasive. Second, they felt that its success depended on how adroitly a propagandist used subtle rhetorical tricks in a communication (later called *message factors* by Janis and his colleagues; cf., 1959). And finally, they assumed the audience was captive, attentive, and gullible. The days of skeptical, "cracker barrel" discussions in the crossroads store were over, they felt. Now the citizenry sat glued to the radio, helpless victims.

This was a frightening view of electronic propaganda as persuasive, subtle, and omnipotent. These critics confidently asserted it. But, they proceeded by intuition and casual analysis, rather than by systematic empirical research. For example, they did not measure persuasive impact directly but inferred it indirectly from the size of the audience. However, there were significant alternatives to the institute's ominous view. For example, it might be that the audiences were not nearly as attentive as it seemed. The tricks of the trade might have been too subtle for most to notice. Perhaps the audiences were highly patriotic or anti-Semitic to begin with, so that the propaganda really did not greatly increase such attitudes. Clearly, it was important that the effects of propaganda be tested empirically.

Phase Two: The Minimal Effects Model

Soon thereafter, an era of more thorough empirical assessments of communication impact began. And indeed, the initial evidence, from studies done both in the laboratory and in real, daily life, suggested that the Institute for Propaganda Analysis had considerably overestimated the persuasive effects of political propaganda. In fact, major political changes produced by media propaganda seemed to be the exception, rather than the rule. In what was the first in-depth study of voters in a presidential election using the newly developed methods of public opinion polling, Lazarsfeld, Berelson, and Gaudet (1948) found that the media had very little direct influence over voting preferences. Audiences for mass communications seemed rather strongly self-selected in that most of those paying attention tended to already agree with the message. So voters primarily received propaganda supporting their own candidate. Moreover, people tended to interpret what they heard about the campaign very selectively, so that nearly every communication was perceived by them as supporting their prior preference in some way. The major implication, then, was that the media primarily *reinforced prior attitudes*.

Experimental social psychologists added to this impression of limited mass communication impact. During World War II, the U.S. army, as part of its attempt to indoctrinate new draftees, prepared special orientation films for them. An extensive and well-controlled series of studies found that the films were highly effective in passing along information about the war effort but were not as effective in changing opinions. Similarly, they produced little change in behavioral intentions, such as increased desire to join combat units (Hovland, Lumsdaine, & Sheffield, 1949). Such minimal effects occurred despite the advantages of this forced exposure over the sporadic and selective exposure characteristics of everyday political propaganda. The conclusion was that even a so-called captive audience will not necessarily be persuaded by mass communications, no matter how carefully the communications have been prepared.

A considerable volume of research on such matters was done in the 1940s and 1950s. It was ably reviewed by Klapper (1960) in his book, *The Effects of Mass Communications*. There he developed an influential viewpoint that came to be known as *the minimal effects model*. He proposed that media propaganda rarely *changes* one's attitudes but instead often serves to *strengthen* one's existing attitudes. The image of a captive and gullible citizenry, the isolated, helpless victims of the tricks of the propagandist, was replaced by Klapper with one of an audience quite capable of ignoring or reinterpreting messages inconsistent with their prior predispositions.

Schramm and Carter (1959) offered a classic example of the media's minimal effects. They conducted a study of a 20-hour telethon starring Senator William F. Knowland, a Republican and majority leader of the U.S. Senate, at the end of his 1958 campaign for the California governorship. The results, for Knowland, were dismal. First, selective exposure hurt him tremendously: The audience was small and biased toward his own supporters. Of the barely 11% who saw any of the telethon at all, Republicans were much more likely to watch, and to watch longer than Democrats. Selective perception also hurt him: Of the new Democrats who did happen to see some of the telethon, nearly half said "nothing" had impressed them. In all, only 2 out of Schramm and Carter's sample of 563 voters said the program had helped them to make up their minds, one to vote for Knowland and the other to vote against him. This amounted to no net gain at all for Knowland after 20 hours of televised propaganda.

The same minimal effect is easily observed in this era in televised presidential debates. Often billed as *decisive*, the data from the debates of 1960, 1976, and 1984 generally suggest that viewers' judgments of "who won" were strongly determined by their predispositions. (See Figure 11-3, as well as Chapter 4 by Fazio and Roskos-Ewoldsen for a discussion of this *selective perception* process.) Democrats tended to think the Democratic candidate won, Republicans tended to think the Republican won, and the undecided most often perceived the debate as dead even!

There are notable exceptions, as in the victory for Mondale in the first debate of the 1984 campaign, and a slight edge for Kennedy in 1960. But these seem to require quite dramatic differences in performance between the two candidates and even further inflation of those performance differences by the media, who typically emphasize "who won" over more substantive concerns. In 1984, even Ronald Reagan's campaign aides eventually succumbed to the admission that the debate was "not the president's best." Obviously, however, debates rarely move more than 10% of committed partisans into accepting that the "other guy" won. Thus, one can see why, given its basis in scientific research, the minimal effects model quickly became the dominant model of mass communication effects. The propaganda scare simply did not seem to pan out in terms of the data.

Factors That Limit Persuasion

Minimal media effects should not seem surprising in light of the difficult process of persuasion. In order for any sort of persuasive appeal to have an effect, it must first be received by the audience; to paraphrase a familiar expression, "What you don't hear can't persuade you." This is rarely an easy task, especially if one's target is the mass audience. Then, when and if the appeal manages to make its way to the audience relatively intact, it must overcome several sources of resistance before it

THE FIRST NIXON-KENNEDY DEBATE (1960)

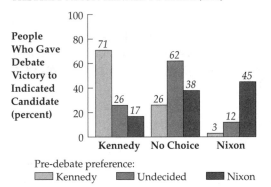

People Who Gave Debate Victory to Indicated Candidate (percent)

Pre-debate preference:
Kennedy   Undecided   Nixon

THE FIRST CARTER-FORD DEBATE (1976)

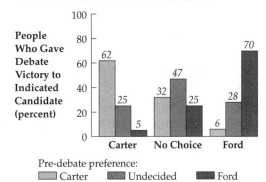

People Who Gave Debate Victory to Indicated Candidate (percent)

Pre-debate preference:
Carter   Undecided   Ford

THE CARTER-REAGAN DEBATE (1980)

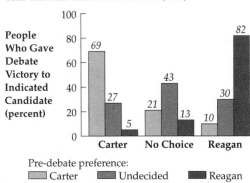

People Who Gave Debate Victory to Indicated Candidate (percent)

Pre-debate preference:
Carter   Undecided   Reagan

THE FIRST MONDALE-REAGAN DEBATE (1984)

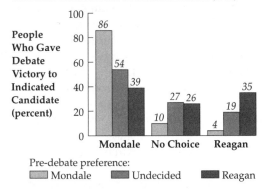

People Who Gave Debate Victory to Indicated Candidate (percent)

Pre-debate preference:
Mondale   Undecided   Reagan

THE SECOND MONDALE-REAGAN DEBATE (1984)

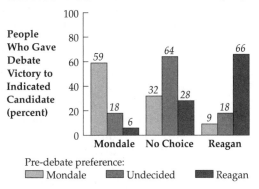

People Who Gave Debate Victory to Indicated Candidate (percent)

Pre-debate preference:
Mondale   Undecided   Reagan

FIGURE 11-3   Who did the better job in each debate? Viewers' judgments of debate performance were greatly affected by their predebate preferences.

Source: Nixon-Kennedy data from Sears and Whitney (1973); Carter-Ford data from *Ann Arbor News*, Sept. 24, 1976, p. 1; Carter-Reagan data from CBS News release, Oct. 29, 1980; Mondale-Reagan data from CBS News/*New York Times* polls, Oct. 7, 9, 21, 24, and 25, 1984.

is accepted. Political attitudes are often rather stubborn entities and, hence, new information is frequently encountered with great prejudice. Thus, it seems useful to distinguish these two stages in the impact of mass communications: *reception* of the message and *acceptance* of it (Sears & Whitney, 1973; see also McGuire, 1985, and Chapters 7 and 10 in this volume).

Reception: Low Levels of Exposure and Attention

Let us start with reception. Consider the case of Father Coughlin's radio broadcasts in the 1930s. His effectiveness depended first of all on people turning their radios on, tuning to his program, and paying attention. For those who were with him this far, Father Coughlin then had to make his message clear and understandable. But, of course, even then he had no guarantee it would be accurately perceived.

Television

Television is widely thought to have *the* most extensive influence over public opinion today. Social critics are able to amass huge quantities of frightening statistics to demonstrate television's power to command vast audiences. For example, it is said that in the United States, 97% of the households possess at least one television receiver; the average set operates about seven hours per day; by the age of 65, the average male viewer will have spent about nine years of his life watching television; the average child has spent more time (about 20,000 hours) in front of the set by the age of 18 than in classrooms, churches, and all other educational and cultural activities combined; and on and on (e.g., Comstock, Chaffee, Katzman, McCombs, & Roberts, 1978; Minow, Martin, & Mitchell, 1973).

However, these statistics are poor measures of exposure (i.e., the extent to which viewers are actually present during the broadcast) and do not measure attention at all (i.e., whether people are actually watching). Such data are typically based on the wide distribution of *television sets* and on rating services' reports about how much of the time televisions are in operation, not on careful observation of actual viewing behavior on the part of people. Other studies have video-recorded the area in front of the family's television. They have found that for as much as 40% of the time the set is operating, no person is in the room or no one is watching the set (Allen, 1965).

Even when someone is watching, television viewing is often a secondary activity—second to an astonishing variety of other activities, such as eating, conversation, dancing, sorting wash, playing Monopoly, scolding children, and reading, to mention only some of the mentionable ones (Szalai, 1972; see Comstock et al., 1978, p. 144). In fact, television watching was a primary activity for the average adult only 91 minutes a day (Comstock et al., 1978). Moreover, even when television viewing is a primary activity, people still report feeling more passive and less alert than in almost any other daily activity except resting and "doing nothing" (Kubey & Csikszentmihalyi, 1990, p. 171).

Although such viewing habits may have much to say about the role of television in how people spend their leisure time (Kubey & Csikszentmihalyi, 1990), these initial problems of exposure and attention are especially troublesome for political persuasion, because politics generally seems too distant to most people to attract their attention. For example, Cantril (1965) found that only 2% mentioned some political matter as their "fondest hope" and 5% as their "worst fear" (mostly issues of war and peace, in the latter case).

Consequently, the public as a whole normally finds political programming considerably less interesting than the entertainment programs that fill most of prime time. Indeed, one recent survey showed that 50% of Americans knew that Judge Joseph Wapner presided over *The People's Court*, a popular courtroom television show, whereas only 12% could identify Chief Justice William Rehnquist of the United States Supreme Court (Kubey & Csikszentmihalyi, 1990, p. 176). Motives for following politics on television generally tend to be simple ones: keeping up with the issues at some modest level and evaluating leaders and candidates for office (McLeod & Becker, 1974). There is an attentive public (at most, 20% of the adult population) who pay closer attention, much as there are dedicated sports fans who watch games regularly. But this segment of the population is far outnumbered by persons for whom politics is rather peripheral.

Nevertheless, ingenious media consultants have designed political programs in forms that can build up the size of their audiences quite markedly. Lengthy, paid partisan programs, such as Senator Knowland's last-minute telethon, sometimes appear as part of political campaigns but more often as political entertainment programs. Also, political candidates vie for the attention of the news media to ensure that their campaigns are given precious time in televised news programs (Ansolabehere, Behr, & Iyengar, 1991). Sometimes the networks give considerable amounts of air time to political events as a public service, such as with the Watergate (see Figure 11-4) or Iran-Contra hearings, political conventions, election-night coverage, the State of the Union Address, and presidential debates. Political emergencies sometimes preempt all other programming, such as the four days of virtually uninterrupted coverage of the events associated with President Kennedy's assassination. And it should be remembered that some entertainment programs and series (e.g., *All in the Family*, *Roots*, and *Holocaust*) also have strongly political themes.

For most people, however, some of the most familiar vehicles for political persuasion are the nightly network television news programs that appear at regular and normally uninterrupted scheduled times. Americans' interpretations of political events are widely assumed to be heavily influenced by these nightly news programs. They do contain the most political news and attract the highest ratings of any standard political programs. But they are aired at exactly the same time most families are drinking cocktails, feeding their children, preparing dinner, and often reading the mail and newspaper. Not surprisingly, then, regular exposure to these programs is less common than one might think. Robinson (1971) found that in a large, national sample of adults, only about one in four persons watched a network evening news program on an average weekday; over half the sample watched none at all in the two-week period of the study. Only about 20% were "regulars," watching at least every other day.

FIGURE 11-4   The Senate Select Committee on Presidential Campaign Activities, chaired by Senator Sam Ervin, Jr., of North Carolina, prepares for another day of investigation into the Watergate scandal. The cameras were rolling, as they were throughout the long series of hearings.

Source: UPI/Bettmann Newsphotos.

And even among the minority who does watch the nightly news, close attention is less common than one might think. One study found that people were less likely to watch an operating television set when the news was on than any other kind of programming (Bechtel, Achelpohl, & Akers, 1972); almost half the time the news was on, no one was watching! Only commercials were so frequently ignored. Similarly, Neuman (1976) found that for San Francisco Bay area residents who had watched one of the network news programs earlier in the evening, an average of only 1.2 stories could be correctly recalled out of the 20 or so typically covered. Memory improved when the interviewer reminded the viewer of the program's headlines, but even then, half the stories were completely forgotten. In Robinson and Levy's (1986) more recent analysis, as many as one-third of their viewers had virtually no recall of any stories, even when cued with headlines! In short, the net-

work news mainly reaches that minority of people who have unusually great interest in public affairs. And even when people are supposedly watching the news,
they tend to pay only superficial attention to it.

Another important fact about television audiences is that they are seg-
mented. On the one hand, the standing attentive public for political affairs runs
at about 20% or 30% of the adult population. This is the group that tries to keep
up with events almost daily year after year (see Jennings & Niemi, 1981). At the
other extreme, we find a fairly substantial "know-nothing" group (estimates
range as high as 20%) that is essentially indifferent to politics and rarely knows
much more than the name of the current president. There is a larger middle
group with only occasional and superficial exposure, whom we might call
"informed laymen." They compose the middle 50% or so who, on the average,
watch the network news once in a while, watch a snatch of a presidential debate
but not from start to finish, and so on. But regardless of the exact percentages, the
problem for political persuasion is obvious: A great many people will simply
never receive the messages, no matter how painstakingly their persuasive effects
were calculated.

Exceptional Cases

There are, of course, exceptions to these generally dreary statistics. On occasion,
the public seems to be engrossed, momentarily, by some political or quasi-political
event. Network television devoted almost four full days to the events surrounding
President Kennedy's assassination; 95% of the public watched some part of the
postassassination programming, and indeed, the average adult spent no less than
34 hours with these events (on television or radio; Sheatsley & Feldman, 1965).
Franklin D. Roosevelt's speech following Pearl Harbor is believed to have reached
80% of the homes in the United States (Minow et al., 1973, p. 30). Gallup reported
that 88% of Americans watched some part of the hearings held on Watergate by the
Ervin Senate Select Committee (O'Keefe & Mendelsohn, 1974). And the classic
series *Roots*, documenting the history of one Black family from its African origins
to the present time, was a smash success. It was said that seven of the eight
episodes rated in the top ten of the all-time television ratings.

Such widespread public attentiveness is also found on occasion for programs
that appear as regular features of the political landscape. The political parties' conventions held every four years have, in the past, been one example. The suspenseful 1960 Democratic convention is testimony to their potential drawing power. It
drew 92% of the household televisions for an average of 15½ hours, according to
one estimate (Katz & Feldman, 1962). Of course, in recent years the many presidential primaries have generally settled presidential nominations long before the
conventions, taking much of their suspense away and reducing their audiences.
Election-night coverage, again when suspenseful or dramatic in some way, is yet
another big draw. In 1964, over 90% of the electorate tuned in (Fuchs, 1966). In
1980, about 80% in one national sample (Jackson, 1983) heard both the projections
of Reagan's victory and the concession speech made by Carter on election night.
Prime-time, three-network presidential addresses can often reach very large por-

tions of the electorate. For example, former President Nixon—known for his well-orchestrated television appearances—attracted audiences of from 40 to 80 million people (Minow et al., 1973, pp. 56–63).

But, at the risk of seeming to be wet blankets, we should note that, even in these occasional cases when much of the United States seems riveted on a common political event, the seeming massiveness of these audiences may be deceptive in terms of actual audience attention. The statistics usually quoted, showing levels of 80% to 95% exposure to such events, reflect audiences at their peaks, and, like stock market highs when one is trying to sell stock, these peaks do not last long. For example, among the largest draws of the occasional, unscheduled political programs are the debates held during presidential campaigns. In 1976, three presidential debates and one vice-presidential debate were held. Exposure was seemingly massive, nearly universal: Nielsen reported 89% of their households were tuned in to at least one of the debates. However, at the most, only about 25% of the public seemed to have watched *all* of *any one* debate (Sears & Chaffee, 1979). And Nielsen suggests that only 42% of the households tuned in to *any part* of *all three* presidential debates.

Selectivity in Reception

A central tenet of the minimal effects model was that other major obstacles to political persuasion were the processes of selective information reception, such as *selective exposure, selective perception,* and *selective learning.* These referred to the notion that people generally avoid, distort, and forget communications that challenge their preexisting attitudes. Presumably, this reflected a general psychological preference for supportive information, a view that fits nicely with the contention in cognitive dissonance theory that nonsupportive information creates unpleasant psychological tensions (Festinger, 1957; see Chapter 5 by Cooper and Scher in this volume).

As the evidence mounted, however, none of these selective processes proved to be as powerful as originally thought. People seemed to deal with discrepant information (information with which they disagreed) more by denouncing it than by avoiding any exposure to it (McGuire, 1969; Sears & Freedman, 1967). Researchers thus began to explore narrower effects in this vein, as opposed to the sweeping rejection of discrepant information originally expected (Frey, 1986; Sears, 1968).

Ultimately, this led to a distinction between two forms of selective exposure: *de facto selectivity* and *motivated selectivity.* De facto selectivity referred to the simple fact that most audiences are composed mostly of people who already agree with the message, which could occur for a variety of reasons. Motivated selectivity, on the other hand, referred specifically to *individuals' psychological preferences* for supportive rather than nonsupportive information (Sears & Freedman, 1967). De facto selectivity can occur without motivated selectivity. For example, readers of the *Wall Street Journal* would tend more than the general population to agree with its conservative editorial positions. That is de facto selectivity. But most readers do not choose to read that newspaper because of its editorials; they read it because of its exhaustive coverage of the financial news. That its editorials are agreeable to them is more like a happy accident; it is not a case of strong, motivated selectivity.

It appeared from the evidence that de facto selectivity was a relatively common phenomenon; that is, audiences did tend to be biased in favor of the messages they heard. But it was less clear that this bias resulted from any kind of motivated selectivity on the part of individuals. Indeed, the evidence for selective exposure on the part of individuals—as well as selective perception and selective retention—seemed much less clear cut than once thought (see Sears, 1968).

The political role of selective exposure, at least in terms of the mass public's exposure to political propaganda on television and in newspapers, seems, if anything, even less prominent today. Whatever obstacle selective exposure used to pose appears to have been largely bypassed by the many changes in the media in recent years. Newspaper, radio, and television coverage are less explicitly partisan today (i.e., Democratic or Republican biases are less apparent), and campaign propaganda mainly takes the form of brief, prime-time political ads that are hard to avoid. The main obstacle to political persuasion today would seem to be the generally low levels of public interest and attention, rather than partisanly motivated selectivity.

Memory

Finally, we come to the last step in the reception of a persuasive appeal: memory. Unfortunately for the propagandist, even the small percentage of people who do pay attention seem to remember relatively little. As we indicated earlier, Neuman's careful study found that viewers of network news programs could remember only 1 in 20 of the stories they had heard earlier that evening; and even what is remembered is probably not retained for very long (Graber, 1987). Memory for presidential debates appears just as superficial. These debates are typically heavily focused on issues, because outstanding journalists are usually chosen to pose questions to the candidates. Even so, viewers' recall emphasizes global impressions rather than the issues that have been laboriously debated. For example, when respondents were asked what they could remember that impressed them about what the 1976 presidential candidates had said in their debates, issues were mentioned by only 28% (Ford) and 16% (Carter). And most of the former (61%) had remembered a seemingly minor comment by Ford regarding Eastern Europe's supposed independence from the USSR. Relatively few viewers had picked up on this comment during the debate itself, but the press had given it great emphasis later on (Sears & Chaffee, 1979).

Thus, the reception of most mass communications seems to be severely dampened in every phase of the process. First and foremost, we noted that the levels of exposure and attention to persuasive messages are usually rather low, and this seems especially true for political programming. Second, in line with Klapper's (1960) original contention, discrepant information that is attended to is rarely perceived in a way that challenges preexisting attitudes much. And now, finally, we see that memory for such messages is often poor indeed. This brings us to the second stage in the impact of persuasive appeals.

Acceptance: Commitment to Preexisting Attitudes

What happens when mass communications are fully received by some portion of their audience? And what factors determine the audience's response?

Political Predispositions

A first answer to this question was hinted at in the original election study by Lazarsfeld et al. (1948) mentioned earlier: *The major effect of most propaganda is to reinforce prior political attitudes.* This conclusion should have a familiar ring to it in light of the broader discussions of attitude change in previous chapters. To the extent that one feels a sense of commitment to a given attitude, incoming information is evaluated in terms of its consistency with that initial attitude. Consistent information is accepted, and, depending on the level of commitment, discrepant information is rejected. In either case, existing attitudes tend to be strengthened. (Of course, as you know from previous chapters, we have simplified what can be a rather complex process.)

Political attitudes vary tremendously in their level of commitment. Some opinions are so superficial and unstable that Converse (1970) labeled them *nonattitudes* (see Chapter 2 by Ostrom et al.). Other opinions are *enduring commitments* acquired early in the life span that are unlikely to change much later in life (Sears & Whitney, 1973; Sears, 1983).

Issues or events that are "hot" enough to attract a large media audience also usually evoke powerful attitudes. That is, the issues people seem to be most interested in are those they already have strong feelings about. Without these strong feelings, the issue is necessarily less interesting. In fact, the combination of heavy attention to the media and weak attitudes is relatively rare. Members of large, attentive audiences tend already to have their minds made up. Hence, when political communications attack weak attitudes, the audience is most commonly inattentive, and when they attract a large audience, they confront attitudes of high commitment.

Again, a good example is the 1976 Carter-Ford debates. Only 3% of those interviewed felt the debates were a decisive factor in their final choice. Instead, the debates appeared to reinforce voters' prior choices. The debates also increased the consistency of the viewers' partisan attitudes about other aspects of the campaign. Issue preferences and candidate images became more consistent with each other, and voters became more certain of the reasons for their preferences (Dennis, Chaffee, & Choe, 1979). To be sure, each debate created some temporary movement toward the candidate generally perceived as the winner, but this dissipated within a few days, restoring the early division of preference (Sears & Chaffee, 1979). This process is less well documented for the other debates we have looked at, but as we saw in Figure 11-3, prior preferences dominated evaluations of debate performance for Nixon-Kennedy in 1960, Carter-Reagan in 1980, and Mondale-Reagan in 1984.

Phase Three: Renewed Respect for Media Effects

We began with the early analysis of political persuasion conducted by the Institute for Propaganda Analysis (e.g., 1939). They were part of the "great propaganda scare" of the era, suggesting that the media deliver very persuasive messages to a captive and gullible mass audience. The research-based analyses of Klapper (1960) and others offered a contrasting view, that the media in fact have only minimal effects. We turn finally to the most recent phase of research, an era perhaps of renewed respect for the media's effects under certain conditions.

The period since the late 1960s has witnessed major social and technological changes in the television industry. Some of these, such as the growth in the number of television sets and in cable television, have increased the availability of television to the general public. Other changes have reflected the growing sophistication of the political uses of television. All this led to a reassessment of its effects. Critiques were published on such topics as "videomalaise" (Robinson, 1976), "presidential television" (Minow, Martin, & Mitchell, 1973), and "the selling of the president" (McGinniss, 1969) as well as on media violence (e.g., Liebert, Neale, & Davidson, 1973) and pornography, with a fairly liberal presidential commission report in 1970 (Keating, 1970) succeeded in 1986 by the quite conservative Meese Commission report (U.S. Dept. of Justice, 1986). And vastly increased amounts of money have been spent on political advertising in campaigns (Ansolabehere et al., 1991).

These changes in the political uses of the media have paralleled important changes in the political environment in its own right (see Blumler, 1977). Most importantly, the public's *party identifications* have become weaker and probably less potent, as well. This is crucial because studies have long shown party identification (i.e., a person's self-identity as a Democrat, Republican, or Independent) to be the major political predisposition determining voting and therefore the predisposition through which media-generated political information was filtered. At the same time, much of the political content on television is now viewed by people with only minimal levels of interest in politics (e.g., viewing political ads that are sandwiched between entertainment programs).

Finally, the media themselves have become less partisan. In response to government regulations calling for fairness and equal opportunity in coverage of controversial issues and political candidates, television news programming is now deliberately balanced and not nearly so likely to provide reinforcement for the committed partisan. Newspapers, too, have attempted to become more balanced in their news coverage (Schultz, 1986). All this suggests that those conditions thought to be rare but yet most conducive to persuasion by the minimal effects model—heavy exposure to the media on issues evoking only weak attitudes—have recently become more common.

This era of a less partisan citizenry more inescapably confronted by modern political programming has led to renewed attention to the media and to renewed respect for media effects. Massive exposure along with weak commitment would seem to create the most favorable environment for political persuasion. But rather than look for massive persuasive effects of individual programs, which have continued not to be very strong, academic researchers have begun to look for a variety of different kinds of media influence. This shift in research focus is significant in that it examines some of the subtler factors contributing to the media's effectiveness.

Long-Term Effects

Researchers have, for one thing, begun to explore changes in public opinion over extended periods of time, rather than the effects of one-shot media events. The long-term effects of media coverage are not as easy to assess, of course. Media coverage over long periods is mixed with the many other events occurring over that time. So it is difficult to distinguish the particular effects of the media from those of the other events and changes of the times. Nevertheless, there are some interesting relationships.

Casualties, the Economy, and Campaign Expenditures

Some analyses examine media effects indirectly by looking at the effects of long-term variables that are very likely to influence opinion through the media. For example, Mueller (1973) found that support for the Vietnam War fell rather steadily and gradually as a function of the increase in American casualties after the official U.S. commitment to the war in 1964 (see Figure 11-5). He did not demonstrate a direct role for the media, but this presumably reflects a long-term effect of media coverage, since the information about casualties was probably communicated to the public primarily through mass media. There were also significant oscillations in support for the war following major developments such as the Tet offensive or the Cambodian invasion, developments that were major media events.

Another indirect index of long-term media impact is the effect of money spent in election campaigns. The most obvious assumption would be that the more money candidates spend on their campaign, the more popular they should become, because they can purchase more media advertising. Grush, McKeogh, and Ahlering (1978) argued that such an effect does exist but only under certain conditions. They predicted that the amount of campaign expenditures ought to be decisive only when little is known about the candidates and the choice is moderately confusing, such as when several unknown candidates are running. Testing this hypothesis on congressional elections, they indeed found that campaign expenditures were strongly related to the vote under these limited conditions. However, when the contests involved well-known candidates or only two candidates, money was not so important. Apparently, the reputations of well-known candidates tend to override the effects of media expenditures. And when only two candidates are running, the media cannot be as decisive as it can be in bringing one or two of them out of a crowded pack (see Figure 11-6).

The likely reason for these effects was the unmeasured mechanism of the media. That is, campaign expenditures translate into media exposure, which, in turn, attracts votes, presumably. But even very high media expenditures are not sufficient to overcome a very well-known, popular, single opponent. The key to

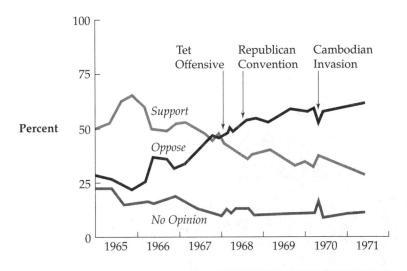

FIGURE 11-5   Support for the Vietnam War declined nearly every year after the official U.S. commitment in 1964. Increases in casualties, presumably communicated via the media, seemingly played a significant role in this decline. Note that the number of persons opposed to the war exceeded the number in favor in 1968 following the Tet offensive, a very successful surprise attack on South Vietnamese and U.S. forces. The nomination of a "hawkish" Richard Nixon later that year also increased opposition. The Cambodian invasion in 1970, which the Nixon administration explained as crucial to halting the expanding communist movement, only temporarily increased support for the war.

Source: From *War, presidents and public opinion* (p. 56) by J. E. Mueller, 1973, New York: John Wiley & Sons. Copyright 1973 by J. E. Mueller. Reprinted by permission.
Note: In fact, the first U.S. forces were sent to Vietnam in 1961; however, the Tonkin Gulf resolution in 1964 marked the United States' official commitment to the conflict.

media effects, again, is massive exposure when the political choices are initially quite confusing or ambiguous, as would be expected by the minimal effects model.

A final point to bear in mind in the analysis of media persuasion is the frequent difficulty in separating the persuasive impact of the communication from that of the event itself. Most political events occur at some considerable distance from the citizenry, and the media are the natural means of bringing the citizenry close to these events. Indeed, how are most people, most of the time, ever to learn anything about political events *except* through the media? Thus, when the level of Vietnam casualties appeared to be associated with declining support for the war, was this impact (such that it was) due to the media reports themselves or to the reality of the casualties? Is decline in presidential popularity due to unfavorable news or to the

"I was packaged by Candidates Limited. Who packaged you?"

FIGURE 11-6   Most candidates for higher office today hire media consultants to help them forge winning images. But it appears that media advertising (and the money to pay for it) is crucial only under certain specified conditions.

Source: Drawing by Handelsman; © 1970 The New Yorker Magazine, Inc.

mistake that led to the news? It is hard to pin these effects on some special additional influence of the media presentation beyond the sole impact of the event itself, which the person could hear about in a variety of ways (say, from friends).

Agenda Setting

The notion that the media exercise considerable control over the public agenda harks back to Walter Lippmann's (1922) early warning that the population at large is very dependent on the media for awareness of those events beyond personal experience. But the effect is not one of persuasion—of inducing the public to agree with a particular position. It is one of *agenda setting*—of focusing the public's attention on some particular issue. "The mass media may not be successful much of the time in telling people what to think, but the media are stunningly successful in telling their audience what to think about" (Cohen, 1963, p. 16).

It is true that one can identify cases in which the media was influential in just this way. At the national level, Funkhouser (1973) found that the volume of news coverage given various issues was an important determinant of the public's sense of issue priorities in the 1960s, even more important than reality (e.g., actual number of troops in Vietnam, the crime rate, etc.). And MacKuen (1981), following this with a more sophisticated, dynamic model of almost exactly the same data, found strong agenda-setting media effects for at least four of the issues he examined: race, campus unrest, the Vietnam War, and energy. That is, each issue was thought to be the most important by the public in the period when it had just been given a great deal of media coverage.

More generally, to support this view, researchers have found significant correlations between the volume of media coverage on particular issues and the public's perceived importance of those issues (e.g., McCombs & Shaw, 1972; Iyengar, 1979). In laboratory situations, increased television news coverage has been shown to induce higher issue salience in viewing subjects (i.e., increase the prominence of the issue in the subjects' thinking). Moreover, these experimental media presentations can apparently determine which *specific* issues the president will be judged on when subjects are asked to evaluate his performance *overall* (Iyengar & Kinder, 1987). A similar effect has been observed outside the laboratory, as well. General assessments of former President Reagan's performance became much more tightly linked to support for the rebels in Nicaragua, known as the *Contras*, after it was revealed that they had received funds from a secret Iranian arms deal, and a media frenzy over the Iran-Contra scandal ensued (Krosnick & Kinder, 1990).

This last point is important since it suggests that the media's focus on particular issues can have powerful political effects: The electorate will give extra weight to those prominent issues in making quite general evaluations of presidential performance. And, of course, the political parties behave as though they understand this. The party of the challenger attempts to keep attention focused on issues of presidential failure, while the party of the incumbent normally only emphasizes issues of presidential success. This characterizes a large component of the ongoing partisan debate (Budge & Farlie, 1983).

However, all this suggests a somewhat exaggerated portrait of the agenda-setting effect. The real causal flow may be in the reverse direction: The media may simply be dutifully reflecting the public's sense of issue importance and giving the public what it wants. This possibility does not explain away all the agenda-setting findings, however. MacKuen's (1981) analysis suggests that the public's priorities, at least sometimes, stem from intense media coverage. He found that, over time, a rise in media coverage of issues *preceded* a rise in public concern about them, which would seem to indicate an agenda-setting effect. This conclusion is very much in line with Rogers and Dearing's (1988) recent review. They found traces of significant agenda-setting effects in the majority of over-time studies they examined.

Fairly straightforward agenda-setting effects do emerge in long-term studies and in laboratory experiments, however. In these cases, of course, the media dose is typically relatively strong. So once again, reliable media effects emerge primarily under conditions of *massive exposure*. Agenda setting in the real world would seem to require somewhat of a blockbuster, most often occurring only when some issue or event makes the headlines over an extended period. One relatively recent example of this may be coverage of the AIDS crisis (see Chapter 10 by Leventhal and Cameron). The media devoted a great deal of front-page, top-story coverage to this problem and eventually brought it to the forefront of public concern (particularly following the death of movie star Rock Hudson). Without extensive media attention, it is perhaps unlikely that AIDS would have been perceived by most people as a crisis so quickly. Initially, AIDS seemed primarily confined to homosexuals and intravenous drug users, posing little immediate threat to those outside these groups. Certainly, this virus has led to great tragedy, which should not be diminished, but the media perhaps changed the perception of the actual threat faster than the threat itself changed. Thus, although it takes time to develop, the agenda-setting effect can be quite consequential.

Hoopla

Ideally, mass media news is intended to convey political information. Yet a major problem for television news is that its informational content is so skimpy. Typically, complex political issues are given little time amidst the commercial breaks, entertainment features, and so on. Coverage of political campaigns is also subject to these time pressures and entertainment motives. And, critics charge, emphasis is therefore given to the "horserace" or "hoopla" aspects of the campaign, rather than to the issues. That is, in an effort to be entertaining in the fraction of the half-hour news show devoted to the campaign, television networks give the backseat to issue-oriented information relative to whatever developments appear more exciting.

A case in point was the Nixon-McGovern campaign in 1972. Many believed that this promised to be an issue-oriented race, since there were such clear differences between the candidates. On the heels of the antiwar protests and general social upheaval of the late 1960s and the early 1970s, the Democrats had nominated an extremely liberal candidate who challenged Nixon's more conservative views on almost every issue, from Vietnam to abortion and busing. However, an analysis of nightly network news content performed by Patterson and McClure (1976) showed little attention to these dramatic differences. From mid-September to election day, a six-week period, each network devoted a total of two hours to the contest—poll results, strategies, and motorcades and rallies—while averaging just over one-half hour on the issues. As a result, regular news viewers showed no greater increase over the course of the campaign in awareness of candidates' issue positions than did nonviewers (Patterson & McClure, 1976, p. 50). The same was true in the 1976 campaign (Patterson, 1980, pp. 160–161). On the other hand, both television and newspaper exposure contribute to more accurate perceptions of which candidate is leading or trailing, and these in turn contribute to voter choices on the basis of who looks viable (Patterson, 1980, Ch. 11).

The media seem to have always been transfixed by the horserace aspects of campaigns. Indeed, Sigelman and Bullock (1991) reviewed front-page stories about the 1888 presidential campaign in the *New York Times* and found that one out of every three paragraphs discussed candidate standings or the likely outcome of the election. This emphasis seems only further magnified with the advent of television and overnight public opinion polls. By 1988, focus on the horserace accounted for the majority of campaign news coverage (Lichter, Amundson, & Noyes, 1988).

One apparent consequence of this fixation on "who's ahead" is the wildly disproportionate attention given to the early Iowa and New Hampshire presidential primaries. Although neither Iowa nor New Hampshire has much significance in terms of electoral votes, together, they accounted for 32% of all primary coverage in 1984 and 34% in 1988 (Adams, 1987; Lichter et al., 1988). And those candidates who win this early media attention—by winning the primary or by beating expectations—have much to celebrate. Winners typically make substantial gains in nationwide polls. In 1984, Gary Hart's standing jumped from 3% to 30% after a surprise second-place showing in Iowa and victory in New Hampshire, followed by a deluge of press and television coverage (Mayer, 1987; see also Orren & Polsby, 1987).

Hoopla news coverage giving inordinate attention to "the contest" is also notable following presidential debates. An analysis of the content of the Carter-Ford debates in 1976 revealed that although the reporters had asked the candidates issue-oriented questions 92% of the time, the media covering the debates focused as much on who won as on the issues (see Sears & Chaffee, 1979; Patterson, 1980). And voters' judgments of who won the debate—like who's ahead in the polls—can themselves have a significant (if not always long-lived) persuasive impact upon presidential preference (Sears & Chaffee, 1979).

Thus, hoopla creates a horserace atmosphere in which people want to bet on a winner or root for the underdog, but either way, the issue is not the *issues*. In this manner, hoopla, like agenda setting, may have a rather subtle, long-term persuasive impact. That impact may not necessarily be one of *changing* political preferences but of affecting which attitudes are important and which lie dormant in the public's political thinking (see Figure 11-7).

Political Advertising

In the early years of radio and television, political communications mainly took the form of lengthy, paid political programs. The candidate's full-length speeches to political audiences were broadcast over radio and television, or lengthy programs were prepared especially for the media, such as FDR's fireside chats or the Knowland telethons discussed earlier. Even in more recent years, such full-length political programs were a major tool for communicating with the public, as in the news conferences held by JFK, former President Nixon's prime-time television speeches, and former President Reagan's weekly Saturday radio addresses.

But the paid half-hour or one-hour campaign speech had all the exposure problems we have already discussed. Relatively few voters had the great interest in politics required to tune in and listen to such lengthy political speeches, and

FIGURE 11-7   Voters rally for their candidate in California. The media often seem to find such events more exciting and hence more newsworthy than issue-oriented coverage. Indeed, the public also seems as interested in the "hoopla" of the campaign as in the issues.

Source: Los Angeles Times Photo, 1986. Photographer: Joe Kennedy.

often those who did were the candidate's already committed supporters. Moreover, the expense of such presentations began to rise with the increased size of television audiences. As a result, as early as the 1950s, these lengthy campaign programs began to give way to shorter presentations modeled on conventional television or radio commercials.

Some experimental studies have suggested that carefully constructed ads that target particular routes to persuasion may be worth the extra effort and expense (see Chapter 6 by Petty et al. in this volume). What specific images are presented seem to be of utmost importance. In one study using only photographs and written descriptions of ostensibly real candidates, Rosenberg and McCafferty (1987) found that rather subtle differences in how the candidates appeared in their photos (e.g., smiling versus no expression, good versus poor lighting) could completely change the outcome of a mock election, even when their party identification and major issue positions were exactly the same.

Along similar lines, Kosterman (1991) presented his subjects with 30-second television spots, some of which had been specially edited to contain *symbolic cues.*

These cues were designed to be highly involving video images that would tie in to long-standing emotional feelings about certain issues. For example, when an ad addressed the problems of drugs and crime, the symbolic-cue video featured minority gang members and graffiti-covered buildings. Presumably, such images elicit the underlying associations many make between drugs and crime and racial stereotypes and thus arouse strong feelings. Indeed, those who viewed these symbolic-cue ads reported feeling more aroused and less thoughtful than those who saw more generic ads (with candidates shaking hands, giving speeches, etc.). But more importantly, the addition of these symbolic images consistently enhanced evaluations of the candidate and likelihood of voting for him, even when the audio portion of the ad presented relatively weak arguments in favor of the candidate and even when subjects believed that the winner might directly impact their well-being (by doubling their tuition)! This finding is important since it suggests that the real substance of an ad—reasons why you should vote for the candidate—can be overwhelmed by emotionally arousing images that bear virtually no direct relevance to the candidate's issue positions or general merit.

Still, much of what we have said about the effects of mass communications presumably applies to these political ads, as well. They are successful in overcoming many of the exposure problems we have discussed, because they are sandwiched in among entertainment and sports programs that are watched for other reasons. But they, too, can produce flagging attention, whether to get a snack, go to the bathroom, or whatever. To counteract such loss of attention, candidates try to saturate the airwaves close to election time. However, they are vulnerable to the selective perception we have discussed; they tend to be rejected by the opponents' sympathizers and applauded by the candidate's own sympathizers, whose preferences they reinforce. Thus, they most likely have their strongest effects in races with unfamiliar candidates or in races with no strong predispositions, such as nonpartisan races or primaries.

It must be remembered that the effect that candidates care about is whether they win or lose. In a close election, say, in a state narrowly divided between the two parties, a relatively small shift could prove decisive in determining the outcome. Many important elections are settled by a margin of only 1% or 2%. So even a relatively small swing to one side or the other could prove decisive. Imagine, then, that some candidate's program of political ads has the typical reinforcing effect upon a candidate's sympathizers, perhaps increasing their enthusiasm and therefore their likelihood of going to the polls; that it attracts some undecided voters who usually vote for that party anyway; and that it attracts a few voters, say, 3% or 4%, from the opponent.

Throughout this chapter, we have described this pattern of effects as typical of the minimal effects model: Mainly, the ads have reinforced prior preferences and have changed only a few attitudes. Yet imagine that such an effect succeeds in putting the candidate over the top. He or she will happily pay off the media consultant's bills! So we must distinguish between our goal here as academic researchers, which is to uncover the most general laws of human behavior that account for the largest and most powerful features of behavior, and the goal of the media consultant, which may be to tilt an election a little this way or that. What counts as a minimal effect for us may not be for him or her!

Some Rare Exceptions to Minimal Effects

The minimal effects model suggested that most one-shot media communications tend more often to reinforce prior attitudes than to change them. That still seems to be mostly true. But there are always exceptions. Here we note a few remarkable cases in which major and important changes in public opinion appear to have been produced by communications in the media presented over a relatively short period of time.

One of the biggest political television events ever was the so-called Four Days following the assassination of John F. Kennedy. Beginning with his shooting at about 12:30 P.M. (CST), on Friday, November 22, 1963, the networks covered the various related events virtually nonstop through his funeral, held the next Monday. The coverage ranged from 60 to 71 hours across the three networks (Rubin, 1967). They covered the subsequent Oswald assassination, two processionals, the requiem service, the cortege to the gravesite, and endless retrospectives and interviews with prominent people.

The average American adult watched almost half of this assassination-related programming—a full 34 hours. Again, it is impossible to separate the effects of the media coverage from those of the event itself, but their combined emotional and attitudinal effects were extraordinary. A survey completed within the following week (Sheatsley & Feldman, 1965) found that only 10% of the public said they had carried on "pretty much as usual"; 40% said they felt more upset than most people (and only 8% less); 48% said that they had trouble sleeping (compared to the roughly 20% who did under normal circumstances); and over half those interviewed, 53%, said they had cried. The attitudinal effects were no less impressive: Half the population called Kennedy one of the best two or three presidents in history, while only 2% said he was "somewhat below average." This, it should be remembered, was a president who had barely won the election in 1960. Moreover, through his abbreviated term, Kennedy's approval ratings were not unusually high (see Mueller, 1973), and historians have subsequently judged him to be somewhere in the middle of the pack. Clearly, there was a major shift in public opinion as a result of all this, and the massive television coverage was instrumental in creating this shift.

Another one of the most dramatic events or series of events in recent American history was the Watergate scandal. Over the many months of revelations, the public had moved with glacial caution toward support for impeachment. But there was evidence of significant attitude change toward former President Nixon in a relatively short time span at the very end of the crisis. Just before Nixon's resignation, a recording came to light that clearly indicated his foreknowledge of the Watergate cover-up. This was called the "smoking gun" tape because it was regarded as finally producing conclusive evidence of his guilt. One study showed that media reports about this tape produced an increase of 15% in those desiring impeachment over a period of just three days (Lang & Stevenson, 1976; see also Chaffee, 1975; Kraus & Chaffee, 1974; Miller et al., 1975). Nixon himself long felt that he "only needed a public relations solution" (Nixon, 1978, p. 773). Whether or not that was true, revelation of this tape was certainly a public relations disaster.

More recently, former President Reagan's approval ratings took a sharp, sudden dive with the initial revelations of the Iran-Contra scandal (Krosnick & Kinder, 1990). Some polls indicated a drop of nearly 20 points within weeks. Although it was clearly another public relations disaster, Reagan, the "Great Communicator," managed to complete his term in office with relatively broad approval.

Conclusion

Social science research relevant to political persuasion has gone through three markedly different phases since the dawn of the electronic media in the 1920s. Predominantly liberal, academic social scientists were initially horrified by the prospect of right-wing propagandists virtually brainwashing the masses through the omnipotence of the mass media. As the data began to accumulate through the 1940s and 1950s, however, it became clear that this image was overdrawn. In fact, for some time, the opposite view was in vogue: that the media are rarely effective in producing large changes in public opinion. This general idea of minimal media effects still has much truth today, although recent research has identified some long-term effects and highlighted the commonalities among the rare instances of short-term effects.

We will conclude with what seem to be the major elements of our current view of political persuasion following some 40 years of relevant research:

1. *Low levels of exposure and attention.* Real public exposure to political communications in the mass media is usually modest, both in the size of the audience and in the level of attention of those who do watch.

2. *Reinforcement of prior attitudes.* Messages that are attended to have difficulties producing actual attitude change because any issue "hot" enough to attract attention usually encounters enduring prior attitudes. In fact, further strengthening of the prior attitudes often takes place.

3. *Exceptions: massive exposure and weak prior attitudes.* Exceptions to the minimal effects model usually depend upon massive exposure (as in long-term, repetitive coverage or a short-term barrage) combined with weak prior attitudes (as with a complex issue or a crowded field of candidates). Similarly, the citizenry is often faced with lower-level political decisions for which their predispositions serve as poor guides (e.g., voting for local nonpartisan judges, voting in a Democratic primary, etc.). In these cases, television ads and newspaper coverage may indeed have substantial influence on the outcomes.

References

Adams, W. C. (1987). As New Hampshire goes . . . In G. R. Orren & N. W. Polsby (Eds.), *Media and momentum: The New Hampshire primary and nomination politics* (pp. 42–59). Chatham, NJ: Chatham House.

Allen, C. L. (1965). Photographing the TV audience. *Journal of Advertising Research, 5*, 2–8.

Ansolabehere, S., Behr, R., & Iyengar, S. (1991). Mass media and elections: An overview. *American Politics Quarterly, 19*, 109–139.

Bechtel, R. B., Achelpohl, C., & Akers, R. (1972). Correlates between observed behavior and questionnaire responses on television viewing. In E. A. Rubinstein, G. A. Comstock, & J. P. Murray (Eds.), *Television and social behavior, Vol. 4. Television in day-to-day life: Patterns of use* (pp. 274–344). Washington, DC: Government Printing Office.

Blumler, J. G. (1977). The political effects of mass communication. In *Social sciences: A third level course, Mass communication and society block 3, units 7–8*. Milton Keynes, Great Britain: The Open University Press.

Budge, I., & Farlie, D. J. (1983). *Explaining and predicting elections: Issue effects and party strategies in twenty-three democracies*. London: George Allen & Unwin.

Cantril, H. (1952). *The invasion from Mars*. In G. E. Swanson, T. E. Newcomb, & E. L. Hartley (Eds.), *Readings in social psychology* (rev. ed., pp. 198–207). New York: Holt.

Cantril, H. (1965). *The pattern of human concerns*. New Brunswick, NJ: Rutgers University Press.

Chaffee, S. H. (Ed.). (1975, October). *American Politics Quarterly, 3*.

Cohen, B. (1963). *The press and foreign policy*. Princeton, NJ: Princeton University Press.

Comstock, G., Chaffee, S., Katzman, N., McCombs, M., & Roberts, D. (1978). *Television and human behavior*. New York: Columbia University Press.

Converse, P. E. (1970). Attitudes and non-attitudes: Continuation of a dialogue. In E. R. Tufte (Ed.), *The quantitative analysis of social problems* (pp. 168–189). Reading, MA: Addison-Wesley.

Dennis, J., Chaffee, S. H., & Choe, S. Y. (1979).

Impact on partisan, image and issue voting. In S. Kraus (Ed.), *The great debates: Carter vs. Ford 1976* (pp. 314–330). Bloomington: Indiana University Press.

Doob, L. W. (1935). *Propaganda, its psychology and technique* (pp. 29–35). New York: Holt.

Festinger, L. (1957). *A theory of cognitive dissonance*. Evanston, IL: Row, Peterson.

Freud, S. (1922). *Group psychology and the analysis of the ego*. London: Hogarth Press.

Frey, D. (1986). Recent research on selective exposure to information. In L. Berkowitz (Ed.), *Advances in experimental social psychology* (pp. 41–80). Orlando, FL: Academic Press.

Fuchs, D. A. (1966). Election-day radio-television and Western voting. *Public Opinion Quarterly, 30*, 226–236.

Funkhouser, G. R. (1973). The issues of the sixties: An exploratory study in the dynamics of public opinion. *Public Opinion Quarterly, 37*, 62–75.

Graber, D. (1987). *Processing the news: How people tame the information tide* (2nd ed.). New York: Longman.

Grush, J. E., McKeough, K. L., & Ahlering, R. G. (1978). Extrapolating laboratory exposure research to actual political elections. *Journal of Personality and Social Psychology, 36*, 257–270.

Hovland, C. I., Lumsdaine, A. A., & Sheffield, F. D. (1949). *Experiments on mass communication*. Princeton, NJ: Princeton University Press.

Institute for Propaganda Analysis (1939). *The fine art of propaganda: A study of Father Coughlin's speeches*. New York: Harcourt and Brace.

Iyengar, S. (1979). Television news and issue salience. *American Politics Quarterly, 7*, 395–416.

Iyengar, S., & Kinder, D. R. (1987). *News that matters*. Chicago: University of Chicago Press.

Jackson, J. E. (1983). Election night reporting and voter turnout. *American Journal of Political Science, 27*, 615–635.

Janis, I. L., Hovland, C. I., Field, P. B., Linton, H., Graham, E., Cohen, A. R., Rife, D., Abelson, R. P., Lesser, G. S., & King, B. T. (1959). *Personality and persuasibility*. New Haven, CT: Yale University Press.

Jennings, M. K., & Niemi, R. G. (1981). *Generations and politics*. Princeton, NJ: Princeton University Press.

Katz, E., & Feldman, J. J. (1962). The debates in the light of research: A survey of surveys. In S. Kraus (Ed.), *The great debates* (pp. 173–223). Bloomington: Indiana University Press.

Keating, C. H., Jr. (1970). Report of Commissioner Charles H. Keating, Jr. In *The Report of the Commission on Obscenity and Pornography*. New York: Random House.

Klapper, J. T. (1960). *The effects of mass communications*. Glencoe, IL: Free Press.

Koch, J. (1967). *The panic broadcast: Portrait of an event*. Boston, MA: Little, Brown.

Kornhauser, W. (1959). *The politics of mass society*. Glencoe, IL: Free Press.

Kosterman, R. J. (1991). *Political spot advertising and routes to persuasion: The role of symbolic content*. Unpublished doctoral dissertation, University of California, Los Angeles.

Kraus, S., & Chaffee, S. H. (Eds.). (1974). *Communication research*. Beverly Hills, CA: Sage.

Krosnick, J. A., & Kinder, D. R. (1990). Altering the foundations of support for the president through priming. *American Political Science Review, 84*, 497–512.

Kubey, R., & Csikszentmihalyi, M. (1990). *Television and the quality of life: How viewing shapes everyday experience*. Hillsdale, NJ: Erlbaum.

Lang, R. D., & Stevenson, R. (1976). Public opinion trends in the last days of the Nixon administration. *Journalism Quarterly, 53*, 294–302.

Lazarsfeld, P. F., Berelson, B., & Gaudet, H. (1948). *The people's choice* (2nd ed.). New York: Columbia University Press.

LeBon, G. (1896). *The crowd: A study of the popular mind*. London: Ernest Benn.

Lichter, R. S., Amundson, D., & Noyes, R. (1988). *The video campaign: Network coverage of the 1988 primaries*. Washington, DC: American Enterprise Institute.

Liebert, R. M., Neale, J. M., & Davidson, E. S. (1973). *The early window: Effects of television on children and youth*. New York: Pergamon Press.

Lippmann, W. (1922). *Public opinion*. New York: Macmillan.

MacKuen, M. B. (1981). Social communication and the mass policy agenda. In M. B. MacKuen & S. L. Coombs (Eds.), *More than news: Media power in public affairs* (pp. 19–144). Beverly Hills, CA: Sage.

Mayer, W. G. (1987). The New Hampshire primary: A historical overview. In G. R. Orren & N. W. Polsby (Eds.), *Media and momentum: The New Hampshire primary and nomination politics* (pp. 9–41). Chatham, NJ: Chatham House.

McCombs, M. E., & Shaw, D. L. (1972). The agenda-setting function of the media. *Public Opinion Quarterly, 36*, 176–187.

McGinniss, J. (1969). *The selling of the president, 1968*. New York: Trident Press.

McGuire, W. J. (1969). The nature of attitudes and attitude change. In G. Lindzey & E. Aronson (Eds.), *The handbook of social psychology* (2nd ed., pp. 136–314). Reading, MA: Addison-Wesley.

McGuire, W. J. (1985). Attitudes and attitude change. In G. Lindzey & E. Aronson (Eds.), *Handbook of social psychology* (Vol. 2, 3rd ed., pp. 223–346). New York: Random House.

McLeod, J. M., & Becker, L. B. (1974). Testing the validity of gratification measures through political effects analysis. In J. G. Blumler & E. Katz (Eds.), *The uses of mass communications: Current perspectives on gratifications research* (pp. 137–166). Beverly Hills, CA: Sage.

Miller, A. H., Brudney, J., & Loftis, P. (1975). Presidential crises and political support: The impact of Watergate on attitudes toward institutions. Paper presented at the annual meeting of the Midwest Political Science Association, Chicago.

Minow, N. N., Martin, J. B., & Mitchell, L. M. (1973). *Presidential television*. New York: Basic Books.

Mueller, J. E. (1973). *War, presidents, and public opinion*. New York: John Wiley & Sons.

Neuman, W. R. (1976). Patterns of recall among television news viewers. *Public Opinion Quarterly, 40*, 115–123.

Nixon, R. M. (1978). *RN: The memoirs of Richard Nixon*. New York: Grosset & Dunlap.

O'Keefe, G. J., Jr., & Mendelsohn, H. (1974). Voter selectivity, partisanship, and the challenge of Watergate. *Communication Research, 1*, 345–367.

Orren, G. R., & Polsby, N. W. (1987). *Media and*

momentum: The New Hampshire primary and nomination politics. Chatham, NJ: Chatham House.

Patterson, T. E. (1980). *The mass media election: How Americans choose their president.* New York: Praeger.

Patterson, T. E., & McClure, R. D. (1976). *The unseeing eye.* New York: G. P. Putnam's Sons.

Robinson, J. P. (1971). The audience for national TV news programs. *Public Opinion Quarterly, 35,* 403–405.

Robinson, J. P., & Levy, M. R. (1986). *The main source: Learning from television news.* Beverly Hills, CA: Sage.

Robinson, M. J. (1976). Public affairs television and the growth of political malaise: The case of "the selling of the Pentagon." *American Political Science Review, 70,* 409–432.

Rogers, E. M., & Dearing, J. W. (1988). Agenda-setting research: Where has it been and where is it going? In J. A. Anderson (Ed.), *Communication Yearbook* (Vol. II). Newbury Park, CA: Sage.

Rosenberg, S. W., & McCafferty, P. (1987). The image and the vote: Manipulating voters' preferences. *Public Opinion Quarterly, 51,* 31–47.

Rubin, B. (1967). *Political television.* Belmont, CA: Wadsworth.

Schramm, W., & Carter, R. F. (1959). Effectiveness of a political telethon. *Public Opinion Quarterly, 23,* 121–127.

Schultz, C. K. (1986). The belligerent neutrality of the news: Creating an environment of informed confusion. Unpublished doctoral dissertation, University of California, Los Angeles.

Sears, D. O. (1968). The paradox of de facto selective exposure without preferences for supportive information. In R. P. Abelson, E. Aronson, W. J. McGuire, T. M. Newcomb, M. J. Rosenberg, & P. H. Tannenbaum (Eds.), *Theories of cognitive consistency: A sourcebook* (pp. 777–787). Chicago: Rand-McNally.

Sears, D. O. (1983). The persistence of early political predispositions: The roles of attitude object and life stage. In L. Wheeler & P. Shaver (Eds.), *Review of personality and social psychology* (Vol. 4, pp. 79–116). Beverly Hills, CA: Sage.

Sears, D. O., & Chaffee, S. H. (1979). Uses and effects of the 1976 debates: An overview of empirical studies. In S. Kraus (Ed.), *The great debates, 1976: Ford vs. Carter* (pp. 223–261). Bloomington: Indiana University Press.

Sears, D. O., & Freedman, J. L. (1967). Selective exposure to information: A critical review. *Public Opinion Quarterly, 31,* 194–213.

Sears, D. O., & Whitney, R. E. (1973). Political persuasion. In I. deS. Pool, W. Schramm, F. W. Frey, N. Maccoby, & E. B. Parker (Eds.), *Handbook of communication* (pp. 153–289). Chicago: Rand McNally.

Sheatsley, P. B., & Feldman, J. J. (1965). A national survey of public reactions and behavior. In B. S. Greenburg & E. B. Parker (Eds.), *The Kennedy assassination and the American public* (pp. 149–177). Stanford, CA: Stanford University Press.

Sigelman, L., & Bullock, D. (1991). Candidates, issues, horse races, and hoopla: Presidential campaign coverage, 1888–1988. *American Politics Quarterly, 19,* 5–32.

Szalai, A. (Ed.). (1972). *The use of time: Daily activities of urban and suburban populations in twelve countries.* The Hague, Netherlands: Mouton.

U.S. Department of Justice. (1986). Attorney General's Commission on Pornography. Washington, DC.

12

THE SUBLIMINAL PERSUASION CONTROVERSY

Reality, Enduring Fable, and Polonius's Weasel

LAURA A. BRANNON
The Ohio State University at Lima

TIMOTHY C. BROCK
The Ohio State University

The subliminal "air-raid" alarm was turned on in the late 1950s (Cousins, 1957; Packard, 1957) and the sirens never stopped wailing; there has never been an "all clear!" Instead, popular belief in subliminal manipulation, and corresponding fears, have steadily increased (Block & Vanden Bergh, 1985; Synodinos, 1988a, 1988b; Zanot, Pincus, & Lamp, 1983). The writer and lecturer most responsible for this trend is W. B. Key (1973, 1977, 1981, 1989). According to Key:

> *Subliminal indoctrination may prove more dangerous than nuclear weapons. The substitution of cultural fantasies for realities on a massive, worldwide scale threatens everyone in this precarious period of human evolution. Present odds appear to favor total devastation. (1989, p. xviii)*

What Effects Are Subliminal Techniques Alleged to Be Having on You?

No issue in the psychology of persuasion has elicited more continuing controversy than the alleged efficacy of subliminal or similar techniques. These techniques refer to any devices used to convey or attempt to convey a message by means of images or sounds of a very brief or hidden nature that cannot be perceived at a normal level of awareness. Have manipulative communicators been influencing you by using subliminal techniques?

• You are watching a movie at a local theater, and all of a sudden, you have a strong craving for popcorn; you get up and purchase a large bucket of popcorn with extra butter and devour it all—despite the fact that you are on a diet! Was the movie altered so that certain frames, appearing too fast for you to consciously perceive them, suggested some word or phrase, such as "Eat popcorn"?

• During an argument one day with your mother, you say several cruel and belittling things, despite the fact that you do not really mean them. Were your cruel words caused by spoken messages (e.g., "Rebel!") hidden in the rock music you had been listening to earlier that day?

• You have been trying to quit smoking for months. Yet despite all of your best efforts, you cannot seem to resist your cravings for cigarettes. Is your compulsion to smoke partly due to the magazine advertisements you read and the billboards you see on the way to work? Do these displays have suggestive words or body forms (with sexual connotations) embedded in their pictures? Is the artwork for these prompts and suggestions so subtle that even an eagle-eyed detective would have to be given a hint or two to know what is happening? To illustrate, recall your last sighting of a Joe Camel ad or billboard. Do you think the camel's nose looks like a penis, and does the mouth resemble female genitals? That's what subliminal persuasion alarmist Wilson Brian Key (as cited in Bream, 1989, p. C11) would have you believe![1]

Scratchmarks on the Private Parts of the Human Mind

Thirty-seven years ago, in "Smudging the Subconscious," the editor of *Saturday Review* described a new device that "thrusts images or messages onto a motion picture or TV grid. The images are invisible to the human eye. They are 'subliminal'; that is, they are beamed into the mind below the threshold of awareness" (Cousins, 1957, p. 20). The device was alleged to increase popcorn sales at a movie theater by flashing "Eat popcorn" and to alter perceptions of a face by projecting "Happy" or "Unhappy" subliminally underneath the face. If it is possible to affect yearning for popcorn or judgments of happiness, perhaps the device could be used to "break into the deepest and most private parts of the human mind and leave all sorts of scratchmarks" (Cousins, 1957, p. 20). The subliminal alarmists emphasized that what we do not see and what we do not know *can* hurt us. In the wrong manipulative hands, subliminal persuasion could be used to destroy the saintly reputation of a Mother Theresa or to enhance the "good name" of a Mafia hoodlum.

Rock Bands and Suicide

The parents of two men who killed themselves after listening to an album by the heavy metal band Judas Priest contended that the suicides were caused by a subliminal message. The message, contained in a song portraying a hopeless view of life, was "Do it!" (Goleman, 1990). Testifying at the trial of the band, University of Michigan psychologist Dr. Howard Shevrin stated, "As I read the evidence, including my own work, the subliminal message could have been a contributory cause to the suicide" (Goleman, 1990, p. B7).

Although the Judas Priest band was acquitted, the final summary of the judge "found that subliminals were there but only found that they were unintentionally placed there" (Larsen, 1990, p. C1). That is, the band was not held responsible for the potentially deadly effects of the subliminal messages. Thus, the Judas Priest verdict left open the possible relationship between a subliminal message and suicide. This possibility is the object of another current suit that alleges that another rock album, *Blizzard of OZ*, contributed to the deaths of two teenagers (Larsen, 1990, p. C1).

Subliminal Audiotapes and Human Improvement

The ability to cause evil that is attributed to subliminal messages is more than matched by their alleged ability to make things better and by the ensuing multimillion dollar self-help industry.

Subliminal audiotapes are now widely marketed and advertised. They are sold in major bookstores, including those operated by many colleges and universities (Merikle, 1988). Consider a typical statement by a manufacturer:

> *You must understand . . . when you listen to these tapes, the only sound you will hear is the restful, pleasant splash of ocean waves as they break on the sandy beach, then go rushing back to join the sea. At least that is what you THINK you hear. But, beneath the gentle sounds of waves*—inaudible to your conscious hearing, but loud and clear to your subconscious—*are carefully researched words and phrases to soften and reverse your stubborn subconscious.*
>
> *The volume can be set at any level—as long as you can hear the sound of the waves even slightly, your subconscious will pick up the embedded suggestions effectively. For best results use your tapes regularly, up to a maximum of four times per day. Since subliminals contain powerful self-programming suggestions, it is not recommended to play them when other people are present.*
>
> *Just relax, watch TV, or enjoy your favorite hobby, as the tapes work secretly below the level of conscious awareness, to reach deep within your subconscious mind. You'll feel better, more relaxed, and confident about your life. As many as 85,000 positive suggestions (affirmations) can be transmitted in just one 60-minute cassette tape.*

This is why more Doctors, Psychologists and professionals choose [name of company]. (Merikle, 1988, p. 356)

Taking Sides in the Controversy: Chapter Overview

Has the privacy of the human soul been breached without a fight? If so, how much is at stake? Is more involved than popcorn sales or a politician's reputation? More than the lives of susceptible teenagers? Does civilization teeter precariously on the menacing cusp of a subliminal mind-warp?

The other side of the controversy is the one adopted in this chapter, namely, that subconscious messages are either entirely absent or too weak to work in the ways alleged. In addition to a selective review of the impact of messages outside of the focus of a person's awareness, in this chapter we will explain the psychology of belief in subliminal persuasion and why the belief will thrive indefinitely.

Introduction

Ironies surround research on subliminal effects. First, one of the interesting aspects of the history of subliminal research is that a researcher can initially find support for a subliminal influence. Even if other researchers fail to reproduce that effect, the popular media publicizes the dubious effect and the general public accepts the media's conclusion (Pratkanis & Greenwald, 1988). Moore (1982) argued that subliminal advertising could not be successful because (1) subliminal stimuli are usually too weak to be observed, and even if they are observed, they would be overwhelmed by other stronger stimuli, and (2) people can control their own responses and can resist any attempts at subliminal influence. Ironically, Saegert (1987) notes that the public's fears of subliminal advertising are based on the assumption that it

> *is effective precisely because the stimulus is weak and because it can circumvent normal screening. . . . Conventional folklore maintains that these unnoticeable messages "take control" of consumers' minds and cause them to do things that they would otherwise forgo if their normal vigilance had not been circumvented. (p. 110)*

Let us take a closer look at alleged subliminal inputs, beginning with subliminal sounds and ending with subliminal sights.

Motivational Audiotapes

Motivational audiotapes are sold nearly everywhere—offered at bookstores, airports, by direct mail, and at supermarkets. They are advertised on television and in magazines. Yet their efficacy is doubtful. Merikle (1988) found that audiotapes, which were supposed to contain inspirational exhortations, in fact contained little more than music, wave sounds, cricket chirps, and bird calls. Sound engineers analyzed commercial audiotapes and found no signs of speech insertions apart from evidence for the nature sounds. Of course, the important question is not whether differences in tapes can be detected by ordinary consumers or even by sophisticated sound engineers. The real issue is whether tapes deliver the therapeutic effects they promise. Not surprisingly, Merikle showed that people reacted the same to subliminal message tapes as they did to placebo, no-message tapes.

Greenwald et al. (1991) recently conducted the most extensive tests of claimed therapeutic effects of audiotapes with subliminal verbal content. In some of these tests, both the listeners and their supervisors did not know what the content of the tapes was. That is, they did not know whether the tapes were supposed to improve memory or to increase self-esteem. The findings clearly showed that subliminal audiotapes designed to improve memory and to increase self-esteem did not produce effects associated with their alleged subliminal content. These findings mean that any effect of an audiotape must be attributable entirely to the listener's perception of the tape's content. Maybe it is true that you cannot tell a book by its cover, but Greenwald et al.'s (1991) research suggests that you can predict a motivational audiotape's effect *only* by its cover—not by the content of the cassette itself.

Merikle concluded:

> In spite of our failure to find any support whatsoever for the many and varied claims concerning these cassettes, it is probably safe to predict that the present evidence will be completely ignored by everyone who wishes to continue to believe in the mystical nature of subliminal perception. (1988, p. 371)

Backward Messages

Continuing with our closer look at subliminal sounds, consider another phenomenon: Messages embedded in rock songs are supposed to be evident when the music is played backwards. When the recordings are played normally (forward), critics claim that the messages are heard subliminally (*backmasking*). The typical criticism is that youthful listeners of rock music are unknowingly "led down a path of loose morality and behavioral aberration" (Vokey & Read, 1985, p. 1231). Belief in the effects of backmasking is so strong that Arkansas and California have passed bills demanding that records and tapes with backmasking have prominent warning labels. Indeed, the state of Texas and the Canadian parliament have funded investigations of backmasking.

To see if backmasking had any impact on listeners, Vokey and Read (1985) first had to confirm that it was more than "people's capacity to spontaneously supply or fill in appropriate speech sounds when they are missing or altered" (Moore, 1988, p. 306). Vokey and Read found that listeners were able to distinguish the sex of the singer when rock music was played backwards but nothing more. When rock music was played backwards, the source of the message was the listener herself rather than some external force (e.g, Satan or evil musician). If listeners were told what they would hear, they heard what they were told to hear. If there was no prompting, they did not hear any messages.

Even though listeners were poor detectors of backmasking, it was still possible that they were affected by the backmasking; after all, a person can die from eating food with an undetectable poison. However, there was "no evidence that listeners were influenced, consciously or unconsciously, by the content of the backward messages" (Moore, 1988, p. 1236). Vokey and Read partly blame the media for confusion about subliminal sound messages. The media often fail to distinguish between the existence of a phenomenon (e.g., backmasking) and evidence that the phenomenon is having any effect.

Subliminal Perception

What about subliminal sights?

In 1957, the messages "Drink Coca-Cola" and "Eat popcorn" were superimposed on movies in progress. The theater audiences were unaware because the exposure times were so short that the flow of the films was unimpeded. The marketing firm responsible reported a dramatic increase in Coke and popcorn sales but provided no empirical evidence for these increases (Moore, 1982).

Subsequently, an academic researcher (Hawkins, 1970) conducted an experiment in which messages were presented subliminally. Hawkins used a device that illuminated printed statements for very short time periods. The device could illuminate two statements at the same time (as in current television monitors with inserts in part of the screen from another channel); it could also mix statements so that they appeared as a single image. The presentation of the subliminal statements took place during another experiment, the cover experiment. The cover experiment had the stated purpose of establishing recognition thresholds for various (automotive) brand names; for example, how quickly would subjects recognize *Ford*? Group I, the control group, received a nonsense syllable (four letters with no meaning, e.g., NYTP) at the subliminal exposure time of 2.7 milliseconds. Group II was subliminally presented with the word *Coke* in the cover experiment. That is, *Coke* appeared very briefly alongside the normal presentation of an automotive brand name (e.g., *Ford*). Each group was presented with its particular subliminal message 40 times over approximately 15 minutes. The subjects then filled out questionnaires in which they indicated how long it had been since they had anything to drink and how thirsty they were at the present time.

"The results were statistically higher thirst ratings for the group exposed to the subliminal stimulus COKE compared to the group exposed to the subliminal presentation of a nonsense syllable" (Beatty & Hawkins, 1989, p. 6). Hawkins concluded that "a simple subliminal stimulus can serve to arouse a basic drive such as thirst" (Hawkins, 1970, p. 324).

Now consider an apparent laboratory corroboration of the kind of effect reported by Hawkins (1970). Kunst-Wilson and Zajonc (1980) displayed bursts of lights on a screen to viewers; the bursts were really octagons shown too fast to see. A few minutes later, the viewers filled out questionnaires in which they indicated their liking for various geometrical shapes, including octagons. Their questionnaire responses indicated they clearly preferred the octagons that were flashed to other shapes that were not flashed. Although the Kunst-Wilson and Zajonc results have been independently reproduced, their support for the possibility of subliminal persuasion is actually quite tenuous, as we shall see below.

Whether subliminal influence can cause changes in behavior is still an open question. Bornstein et al. (1987) found that subjects agreed more with an accomplice of the experimenter if that accomplice's face had previously been subliminally presented; they agreed less when they were seeing the accomplice for the first time, that is, without prior subliminal viewings. Unfortunately, the effect was not strong, and it did not affect other measures of behavior. Thus, the findings did not advance the likelihood of real-world subliminal persuasion.[2]

In sum, several important question marks surround subliminal influence. First, although people liked the shape of octagons better than other shapes, advertisers do not want consumers merely to like the word *popcorn*; they want consumers to be motivated to act, to *buy* popcorn. Subliminal repetition of communicators' faces may make those communicators more persuasive in the next few minutes, but would those subliminally enhanced faces be more persuasive the next day, the next week? Linkage from a subliminally induced preference to a subsequent supermarket aisle or voting booth decision has yet to be documented. There is no evidence that a message registered below threshold (i.e., below one's level of awareness) can have effects persisting longer than a few minutes. And finally, ask yourself, When does a persuasion practitioner (such as a television advertiser) have the luxury of a captive audience whose attention can be trained on an unimpeded subliminal message? Even if this direct pipeline to the mind were possible, however, there is no evidence that weak stimuli can countervail strong stimuli, that is, the other strong sights and sounds and internal thoughts reaching the mind of the recipient.

Embedded Messages

Subliminal persuasion alarmist Key (1977) argued repeatedly that advertisers embed the word *sex* in their advertising copy to obtain enhanced recall and recognition through implicit sexual association. To test this hypothesis, Vokey and Read (1985) produced three sets of slides of vacation experiences: in the first, the word *sex* was embedded three or four times; in the second, a three-letter nonsense syllable was inserted; and in the third, there were no embeds. Viewers examined an equal number of each type of slide before being tested for their ability to remember aspects of the vacation scenes. None of the viewers reported seeing the word *sex*, so the embedding was not noticed. Viewers could only see *sex* if it was pointed out to them. (We return later to the insight that subjects see Key's sexual objects in advertisements only when these shapes and forms are pointed out.) Key's claim was not supported. Slides that had been *sex* embedded during initial exposure were not better recognized than slides with nonsense syllables or no embeds. There was no improvement when another test was administered two days later (see Figure 12-1).

Contemporary Issues in Subliminal Research

Pratkanis and Greenwald (1988) noted that "researchers have failed to produce reliable subliminal effects for at least three reasons: (a) inconsistent use of the term subliminal, (b) lack of adequately precise and standardized methods, and (c) lack of an adequate conception of unconscious processes." They further noted that, "as a consequence of these problems, it has not yet been possible to

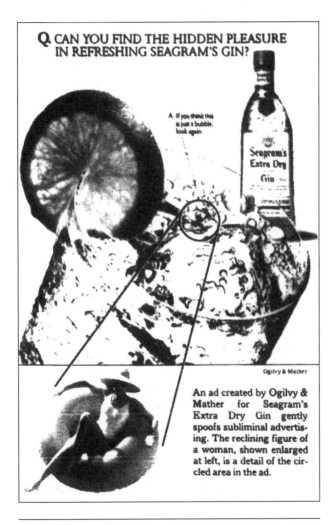

FIGURE 12-1   All the world's a glass of gin when your true love waits therein!

describe, with confidence, conditions under which subliminal effects are likely to occur" (p. 339).

What Is Subliminal?

One of the major problems in determining the effect of subliminal messages is precisely defining what is meant by *perception without awareness* (Moore, 1988; Synodinos, 1988b). The term *threshold* is used to refer to the point at which awareness of a stimulus (e.g., the word *Coke*) is reported or at which unreported awareness has a measurable effect on some subsequent behavior. To illustrate, detection of vodka in a vodka-and-tonic will vary among drinkers. Each drinker's vodka-reporting threshold can be defined in terms of a proportion of vodka to tonic. *Subjective* awareness thresholds consist of subjects' self-reports as to whether they were aware of the stimulus; *objective* awareness thresholds, on the other hand, are determined by subjects' ability to distinguish whether a stimulus was actually presented (Cheesman & Merikle, 1986).

Here is one respected technique for establishing *objective* thresholds of awareness. Observers must distinguish between the presence of a stimulus (e.g., a word) and its absence (e.g., a blank slide). Subliminality is achieved when the observer is unable to distinguish the word's presence from its absence (Eriksen, 1960). According to Moore (1988), the most serious problem with research attempting to demonstrate subliminal effects is carelessness in ensuring that messages are truly subliminal. "Some messages that are assumed to be subliminal may be either partially available to consciousness some of the time or may be so far below an objective threshold of awareness that they are operatively nonexistent" (Moore, 1988, p. 311).

Setting up conditions that rule out the availability of a stimulus to consciousness and, at the same time, allow for some operative, measurable effect has proven very difficult for research scientists. Let us return to your vodka-and-tonic. Suppose we wanted to demonstrate that vodka impairs your performance on a video game; at the same time, we want you to be completely convinced that your drink contains nothing but tonic water. Quantities of vodka minute enough not to be detectable to the most sensitive palate and small enough to evoke none of the usual sensations of alcohol (euphoria, warmth, etc.) might be too tiny to have any effect on your performance on a video game or any other measurable task. Few investigations of subliminal persuasion have achieved the requisite fine-tuning of stimulation necessary for a fair test of the phenomenon.

But We All Believe in It!

Although scientists have not been able to provide reliable recipes for subliminal omelets, the average person has subliminal egg on his or her face and likes it! At the outset of this chapter, we noted that popular belief in subliminal manipulation is steadily increasing. How come? (Gentle reader, perhaps you are one of the believers!)

Speculation Regarding the Psychology of Belief in Subliminal Persuasion

Social psychologists have uncovered five human tendencies that may account for the widespread acceptance of the efficacy of subliminal persuasion. The first is the propensity to attribute our unfavorable outcomes to external causes (Weary Bradley, 1978). Given that most consumers are not completely satisfied with their purchases of advertised products, they might be ready to attribute, or blame, external causes.

One way of accounting for dissatisfactions would be to attribute purchase choices to forces beyond one's control, that is, to manipulative advertising. This speculative account is testable. Propensity to believe in subliminal manipulation should be higher, other things equal, for products (and/or product categories) that are more disappointing. Similarly, subliminal manipulation is more likely to be imputed to advertising for products that are enjoyable but unhealthful (cigarettes, alcohol, calorie-rich foods, etc.). People can justify their consumption of cigarettes, rich foods, and so forth by telling themselves that outside forces compelled them to do these things. If it was not the devil that made them do it, then perhaps it was subliminal advertising.

The second account deals with the propensity for false beliefs to persevere (Ross, Lepper, & Hubbard, 1975). Most consumers appear to be aware of aspects of the controversy surrounding subliminal persuasion (Synodinos, 1988a). Indeed, because these aspects receive fervent media attention, consumers have frequently processed the term *subliminal* in conjunction with terms such as *persuasion*, *advertising*, and the like. Consider how these consumers will now react to the following quotation from Anthony Pratkanis in the *New York Times*:

> *Subliminal tapes are today's snake oil. There's no evidence that there is subliminal perception of their message. There's no evidence of any perception at all, let alone evidence that they work. (Goleman, 1990, B9)*

Knowing that Pratkanis's statement was based on a careful empirical test of such tapes' effectiveness and knowing that subliminal tape companies support their claims only through testimonials from satisfied customers may not be sufficient to change long-standing and long-processed beliefs about the power of subliminal messages. People will have many other beliefs and experiences connected in their minds with the original supportive beliefs; these connections will make the original beliefs salient and easy to think about. Thus, the original beliefs may easily override any new information. Moreover, it will not be long before the media supplies consumers with new allegations or so-called evidence attesting to subliminal power.

A third account stems from the everyday experience of responding with feelings of like/agree versus dislike/disagree to incomprehensible or even unintelligible messages (Padgett & Brock, 1987). Indeed our initial social experience involves exposure to unintelligible communications; infants first hear vocalizations from parents and eventually associate these novel sounds with meaning. As adults, we use contextual cues to interpret and respond to messages in incomprehensible foreign languages. For example, crowds chanting in Russian in Moscow and Leningrad during the 1991 coup attempt elicited immediate understanding from observers everywhere in the world.

A fourth account stems from the equally common experience of having beliefs, attitudes, and the like for which one cannot recall the source. A central assumption of the cognitive response approach to persuasion is that audiences are active in the persuasion process, providing material not in the original message (see Chapter 6 by Petty et al. in this volume). Further, the persistence of persuasion depends on the extent to which one rehearses these self-generated cognitive responses (Greenwald, 1968), rather than rehearsing responses based on the communication, such as paraphrases of message content. Hence, a message that maximizes self-generated responses will have more long-term effectiveness than one that does not. Forcing a recipient of a persuasive message to rely on self-generated cognitive responses (rather than on remembering the message) therefore may increase the effectiveness of that message. But this experience could also reinforce an impression of having been the target of subliminal manipulation because the original message that instigated one's responses has been forgotten, and one may find oneself agreeing with unretrievable message points.

Finally, a fifth determinant of belief in subliminal persuasion may be the "fallacy that presence implies effectiveness" (Vokey & Read, 1985, p. 1232). Once it has been acknowledged that some incoming stimulation is actually there, although below the level of one's awareness, then it is assumed that such stimulation is having an impact on one's beliefs and behaviors. Since we often surmise—sometimes correctly—that very small amounts of chemicals and foodstuffs can have important effects on our well-being, perhaps it is consistent to suppose that quite undetectable symbolic stimulation in the form of very brief sights and sounds may also have some serious consequences.

In sum, belief in the efficacy of subliminal persuasion may be determined by the following factors, singly or together:

- The tendency to attribute unfavorable outcomes to external causes
- The perseverance of long-held beliefs in spite of countervailing evidence
- Wide experience in responding to unintelligible messages
- Wide experience in responding to a topic after forgetting the original message on that topic
- The belief that if something exists it must be having an effect

Conclusions

Pratkanis and Greenwald (1988) summarized research on subliminal influence:

> *There continues to be no reliable evidence in support of the more sensational claims for the power of subliminal influence. Further, those subliminal findings that appear to be replicable (a) tend to involve only low levels of cognitive processing, levels that are of*

little value to the marketer, (b) are difficult to implement in mass media settings, and (c) might just as (or more) easily be implemented using supraliminal (observable/detectable) techniques. (p. 349)

Although there are some mild, reliable effects, it appears that the only way that the marketing industry is profiting from subliminal persuasion is by exploiting the public's widespread belief in its efficacy (by selling self-help audiotapes, for example).

Epilogue: The Story That Is Bound to Be Repeated

We conclude with a true fable. The term *fable* is used because we expect that the sequence of events and the meaning of the sequence will persist indefinitely. Recall that Hawkins's (1970) research appeared to corroborate the observation of the market researchers that subliminal directives can have the power ascribed to them. Indeed, for the next two decades, Hawkins's study has been one of the most widely cited classics in consumer behavior journals and textbooks.

We come now to the end of the fable, an attempt by Hawkins to reproduce his own 1970 findings (Beatty & Hawkins, 1989). *Every effort was made by Beatty and Hawkins to duplicate exactly the original experiment*, but the results showed no differences in thirst ratings between the experimental group (*Coke*) and the control group (nonsense syllable; see the description earlier). In considering explanations for their failure to repeat the original results, the authors speculated that, in the original experiment, "the treatments had no effect but the control group reported lower thirst ratings due to chance (sampling error). . . . In conclusion, *this study casts serious doubts on the validity of one of the few studies to provide empirical evidence of subliminal effects in an advertising context*" (Beatty & Hawkins, 1989, p. 7).

We expect that the Hawkins-Coke fable will be repeated over and over again in the future and with the same three-act drama: first act, an observation of an apparent subliminal effect in the field; second act, demonstration of the effect by an enthusiastic researcher in a laboratory analogue; and third act, subsequent failure by other researchers to reproduce the effect. It is noteworthy and praiseworthy that Hawkins himself published a retraction of his findings (Beatty & Hawkins, 1989). Nevertheless, it is safe to predict that Hawkins's 1970 classic will continue to be cited as proof of subliminal persuasion in the next best-seller by Wilson Brian Key and/or his successors. Further proof of subliminal manipulation will be provided using the same old "see-something-in-the-icecubes" trick (see Figure 12-2).

Remember Hamlet's verbal jousting with Polonius (Act III, 2):

Hamlet: "Do you see yonder cloud that's almost in the shape of a camel?"

Polonius: "'Tis like a camel indeed."

Hamlet: "Methinks it is like a weasel."

PEOPLE HAVE BEEN TRYING TO FIND THE BREASTS IN THESE ICE CUBES SINCE 1957.

The advertising industry is sometimes charged with sneaking seductive little pictures into ads.

Supposedly, these pictures can get you to buy a product without your even seeing them.

Consider the photograph above. According to some people, there's a pair of female breasts hidden in the patterns of light refracted by the ice cubes.

Well, if you really searched you probably *could* see the breasts. For that matter, you could also see Millard Fillmore, a stuffed pork chop and a 1946 Dodge.

The point is that so-called "subliminal advertising" simply doesn't exist. Overactive imaginations, however, most certainly do.

So if anyone claims to see breasts in that drink up there, they aren't in the ice cubes.

They're in the eye of the beholder.

ADVERTISING

ANOTHER WORD FOR FREEDOM OF CHOICE.

American Association of Advertising Agencies

FIGURE 12-2   Are suggestive stimuli hidden in ads?

Source: Courtesy of the American Association of Advertising Agencies.

Polonius: "It is backed like a weasel."

Hamlet: "Or like a whale?"

Polonius: "Very like a whale."

Notes

1. As we will consider later in this chapter, scientific findings have challenged the opinions of Wilson Brian Key as well as those of others who point to the insidiousness of subliminal manipulation. Nonetheless, Key's views are extremely well known and he is widely read, as evidenced by the instant popularity of his four books. (See the References to this chapter, namely, Key, 1973, 1977, 1981, 1989.)

2. "Recent attempts to demonstrate the marketing relevance of subliminal stimuli [Cuperfain & Clarke, 1985; Kilbourne, Painton, & Riley, 1985] contain so many methodological flaws that they cannot be said to have advanced the case regarding any possible advertising application" (Moore, 1988, p. 309).

Acknowledgment

We are indebted to Michael Lynn for his help in searching the literature and proposing issues for this chapter.

References

Beatty, S. E., & Hawkins, D. I. (1989). Subliminal stimulation: Some new data and interpretation. *Journal of Advertising, 18,* 4–8.

Block, M. P., & Vanden Bergh, B. C. (1985). Can you sell subliminal messages to consumers? *Journal of Advertising, 14,* 59–62.

Bornstein, R. F., Leone, D. R., & Galley, D. J. (1987). The generalizability of subliminal mere exposure effects: Influence of stimuli perceived without awareness on social behavior. *Journal of Personality and Social Psychology, 53,* 1070–1079.

Bream, M. (1989). Subliminal seduction. *Marketing, 2,* C10–C11.

Cheesman, J., & Merikle, P. M. (1986). Distinguishing conscious from unconscious perception. *Canadian Journal of Psychophysics, 40,* 343–367.

Cousins, N. (1957). Smudging the subconscious. *Saturday Review, 40,* 20.

Cuperfain, R., & Clarke, T. K. (1985). A new perspective of subliminal perception. *Journal of Advertising, 14,* 36–41.

Eriksen, C. W. (1960). Discrimination and learning without awareness: A methodological survey and evaluation. *Psychological Review, 67,* 279–300.

Goleman, D. (1990, August). Research probes what the mind senses unaware. *New York Times,* pp. B7–B8.

Greenwald, A. G. (1968). Cognitive learning, cognitive response to persuasion and attitude change. In A. G. Greenwald, T. C. Brock, & T. M. Ostrom (Eds.), *Psychological foundations of attitudes* (pp. 147–170). New York: Academic Press.

Greenwald, A. G., Spangenberg, E. R., Pratkanis, A. R., & Eskanazi, J. (1991). Double-blind tests of subliminal self-help audiotapes. *Psychological Science, 2,* 119–122.

Hawkins, D. (1970). The effects of subliminal stimulation on drive level and brand preference. *Journal of Marketing Research, 7,* 322–326.

Key, W. B. (1973). *Subliminal seduction: Ad media's manipulation of a not so innocent America.* New York: Signet.

Key, W. B. (1977). *Media sexploitation.* New York: Signet.

Key, W. B. (1981). *The clam-plate orgy and other subliminal techniques for manipulating your behavior.* New York: Signet.

Key, W. B. (1989). *The age of manipulation: The con in confidence, the sin in sincere.* New York: Henry Holt.

Kilbourne, W. E., Painton, S., & Ridley, D. (1985). The effect of sexual embedding on responses to magazine advertisements. *Journal of Advertising, 14,* 48–56.

Kunst-Wilson, W. R., & Zajonc, R. B. (1980). Affective discrimination of stimuli that cannot be recognized. *Science, 207,* 557–558.

Larsen, D. (1990, December 2). Test of their metal. *Dayton Daily News,* C1.

Merikle, P. M. (1988). Subliminal auditory messages: An evaluation. *Psychology and Marketing, 5*(4), 355–372.

Moore, T. E. (1982). Subliminal advertising: What you see is what you get. *Journal of Marketing, 46,* 38–47.

Moore, T. E. (1988). The case against subliminal manipulation. *Psychology & Marketing, 5*(4), 297–316.

Packard, V. (1957). *The hidden persuaders.* New York: McKay.

Padgett, V. R., & Brock, T. C. (1987). Do advertising messages require intelligible content?: A cog-

nitive response analysis of unintelligible persuasive messages. In S. Hecker & D. W. Stewart (Eds.), *Nonverbal communication in advertising* (pp. 185–203). Lexington, MA: Lexington Books.

Pratkanis, A. R., & Greenwald, A. G. (1988). Recent perspectives on unconscious processing: Still no marketing applications. *Psychology and Marketing, 5*(4), 337–353.

Ross, L., Lepper, M. R., & Hubbard, M. (1975). Perseverance in self-perception and social perception: Biased attributional processes in the debriefing paradigm. *Journal of Personality and Social Psychology, 32,* 880–892.

Saegert, J. (1987). Why marketing should quit giving subliminal advertising the benefit of the doubt. *Psychology and Marketing, 4,* 107–120.

Synodinos, N. E. (1988a). Subliminal stimulation: What does the public think about it? *Current Issues and Research in Advertising, 11,* 157–185.

Synodinos, N. E. (1988b). Review and appraisal of subliminal perception within the context of signal detection theory. *Psychology and Marketing, 5*(4), 317–336.

Vokey, J. R., & Read, J. D. (1985). Subliminal messages: Between the devil and media. *American Psychologist, 40,* 1231–1239.

Weary Bradley, G. (1978). Self-serving biases in the attribution process: A reexamination of the fact or fiction question. *Journal of Personality and Social Psychology, 36,* 56–71.

Zanot, E. J., Pincus, D. J., & Lamp, E. J. (1983). Public perceptions of subliminal advertising. *Journal of Advertising, 12,* 39–45.

GLOSSARY

LAURA A. BRANNON
The Ohio State University at Lima

The purpose of this glossary is to provide quick understanding of technical terms. Although the definitions are usable across chapters, further clarification of a term requires considering its use in context. Formal definition has been eschewed in favor of fast, intuitive communication of the gist of the term. Thus, this glossary does not replace either dictionary or encyclopedia treatments. Wherever possible, the chapter authors' definitions have been respected and incorporated in the glossary. In some cases, a short additional paragraph reminds the reader of the theoretical meaning of the term, for example, how the term is used in theoretical relationship with another term.

Three criteria were used to determine which terms to include. A term was included first, if it was considered an important concept in the psychology of persuasion; second, if it was considered a key concept for at least one chapter in the present volume. The third criterion for inclusion was that the layperson's definition for the term did not sufficiently convey the term's technical meaning in this volume. Hence, terms whose ordinary dictionary definitions (for example, definitions from the *American Heritage Dictionary*, 2nd College Edition) are close enough to their meanings in the context of this volume were not included. For example, *attention* and *comprehension* are frequently referred to in many of the present chapters. However, because their common definitions—"concentration of the mental powers upon an object; observant consideration; notice" and "to understand" respectively—convey the terms' meanings here, they were not defined. On the other hand, terms such as *attitude* (commonly defined as "a position of the body or manner of carrying oneself, indicative of a mood or condition; a state of mind or feeling with regard to a person or thing") are defined because they have an altered meaning and play an important role in the psychology of persuasion.

Finally, some potential entries were composites of two or more terms. In those instances in which the composite's meaning is straightforward or easily derivable, once the meaning of the individual terms is understood (e.g., *attitude change*), no definition is provided. On the other hand, when the composite's meaning is not readily derivable (e.g., *elaboration likelihood*) the composite entry is defined.

Italicized words or expressions within definitions refer to terms defined elsewhere in the glossary.

accessibility of an attitude—How easily the *attitude* comes to mind. One measure of how accessible an *attitude* is from memory is how long it takes people to answer whether they like or dislike something. Highly accessible *attitudes* are more predictive of behavior than less accessible *attitudes*. In addition, this approach can be used to distinguish *attitudes* from *nonattitudes*, because people with a long delay are thought of as not having an *attitude* prior to the question being asked.

accessible—Salient and easily brought to mind.

accomplice (experimental)—A helper of the experimenter who plays a role given to him or her by the experimenter.

acquiescence bias—The tendency to agree with everything, regardless of what a question asks.

activation (e.g., of an attitude)—The bringing of an item, category, or *attitude* from memory into consciousness.

activation (of sympathetic nervous system)—Alerting a bodily system (in this case, the *sympathetic nervous system*) for action.

affect—Emotional feelings.

affective-cognitive consistency—See *evaluative-cognitive consistency*.

affective direction—The direction (positive or negative) of an *affective* reaction.

affective intensity—The magnitude of an *affective* reaction.

affective responses—The emotional feelings and physiological consequences of encountering or thinking about an *attitude* object. These feelings vary from positive to negative on the evaluative *attitude* dimension.

agency—So-called masculine characteristics such as dominance and assertiveness; attributes linked to resisting influence.

agenda setting—Focusing the public's attention on a particular issue; the mass media is often attributed the ability to set the public agenda.

agentic concerns—Concern with self-assertion, self-expansion, and the urge to master.

argument—A piece of information regarding the merits of a position; a proposition in a persuasive message.

arousal—A state of readiness for action.

associative network—Several beliefs and experiences connected in memory, such that *activating* one item from the network of beliefs makes other beliefs in the network salient (*accessible*).

attitude—A general and enduring positive or negative feeling about some person, object, or issue (Petty & Cacioppo, 1981).

attitude (within the attitude-to-behavior process model)—An association in memory between the *attitude object* and one's evaluation of the object; the strength of this association can vary and determines the *accessibility* of the *attitude* from memory.

attitude-behavior consistency—See *attitude-behavior correspondence.*

attitude-behavior correspondence—In order to examine the relationship between *attitudes* and behavior, the *attitude* and the behavior must be measured at equivalent levels of specificity. A specific behavior is best predicted by an attitudinal question that is equally specific to the action in question, the target of the action, the context in which the action is performed, and the time of the action. In contrast, a general pattern of behavior is best predicted by a general *attitude measure*. Similarly, in order to examine the relationship between personality variables and behavior, the personality variables and the behavior must be measured at equivalent levels of specificity.

attitude-congruent knowledge—Knowledge supporting an individual's *attitude.*

attitude dimensionality—The different belief clusters that are present in a person's set of beliefs; the complexity of the underlying beliefs.

attitude measurement—Assigning a number to an *attitude* that reflects its evaluative character.

attitude object—Simply put, the object of an *attitude*. People hold *attitudes* toward all kinds of objects: specific persons, social groups, policy decisions, personal action decisions, abstract concepts, consumer products, and the like.

attitude properties—*Attitudes* have a variety of characteristics, for example, *evaluative* and *nonevaluative* properties.

attitude relevance cues—Prompts that lead an individual to consider the relevance of his or her *attitude* in the immediate situation.

attitude response domain—Observable (and therefore measurable) *responses* used to assess *attitude properties*; these may be *affective, cognitive,* or *conative.*

attitude strength—Refers to the apparent influence that the *attitude* has upon the individual's behavior; related to the *accessibility* of the *attitude.*

attitude structure—When an issue is of high importance to a person and he or she has thought about it repeatedly and organized his other beliefs, feelings, and experiences into a coherent position, the person is likely to have a well-articulated stance with an easy-to-recall basis. On the other hand, when the person knows little about an issue or it is unimportant to him or her, the person's reactions are not likely to be organized in memory in a meaningful way, and he or she may not be readily able to recall relevant information.

attitude-to-behavior process model—A model of *attitude-behavior consistency* that maintains that whether an *attitude* directs behavior depends upon whether the *attitude* is *activated* from memory and the extent to which the *attitude* colors the individual's *definition of the event*. The *attitude* must be *activated* from memory when the individual sees the *attitude object*, if the *attitude* is to exert any influence. If the *attitude* is *activated* from memory, then it serves as a filter through which the object is viewed at that moment in time. As a result, immediate perceptions of the *attitude object* will be consistent with the *attitude*. In contrast, if the *attitude* is not *activated*, then the immediate perceptions will be based on momentarily noticeable features of the *attitude object* that may not be consistent with the *attitude*. According to the model, then, the initiation of the attitude-to-behavior process depends upon whether the *attitude* is activated from memory. The model predicts that *attitude accessibility* will determine the relation between *attitudes* and perceptions, or judgments, of an object. The relation is expected to be stronger if the *attitude* is *accessible* from memory than if not. The model makes a similar prediction regarding the attitude-behavior relation.

attitudinal component (in the theory of reasoned action)—According to the *theory of reasoned action*, one of the components that forms a *behavioral intention*; a combination of both the person's beliefs concerning the likely outcomes to result from performing the behavior and the person's positive or negative feelings about those outcomes.

attitudinal familiarity—The extent to which an *attitude* is encountered frequently in everyday life.

attribution—An inference about the causes of behavior or *attitudes*.

authority principle—Legitimately constituted authorities are influential because of their superior information and power.

authority rule for compliance—One should be more willing to follow the suggestions of someone who is a legitimate authority.

autistic persuasion—Social influence occurring with minimal social interaction, primarily within the mind of the recipient of influence.

autokinetic effect—An optical illusion in which, after focusing attention for several seconds on a pinpoint of light in an otherwise completely dark room, the light appears to move erratically, even though the light is actually stationary.

aversive consequences—Negative or unpleasant consequences; a behavior must result in aversive consequences in order for *cognitive dissonance* to be aroused.

backmasking—Alleged *subliminal messages* embedded in rock songs. The messages are supposed to be evident when the music is played backward. When the recordings are played normally (forward), critics of such songs claim that the messages are heard *subliminally*.

bait-and-switch procedure—A variation of the *commitment/consistency rule for compliance* in which a retailer may advertise certain merchandise at a special low price. When the customer arrives to take advantage of the special, he or she finds the merchandise to be of low quality or sold out. However, because customers have by now made an active *commitment* to making a purchase at that particular store, they are more willing to agree to examine and, consequently, to buy alternative merchandise there.

bandwagon—A propaganda technique that consists of leading recipients to believe that everyone believes a particular idea.

behavioral intention—According to the *theory of reasoned action*, the single best predictor of a person's eventual behavior. In forming a behavioral intention, the individual considers, weighs, and combines his or her *attitude* toward the behavior in question with *subjective norms* regarding the behavior.

behavioral style—Behavioral *responses* organized in a consistent pattern: for example, a consistent behavioral style is a source of *minority influence.*

belief conversion effect—When a minority in a group is behaviorally consistent, it can sometimes influence majority members' private beliefs, even when the minority is still publicly rejected or ignored. In such instances, a minority can produce conversion in the private beliefs of majority members without any apparent influence on what they say overtly or publicly. This effect is probably mediated by issue-relevant thoughts in members of the majority, thoughts generated in an attempt to explain the minority's behavior.

belief perseverance—The tendency to continue to hold a belief even after the original basis for the belief has been disconfirmed.

biased message processing—When a message recipient's cognitive responses to a message are not objective but are biased in a particular direction (pro or con).

blind judgment—A judgment made by an experimenter without knowing to which conditions the judged items or behavior belong.

bodily cues—*Nonverbal measures of attitudes* in which *affect* is conveyed through shrugs, gestures, foot tapping, self-touching, self-scratching, and so on.

bogus pipeline—A technique of measuring *attitudes* in which people are led to believe that a machine can precisely measure the direction and intensity of their *attitudes*; this is done to get them to reveal information that they might normally be unwilling to report.

bolster (an attitude)—A method of resolving cognitive inconsistency, which consists of developing additional, consistent cognitions to support an *attitude.*

brain waves—The electrical signals that the brain generates while processing information.

catharsis—The therapeutic release of tension or anxiety.

cathartic reactions—See *catharsis.*

central route to persuasion—According to the *elaboration likelihood model*, persuasion resulting from careful thinking about and *elaborating* upon the *arguments* presented by the message; the recipient must be both motivated and able to evaluate the message *arguments'* merits. *Attitudes* formed via this route tend to be stable over time, predictive of the person's *attitude-relevant behavior*, and resistant to change from competing messages.

channel—The medium in which a communication is transmitted (e.g., a magazine advertisement).

choice dilemmas—Hypothetical problems used to study *group polarization* effects. Each of these problems entails a protagonist who must choose between two courses of action, one of which is riskier than the other.

classical conditioning—Learning to associate an initially neutral *stimulus* (a *conditioned stimulus*) with some evocative *stimulus* (*unconditioned stimulus*). Repeated pairings of the *conditioned stimulus* with the *unconditioned stimulus* result in the *conditioned stimulus* evoking the same response (*conditioned response*) as does the *unconditioned stimulus.*

classically conditioned physiological responses—The notion that a physiological response could be linked uniquely to a particular concept, such as "good." By artificially creating a unique link between a physiological *response* and a concept such as "good," one could then measure a person's *attitudes* toward an object, person, or issue by recording the size of the physiological response that followed the presentation of the *attitude object*.

cognitive approaches to health persuasion—Approaches to health persuasion that emphasize cognition and thought, rather than the acquisition of the skills needed for performing healthy behaviors. There are two types of cognitive approaches: those that make use of formal decision models entailing cost-benefit analyses of health behavior and those focused on the *commonsense attitudes* about health threats that motivate *self-regulatory efforts* to reduce personal risk.

cognitive dissonance theory—Whenever a person holds two cognitions or thoughts that are inconsistent or in conflict with one another, the person will feel tension (cognitive dissonance). The tension will be experienced as a *drive* and will result in efforts to reduce the inconsistency between these two cognitions. The amount of dissonance experienced (and therefore the intensity of the *drive* to reduce the dissonance) will be based on the number of discrepant cognitions one has (weighted by the importance of those cognitions), divided by the number of consistent consonant cognitions one has (weighted by their importance). When people feel *personally responsible* for unwanted or *aversive consequences*, cognitive dissonance is aroused, which can result in *attitude* change.

cognitive processes—The mental functions associated with perception, learning, and thinking.

cognitive responses—The beliefs, inferences, and assumptions made about an *attitude object*; also refers to the thoughts generated in response to a message, which vary from favorable to unfavorable on the evaluative *attitude* dimension.

cognitive response analysis—A method for analyzing the persuasive effects of a message in which respondents jot down their attitude-relevant thoughts immediately after hearing or reading a persuasive message. These *responses* are then scored (by either the respondent or by several independent raters) as being positive or negative toward the *attitude object*. An overall *attitude* score for each respondent is obtained.

cognitive response approach to persuasion—See *cognitive response analysis*.

cognitive schema—A knowledge structure that allows people to use prior knowledge to interpret new information. Schemata contain both the attributes of a concept and relations among the attributes. Schemata are thought to guide the perception of new information, recall of old information, and social inferences. People with high *affective-cognitive consistency* and good *accessibility of attitude-relevant information* can be thought of as individuals with this kind of organized knowledge structure on a particular issue. These people find it relatively easy to generate counterarguments to a persuasive message.

cognitive style—A consistent difference among individuals in the way they process information.

collective representations—A complex amalgam of social, cultural, and historical events and underlying ideas.

commercial compliance professionals—Those individuals whose business or financial well-being is dependent on their ability to induce *compliance* (e.g., salespeople, fundraisers, advertisers, political lobbyists, cult recruiters, con artists).

commitment—A method of eliciting *compliance* that relies on the principle that, once a person makes a commitment (takes a stand or goes on record), there is a natural tendency to behave in ways that are stubbornly consistent with the stand. See *consistency principle* and *commitment/consistency rule for compliance*.

commitment/consistency rule for compliance—After *committing* oneself to a position, one should be more willing to *comply* with requests for behaviors that are *consistent* with that position.

commonsense beliefs—What people know from what they see, hear, and feel in their everyday life.

communal concerns—Orientation toward selflessness, concern for others, and a desire to be at one with others.

compliance—Action that is taken only because it has been requested; the process of generating compliance is the process of getting others to say yes to a request.

conative responses—The *behavioral intentions* and overt actions taken in regard to an *attitude object*.

conditioned response—According to *classical conditioning*, the acquired *response* to a *conditioned stimulus*.

conditioned stimulus—An originally neutral *stimulus* that, through repeated associations with an *unconditioned stimulus*, comes to elicit the same (or similar) *responses* as the *unconditioned stimulus*.

conformity—Changing behavior as a result of having been exposed to opinions, behaviors, or preferences of other individuals in a group. The source of influence is often a majority within a group, and the recipient of influence is often a minority. The influence results mostly in public *compliance* without private acceptance.

consistency principle—People are motivated to appear consistent, because consistency within one's thoughts, words, and actions is highly valued in American society.

consonant cognitions—Thoughts and beliefs that agree with or are consistent with other cognitions.

content analysis—An approach to analyzing *protocol* data that tries to identify the variety of themes that are expressed by respondents. This involves thoughtful reading of all the *protocols* with the purpose of inferring the underlying categories of moral, practical, and psychodynamic concerns that are expressed there. Once a set of categories is developed, it is taught to a small set of coders who then read through all the *protocols* and count the number of times each underlying category appears in each *protocol*.

context—Setting.

control condition—A group of *subjects* that is exposed to the experimental setting, but not the experimental treatment.

correlation coefficient—A statistical measure of the direction and magnitude of relationship between two variables (e.g., attitude and behavior), ranging from –1 (a strong negative relationship, as one variable increases or becomes more positive, the other decreases) to +1 (a strong positive relationship, as one variable increases or becomes more positive, the other variable increases also).

counterattitudinal message—A message that advocates a position contrary to one's own.

CR—See *conditioned response*.

criminal ideology—A set of systematically interrelated *attitudes* about crime and criminal activity.

CS—See *conditioned stimulus*.

cue—See *peripheral cue*.

deadline technique—A variation of the *scarcity rule for compliance* in which an official time limit is placed on the customer's opportunity to get what is being offered.

decision approaches to health persuasion—See *cognitive approaches to health persuasion*.

de facto selectivity—A form of *selective exposure*, referring to situations in which an audience for a message is composed mostly of people who already happen to agree with the message. For example, Rotary Club members are exposed to probusiness messages; they are rarely exposed to socialist messages. Because of the fact of their group membership, the messages they hear are selected for them. Thus, they are already biased in favor of the messages they hear.

definition of the event—Within the *attitude-to-behavior process model*, the definition of the event consists of two components—the individual's perceptions of the *attitude object* in the immediate situation and the individual's *definition of the situation*.

definition of the situation—Within the *attitude-to-behavior process model*, the storehouse of knowledge that an individual possesses concerning behaviors that are to be expected and that are appropriate in the particular situation.

dependent variable—The aspect of behavior that the experimenter expects will be affected by the *independent variable*. It is called this because if a relationship exists, its value will depend on the *independent variable*. For example, performance in a flight simulator, the dependent variable, may depend on the number of cups of coffee consumed, the *independent variable* (see *factorial design*).

diffusion of responsibility—Spreading the responsibility for a negative outcome among as many people as possible, in order to reduce *personal responsibility*.

dimensions of responsibility—Aside from free choice and foreseeability, Shaver (1985) identified other aspects of *personal responsibility*. A person will be seen as responsible for an action to the extent that a person is seen as the cause of some outcome, that the action was intended, and that the person had an appreciation of the moral wrongfulness of his or her conduct.

direct verbal measures—Directly asking a person how he or she feels about the *attitude object*. These can be divided into two categories: *structured* and *unstructured* scales.

dispositions—Inner feelings or attributes of a person.

dissonant cognitions—See *cognitive dissonance*.

distraction—A *stimulus* that causes reduced attention to a task; a variable that disrupts whatever the dominant thoughts are in response to a communication.

door-in-the-face technique—See *reciprocal concessions procedure*.

drive—A state of organic tension (e.g., hunger) that people are motivated to alleviate through taking some action (e.g., eating).

eccrine glands—A particular class of sweat glands.

EDRs—See *electrodermal responses*.

EEG—See *electroencephalography*.

effort justification—According to *cognitive dissonance theory*, people come to like things better the more they suffer to attain them (*attitudes* change to justify the effort expended).

ego involvement—See *personal relevance*.

elaboration (of message arguments)—Carefully thinking about message information and relating it to things the person already knows; generating *cognitive responses* to message *arguments*.

elaboration likelihood—The likelihood that a person will engage in *elaboration of message arguments*.

elaboration likelihood model of persuasion—A model of the persuasion process that describes two routes to persuasion: a *central route* and a *peripheral route*.

electrodermal activity—Sweating.

electrodermal measure—A procedure for measuring sympathetic activation involving the measurement of sweat gland activity. A very small electrical current is applied across two electrodes that are attached to the hand. Changes in the resistance of the skin to the flow of electric current reflect changes in the *activation* of the *eccrine sweat glands*. The more these glands are *activated*, the more filled they are with sweat (a good conductor), and the lower the resistance to current flow. Larger electrodermal responses (increased sweating) are associated with stress and emotion.

electroencephalography—A method of recording, from the scalp, the electrical signals (*brain waves*) that the brain generates while processing information.

electromyographic responses (as a function of affective direction)—Emotional reactions that are too fleeting or subtle to evoke an outward expression can nevertheless be measured physiologically. Electromyography is a method of detecting neural *activation* of the *striated* (e.g., facial) *muscles* that result in electrical impulses, even when there are no perceptible facial muscle contractions.

ELM—See *elaboration likelihood model of persuasion*.

embeds—An alleged form of *subliminal persuasion* in which words or body forms are inserted in a print message by the use of shadows or shading.

EMG—See *electromyography*.

epidemiological (epidemiology)—The study of the relationship between various pathological conditions and factors such as environment and heredity.

evaluative-cognitive consistency—The correspondence between a person's emotional responses to an issue and the person's beliefs about it. This correspondence is *topic bound*, in that if people are high in consistency on one issue, this indicates little about their consistency on another topic. In general, *attitudes* high in consistency appear to be more stable over time and resistant to persuasion attempts than those low in consistency. This may be due to the fact that a person with high affective-cognitive consistency on a particular topic will probably be aware of all positions on an issue; in addition, people with high levels of consistency may have their beliefs and ideas about an issue organized in a way that is highly *accessible*. Therefore, high-consistency people are more likely and able spontaneously to counterargue opposing information.

evaluative property of an attitude—How positively or negatively a person feels toward an *attitude object*.

even-a-penny-would-help technique—See *legitimization-of-paltry favors*.

event-related brain potentials—Changes in brain activity that are linked to some event (e.g., the presentation of a tone or an *attitude object*).

facial cues—*Nonverbal measures* of attitudinal affect, in which feelings of pleasure and disgust are expressed through the eyes, nose, mouth, and brows. Research has found that facial expressions carry similar meanings across a variety of cultures.

factorial design—An experimental design with two or more *independent variables*. For example, the first *independent variable* could be trainee pilots' experience in a flight simulator—two weeks versus ten weeks of experience. The second *independent variable* could be number of cups of coffee consumed prior to a flight simulator test—two cups versus six cups. The number of errors made by the trainees at each level of experience and each dosage of coffee would be the *dependent variable*.

fear-drive model—A message-learning model that assumes that threatening message content provokes fear, which motivates the recipient to form and *rehearse* a mental plan for protective action and that creating and acting on such a plan would make the individual feel less frightened. The reduction of fear is assumed automatically to lead to the learning or *reinforcement* of these protective reactions.

focus groups—A small group of people who are recruited to discuss an issue or consumer product among themselves. This focused interaction among group members often brings out subtleties and nuances in *attitudes* that would otherwise be missed.

foot-in-the-door technique—A variation of the *commitment/consistency rule for compliance* in which a solicitor will first ask for a small favor that is virtually certain to be granted. The initial *compliance* is then followed by a request for a larger, related favor. People who have agreed to the initial, small favor are more willing to do the larger one.

forced-compliance paradigm—Another term for the *induced-compliance paradigm*.

forearm flexors—Muscles that make the forearm bend.

forewarning of persuasive intent—Informing a recipient in advance that a speaker is deliberately going to try to persuade him or her. According to the *elaboration likelihood model*, this leads to *biased processing*, in which the recipient is motivated to defend his or her original position.

four-walls technique—A variation of the *commitment/consistency rule for compliance* in which a potential customer is asked a series of questions to which the answer will very likely be "yes." To be *consistent* with the previous answers, the customer must then say "yes" to the crucial final question.

friendship/liking rule for compliance—One should be more willing to *comply* with the requests of friends or other liked individuals.

generalization—Making identical *responses* to similar *stimuli*.

GKT—See *guilty knowledge test*.

great propaganda scare—An early perspective on media effects (late 1930s), in which social scientists closely examined the rhetoric of articulate propagandists and described the psychological dynamics behind their effectiveness. Social scientists assumed that mass political propaganda was in itself highly persuasive; its success depended on how adroitly a propagandist used subtle rhetorical tricks in a communication; and the audience was captive, attentive, and gullible.

group-induced opinion shift—Opinion changes produced by participating in group discussion.

group polarization—The phenomenon in which group discussion produces opinions that are more extreme than those held by the members before they entered into the discussion.

group-pressure conformity studies—A particular form of *conformity* study in which *subjects* are usually informed that other people in their experimental group hold a belief or *attitude* that is different from *subjects'* own positions. These other members have surveillance over subjects' *responses*; that is, these other members know (or appear to know) whether *subjects conformed* to their views.

groupthink—According to Janis (1971), "The mode of thinking that persons engage in when concurrence-seeking becomes so dominant in a cohesive *ingroup* that it tends to override realistic appraisal of alternative courses of action." When members' desire to agree with each other becomes excessive, they tend to generate *arguments* that allow the group as a whole to rationalize their preexisting positions. Dissent is not welcome. The members, as a result, become extremely reluctant to communicate disagreements with the established group *norm*. These *biases*, deriving from each individual's desire to secure social approval from the group, lead to an illusory confidence in the group's position and sometimes to disastrous decisions.

guilty knowledge test—A deception-detection technique based upon the *significant information test*, in which criminal subjects are asked a series of questions about a crime, with multiple-choice alternatives including the correct answer as well as other plausible but incorrect choices. Only an individual who knows the details of the crime is expected to respond physiologically to the correct answer because this information has special significance to the guilty individual, and its presentation threatens to expose the individual's guilt.

habit—An almost automatic pattern of learned behavior.

"hoopla" news coverage—In an effort to be entertaining during news coverage of a political campaign, television networks give less play to issue-oriented information in comparison to whatever developments appear more exciting. In this way, the media may have an impact on which *attitudes* are considered impor-

tant and which lie dormant in the public's political thinking, in a manner similar to *agenda setting.*

"horserace" news coverage—News coverage that emphasizes who is ahead in political contests, in polls, and the like. A "horserace" atmosphere is created in which people may want to "bet on a winner" or "root for the underdog."

ideology—A systematic scheme or coordinated body of ideas or concepts especially about human life or culture (*Webster's Third*, 1966).

independent variable—The variable, or treatment, that is controlled or manipulated by the experimenter; for example, the number of cups of coffee subjects are given in a flight simulator test (see *factorial design*).

indirect attitude measures—People are likely to misrepresent their *attitudes* when it is in their self-interest to do so; therefore, indirect measurement techniques are developed to overcome problems that arise when respondents are either too embarrassed or worried about their attitudes being used against them.

individual difference—A trait or other characteristic that can be used to distinguish individuals from one another (e.g., level of self-esteem).

induced-compliance paradigm—An experimental paradigm in which a person is induced to comply with a request that is contrary to his or her attitude.

information error test—A type of *indirect attitude measure* in which respondents answer a series of factual questions in a multiple-choice test format. Although the test is presented to the respondent as being a test of factual knowledge, in reality, all of the alternatives for each question are incorrect. The set of alternatives vary in how favorable or unfavorable they are toward the *attitude object.* Since respondents will not know the correct answer, it is assumed that they will draw upon their *attitude* when selecting an alternative to each question.

informational influence—Social influence occurring because the group member wants to be correct and interprets the behavior of other group members as information about what position is correct. When a unanimous majority endorses one position, this suggests that the position must be correct. Therefore, individuals give up trusting their own senses and instead *conform* to the majority.

information-processing model of persuasion—According to McGuire, persuasion is the result of a series of sequential steps. First, the recipient must attend to the message, then comprehend its content, and finally, yield to the persuasive suggestion. Attention to and comprehension of the message have usually been combined into a single variable labeled *reception.*

ingroup—The group that one belongs to and with which one identifies.

Institute for Propaganda Analysis—Formed during the *great propaganda scare* of the 1930s by social scientists to put out regular newsletters as well as detailed exposés of the propagandistic devices used by effective orators. They analyzed the content of speeches in order to scrutinize systematically the tricks of propaganda.

interaction—The situation in a *factorial design* where one *independent variable* has a different effect at different levels of another *independent variable.* For example, amount of experience that pilot trainees have had in a flight simulator—two weeks versus ten weeks—may have no effect on their performance if they only consumed two cups of coffee prior to the test. However, if the trainees consumed six cups of coffee, amount of experience may have a strong effect (i.e., the more experienced trainees may perform better than the less experienced trainees).

internalization (of group norm)—The incorporation of others' *attitudes* and standards into the self.

interpersonal influence—The ways in which one individual can influence another individual's *attitudes*, beliefs, perceptions, or behaviors.

issue salience—The prominence of an issue in a person's thinking.

law of natural selection applied to the compliance profession—Those *commercial compliance professionals* who use procedures that work well to elicit *compliance responses* will survive and flourish. Further, they will pass these successful procedures on (somewhat like genes) to succeeding generations (e.g., trainees). Unsuccessful compliance procedures will not be passed on to newer generations.

learning approaches to health motivation—Models that emphasize the acquisition of the skills needed for performing preventive and compliance behaviors, for example, the *fear-drive model* and communication to instill the skill needed for health action.

legitimization-of-paltry-favors (even-a-penny-would-help) technique—A variation of the *commitment/consistency rule for compliance* in which a fundraiser who makes a request that legitimizes a paltry amount of aid ("even a penny would help") makes it difficult for a target to refuse to give at all. The request makes a minuscule form of aid acceptable, thereby reducing the target's ability to give nothing and still remain consistent with the desirable image of a helpful person.

level of moral reasoning—Higher levels of moral reasoning are characterized by basing conduct on one's general principles of ethics. Lower levels of reasoning focus on the consequences of a particular action or on simple adherence to social or legal rules.

Leventhal's self-regulatory model of illness behavior—A *self-regulation model of health persuasion* that emphasizes the need to understand how an individual perceives a health threat in order to change his or her *attitudes* and behavior. Messages that provoke feelings of fear and loss of hope or competence may deter action, whereas messages that create the view that inaction will lead to danger, fear, and loss of hope may stimulate action. In addition, individuals often behave according to *commonsense beliefs* about illnesses (such as the belief that one feels pain and other symptoms when ill). Therefore, they will be at risk whenever the *commonsense belief* and the disease process are at variance with one another.

liberating effect—The presence of a small minority can subvert the power of the majority. The minority's dissent frees members to express the correct opinion, as they would in the absence of an incorrect majority. This liberating effect can occur for two reasons: A minority breaks the unanimity of a majority; and a minority can provide social support for one's dissenting position.

life skills training program—A *learning approach* to smoking prevention in which subjects are provided with both strategies to avoid smoking and messages to generate skills for handling stress. Improvement in the management of daily life situations can reduce the failure-induced anxiety and distress that produce the urge to smoke.

Likert scale—A type of *multiple-item scale* in which the researcher begins by generating a large pool of belief statements for *pretesting*. The entire set of items is given to a sample of *pretest* subjects to indicate how much they agree or disagree with each item. Each *subject* is presented with the statements and instructed to check only one of (usually) five possible responses for each statement (Strongly Agree, Agree, Undecided, Disagree, Strongly Disagree). A provisional *attitude* score is computed for each of these *subjects* based on their answers to the entire item set. Only those individual items that *correlate* the highest with the provisional score are selected for inclusion in the final scale.

liking principle—People are more favorably inclined toward the opinions and requests of those they know and like.

liking rule for compliance—See *friendship/liking rule for compliance*.

limited-number tactic—A variation of the *scarcity rule for compliance* in which a customer is informed that membership opportunities, products, or services exist in a limited supply that cannot be guaranteed to last long in order to convince prospects of an item's *scarcity* and thereby increase its immediate worth in their eyes.

list technique—A variation of the *social validation principle* that involves asking for a request only after the target person has been shown a list of similar others who have already *complied*.

locus of control—The amount of control that people perceive themselves as having over their life and environment. Individuals with an external locus of control perceive the environment and events external to themselves as tending to control their lives. Individuals with an internal locus of control tend to feel that they govern their lives and environment.

long-term media effects—Changes in public opinion over an extended time, rather than the effects of one-shot media events.

low-ball technique—A variation of the *commitment/consistency rule for compliance* in which a salesperson obtains a *commitment* to an action and then increases the costs of performing the action.

majority influence—See *conformity*.

mass society—Kornhauser (1959) contended that modernization and industrialization led to the breakdown of primary-group ties, and the psychic void created by the loss of these ties was filled by the unstable, volatile swings of the masses from one extreme to another. The mass media presumably provided an important mechanism by which the masses could be manipulated.

material self-interest—A *compliance* principle appealing to the desire to maximize one's material benefits and minimize one's material costs.

message-based Likert scale—A type of *Likert scale* that bypasses the usual first step of *pretesting* a large group of items. This approach is taken when the researcher wants to know respondents' reactions to the specific *arguments* and conclusions presented in a persuasive communication. The investigator prepares a small number of belief statements, each of which relates to an *argument* in the message. In this manner, a scale of only a few items may be prepared. For this type of scale to be *reliable*, all of the items must show positive *correlations* with one another.

mind guard—A group member who protects a leader from a potential threat to his positions, *arguments*, and beliefs, just as a body guard protects him or her from physical assault.

minimal effects model—Phase two of the perspectives on media effects (popular during the 1940s and 1950s), in which social scientists attempted empirical assessment of mass communication impact. They concluded that major political changes produced by media propaganda were the exception rather than the rule and that the media primarily *reinforced* prior *attitudes*. In a review of the literature, Klapper (1960) formally developed the minimal effects model, which proposed that media propaganda rarely changes one's *attitude* but instead often serves to strengthen one's existing *attitudes*.

minority influence—The process by which a minority in a group may alter the beliefs and behaviors of the majority.

misattribution cue—An event that provides an incorrect alternative explanation for some experience or feeling; for example, a person feels afraid and attributes the fear to seeing a black cat.

mob psychology—The notion that people tend to lose their inhibitions and be swept into action by the emotions of a crowd.

moderating variable—A condition or treatment that can affect the extent of relationship between two other variables. For example, age may influence how pilot-training experience affects performance in a flight simulator: The more experience, the better the performance. But this relationship may be stronger for younger than for older trainees. Age moderates the relationship between training and performance.

motivated selectivity—A form of *selective exposure*, referring to cases in which individuals exhibit psychological preferences for supportive rather than nonsupportive information. For example, after buying a particular car, people may seek out information that supports the car they bought (e.g., wanting to talk to other owners of that car) and may avoid information about cars that they rejected (avoiding the owners of competing cars).

motivation—A general term to denote a readiness to take action that stems from a person's conscious intentions, goals, or needs.

motivational audiotapes—Audiotapes that offer self-help or self-improvement.

multiple-item scales—A type of *structured scale* for *attitude measurement* consisting of multiple questions that cover a variety of feelings and beliefs a person may have toward an *attitude object*. Averaging across multiple separate items provides a more *valid* index of the underlying *attitude* than a *single-item scale*, because the bias affecting any single item will have a relatively small effect on a person's total test score.

name-calling—A propaganda technique that consists of giving an idea a bad label.

need for cognition—An *individual difference variable* that differentiates people who generally enjoy thinking in a wide variety of situations (those high in need for cognition) from those who do not (those low in need for cognition). According to the *elaboration likelihood model of persuasion*, those high in need for cognition are more likely to process messages via the *central route*.

neural impulses—Electrochemical waves propagated along a chain of neurons, which transmit and receive signals from the nervous system.

nonattitudes—Opinions that people express that do not reflect a preexisting view they had on the issue. Rather, they concocted a response on the spot, often based on little or no information about the issue. These nonattitudes can be a source of bias in *attitude measurement*.

nonsense syllables—Meaningless groups of letters or speech sounds. They are often used as *stimuli* in experiments—for example, to examine how preferences for any object (including nonsense syllables) are influenced by the number of times a person is shown the object.

nonverbal communication—Communicating ideas without using either written or spoken language.

nonverbal measures—*Observational measures* based on *paralinguistic, facial,* and *bodily cues* that convey *attitudes* that may contradict a respondent's verbalizations.

norm—Beliefs about how one should or is expected to behave in a given situation.

normative influence—Social influence that is driven by the *motive* of social approval. When a group member wants to be liked and approved by others, he or she may adjust his or her opinion to that of others in order to gain approval or avoid rejection.

objective awareness thresholds—Determined by subjects' ability to distinguish whether or not a *stimulus* was actually presented. A *stimulus* is below the objective threshold if subjects' guesses about what was presented are at no better than chance level.

objective message processing—Message processing motivated by a desire to seek the truth, whatever it is. In order to process a message in an objective manner, the person must have the requisite skills and opportunity to consider the *arguments* impartially.

observational measures of attitudes—Assessing *attitudes* by observing the overt actions, facial expressions, and physiological responses of the respondent.

opinion thermometer—A *single-item self-rating scale of attitudes* in which gradations in temperature are used to represent gradations in attitude.

outgroups—Groups other than the group to which a person belongs or identifies.

overarching compliance principles—Those principles that (a) occur in many versions, (b) appear across the range of *compliance* professions, (c) are employable by the greatest number of *compliance practitioners*, and (d) have been successfully used historically. They are *reciprocity, social validation, commitment/consistency, friendship/liking, scarcity,* and *authority*.

overt behavior—As a measure of *attitude*, the investigator records whether certain activities are engaged in by the respondent. Social behaviors are selected that reflect either a favorable or unfavorable orientation toward the *attitude object*. These refer to the kinds of actions that are supportive or antagonistic to the *attitude object*. Supportive behaviors are assumed to reflect favorable *attitudes*, whereas antagonistic behaviors are assumed to reflect unfavorable *attitudes*.

overt bodily response (as a function of affective direction)—A person's physical actions and expressions (e.g., smiles, posture, interpersonal spacing) that can reveal whether one feels positively or negatively about an object or person.

paralinguistic cues—*Nonverbal measures of attitudes* that include all audible characteristics of speech other than verbal content. Research has shown that deceptive verbalizations have a distinctive sound. Some studies suggest that lies are high pitched, punctuated by hesitations, and contain many speech errors, such as mispronunciations and the use of "ums" and "ahs."

parsimonious explanation—A simple explanation of a phenomenon; scientific theories strive for parsimony.

perceptual grouping (of majority members)—Individuals automatically categorize similar things. In the social domain, individuals may be seen as part of a single category, especially when the number of individuals increases and the individuals are similar to each other. This perceptual grouping phenomenon is used to explain the common result of *conformity* studies that a rather small majority has as much power over an individual as does a large majority. When there are more than three or four individuals advocating the same position, these individuals are no longer perceived as separate individuals but rather as a clique.

peripheral cue—An aspect of a message (e.g., a celebrity endorser) that may indicate little or nothing about the true merits of a message but nevertheless may prompt *attitude* formation in the absence of diligent consideration of the true merits of the person, object, or issue under consideration.

peripheral route to persuasion—According to the *elaboration likelihood model*, persuasion resulting from reliance on a relatively simple *cue* in the situation, rather than on extensive cognitive effort. *Attitudes* formed via this route are less persistent, less predictive of behavior, and less resistant to competing messages than are *attitudes* formed or changed by the *central route*.

personal relevance—Whether a persuasive message has direct personal implications for the recipient. According to the *elaboration likelihood model*, greater personal relevance should increase the likelihood of *central-route* message processing.

personal responsibility—In order for a person to feel personally responsible for the negative consequences of an action, he or she must at least feel that the behavior was freely chosen and that the negative consequences were foreseeable (although there may be other *dimensions of responsibility*). A person must feel personally responsible for producing *aversive consequences* in order for *cognitive dissonance* to be aroused.

persuasive argument theory—A theory of *group polarization* that assumes that it is issue-relevant thought exchanged during discussion that leads to opinion polarization. According to the theory, on any given issue, there is a pool of *arguments* available in the culture, some of which favor one position and the others of which favor the alternative position. These *arguments*, however, are not always shared; any given person usually thinks of only some of these *arguments*. Through group discussion, initially unshared *arguments* are exchanged and become widely available. As a consequence, each member gains additional *arguments* that did not come to mind before. It is these *arguments*, newly gained in discussion, that lead to polarization. *Group polarization* is thus a consequence of the argumentation that occurs in group discussion. *Group polarization* occurs in the direction of a position that is shared by members prior to discussion, because such a position elicits more numerous and persuasive supporting *arguments* than the alternative position. The theory emphasizes the role of issue-relevant thinking and views *group polarization* as due to *informational influence*.

physiological activation—See *activation of the sympathetic nervous system*.

physiological arousal—Activation of the sympathetic nervous system. Such activation may be reflected in increased heart rate, blood pressure, breathing rate, sweating, and feelings of tension.

physiological indicators of affective direction—Physiological measures, including *overt bodily responses* and *electromyographic responses*, that reflect the positive or negative nature of emotional reactions.

physiological measures of attitude—See *physiological indicators of affective direction*.

pluralistic ignorance—A social phenomenon in which each member of a group believes that every other member shares the same opinion or the same reason for a course of action. In fact, opinions and reasons differ, and members are ignorant of these differences.

polygraph—A device that measures blood pressure, respiration, pulse, and *electrodermal activity* in an attempt to detect whether a person is telling the truth.

precious mistake phenomenon—An example of the *scarcity principle* in which flawed items (e.g., a blurred stamp) are sometimes the most valuable of all.

presence-implies-effectiveness fallacy—The incorrect assumption that if some incoming stimulation is actually there, although below one's awareness (*subliminally*), it must be having an impact on one's beliefs and behaviors.

pretest—A preliminary study whose results are used to develop measures or procedures to be used in a later study.

primacy effect—An effect of order of presentation of messages or of response alternatives. Refers to situations in which the first message of two is more effective or, in closed-response questions, situations in which respondents are biased toward choosing one of the first answer choices they hear.

primary prevention (of health problems)—Avoiding behaviors that lead to health problems (e.g., dieting and exercising), rather than treating existing problems.

principles of propaganda—A list of the persuasive methods used by effective propagandists supposedly to win unsuspecting listeners over to their cause. The list was created by social scientists during the *great propaganda scare*.

proattitudinal message—A message that advocates a position similar to one's own.

projective test—A type of personality test based on responses to ambiguous *stimuli*. It assumes that people unconsciously interpret ambiguous *stimuli* in terms of their own *attitudes* and feelings.

protocol—A typed transcription of an open-ended or unstructured interview with a respondent.

psychological reactance—One of the sources of power for *scarcity* appeals. Whenever our freedoms are limited or threatened, the need to retain them makes us want them (as well as the goods and services associated with them) significantly more than previously. So, when increasing *scarcity*—or anything else—interferes with our prior access to some item, we will react against the interference by wanting and trying to possess the item more than before.

psychophysiology—The scientific study of human thought, emotion, and behavior as revealed or implemented in physiological events.

question-order effects—A source of bias in *attitude measurement* reflecting that the order in which questions are asked can have a substantial effect on answers. The answers people give to an *attitude* question in a survey can be partly influenced by the questions that came before it.

"rally-'round-the-flag" effect—The frequent tendency for the public to rally behind a president's controversial actions in foreign affairs. It demonstrates how general predispositions, such as patriotism, can increase the amount of *attitude* change; it is an example of *reinforcement-of-prior attitudes*.

rational decision models (of health persuasion)—According to this *cognitive model of health persuasion*, individuals' reactions to a health message are based upon their awareness of personal vulnerability to the health threat, combined with the negative consequences associated with the threat.

recency effect—An effect of order of presentation of messages or of response alternatives. Refers to situations in which the second message of two is more effective or, in closed-response questions, situations in which respondents are biased toward choosing one of the last answer choices they hear.

reception (of a message)—Attention to and comprehension of a message (see also *information-processing model of persuasion*).

reciprocal concessions procedure (also known as the door-in-the-face technique)—A variation of the norm for *reciprocity* of favors in which a requester begins with an extreme request that is nearly always rejected and then retreats to a more moderate favor—the one that the requester had in mind from the outset. The requester hopes that the retreat from the extreme to moderate request will spur the target person to make a reciprocal concession—by moving from initial rejection of the larger favor to acceptance of the smaller one.

reciprocation rules of compliance—One should be more willing to *comply* with a request from someone who has previously provided a favor or concession.

reciprocity—A societal rule obliging people to give back the form of behavior they have received. For example, gifts are to be met with return gifts, favors with return favors, benefits with return benefits, and the like.

reference group—A group whose values have been adopted by a person; the values can be those of an actual group (e.g., a teenage gang) or an imagined group (e.g., "liberals").

rehearsal—Repeated thinking or verbaliziing in order to enhance recall.

reinforcement—Any experience that increases the strength or likelihood of a *response*.

reinforcement of prior attitudes—Making prior attitudes even stronger and more resistant to change. Political messages that are attended to often fail to produce actual *attitude* change because any issue "hot" enough to attract attention usually encounters enduring prior *attitudes*. In fact, further strengthening of the prior *attitude* often takes place.

reliability—The stability of a test or an effect. A reliable test is one that gives similar results on a second measurement. Similarly, a reliable effect is one that occurs consistently over time.

renewed respect for media effects—Phase three of the perspective on media effects (the period since the late 1960s) in which social scientists have begun to examine subtler factors contributing to the media's effectiveness.

response—A reaction to a *stimulus*.

response latency—The length of time between the onset of a *stimulus* and the *response* onset.

response-order effect—A source of *bias* in *attitude measurement* in which presenting *response* alternatives in different orders can lead respondents to give different answers, even though the questions seem to ask the same thing. For example, if a person were asked, "What is the most important problem facing the nation today: crime, drugs, the economy, or the environment?" her response may be different than if the list of problems were read in another order. There are two types of response order effects: *primacy* and *recency*.

responsibility attribution—How people decide who is responsible for or who caused an outcome.

right-now-deadline technique—A variant of the *scarcity rule of compliance* in which customers are told that, unless they make an immediate purchase decision, they will have to buy the item at a higher price or they will not be able to purchase it at all.

risky shift—An example of *group polarization* in which opinions become riskier after group discussion.

role theory—People's expectations of others are based largely on the *social roles* in which they are encountered. These expectations are communicated to others through both *verbal* and *nonverbal channels*, and people are *reinforced* when they meet these expectations.

scarcity principle—Rare or scarce opportunities, objects, information, and experiences are seen as being valuable and desirable.

scarcity rule for compliance—One values those opportunities and objects that are scarce or dwindling.

schema—A cognitive structure that represents one's organized knowledge about a concept, including both the attributes of a concept and relations among the attributes. A schema guides message processing and recall of information about the concept.

secondary prevention (of health problems)—Behaviors that minimize illness through early detection and treatment.

selective attention—The propensity to avoid paying attention to information or *stimuli* that challenge preexisting *attitudes* or beliefs; in other words, attention to supportive stimuli in the environment. (See also *selective reception*.)

selective exposure—The propensity to avoid being exposed to information or *stimuli* that challenge preexisting *attitudes* or beliefs; in other words, exposing oneself to supportive information in the environment. There are two forms: *de facto selectivity* and *motivated selectivity*. (See also *selective reception*.)

selective interpretation—The propensity to distort information or *stimuli* that challenge preexisting *attitudes* or beliefs; in other words, interpreting information in the environment as being supportive of one's preexisting *attitudes* or beliefs. (See also *selective reception*.)

selective perception—See *selective interpretation*.

selective reception—One of the tenets of the *minimal effects model* was that major impediments to political persuasion included the processes of selective information reception, such as *selective exposure* and *selective perception*. The notion that people generally avoid, distort, and forget communications that challenge their preexisting *attitudes*.

self-affirmation theory—A theory that assumes that people are motivated to take actions to bolster important aspects of their *self-concepts*.

self-censorship—One of the symptoms of *groupthink* in which group members are reluctant to communicate disagreements with the group *norm*, in the service of maintaining consensus in the group, and to avoid potential social rejection by other group members.

self-concept—A person's view of himself or herself, including self-evaluations of his or her personal worth, values, goals, and abilities.

self-esteem—A personal estimate of worthiness or an evaluation of oneself in a positive or negative way. High self-esteem reflects an overall positive evaluation of oneself, and low self-esteem reflects a negative evaluation.

self-identification theory—A theory that assumes that people are motivated to take actions that reflect their view of their own identity.

self-image—See *self-concept*.

self-monitoring—An *individual difference variable* differentiating individuals who are guided by their inner states from those who are guided by situational cues. Individuals low in self-monitoring are guided by their inner states, attributes, and *attitudes*. In contrast, individuals high in self-monitoring are guided by a pragmatic concern with what is appropriate in each situation; they monitor the impression that they make on other people and adjust that impression to fit with others' expectations.

self-regulation—The process of controlling one's own behavior.

self-regulation models (*of health persuasion*)—*Cognitive models* of health persuasion that consider the intuitive, *commonsense beliefs* that people have about illness, in addition to their more rational, logical thinking. People's intuitive beliefs are assumed to affect the perceived meaning or interpretation of health messages, their acceptance, and their impact on behavior.

self-relevance—See *personal relevance*.

self-report measures—See *direct report measures.*

self-serving bias—The tendency to interpret information in a way that supports a positive self-image.

semantic conditioning—A variation of *classical conditioning* in which the *conditioned stimulus* is a word or phrase.

semantic generalization—A special case of *stimulus generalization* in *semantic conditioning* in which words and objects similar in meaning to the *conditioned stimulus* can also evoke a *response* similar in form to the *conditioned response.*

sensitization to commitments procedure—A variation of the *commitment/consistency rule for compliance* in which, rather than inducing a new *commitment* to a product or service, practitioners point out existing *commitments* within potential customers that are consistent with the product or service being offered. In this way, desirable existing *commitments* are made more visible to the customer, and the strain for *consistency* directs behavior.

short-term media effects—Although most one-shot media communications tend more often to *reinforce* prior *attitudes* than to change them, there have been a few remarkable cases in which major and important changes in public opinion appear to have been produced by communications in the media presented over a short time.

significant information test—A deception detection method that assumes that a *stimulus* that is (or is made) highly significant to a person (e.g., a murder weapon) evokes stronger physiological responses than does a stimulus that is not significant. In guilty individuals, presentation of the *stimulus* is associated with greater physiological responsivity to the extent that it is familiar and threatens to expose the guilty individual. In *attitude* assessment, various *attitude* positions are presented to the *subject*; the *subject's* true *attitude* position is expected to evoke more physiological responsivity than other positions because the person's own *attitude* has the greatest familiarity and personal significance.

single-item self-rating scale of attitudes—A *structured scale of attitudes* in which the pro-to-con attitude dimension is described to respondents who are then asked to check the category that best describes their overall *attitude.* Other scales provide a single statement of *attitude* or belief and ask how much the person agrees or disagrees with it.

SIT—See *significant information test.*

social comparison theory—Applied to *group polarization*, social comparison theory draws on the assumption that individuals compare their opinions to others' opinions and shift their opinions so as to gain approval or to be accepted by other group members. (In other words, *group polarization* is due to *normative influence.*)

social labeling technique—A variation of the *social validation rule for compliance* in which a person is informed that certain others have labeled him or her in a specific way. Later, the person is found to be more willing to comply with requests that are in keeping with that label. For example, people who are labeled as charitable will subsequently donate more money to charity than those who were not so labeled.

social norms—*Norms* defined by a specific group.

social roles—Social positions (e.g., leader) that are associated with expected *attitudes* and behaviors.

social validation—Refers to the process of trying to determine what is correct by finding out what other people think is correct. Thus, we may view a behavior as more correct in a given situation to the degree that we see others performing it.

social validation rule for compliance—One should be more willing to comply with a request for behavior if it is consistent with what similar others are thinking or doing.

spreading of alternatives—According to *cognitive dissonance theory*, every time we choose between two or more alternative courses of action, we experience some *dissonance*. The *dissonance* is caused by the negative elements of the course of action chosen and the positive elements of the course that was not chosen. When people are asked to choose between two equally desirable alternatives, they eventually may come to see the chosen alternative as more desirable than it had initially been rated and the foregone alternative as being less desirable than it had initially been rated (i.e., spreading their desirability apart). This is due to the person's attempt to reduce *cognitive dissonance* by adding thoughts that are consistent with the chosen alternative (positive aspect of the chosen alternative and negative aspect of the foregone alternative).

stair-step scale—A *single-item self-rating scale of attitudes* in which gradations in height parallel gradations in *attitude*.

stimulus (stimuli)—Any external or internal event that elicits a response.

stimulus ambiguity—Any situation or happening for which there is no obviously correct or appropriate response; the absence of any clear physical or objective reality.

stimulus generalization—Refers to process by which *stimuli* that are similar to a *conditioned stimulus* can also evoke a *response* similar in form to the *conditioned response*.

striated muscles—Those muscles used in voluntary activity; activity that we will to occur in a certain way and with a certain effect.

structured scales—A form of *direct verbal measurement* in which the respondent is given a limited number of answers to select from when responding to a question.

structured settings—Situations that provide clear guides to appropriate action and are likely to be perceived and evaluated in a similar manner by most people.

subconscious—Memories, events, or mental processes that are beneath conscious awareness.

subject—In social psychology, a person who is being observed, either in an experimental or field situation.

subjective awareness thresholds—Subjects' self-reports as to whether they were aware of a *stimulus*, regardless of whether a stimulus was actually presented.

subjective norm—According to the *theory of reasoned action*, one of the components that forms a *behavioral intention*. It is a combination of both the person's beliefs about what important others think should be done and the person's motivation to comply with the wishes of these others.

subliminal message presentation—Any devices used to convey or attempt to convey a message by means of images or sounds of a very brief or hidden nature that cannot be perceived at a normal level of awareness. Forms of subliminal messages include modifying a movie film so that frames appear at a speed at which the observer cannot consciously perceive their presence but *subconsciously* the word, phrase, or scene is registered (and may thus have a persuasive effect). Alternatively, spoken messages are accompanied by other sounds that hide the message and make it inaudible to an attentive listener. Another form is alleged to be the insertion of words or body forms (*embeds*) into a message by the use of shadows or shading.

subliminal perception—The perception of *stimuli* that are below one's level of awareness.

subliminal persuasion—See *subliminal message presentation*.

supraliminal message presentation—The presentation of observable and detectable material.

sympathetic nervous system—The branch of the autonomic nervous system that functions as the arousal center during emergencies or stress situations. (The autonomic nervous system regulates the mostly involuntary functions of the internal muscles and glands.)

tertiary prevention (of health problems)—Behaviors that control or reduce the complications of illness.

testimonial—A propaganda technique that consists of attributing an idea to a trustworthy or an evil source.

"that's-not-all" technique—A variation of the norm for *reciprocation* of favors in which, after making a first offer but before the target can respond, the requester betters the deal with an additional item or a price reduction.

Thematic Apperception Test—A *projective test* in which *subjects* are asked to describe what is going on in ambiguous pictures. This test can be used as an indirect *attitude measure* if powerful *attitudes* influence the stories that respondents tell about the ambiguous pictures.

theory of reasoned action—A theory of *attitude-behavior consistency* that assumes that an individual's *behavioral intention* is the single best predictor of the person's eventual behavior. In forming a *behavioral intention*, the individual considers, weighs, and combines his or her *attitude* toward the behavior in question and *subjective norms* regarding the behavior.

threshold of awareness—Level of awareness.

topic-bound approach to individual differences—Refers to predispositions that make people change their minds in response to a given message topic but that may not predict responses on another topic.

unconditioned response—In *classical conditioning*, a natural, unlearned *response* to an *unconditioned stimulus*.

unconditioned stimulus—In *classical conditioning*, a *stimulus* whose presentation alone evokes a *response* of some kind (*unconditioned response*).

UCR—See *unconditioned response.*

UCS—See *unconditioned stimulus.*

unintelligible message—A meaningless message; gibberish.

unobtrusive measure—An observational measure of *attitude* in which the respondents do not know that they are being observed; used because people have no reason to distort their behaviors if they are unaware that others are watching and listening.

unsolicited gift technique—A variation of the *reciprocation rule of compliance* in which a solicitor gives a small gift, accompanied with a request for a donation. The technique relies on the fact that most people do not go to the trouble of returning the gift and feel uncomfortable about keeping it without reciprocating in some way. It also relies on the willingness of people to make a contribution that is larger than the cost of the gift they received.

unstructured scale—A form of *direct verbal measurement* in which respondents are asked open-ended questions and can elaborate their thoughts as fully as they wish when answering each question.

unstructured settings—Ambiguous situations that offer few guides to behavior; such situations can occur when the usual constraints on a social situation are unexpectedly lifted.

validity—Accuracy. A valid test is one that measures what it is intended to measure.

variables affecting ability to process a message—Factors affecting whether the person has the necessary skills, knowledge, and opportunity to evaluate a message.

variables affecting motivation to process a message—Factors affecting a person's conscious intentions and goals in processing a message.

verbal measure of attitudes—A measure that involves asking a respondent direct questions, such as through questionnaires and surveys, in order to assess *attitudes*. There are *direct* and *indirect* verbal measures.

verbal reports (of attitudes)—See *verbal measures of attitudes.*

vested interest—A person has a vested interest in an issue when actions relevant to that issue could have an impact on the individual. (See also *personal relevance.*)

working knowledge—The extent of attitude-relevant beliefs and experiences that people spontaneously bring to mind when confronted with an *attitude object*. These beliefs may or may not be objectively accurate. They reflect one's subjective understanding of the *attitude object* or topic. It is relatively difficult to change the opinions of knowledgeable people compared to people with little knowledge about a topic.

zeitgeist—The social and political "spirit of the times."

NAME INDEX

SUBJECT INDEX